THE TWO HORIZO[...]

J. GORDON MCCONVILLE and CRAIG BARTHOLOMEW, *General Editors*

Two features distinguish THE TWO HORIZONS OLD TESTAMENT COMMEN-
TARY series: theological exegesis and theological reflection.

Exegesis since the Reformation era and especially in the past two hundred
years emphasized careful attention to philology, grammar, syntax, and concerns
of a historical nature. More recently, commentary has expanded to include
social-scientific, political, or canonical questions and more.

Without slighting the significance of those sorts of questions, scholars in
THE TWO HORIZONS OLD TESTAMENT COMMENTARY locate their primary
interests on theological readings of texts, past and present. The result is a para-
graph-by-paragraph engagement with the text that is deliberately theological
in focus.

Theological reflection in THE TWO HORIZONS OLD TESTAMENT COM-
MENTARY takes many forms, including locating each Old Testament book in
relation to the whole of Scripture—asking what the biblical book contributes
to biblical theology—and in conversation with constructive theology of today.
How commentators engage in the work of theological reflection will differ from
book to book, depending on their particular theological tradition and how they
perceive the work of biblical theology and theological hermeneutics. This het-
erogeneity derives as well from the relative infancy of the project of theological
interpretation of Scripture in modern times and from the challenge of grappling
with a book's message in Greco-Roman antiquity, in the canon of Scripture and
history of interpretation, and for life in the admittedly diverse Western world
at the beginning of the twenty-first century.

THE TWO HORIZONS OLD TESTAMENT COMMENTARY is written pri-
marily for students, pastors, and other Christian leaders seeking to engage in
theological interpretation of Scripture.

Micah

Stephen G. Dempster

WILLIAM B. EERDMANS PUBLISHING COMPANY

GRAND RAPIDS, MICHIGAN

Wm. B. Eerdmans Publishing Co.
2140 Oak Industrial Drive NE, Grand Rapids, Michigan 49505
www.eerdmans.com

26 25 24 23 22 21 20 19 18 17   1 2 3 4 5 6 7 8 9 10

ISBN 978-0-8028-6513-7

Library of Congress Cataloging-in-Publication Data

Names: Dempster, Stephen G., author.
Title: Micah / Stephen G. Dempster.
Description: Grand Rapids : Eerdmans Publishing Co., 2017. | Series: The two horizons
     Old Testament commentary | Includes bibliographical references and index.
Identifiers: LCCN 2017023223 | ISBN 9780802865137 (pbk. : alk. paper)
Subjects: LCSH: Bible. Micah—Commentaries.
Classification: LCC BS1615.53 .D46 2017 | DDC 224/.9307—dc23
     LC record available at https://lccn.loc.gov/2017023223

Contents

Contents

Preface

A while ago I received an invitation to teach a Bible Study group on the topic of Mic 6:1–8. About a week after I taught the study I received an invitation to write this commentary. One of the important messages of Mic 6 is that where one serves God is not as important as how.

I wrote the majority of this commentary—the first draft—on sabbatical from Crandall University and while serving as a consultant for the Cameroonian Association of Bible Translators and Literacy (CABTAL) in Yaounde, Cameroon, with two exegetes, the Reverend David Ngole and Pastor Ervais Fotso. It was a joy working with these fine scholars, who had a great passion for the work of the translation of Scripture into two of the many mother tongues of their country: Bakweiri and Bakoko. I learned countless lessons about translation, and my family and I were warmly welcomed and embraced by not only these exegetes but by their families and the entire CABTAL family, under the leadership of their "Papa," Efi, and their "Mama," Leah.

Cameroon is an absolutely beautiful country and the people are amazing. It was one of the highlights of my life to be there and research and write in this microcosm of Africa. However, while issues of injustice occur in the world in many places, they are virtually omnipresent in the beautiful country of Cameroon. The most obvious injustice was the opulent wealth of the leadership juxtaposed with the poverty of the marginalized majority. Bribes, corruption in the courts, oppression of the spirit and the flesh, and the presence of a growing prosperity gospel among the churches—all of which were the hallmarks of Micah's age—are all too prevalent in Cameroon. At the same time a growing evangelical sector is passionate about God and needs to be more passionate about justice. Spending time with Micah in Africa was a tonic for my soul but also a goad to my conscience. It made me also much more aware of the opulence and affluence of the West and the need "to live simply so that others may simply live." I trust that spending time with my commentary on this remarkable book may help every reader to have a heart set aflame with a deeper and fuller and more comprehensive love for God in doing justice, loving mercy, and walking humbly with him.

I would like to acknowledge the following: Gordon McConville, who helped this commentary be much better as a result of his editorial work and suggestions; Andrew Knapp and his staff at Eerdmans for their labors of editorial supererogation; Crandall University and the supportive and collegial environment that provides encouragement where one can think freely about the great issues of the Bible and the world and receive financial support for a sabbatical—thanks to the Steeves Foundation; Drs. Seth Crowell and Jim Rusthoven, my academic deans at the time, who encouraged me in this project; Andrew Marshall, the librarian at Crandall, who went above and beyond the call of duty in acquiring articles and books for my research; Dr. Byron Wheaton, whose invitation to speak at Ryle Theological College helped give me an opportunity to address some of the themes of Micah and clarify some of them; Peter Gentry, Ted Newell, and Bruce Waltke for being stimulating sounding boards; my students, who persevered in my Old Testament classes at Crandall University and Toronto Baptist Seminary in Canada and Westminster Theological Centre in the United Kingdom as together we thought through the exegetical issues of Micah and their application; and the members of study groups in Moncton, Canada, and Yaounde, Cameroon, who gently nudged me to think through some of the applications of Micah to contemporary life. It is a privilege to offer my humble contribution to the list of many commentators to whom I am indebted.

I dedicate this book to Jessica Sinclair, our daughter, who encouraged and guided us through the process of going to Cameroon to serve God there under the auspices of Wycliffe Bible Translators; Bob Lane, who became a fast friend with me in Cameroon and whose life verse was Mic 6:8 (Bob died shortly after we left Cameroon but in the short time that I knew him we had become soul mates; he lived his life verse); and the wonderful brothers and sisters at CABTAL, who give of themselves selflessly in the mission of bringing the word of God to the people of Cameroon in their own languages.

Whatever defects are in this book, I alone am responsible for them. I look forward to the day when God's dream as reflected in Mic 4:1–4 will be finally realized. Until then . . .

כִּי כָּל־הָעַמִּים יֵלְכוּ אִישׁ בְּשֵׁם אֱלֹהָיו
וַאֲנַחְנוּ נֵלֵךְ בְּשֵׁם־יְהוָה אֱלֹהֵינוּ לְעוֹלָם וָעֶד
(Mic 4:5)

Introduction to the Book of Micah

The Prophet and His Times

Micah may have been a short,[1] popular name for boys in ancient Judah, but its meaning carried heavy theological freight.[2] This name captures the sense of his small collection of speeches. When his book is compared with that of his contemporary, Isaiah of Jerusalem, it is easy to see why Micah is classed as one of the Minor Prophets.[3] But that being said, the brevity of his name, as well as the terseness of his discourse, was anything but minor. For his name—a four-letter word in Hebrew[4] (מִיכָה/*mîkâ*)—is a rhetorical question: "Who is like Yahweh?" As such, it is an exclamation of praise, "an expression of adoration and wonder at the incomparable God of Israel."[5] Over the course of time, it is easy for theological concepts to lose their evocative power, but the use of

---

1. A longer form had twice as many syllables.

2. Eleven other people had this name or a variation of it in biblical times: Judg 17:1; 1 Kgs 22:8; 1 Chr 5:5; 8:34; 9:40; 23:20; 2 Chr 34:20; Neh 10:11; 11:17; 12:35; Jer 36:11.

3. "Beside the majestic figure of Isaiah the figure of his contemporary Micah appears small"; Julius A. Bewer, *The Literature of the Old Testament* (New York: Columbia University Press, 1962), 117. It should be remembered that the "minor" in the Minor Prophets refers only to the relative size of their message when compared to that of the Major Prophets: Isaiah, Jeremiah, Ezekiel. The Hebrew system of ordering the books refers to the Minor Prophets as the Twelve. All of the "minor" prophets comprise one book in this system. One of the earliest mentions of the Minor Prophets as minor because of size is St. Augustine (*City of God* 18.29): "The prophecy of Isaiah is not in the book of the twelve prophets, who are called the minor from the brevity of their writings, as compared with those who are called the greater prophets because they published larger volumes." Hilary of Poitiers mentions the same idea a few decades earlier in the introduction to his commentary on the Psalms.

4. Jer 26:18 has an intermediate form between the short form (four letters) in Micah and the long form (six letters) in 2 Chr 13:2.

5. Mays, *Micah*, 1.

Micah's name at the beginning and ending of his work (1:1–4; 7:18) sustains the wonder. In the book Micah loses no time in presenting the incomparable God in his awesome transcendence. This God emerges from the throne room of the universe to make a steep, breathtaking, descent to the heights of planet Earth, where the massive mountains dissolve underneath his feet like wax before a burning fire, like water gushing down a slope (1:3–4). For Western thinkers God's transcendence is often described with abstract ideas like omnipotence, omnipresence, and omniscience, but for Micah transcendence was no abstraction. Yahweh's presence immediately dissolves the most enduring elements of material reality, instantly revealing the enormous ontological gap between the infinite and finite. Who is like Yahweh? What is like Yahweh? If no one knows, this first speech provides a quick unforgettable lesson in two short verses.

Throughout the collection of Micah's speeches the audience of Micah, whether ancient or modern, learns a great deal about this God. He is a God who takes his covenant with his people seriously (1:5), who will brook no rivals to transcendence (1:6–7), and who controls the nations—even the dreaded Assyrian army (1:6–16). Yet he is concerned with the plight of the "little people" and their exploitation at the hands of the covetous rich (2:1–3, 8–9; 3:1–3), with telling the truth (2:6–11; 3:5–8), with a just society and the importance of human rights (6:6–8), with the terrible blight of war in the world (4:1–5), and with what it means to be human (6:6–8). In addition, this God is not a dispassionate, distant figure but one who suffers the pain of the victims, is furious with their oppressors (an implication of the many judgment speeches and also 7:18b), and is exasperated with his people because of their failure to respond to his grace (6:3). This is surely a god like no other, a transcendent one—"high and lofty" (this is Isaiah's way of describing transcendence in Isa 6:1), but also concerned with matters of mundane reality like fairness and equity, poverty and wealth, widows and orphans.

If the first short speech describes the transcendence of Micah's God, the last speech concludes on the same note. The final speech (7:18–19) is a hymn sung in answer to the question provoked by Micah's name: Who is like Yahweh? The answer is described in seven characteristics demonstrating ethical transcendence: pardon, forgiveness, cessation of anger, delight in mercy (חֶסֶד/*ḥesed*), conquest of sin, renewal of mercy, and removal of sin. It is interesting that these qualities of God are mentioned at the end of the book, after the sins of the people of Judah have been graphically depicted. Much judgment has been described throughout the text, but the last word is one of grace. But it is certainly not cheap. Forgiveness and pardon have definitely not been severed from justice, as shown by the reference to divine anger.[6]

---

6. As if it were possible to sever forgiveness from justice. Indeed true forgiveness assumes

Thus this forgiveness and pardon are costly; neither does the relinquishment of anger come without a price. But at the end of the book, there is also an end to the divine anger.

The seven qualities have as their structural center an attribute that is central to the divine character, a quality that wells up from within Yahweh's heart and fills his being—חֶסֶד/*hesed*. This word is variously translated "mercy," "loyalty," "covenant love," "fidelity," and "loving-kindness" and is frequently viewed as an obligation placed on a covenant member, particularly the stronger party, to help in a dire situation; but there is also an element of grace and magnanimity extended to the weaker party, much beyond the "call of duty."[7] This is the principal characteristic of Yahweh's heart and personality, for this is what he most delights in. Yahweh never delights in anger but rather *hesed*. This is how he defines his reputation! And so at the end of the book as well as the beginning, Micah states that no creature can compare to God. "Though they [Israelites] are sinners, justly under punishment, YHWH is incomparable as the one whose forgiveness is more powerful than their sins. He delights in mercy and will not persist in anger. Their salvation depends, not on them, but on something in him."[8] This small book of speeches is a miniature mirror image of the theological Mount Everest of Isaiah.

There is another sense in which the rhetorical question posed by Micah's name is not an exclamation of praise but perhaps a cry of desperation. Who is like Yahweh? No one! That is not a cry of doxological wonder, but also perhaps a sense in which it is a lament.[9] For although Micah's people, the people of Judah

---

that there has been a wrong—someone's rights have been violated. Thus forgiveness assumes a just order and retributive justice. See the important study by Nicholas Wolterstorff, *Justice: Rights and Wrongs* (Princeton: Princeton University Press, 2008), 96–108.

7. For the stress on obligation see Nelson Glueck, *Hesed in the Bible* (Cincinnati: Hebrew Union College, 1967); Katharine Doob Sakenfeld, *Faithfulness in Action: Loyalty in Biblical Perspective*, Overtures to Biblical Theology (Eugene: Wipf & Stock, 2001). For a more nuanced and wholistic perspective see Francis I. Andersen, "Yahweh: The Kind and Sensitive God," in *God Who Is Rich in Mercy: Essays Presented to Dr. D. B. Knox*, ed. P. T. O'Brien and D. G. Petersen (Grand Rapids: Baker, 1986), 41–88; Gordon R. Clark, *The Word Hesed in the Hebrew Bible* (New York: Continuum, 1993). One of the most insightful meditations on this word is a thanksgiving song that begins the final book of the Psalter (Ps 107). It begins with the theme that Yahweh is to be praised because he is good. But why is he good? The answer is clear—his *hesed* lasts forever (107:1). Then the meaning of *hesed* is demonstrated: four exemplary situations of absolute and utter helplessness are described. When the people in these exigencies are at the end of any and every human resource, they cry out to God, who shows them *hesed* by delivering them. The psalm concludes with an exhortation for the wise to consider and ponder the *hasdê yhwh* (107:43).

8. Mays, *Micah*, 11.

9. I thank Jewel Maclellan in particular for this insight, which she presented in a Bible study on Micah.

in the eighth century BCE, could not compare to God ethically, they were still called to imitate Yahweh and reflect his character and image his personality to the world by sharing and reflecting his values: walking with him and doing justice and loving *ḥesed*. They were supposed to be a channel through which the world would be blessed (Gen 12:3; Ps 67:1–2), a kingdom of priests (Exod 19:1–6), a showcase of God to the surrounding world.[10] God's covenant with Israel aimed at helping the nations to pursue righteousness and justice and thus mirror Yahweh's "way"—his essential mode of being and personality to the world (Gen 18:19). Israel was the beginning of God's salvation project for a world that had hopelessly lost its way. Unfortunately, Judah during Micah's time had also lost its own way. Yet Yahweh did not give up on his people—he called them back to their roots and their fundamental identity, calling, and mission. One of the ways he did this was to raise up the eighth-century prophets, one of whom was Micah of Moresheth. Throughout his collection of speeches Micah laments the paucity of those who are like Yahweh—practitioners of justice and lovers of *ḥesed*. In fact such people have vanished from the land (7:1–2). Judah had become a failed state like modern Somalia and Honduras, where might became right, and the country one vast "Hunger Games,"[11] with the wealthy preying on the rest of the population.

If Micah's name signals important information about his message, little is known about *Micah the person*, and this is not that surprising since the details of the prophets' lives were not nearly as important as their calling and their obedience in being a vehicle for the divine word in history. The reason why we even know something about their personal lives is because of their calling. Who they were was not as important as what they had to say. Ellul makes a comment about this "anonymity" in describing an Israelite slave girl in a foreign household who told her master about a prophet in Israel who could heal him. Once she points her master to the prophet Elisha, she vanishes from the story: "Even her name is not recorded and the rest of her human adventure is without importance. She has borne the Word of God, and this is the decisive event in her life both for herself and others."[12]

10. Note the important study of Israel by Christopher Wright in which he develops these themes. Wright speaks of Israel as being God's "shop window" to the world: "The whole history of Israel . . . is intended to be the shop window for the knowledge of God in all the earth. This is the reason the story is to be told from generation to generation"; *The Mission of God: Unlocking the Bible's Grand Narrative* (Downers Grove: IVP Academic, 2006), 172.

11. See Peter Hitchens's comments about a visit to Somalia as a journalist; *The Rage against God: How Atheism Led Me to Faith* (Grand Rapids: Zondervan, 2010), 92–97.

12. Jacques Ellul, *The Politics of God and the Politics of Man* (Grand Rapids: Eerdmans, 1972), 30–31.

Ellul's remark is also true for the prophets. Their words have been preserved not because of their elegant rhetoric or political astuteness but because they were also the words of the living God.[13] As Wolff observes: "What holds true for all the prophets holds true for Micah: his life has disappeared behind the word which he was sent to proclaim."[14] That being said, some knowledge can be gleaned about Micah the man from the record he left as well as some other sources.

His hometown was Moresheth, which is probably to be identified with Moresheth-gath. Its name means "acquisition" or "inheritance," and it is linked with the Philistine city of Gath probably because of its proximity to this larger center. It is likely to be identified with modern Tell el-Judeideh, about ten kilometers southeast of Gath and about the same distance northeast of Lachish.[15] An ancient line of interpretation identifies it with the nearby town of Mareshah (e.g., the Targum on Mic 1:1; cf. Josh 15:44) but these two towns are distinguished in Mic 1:14–15.

Moresheth was a border town, in the liminal zone between central Judah and Jerusalem on the one hand and the Philistine culture and the Via Maris on the other, and therefore part of the interface between these two major cultures.[16] People from this locale would have been aware of international movements as a result of being near the Via Maris—the main traffic artery between Egypt and Mesopotamia. Growing up in this town would result in exposure to the influences of significant cultural currents from all directions: cultural and political pressure from Jerusalem to the east in order to protect its western boundary; similar pressure from the west as Philistia sought to enlarge its own sphere of influence; international currents from the Mesopotamian north and the Egyptian south as the cultural traffic moved up and down the Via Maris trading in goods and ideas.

Because of its location, situated in the rich and fertile land of the southern hill country of Judah, Moresheth was an important farming community.

---

13. See, e.g., the comments in a similar regard by T. S. Eliot: "The Bible has had a literary influence not because it has been considered as literature but because it has been considered the report of the Word of God"; *Selected Prose of T. S. Eliot*, ed. Frank Kermode (New York: Harcourt Brace, 1975), 98.

14. Wolff, *Micah the Prophet*, 4.

15. Eusebius the historian identifies it east of Eleutheropolis (*Onomasticon* 716). The ancient Madaba Map, in the same general location, has a citation: "Morashti, from which the prophet Micah came." Jerome identified it with Eleutheropolis, Beit Jibrin. See further Philip J. King, *Amos, Hosea, Micah—An Archaeological Commentary* (Philadelphia: Westminster, 1988), 60.

16. See Ron Tappy's work for the importance of such sites as being the interface between two worlds; Ron E. Tappy and P. Kyle McCarter Jr., eds., *Literate Culture and Tenth-Century Canaan: The Tel Zayit Abecedary in Context* (Winona Lake: Eisenbrauns, 2008).

It provided not only fruits and vegetables for self-subsistence but also surplus produce for the markets of nearby villages. It was a strategic border town protecting the southwest flank of Judah from invasion. Thus the Chronicler remembers Rehoboam fortifying the nearby village of Mareshah after the secession of the northern tribes from the united kingdom (2 Chr 11:5–12).[17] The king probably feared an attack from Egypt and attempted to provide the Judahite equivalent of a Maginot Line by fortifying a battery of towns. Moreover, the Chronicler described an event later during the reign of Asa, in which an enormous Ethiopian army was stopped in its tracks at Mareshah by a small contingent from Judah, who depended on divine help (14:9–12). If Mareshah and its surrounding towns—including Moresheth, were historical symbols of divine aid in times of national crisis,[18] this would have registered an impact on the local consciousness in the same manner that such national symbols as Gettysburg and Stalingrad shaped American and Russian thought. Finally, the Chronicler depicts a prophet criticizing a king of Judah for making an alliance with an idolatrous king of Israel (20:35–37). This prophet was named Eliezer from Mareshah, and he dared to condemn a commercial and military alliance for theological reasons. If such stories or others like them were available to the residents in the villages nearby, they would have made an impression on young minds as they learned about the heroes of their past and had their worldview shaped accordingly,[19] and Micah would surely have been included in this group.

Micah was probably a farmer in the agrarian community of Moresheth. He certainly identified with the members of his village whose small farms were being swallowed up by wealthy landowners (2:1–4). He frequently uses shepherd imagery in his oracles (2:12–13; 4:6–8; 5:4–5, 8–9; 7:14–15) and farming imagery in his description of the ideal society (4:3–4), as well as descriptions of judgment (4:13), futility curses (6:15), and the widespread corruption in society

17. There is a good possibility that the Gath of 2 Chr 11:8 is a short form for Moreshethgath and has been eliminated because of the next reference to Mareshah. See Carl S. Ehrlich, *The Philistines in Transition: A History from ca. 1000–730 B.C.E.* (Leiden: Brill, 1996), 62; and Yohanan Aharoni, *The Land of the Bible: A Historical Geography* (Philadelphia: Westminster John Knox, 1979), 330–32.

18. The assumption being that these stories are not just later fabrications of the Chronicler, even if they are theologically embellished. See further Anson F. Rainey, "The Chronicler and His Sources—Historical and Geographical," in *The Chronicler as Historian*, ed. M. Patrick Graham, Kenneth G. Hoglund, and Steven L. McKenzie, Journal for the Study of the Old Testament Supplement 238 (Sheffield: Sheffield Academic Press, 1997), 55–58.

19. On such "lived out narratives" as a means of worldview formation, see Christian Smith, *Moral, Believing Animals: Human Personhood and Culture* (New York/Oxford: Oxford University Press, 2003), 63–94.

(7:1–2). He certainly knew the countryside of southwestern Judah (1:8–16)! Like most people growing up in a small farming village, he would have been familiar with the ways and means of agrarian life. Wolff believes that Micah was also a leading elder in the town of Moresheth, which explains his concern for justice and the plight of the small farmer and the poor. This might also explain the possibility of his literacy (cf. 3:1).[20]

One thing that is known for certain about Micah is his courageous proclamation of God's judgment to a nation that would have been shocked by his words. Against Micah was arrayed all the organized structure of a corrupt economic, political, and religious system. But Micah rose to the challenge and flatly contradicted false assurances of prosperity in the face of massive injustice. There was no nuance or political correctness in his speech. To those who urged him to curtail his message of divine judgment, he countered with searing words that they preached an insidious prosperity gospel (2:6–11). To a judicial system that sanctioned "bloody murder," Micah argued that "what goes around comes around" (3:1–4). Economic pirates and landgrabbers, Micah declared, would also one day lose everything, including their own souls (2:1–5). Micah was unafraid to name the "elephant in the room" and speak the plain truth. To priests who argued that the temple was evidence of divine privilege, Micah announced that it could not coexist with blatant injustice. The magnificent temple would crumble into ruins on the ash heap of history (3:9–12).

Micah was the first to announce the destruction of Jerusalem and the sacred temple, the sign of God's presence and blessing among his people,[21] the theological center of the world. Zion was the place of blessing and life forever more (Ps 133), the spiritual home of Israel and the world (Ps 84, 87), with a divine guarantee of "eternal security" (Ps 46–48). To receive this electrifying message of judgment on the nation must have been a stunning revelation to Micah himself; to announce this outrageous news would require almost supernatural empowerment. It is probably no accident that the oracle that announced Micah's miraculous reception of the message and the empowerment to declare it precedes the speech announcing the destruction of Jerusalem and the temple:

> *Nevertheless, I am filled with power—the Spirit of Yahweh—and justice and strength, to declare to Jacob his transgression, to Israel his sin!* Listen now

20. Wolff, *Micah*, 5–9.

21. "He was apparently the first prophet to proclaim the unconditional judgment of Yʜᴡʜ upon Jerusalem"; Mays, *Micah*, 13. As earlier precedents, the tabernacle at Shiloh had been destroyed, and the ark of the covenant captured (1 Sam 4–5). Although the destruction of the tabernacle at Shiloh is never explicitly described elsewhere in Scripture, it can be inferred from other texts (cf. Jer 7:12).

to this, O heads of the house of Jacob, leaders of the house of Israel, you who abominate justice and pervert everything that is right, who build Zion with blood. . . . Therefore because of you, Zion will be ploughed like a field, Jerusalem will become a heap of ruins, and the temple mount will become a high place in the woods! (Mic 3:8–12, my translation; emphasis added)

"This is Micah's task: to proclaim what no one likes to hear."[22]

Micah was not only courageous; he also knew the history and religious traditions of his nation. He was familiar with the motif of a woman having birth pangs and giving birth to a deliverer (Mic 4:9–10; 5:1; cf. Gen 3:15); a covenant with the patriarchs (Mic 7:20)[23] and the patriarchal blessings of healing for the nations and curses on enemies (Mic 5:6–8; cf. Gen 12:1–3); the crippling of Jacob/Israel (Mic 4:6–7; cf. Gen 32:32); the blessing of dew on Jacob (Mic 5:7; cf. Gen 27:28) and a lionlike ruler from the tribe of Judah (Mic 5:8; cf. Gen 49:9; Num 24:9); the exodus (Mic 6:4); the early Israelite leadership of Moses, Aaron, and Miriam (6:4); and the story of Balak and Balaam (6:5). He was aware of the early covenant at Sinai[24] and its foundational stipulations such as the prohibition of coveting (2:2), the early Israelite credo (7:18–19), the conquest and the ban (חֵרֶם/*ḥērem*) (4:13), the apportioning of lands to the tribes and clans of Israel (2:4–5), and the theological notion of the land as a place of security and rest (2:10). He knew about the deaths of Saul and Jonathan and David's dirge in their honor (1:10; cf. 2 Sam 1:20) as well as traditions of David's birthplace in Bethlehem (Mic 5:2) and his hideout in the cave of Adullam while a fugitive (1:15). The Zion traditions were especially important for him (4:1–5:5).[25] He was also cognizant of the basic history of his northern neighbor, Israel, as is shown by his knowledge of the unjust practices of the house of Omri (6:16).

Finally, Micah's oracles exude passion. His first depiction of himself is as a wild animal wailing over the fate of his people. Who is this person who walks naked and barefoot through the countryside, lamenting the destiny of his country before the approaching juggernaut of the Assyrian army (1:8)? Throughout the rest of his oracles, his anger at oppression, his sympathy for victims as he became their lone voice (2:9; 3:1–3; 4:6–7), and his scathing denunciations of injustice show that he was not just an impersonal mouthpiece for God. He even identified himself completely with his people, expressing

22. Wolff, *Micah*, 105.
23. This of course assumes that Micah was the speaker of this oracle.
24. See A. S. van der Woude, "Micah ii 7a und der Bund Jahwes mit Israel," *Vetus Testamentum* 18 (1968): 388–91.
25. See J. J. M. Roberts, "The Davidic Origin of the Zion Tradition," *Journal of Biblical Literature* 92 (1973): 329–44.

grief and woe for their corruption (7:1–6), their future judgment, and hope for vindication.[26]

What about the *times* in which Micah lived? Such a consideration shows the importance of history for understanding the biblical message. Without historical context and color, the word of God would be like a timeless communication dropped from the sky. Calvin reminds his readers of the importance of history when seeking to understand and apply the prophetic message. He mentions that Micah's "sermons would be useless, or at least frigid except his time were known to us, and we be thereby enabled to compare what is alike and what is different to the men of his age and in those of our own."[27] Thus the knowledge of the times of Micah contributes to understanding and application.

The historical context of Micah's prophecies is dated rather precisely to the reigns of three kings of Judah: Jotham, Ahaz, and Hezekiah (1:1). Nowhere in his recorded speeches does Micah explicitly mention any of these kings. There may be an allusion here or there,[28] but nonetheless they remain anonymous. This literary absence might function as a critique of the Davidic dynasty in the interest of highlighting a just Davidide who would someday rule "to the ends of the earth" (5:4). Some suggest that this failure to target the king indicates a naïve support of a righteous king surrounded by evil counselors,[29] or that Micah implicitly supported Hezekiah in his earlier attempts to reform the nation,[30] or that Micah was simply not interested in politics. The first king's rule under whom Micah prophesied was Jotham, who was a coregent with his father, Uzziah, for a number of years before assuming sole kingship around 742 BCE and reigning until 735. He was succeeded by his son Ahaz, who ruled for twenty years, and he in turn was followed by Hezekiah who assumed leadership for twenty-eight years, until 687.[31] This leaves us with a maximum period of fifty-five years for Micah's prophetic activity and a minimum of twenty years. But since it is known from other sources that Micah predicted the destruction of the temple during the crisis of Sennacherib in 701 BCE (Jer 26:18–19), and

---

26. See his constant references to "my people" (1:9; 2:4, 8, 9; 3:3, 5; 6:3 [God], 5 [God]—note also that "my glory" probably refers to Israelite children in 2:9b) and his identification with them in 7:8. But also cf. "this family" (2:3) and "this people" (2:11), where it is clear that he is distancing himself from the evil in his society.

27. Calvin, *Twelve Minor Prophets*, 151.

28. E.g., some scholars think that 5:1 refers to Hezekiah during the time of the Assyrian siege in 701 BCE but he has been demoted to the position of a judge; others think that his help is satirically questioned in 4:9.

29. Hillers, *Micah*, 43.

30. Waltke, *Micah*.

31. His last ten years would have been a co-regency with his son, Manasseh.

since the most likely historical context for the description in Mic 1:8–16 of the devastation coming to southwestern Judah was during this historical period (1:2–16), the minimum period of Micah's prophetic activity would be about thirty-five years.[32] While one cannot achieve certainty in such historical matters, many of the oracles suggest that the period before and leading up to 701 is the most suitable historical context for the present collection of speeches.[33]

When Jotham came to the throne in Judah, a remarkable period of stability and peace ended in both the northern and southern kingdoms. In the north, the long dynasty of Jehu had just finished, and for the next two decades there would be an unbroken sequence of bloody coups.[34] At the beginning of this period there was a dawning awareness of the growing Assyrian threat to the northeast, and there would be political machinations and intrigue among the various powers in the neighborhood of Israel to try to thwart the Assyrian giant as it moved further to the west and south to satisfy its insatiable lust for conquest.

The main Assyrian king who began "to knock on Israel's door" was Tiglath-pileser III, known as "Pul" in the Bible (2 Kgs 15:19). When he entered the Levant, he ruthlessly smashed a coalition army of neighboring states and demanded tribute. Then after a failed attempt by Israel and Aram to stop him, he was able to exact tribute from King Menahem of Israel, who became a puppet ruler. Menahem's brutal reign seems to have ended with natural death, and he was succeeded by his son Pekahiah, who was assassinated by Pekah, who led an equally brief nationalistic revolt resulting in his own assassination by Hoshea, who in turn became another Assyrian marionette. When Tiglath-pileser died, Hoshea seized the opportunity to revolt against Assyria, thinking that he would receive aid from Egypt. It was a fatal mistake. The new Assyrian king, Shalmeneser III, returned with a vengeance, and the northern kingdom of Israel soon became relegated to the historical dustbin. Its capital city, Samaria, managed to survive the death of Shalmeneser but Sargon II applied the *coup de grâce* in 722, mercifully ending Israel's death throes.

In the south, Uzziah's death, which culminated a long period of stability

32. Calvin argues plausibly for a period of about thirty years but he is not dogmatic; *Twelve Minor Prophets*, 151.

33. Many scholars hold to the belief that oracles found in Mic 4–7 come from a much later time than Micah's, being composed and delivered during the exile and postexilic periods. For various reasons, I find their views more speculative than convincing.

34. The grim list of assassinations and coups d'etat leaves little to the imagination: Zechariah (746–745), Shallum (745), Menahem (745–37), Pekahiah (737–736), Pekah (736–732), and Hoshea (732–722), who presided over the destruction of the nation. The only one to die a natural death would have been Menahem. For background on this period see 2 Kgs 15–17; Hos 4:1–3; 13:10–11.

and peace, shook the political foundations of the nation. Isaiah experienced his call during this year and was assured, despite the absence of a stable human king, that the real king of Israel, Yahweh, continued to reign (Isa 6:1–3). But such assurance surely had as its background the mood of insecurity and anxiety produced by Uzziah's death. Around the same time, Micah was called to be a prophet. During this unstable period it is unlikely Micah and Isaiah knew each other very well as one was from a farming village twenty-five miles away from the center of Jerusalem, while the other had close links to palace and temple.

Into this politically volatile situation, Jotham was able to navigate some-what ably after the death of his father. There are records of fortifications of Jerusalem under his reign, as well as fortifications on Judah's southwestern flank (2 Chr 27:3–4). At least one military success is noted against Judah's eastern neighbor, the Ammonites (27:5).[35] But during the last part of his reign, there were attempts by the Arameans and the northern kingdom to enlist Judah in a coalition to withstand the growing Assyrian threat from the north. Jotham seemingly resisted such overtures but also paid the price for his resistance (2 Kgs 15:37). After his death, these states continued to attempt to enlist Jotham's son, the young Ahaz, in their efforts to halt the growing Assyrian threat (Isa 7). They threatened force if he did not comply, with a plan to install a puppet ruler in Jerusalem to grant their every political wish. Ahaz was paralyzed with fear, caught between the devil of his northern neighbors whom he knew and the deep blue sea of the Assyrians whom he did not know nearly as well (a situation well described in 7:1–2). Isaiah encouraged Ahaz not to fear the smoldering firebrands from the north, or to cast his lot in with the Assyrians, but to trust in Yahweh alone (7:1–14). "Isaiah had asked Ahaz to believe that it was neither Pekah nor Rezin nor even the mighty Tiglath-pileser who governed history. The world was in the hands of God."[36] For Ahaz, however, the Assyrian armies and chariots whom he could see were more real than an invisible God: After all, "Isaiah offered words; Assyria had an army."[37] Consequently he called for aid from Assyria, which dealt with his unfriendly neighbors in summary fashion (2 Kgs 16:5–9). Impressed by the religion of the Assyrians, Ahaz had a replica of their altar made to specifications, moved the bronze altar of the temple to a more marginal position, and filled the vacated space with the new Assyrian altar (16:10–18). This was sacrilege, the equivalent of replacing a cross in a central position in a Christian church with a statue of a Buddha or a totem. Although

---

35. In summary comments about Jotham's reign (2 Chr 27:7), the Chronicler also mentions other wars in which Jotham was engaged.

36. Heschel, *Prophets*, 82.

37. Ibid., 80.

Ahaz would use the Israelite altar for personal and private enquiry, the public, national faith was clearly that of the Assyrians.[38] In other words, one could have one's personal devotions with Yahweh in private, but Assyria and its gods ruled the public square. The Chronicler has records that make the evil described in Kings seem rather tame. Ahaz built high places in every town of Judah and even placed an altar on every street corner in Jerusalem (2 Chr 28:24–25)!

Not only was Ahaz influenced by Assyrian faith, but also by the local Canaanite cults dotted throughout the land. One of their more notorious practices was that of child sacrifice, and it had not only influenced the wider population, but left its bloody imprint on the king of Judah as well. While the archeological evidence is disputed, both the Israelite historian (2 Kgs 16:2–4) and Micah the prophet converge together to indicate the prevalence of child sacrifice in Israel during the latter half of the eighth century BCE.[39] Micah probably alludes to both the Canaanite practices of using high places as centers of worship *and* human sacrifice (1:5; 6:7).[40]

Some scholars locate a number of Micah's prophecies in this early period of Ahaz but it is difficult to be certain. Micah prophesied the destruction of Samaria before it happened (1:2–7) during the latter period of the reign of Ahaz.[41]

38. The Assyrians probably did not have an aggressive evangelistic, religious agenda. After all, they were polytheists. At the same time it was clear where the center of religious power was, and that had an impact on Israelite faith. See Mordechai Cogan, *Imperialism and Religion: Assyria, Judah, and Israel in the Eighth and Seventh Centuries B.C.E.* (Missoula: Scholars Press, 1974). Steven Holloway argues that religious imperialism was done in both overt and covert ways. Overt methods would include such activities as "godnapping," the stealing of divine images used by conquered peoples, and covert methods would be attempts made to influence the elite population of a conquered country toward the Assyrian way of life, which of course included religion. See *Aššur Is King! Aššur Is King! Religion in the Exercise of Power in the Neo-Assyrian Empire* (Leiden: Brill, 2002).

39. In the parallel passage in 2 Chr 28:3, Ahaz offers up his sons (plural) in sacrifice. See Mordechai Cogan and Hayim Tadmor, *II Kings* (New Haven: Yale University Press, 1988).

40. Andersen and Freedman make a case that human sacrifice *could* be described in 3:1–4 but this type of human sacrifice resulting in cannibalism would have been improbable in ancient Israel; *Micah*, 354, 533. For examples of cannibalism or anthropophagy born of desperation see Deut 28:52–57 and 2 Kgs 6:26–31. See also the desperation produced by a famine depicted in the Babylonian version of the *Atrahasis Epic* D (i) 36–38 and D (ii) 48–51: "[When the sixth year arrived, they served up] the daughter for meal, they served up the[son for food]; one [house] consumed another." For discussion about cannibalism in the ancient world and a discussion of this text, see Beate Pongratz-Leisten, "Ritual Killing and Sacrifice in the Ancient Near East," in *Human Sacrifice in Jewish and Christian Tradition*, ed. Karen Finsterbusch, Armin Lange, and K. F. Diethard Römheld (Leiden: Brill, 2007), 11–12.

41. But cf. Mays (*Micah*, 25, 46) who thinks the prophecy against Samaria constitutes part of a written redaction in the late seventh century that seeks to produce a unified theme of a prophecy against Samaria and Jerusalem in Mic 1, in order to fulfill the scheme of Micah

This is the only explicit prophecy about Samaria in the prophecy of Micah, and since he was known as a prophet who addressed the northern kingdom as well as the south (1:1), he would have presented many more oracles against Israel that were not written down in his collection of speeches.[42] From the oracle about Samaria that is preserved, it is clear that Micah follows his northern predecessor, Hosea, in viewing the idolatry of the northern kingdom as an expression of adultery and infidelity (1:7).

When Hezekiah became king in 715,[43] he continued some of the same practices as his father. Many of the same social policies and corrupt religious practices in the culture remained in place. It was a time of oppression of the poor by the rich and powerful as well as religious syncretism.[44] Throughout Micah's oracles, there is an awareness of the disenfranchisement of people from their homes and land by creditors and robber barons, trafficking in children, corruption in the courts, along with the support of an immoral religious system that provided a theological rationale for social injustice. A few of Micah's oracles can be reasonably dated to Hezekiah's time. The ominous description of the fate of the cities in southwestern Judah suggests the Assyrian advance on Jerusalem in 701 BCE (1:8–16).[45]

But in Micah's eyes there may have been a warm-up to this campaign

---

prophesying against both capitals, which is noted in the editorial inscription. But why could not Micah have prophesied the destruction of Samaria before it happened? In my judgment this would have given his prophecy against Jerusalem more theological authority. Mays seems to vacillate in his judgment about this text as he writes about it being editorial and then considers that if some of it is original with Micah it would be the only prophecy that could be dated before Hezekiah's accession.

42. Some scholars believe that other oracles of Micah are linked to the northern kingdom and thus Samaria. See, e.g., Shaw, *Speeches of Micah*, 223–25.

43. There are issues with the dating of Hezekiah but I follow Bright and Albright here. For a thorough discussion of the dating problem, see A. K. Jenkins, "Hezekiah's Fourteenth Year: A New Interpretation of 2 Kings xviii 13–xix 37," *Vetus Testamentum* 26 (1976): 285–98.

44. The recent discovery of a seal with the inscription "Hezekiah, son of Ahaz" along with a diagram of a sun with wings and two Egyptian Ankh signs suggests religious syncretism. See Nir Hasson, "Seal Impression with King Hezekiah's Name Discovered in Jerusalem," *Haaretz* (December 2, 2015); available online at haaretz.com/jewish/archaeology/.premium-1.689594.

45. Shaw (*Speeches of Micah*, 222) dates this to a very early period (747) while Wolff (*Micah*, 2–4) to the period shortly after the destruction of Samaria, but most scholars see in this passage the western approach of Sennacherib in 701. Isaiah also describes a northern approach (10:28–32). As a basic point, it can be affirmed that the prophetic book of Micah contains only a small sample of the total extent of the prophesying of Micah. To be a prophet for a period of about twenty-five to thirty years and have speeches that total only about one half hour of speaking would strain credulity. Cf. Rudolph who remarks: "Was wir heute besitzen, kann nur ein Bruchteil der Verkündigung des Propheten sein"; *Micha, Habakuk, Zephanja*, 21.

as the Assyrians under Sargon II quashed a rebellion in which Judah may have been involved in 712/711. Judah was tempted to be a participant with other states, including Moab, and Edom centered in the Philistine city-state of Ashdod. Help was requested from Egypt in their revolt. Isaiah himself went barefoot and naked in Jerusalem as a prophetic sign of what would happen to the rebels (Isa 20). The Assyrians crushed the rebellion and probably attacked Azekah as a warning to Hezekiah to remain submissive to Assyrian rule.[46] But Micah could easily have seen this conquest as a warning to Judah. After all, he had earlier prophesied the conquest of Samaria by the Assyrians, and the enemy was now on Judah's southwest doorstep. Even nearby Gath had been decimated.

The campaign of 701 was probably precipitated by the death of Sargon II in 705 and the accession of Sennacherib. Judah as well as other states would have taken this opportunity to cast off the oppressive Assyrian yoke. The Assyrians first had to suppress a revolt in Babylon, but they eventually came to the west to settle accounts. The vision of Micah in 1:8–16 probably addresses the coming ravaging of the Judean countryside in 701 under Sennacherib. Significantly, there is no mention of the destruction of Jerusalem. The Assyrian war machine comes to a halt outside the city gates. Micah's prediction of the destruction of the temple (3:9–12) seems best suited to this period, and it is independently confirmed one hundred years later. When Jeremiah predicted the destruction of the temple, he was immediately accused of treason and faced execution. He was defended by an individual who remembered the remarkable precedent of Micah's pronouncement of doom a century earlier. Instead of being executed, Micah became a national hero for inspiring repentance led by none other than the king himself:

> Then the officials and all the people said to the priests and the prophets, "This man does not deserve the sentence of death, for he has spoken to us in the name of the LORD our God." And some of the elders of the land arose and said to all the assembled people, "Micah of Moresheth, who prophesied during the days of King Hezekiah of Judah, said to all the people of Judah: 'Thus says the LORD of hosts,
>
> > Zion shall be plowed as a field;
> > > Jerusalem shall become a heap of ruins,
> > > and the mountain of the house a wooded height.'

---

46. Hayim Tadmor, "Philistia under Assyrian Rule," *Biblical Archaeologist* 29 (1966): 86–102.

Did King Hezekiah of Judah and all Judah actually put him to death? Did he not fear the LORD and entreat the favor of the LORD, and did not the LORD change his mind about the disaster that he had pronounced against them? But we are about to bring great disaster on ourselves!" (Jer 26:16–19)

This indicates that Micah's electrifying oracle of judgment evoked repentance in Hezekiah and the people and led to the temple and city being saved during the Assyrian crisis of 701 BCE.[47] The main brunt of judgment oracles was probably spoken before this period of repentance.

That the entire collection of Micah's oracles has been dated to a period of thirty-five years suggests that Micah probably spoke many more oracles than found in the present collection. Moreover, much of that time, except for the crisis that resulted in repentance, was marked by similar social and religious conditions. Presumably this would have been the case for the critique of his people's faith in 6:1–8. That there is no recognition of the momentous impact of Micah's prophesying on the people of Judah within his prophetic book reveals the real interests of the prophets and/or their editors. They had very different goals than modern historians. The words of the prophet were the words of God. The prophet was a vehicle for the word of God in history. Nothing else really mattered. There might well have been sages and analysts in Micah's time who might have given a different perspective on their era but the prophet was an "exegete of existence" from the only perspective that ultimately mattered.[48] This is why his words were preserved. As the words of God, they transcend their original historical context to speak to all who hear and read them.

The Oracles and Their Structure

The speeches in Micah had a preliterary stage.[49] They were probably spoken before they were transmitted in writing and became part of a literary collection. Micah would not have written out his speeches before he delivered them orally,

---

47. Alfaro, *Justice and Loyalty*, 4.

48. Ibid., 1.

49. Although this has been the traditional view, it is increasingly being called into question as some scholars now argue that the book was written by a literary elite and most likely therefore had a literary origin much later than the time mentioned in the historical superscription. Although it was set in the period described in the historical note, this was a literary fiction: "At best it characterizes a monarchic prophet of old, Micah, according to the way he was imagined by the community of literati within which the book was composed, read and reread. The same holds true for the social conditions referred to in the book"; see Ben Zvi, *Micah*, 10.

although there is precedent for this with at least one other prophet (cf. Jer 36).[50] Only a few parts of the book itself have a literary origin, for example, the book's superscription, which functions as the initial part of the prophet's curriculum vitae, providing information about the author, his location, authority, historical period, and the recipients of his messages (1:1; cf. 3:1a). About twenty to thirty independent speeches can be identified, and each of these would have had a specific social and historical context that can no longer be precisely identified.[51] The original oral nature of these speeches is quite clear. As Renaud remarks, "Let us not forget that the oracles have been spoken before being written."[52] Sudden transitions in theme, choppy sentence structure, the use of wordplay and puns that would have been more recognizable to the ear than to the eye, the switch in person and number on verb forms, the use of imperatives and oral interjections, grammatical incongruities, semantic ambiguities, and colloquialisms—these all indicate the oral nature of the original discourse. In other words, the written form of these speeches largely preserved their original oral qualities.[53] Discourse that is first composed in writing has more thematic coherence, more logical structure, more grammaticalization, and more extensive vocabulary to compensate for the loss of paralinguistic features such as tone, gesture, stress, and emphasis.[54]

With the aid of some historical and sociocultural evidence revealed in the various speeches, reasonable conjectures can be made about their original historical context, but that *specific* context has been largely obscured in the

50. But even in this example the original speeches were first oral compositions. Jeremiah did not write them but had his scribe, Baruch, record them on a scroll that was then read to the people on a feast day at the temple. There is also a story of Elijah composing a judgment oracle in a letter and sending it to King Jehoram of Judah (2 Chr 21:12-15).

51. Francis I. Andersen isolates twenty-seven such poetic units; "The Poetic Properties of Prophetic Discourse in the Book of Micah," in *Biblical Hebrew and Discourse Linguistics*, ed. Robert D. Bergen (Winona Lake: Eisenbrauns, 1994), 520-28. My count is lower, due to my thinking that some of his units are stanzas in a poetic composition. Shaw (*Speeches of Micah*, 17-23, 221-25) argues that there are six well-crafted speeches in the book.

52. "N'oublions pas que les oracles ont été parlés avant d'être écrits"; Renaud, *Formation du Livre de Michée*, xviii.

53. Note a similar point made for Mark's Gospel: "[It] is in no way the smooth product of a skilled author seated at his desk, but has all the vividness and peculiar patterns of speech that one finds in actual transcripts of live speeches"; David Alan Black, *Why Four Gospels?* 2nd ed. (Gonzalez, Fla.: Energion, 2010), 67.

54. David Olson, "Oral Discourse in a World of Literacy," *Research in the Teaching of English* 41 (2006): 136-43. I find it remarkable that Ben Zvi can observe these same qualities and argue that they are "consistent with a highly literate text written first to be read and reread by a community of literati, and second to be explained by the literati to other social groups with less than high literacy"; *Micah*, 38.

literary form of the book. The general historical context, of course, is provided by the historical superscription (1:1). Oracles that were originally independent are arranged together in a new literary context that shapes their meaning.[55] Perhaps this new context had a preliterary stage as well. In other words it is difficult to judge whether much of the current literary arrangement had oral precursors. The sequences of oracles abound in catchwords and catchphrases that may have provided a way to link up the oracles orally before fixing them in the permanent medium of writing.[56]

This commentary will attempt to understand the original historical context of the oracles, before considering them in their new literary context. As Waltke notes, the preliterary form of the oracle addressed the original audience in its historical context and the written form of the oracle now addresses all audiences of the book.[57] For example, the oracle against Samaria that opens the book would have had an original context before the destruction of the city in 722 BCE. In its new literary context it begins the book, being paired with an oracle delivered about two decades later in its original context. From a literary point of view both oracles provide examples of God's coming judgment to the two principal recipients mentioned in the titular inscription, Samaria and Jerusalem—in that precise order—and therefore serve to authenticate the prophecies of Micah and stress to all future audiences that these words of his are not ordinary words and that everyone, inevitably, has to do with God.

Similarly the specific historical contexts for the three judgment oracles in Mic 3 would have been different as judicial leaders, prophets, and priests are all addressed. But these three speeches have now been combined into one literary unit that functions to deliver a comprehensive broadside on the civic and religious leadership of Judah. Thus while most of the speeches in the book were spoken at different times and in various places during the timespan indicated in the titular inscription, they have now been fixed in the permanent medium of writing and arranged and edited in such a way that this is a literary accomplishment in its own right. The resulting book is not just a catalog of speeches, arranged without rhyme or reason. There is a strategic design to the overall structure of the book. Thus the book is not a mere anthology of Micah's oral

---

55. For examples of this see Walther Zimmerli, "From Prophetic Word to Prophetic Book," in *"The Place Is Too Small for Us": The Israelite Prophets in Recent Scholarship*, ed. R. P. Gordon (Winona Lake: Eisenbrauns, 1995), 443–52.

56. For a list of the different possibilities see John T. Willis, "Fundamental Issues in Contemporary Micah Studies," *Restoration Quarterly* 13 (1970): 77–90.

57. The leaders at the time (preliterary) and the covenant community throughout its history (literary). See Waltke, *Micah*, 43–44.

proclamations, a sort of "file of sermons,"[58] but it has an intentional design and shape. For example, the only time Micah's name appears in the book is at the beginning; it is hardly coincidental then that there is a wordplay on the prophet's name at the end of the book.[59] That the prediction of the destruction of the temple (3:12) is followed by the prophecy announcing the worldwide exaltation of the temple is surely intentional from a literary point of view (4:1-5). But surely it would not have made sense to pronounce the second oracle immediately after the first as part of one speech in the same place to the same audience!

The literary plan of the book organizes judgment and salvation oracles into three sections of escalating intensity in which the negative notes of judgment gradually are drowned out by the positive notes of salvation, and the final chapter dramatically shifts from a lament to a hymn (see discussion of structure below). This intentional literary strategy shaped the many diverse oral units into a cohesive text. That the first oracle of the book is the only speech that explicitly deals with Samaria is surely a matter of literary design (1:5-7), as is the placement of the only oracle describing the total corruption of Judah near the end of the book (7:1-7). Similarly the summative nature of the final section (7:8-20), bringing to a climax the book's message, is the result of a deliberate editorial plan.

Clearly, then, there is a difference between the presentation of the speeches of Micah in the canonical and literary context of the *book* of Micah and their historical pronouncement as they first came from the *mouth* of Micah. The latter can be regarded as aimed at the *original* audience of the prophet. The former is aimed at the *primary* audience of the prophet. The speeches have now been collected and organized into a new canonical context aimed at a much wider audience, which will have the opportunity to hear or read this new word of God throughout the subsequent generations. Thus from a synchronic point of view, the text is presented as a complete unit from Micah's time. It has also been integrated into a collection of other prophetic writings since "the words of the ancient prophets were important because the Word of God as spoken through the prophets was valid for all time."[60] The prophetic writings were placed into a larger collection of sacred books, which form the Jewish Tanakh or the Christian Bible. This series of contexts could be viewed as ever widening ripples in a lake caused by the original stone (speech) thrown into the water:

---

58. Waltke, "Micah," 13. Although Waltke uses this phrase, he is quick to indicate that this collection is more than an arbitrary collection but it is now a complex literary work in its own right.

59. Micah's name (1:1) means "Who is like Yahweh?" The same question occurs at the end of the book in the sentence "Who is a God like you?" (7:18).

60. Smith, "Book of Micah," 210.

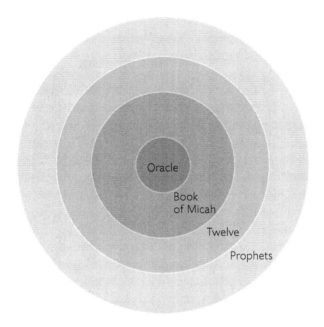

Reasonable judgments about the specific, original social locations of the prophet's many speeches can be made from clues offered in the texts. Thus when Micah is addressing priests it can be assumed he is speaking in a sacred zone like the temple (3:9–12); the speeches to judicial officials imply the courts (3:1–4); the criticism of merchants entails the marketplace (6:9–16).

The book's title (1:1) limits the historical period of Micah's prophesying to approximately thirty-five years. When *the book* was completed is another matter, and when it was integrated into the prophetic collection is still another issue. Suffice it to say that that the book would probably have been written before the time of Jeremiah (one hundred years later) since an oracle of Micah is cited verbatim during this period, and it is presented as originating in Micah's time (Jer 26:18–19). Micah's oracle itself was probably well known since it was used as a precedent to defend Jeremiah's prediction of the destruction of the temple. Its mere citation settled an argument over whether Jeremiah should be executed for blasphemy. It would be reasonable to assume that an edition of Micah's speeches had been in circulation for a long period, sometime after the Assyrian invasion of 701 BCE.

That Micah predicted the destruction of Jerusalem and that the city was spared as a result of national repentance sheds light on the two oracles that begin the book, which essentially authenticate the credentials of the prophet. It is a fact that Samaria and the northern kingdom were destroyed—this prophecy was fulfilled.[61] But the companion oracle depicts the southern kingdom about to be devastated and the Assyrian army at the very gate of Jerusalem. The atmosphere is one of terror as the countryside will witness the progressive onslaught of the Assyrian juggernaut. There is no mention of the capture of Jerusalem, which matches the dire situation of Judah depicted in 2 Kgs 18:13–19:37; Isa 36–37; and Sennacherib's Prism 3.18–46.[62] The salvation of Jerusalem comes at the last possible moment from the Assyrian army—snatched as it were as "a bird from a cage"![63]

Thus both oracles announcing the doom of the capital cities of their respective countries would have probably been placed in first and second position in the book in written form shortly after the titular superscription was written. Both events—the destruction of the northern kingdom and Samaria, and the destruction of the southern kingdom with the exception of Jerusalem—and both predictions of the prophet would have been fresh in the minds of the people of Judah and would have served as nothing else could to authenticate the book of Micah. No explanation would have been necessary for the sparing of Jerusalem from certain destruction since it was already known that Micah's preaching had caused a deep repentance in the nation. So both of these oracles placed together at the beginning of the book would have been most effective if they had been in the relatively recent memory of the editor and his first audience. Their literary transcription and juxtaposition may have coincided with the writing of the book's title (1:1), perhaps the only part of the book that had a literary origin.[64] In my judgment, then, the book was written sometime in the last part of Hezekiah's reign or early in the reign of Manasseh.

This book was probably soon integrated into a collection of the preexilic prophets that gradually evolved. There is uncertainty about when this latter collection was completed, but the last three prophets would have been added in the postexilic period. There is clearly organization in the arrangement of the prophets in the Twelve, and a postexilic redaction probably affected all of the books. It is no accident that Micah is the middle book of a trio that deals with the Assyrian nation in the Hebrew Bible: Jonah, Micah, and Nahum. Each of these books has a meditation on the significance of the divine name for sal-

61. Not in the exact particular details described in Mic 1 but nonetheless the northern kingdom came to an end.

62. See James B. Pritchard, *Ancient Near Eastern Texts Relating to the Old Testament with Supplement*, 3d ed. (Princeton: Princeton University Press, 1969), 287–88.

63. Ibid., Sennacherib's Prism 3.1 27.

64. There clearly is an intentional echo between the use of Micah's name (a rhetorical question) in the superscription and the rhetorical question in the last unit in the book (7:18a).

vation and judgment, a meditation that has significance for the redaction of the book of the Twelve as a whole.[65] In Jonah, the Israelite credo—Yahweh's revelation of the significance of his name to Moses after the debacle of the golden calf (Exod 34:6-7)—is recalled to show that God's heart is merciful to repentant sinners whether they be Israelites or the hated Assyrians (Jonah 4:2). Micah shows that the deliverance of Jerusalem during the Assyrian invasion was certainly due to that same mercy shown the Assyrians, but it also shows the Assyrians have changed and become a warlike people again. And at the end of Micah, there is a clear awareness that because of God's commitment to the covenant, he will not give up on Judah—even after all its evil—but he will purify his people and make them the key to a universal salvation by which his indomitable *ḥesed* heart will triumph over all sin and evil (Mic 7:18-20; 4:1-5). Nahum meditates on the name of God for a now unrepentant and hardhearted Assyria. In the face of unrepentance there is an end to the divine patience, which will by no means acquit the intransigent guilty (Nah 1:2-3). Thus the positioning of this "Assyrian triad" of books is intentional.

It is also part of a deliberate editorial plan that Micah's announcement of the destruction of the temple is found to be the exact midpoint of the Twelve (3:9-12). With this placement the final editors of the Twelve were making a statement about the destruction of the temple and also its resurrection (4:1-5)! This death-and-resurrection temple redaction at the center of the Twelve is roughly paralleled in the other major prophetic books.[66] Thus there is Micah's oracle in Jeremiah about the destruction of the temple that is cited verbatim (Jer 26).[67] The little Book of Comfort soon follows (30-31), which will give the exiles "a hope and a future" (29:11). Similarly, near the center of Ezekiel is an announcement of the destruction of the temple coinciding with the death of the prophet's wife (Ezek 24). After the judgment of the nations (25-32), hope and resurrection comes to the nation and the temple (33-48). And the center of Isaiah is a narrative that announces the coming exile of Judah and Jerusalem at the hands of Babylon (Isa 36-39). Although there is no prediction per se of the destruction of the holy city, it is assumed. This is followed by the coming salvation of not only Judah but the ends of the earth (40-66). This suggests then that the final redaction of the Twelve would have taken place during the postexilic

65. Raymond Van Leeuwen, "Scribal Wisdom and Theodicy in the Book of the Twelve," in *In Search of Wisdom: Essays in Memory of John G. Gammie*, ed. Leo G. Purdue, Bernard B. Scott, and William Johnstone (Louisville: John Knox, 1993), 31-49.

66. For a study of this phenomenon see my unpublished paper, "A Canonical Theology of the Prophets," presented at the 2012 Evangelical Theological Society in Milwaukee. The paper was given in a colloquium on Old Testament theology honoring John Sailhamer.

67. This might explain why there are two temple sermons in Jeremiah!

period, and it helps elucidate the more general structure of the other prophetic books, which probably were redacted earlier: Jeremiah, Ezekiel, and Isaiah.[68]

Scholars have proposed at least eight different literary structures for the book of Micah,[69] ranging from a division of the book into as many as six major sections[70] or as few as two.[71] But the majority of proposals can be reduced to two main alternatives: a bipartite versus a tripartite structure.[72] In the bipartite structure the book is divided into two sections: Mic 1–5 stresses the nations, and Mic 6–7 emphasizes the people of Israel. There are two major alternatives for the tripartite structure of the book: in one view the oracles are roughly divided into speeches of judgment (Mic 1–3), comfort (Mic 4–5), and hope beyond judgment (Mic 6–7); and in the second arrangement each section begins with prophecies of judgment and concludes with oracles of salvation (Mic 1–2, 3–5, 6–7).[73] As the sections unfold, the tempo of judgment decreases while the cadence of salvation increases.

The main arguments favoring a bipartite structure are formal and semantic. The first and second major divisions begin with almost identical wording, with the first addressing the nations and the second addressing the nation of Israel:

Hear, you peoples, all of you. (1:2)	שִׁמְעוּ עַמִּים כֻּלָּם	*šimʿû ʿammîm kullām*
Hear what the LORD says. (6:1)	שִׁמְעוּ־נָא אֵת אֲשֶׁר־יְהוָה אֹמֵר	*šimʿû-nāʾ ʾēt ʾăšer-yhwh ʾōmēr*

The first five chapters then call the nations to hear what God is going to do to Samaria and Jerusalem, and thus they must either submit to his rule (4:1–4) or be punished (5:10–15). The last two chapters challenge the people of Judah to

---

68. E.g., the final redaction of Jeremiah would have taken place at least no earlier than the last historical notation found in the book—the second year of Amel-Marduk's reign (cf. Jer 52).

69. Jacobs, *Conceptual Coherence of the Book of Micah*, 60–62.

70. Shaw, *Speeches of Micah*, 221–25.

71. E.g., see among others, Mays, *Micah*, 2–9; and Jacobs, *Conceptual Coherence of the Book of Micah*, 60–96. Wolff (*Micah*, 17–26, 86) argues for a four-part structure (1–3; 4–5; 6:1–7:7; 7:8–20); Ben Zvi argues (*Micah*, 2–7) essentially for a one-part structure with an introduction (1:1) and conclusion (7:18–20).

72. For a discussion of alternative views, see Mignon R. Jacobs, "Bridging the Times: Trends in Micah Studies since 1985," *Currents in Biblical Research* 4 (2006): 314–15. D. E. Miller's tripartite divisions are 1–3; 4:1–5:8; and 5:9–7:20; and J. R. Wood's are 1:1–16; 2:1–3:12; and 6:1–7:9 with some additions, which functions as a revisor's subplot.

73. See McComiskey, *Micah*, 401; and Waltke, *Micah*, 13–15.

prepare for this coming judgment and to trust in Yahweh who will transform this judgment into the pathway of grace and glory.[74] In the first section the judgment oracles comes first (1–3) followed by the salvation oracles (4–5); in the second division there is a similar pattern (6:1–7:7; 7:8–20).

The main difficulty with this view is that Israel is in the foreground in the first section with the nations in the background. Moreover an oracle of salvation (2:12–13) disturbs the consistent pattern of judgment in Mic 1–3. While there are valiant attempts to understand this oracle as one of judgment and thus consistent with the theme of its context, these attempts are unsatisfying. Third, the final section resumes themes from other parts of the book, particularly with important oracles dealing with the nations (7:11–13, 16–17) and not just the people of God.

Those who discern a tripartite structure of 1–2, 3–5, and 6–7 note how each division begins with a call to hear:

Hear, you peoples, all of you. (1:2)	שִׁמְעוּ עַמִּים כֻּלָּם	*šimʿû ʿammîm kullām*
And I said: Listen, you heads of Jacob. (3:1)	וָאֹמַר שִׁמְעוּ־נָא רָאשֵׁי יַעֲקֹב	*wāʾōmar šimʿû-nāʾ rōʾšê yaʿăqōb*
Hear what the LORD says. (6:1)	שִׁמְעוּ־נָא אֵת אֲשֶׁר־יְהוָה אֹמֵר	*šimʿû-nāʾ ʾēt ʾăšer-yhwh ʾōmēr*

Thus Rudolph sees the book as progressing from judgment to grace,[75] and Waltke entitles the divisions: God gathers (1–2), restores (3–5), and forgives the remnant of his people (6–7).[76]

The proponents of the tripartite division of 1–3, 4–5, and 6–7 claim that the more natural divisions are based on major differences in content.[77] Thus Andersen and Freedman name the respective sections: The Book of Doom, The Book of Comfort, and The Book of Contention and Conciliation.[78] While advocates of the first view might argue that the second view ignores formal links between each of the beginning sections in the interests of semantic content,

74. Mays, *Micah*, 2–11.

75. Rudolph, *Micha, Habakuk, Zephanja*, 21–140.

76. Waltke, *Micah*, 13–16. See also John T. Willis, "The Structure of Micah 3–5 and the Function of Micah 5:9–14 in the Book," *Zeitschrift für die alttestamentliche Wissenschaft* 81 (1969): 191–214.

77. See, e.g., Smith, *Micah, Zephaniah, and Nahum*, 8–9.

78. Andersen and Freedman, *Micah*, 16–27.

those who hold the second view point to the unique use of the narrative verb form in 3:1 linking this section with Mic 1–2; they also observe that the same verb form linking 1:2; 3:1; and 6:1 occurs in 3:9 and 6:9, where it has no larger structural significance.[79]

Other features are used to support this arrangement. Thus beginnings and endings of each major unit echo one another in a head-tail type of linkage. For example, Micah announces "the transgression of Jacob . . . and the sins . . . of Israel" (1:5) at the beginning before the prophecy of the decimation of Samaria into a heap of the field (1:6). At the unit's end, Micah is called "to declare to Jacob his transgression and to Israel his sin" (3:8), and a prophecy of judgment describes Jerusalem becoming a heap in a ploughed field (3:12).

While the strengths of this view can be easily seen, so can its weaknesses. One of its foremost problems is the seamless grammatical connection between 3:12 and 4:1. The sequential verb form indicating the future in 4:1 shows that it is not easily separated from the previous section. Second, as already mentioned, it is difficult to see how 2:12–13 with its positive message fits into the Book of Doom. The two additional uses of the major structural signal that indicates larger divisions of text (1:2; 3:1; 6:1) within a division in 3:9 and 6:9 serve to highlight the stupendous nature of the judgment within each division, dramatizing a radical new departure in the text: first the *temple* (3:9–12) will be destroyed and then the *city* (6:9–16). Finally although the sequential past tense form is used in 3:1 to show the close relationship between Mic 1–2 and Mic 3–5, this form can also be used at the beginning of a major division (cf. Amos 1:2; Lev 1:1). Considerations like these convinced Waltke to change his view from alternative 1 to alternative 2 in his second commentary on the text, written some thirteen years after his first.[80]

In my judgment, then, the first alternative is the most cogent. The three sections (1–2, 3–5, 6–7) are like the three movements of a musical score, with the second and third movements gradually increasing in intensity and volume as the score progresses, with the dark night of judgment gradually fading as the dawn of grace approaches.[81] Each section that begins with judgment ends with

---

79. These points are conceded, e.g., by Willis, "Structure of Micah," 194. See further Jacobs, *Conceptual Coherence of the Book of Micah*, 67–68.

80. Waltke, "Micah," in *The Minor Prophets: An Exegetical and Expository Commentary*, edited by T. E. McComiskey (Grand Rapids: Baker, 1993), 2:591–764; cf. Waltke, *Micah*, 13–16. Sweeney's unique analysis argues for a four-part structure observing a break in syntax in 2:1 and 7:1. Thus his structure is 1, 2–5, 6, and 7. While it is true that there are syntactic breaks in 2:1 and 7:1 these sections are introduced by interjections that tie the oracles to the previous texts, thus supplying reasons for the judgment just pronounced; *Twelve Prophets*, 345–46.

81. Keil does not use this metaphor but he essentially reaches the same conclusion: the three

a note of grace. The first movement announces the judgment of Samaria (1:2–7) and Jerusalem (1:8–16) and the reasons for the impending disaster (2:1–11). It is mainly doom and gloom, and blames the judgment on idolatry, greed, and false prophecy, but it concludes on a note of light and salvation (2:12–13). In the second movement the judgment intensifies as Jerusalem and the temple are razed to the ground, and similarly the reasons for the judgment are amplified: in addition to greed and false prophecy, there is corruption in the courts (3:1–4) and avarice among the prophets (3:5–8) and priests (3:9–12).

However, the flicker of hope that ended the first section becomes fanned into a flame as a future, purified Jerusalem becomes a beacon of hope for the world. But it will not happen until it goes through a crucible of judgment, exile, and purification (4:1–5:15). In the final section there is a further intensification of judgment as God is totally exasperated by the corruption of the people as a whole, not just the leadership (6:1–8). They do not have any of the qualities necessary for covenant life: justice, mercy, and fellowship with God (6:9–16; 7:1–7). But the prophet identifies with the people, and they pass through the fire of judgment. In a summative passage (7:8–20), all the major sections of the book are echoed, and the book ends with a crescendo in which Israel is saved as well as the nations, and God is praised for his justice and his *ḥesed*! In this last section, particularly, there is a concern for the repentance and renewal of Judah coinciding with its salvation. Thus the tripartite structure with its emphasis on repetition, intensification, and progression is an example on a large scale of emphasis—perhaps even an example of the superlative in Hebrew—in which a quality is repeated three times.[82] Yahweh is a God of judgment *and* salvation, and this must never be forgotten, but salvation is the final word!

Two recent studies of the structure of Micah come to some radically different conclusions from the discussion above. First, Ben Zvi views the book of Micah as a parade example of the composition of literature by literati writing a text in postexilic Judah. It contains an introduction (1:1), a body (1:2–7:17), and a conclusion (7:18–20).[83] The book implies a prophet whose ministry can be traced back to the preexilic period. The frequent changes of discourse, the changes in verb number and shifts in gender, and frequent thematic transitions were deliberately composed in writing to reflect the situation of an implied

sections are organically combined "as seen in the clearly marked and carefully planned progressive movement apparent in their contents." Keil says that in the first address the threat of judgment pervades, in the second the messianic salvation, in the third the admonition to repent in order to participate in the coming salvation; *Minor Prophets*, 422–24.

82. See, e.g., Isa 6:3; Jer 22:29; Ezek 21:27; cf. Bruce K. Waltke and Michael O'Connor, *An Introduction to Biblical Hebrew Syntax* (Winona Lake: Eisenbrauns, 1990), 233–34.

83. Ben Zvi, *Micah*, 2–9.

author/speaker. The resulting ambiguity provides an important role for the literati as they seek to interpret the work to their audiences. In other words, they need to make work for themselves, and this is how they do it. There are just a few shades of hermeneutical deconstruction in this approach as Ben Zvi argues that these literati seek to define their roles as "brokers of knowledge" for postexilic Yehud.[84]

Second, Wood makes the case for the book as the script written in the seventh century BCE for a dramatic performance.[85] This explains the changes in mood, speaker, number, gender, and interjections. She argues that a number of exegetical difficulties are readily explained as a speaker's aside to an audience. Many examples are given from Sumerian laments and Greek plays to help elucidate texts in Micah.

While these explanations of the literary evidence in Micah are stimulating, they fail to convince. The same evidence can be explained with the traditional paradigm in which the prophet spoke oracles at various times and places that were later collected and arranged in a literary design. There is no substantial historical evidence for a group of literati who were "brokers of knowledge" for the common people, nor is there evidence of theatrical productions being used in the biblical period. Moreover, such views fail to take into consideration the historical and hermeneutical value of the superscription for the book.

Authorship, Date, and History of Interpretation

Until the advent of the critical period in biblical study, the book was mainly seen as a compendium of speeches of the prophet Micah who lived in the latter part of the eighth century BCE, a contemporary of Isaiah in the southern kingdom of Judah whose ministry overlapped with Hosea and Amos in the northern kingdom of Israel. Early Christian interpretation emphasized Micah as a messianic prophet who heralded the coming Messiah of Israel, who would bring salvation to the world. This emphasis can be gleaned in the New Testament, where the Jewish priests and scribes are depicted as referring to the book of Micah for locating the birthplace of the coming king in Bethlehem in response to a query from Herod: "For so it has been written by the prophet: 'And you, Bethlehem, in the land of Judah, are by no means least among the rulers of Judah; for from you shall come a ruler who is to shepherd my people

---

84. Ibid., 172, 181.

85. Joyce Rilett Wood, "Speech and Action in Micah's Prophecy," *Catholic Biblical Quarterly* 62 (2000): 645-62.

Israel'" (Matt 2:1–6). Similarly the same text in Micah is probably used in John's Gospel to indicate a Jewish expectation that the Messiah would come from Bethlehem: "Has not the scripture said that the Messiah is descended from David and comes from Bethlehem, the village where David lived?" (John 7:42). Other extrabiblical texts from a later period confirm this expectation (Targum Jonathan on Mic 5; Talmud Jerusalem, tractate *Berakot* 2.4, 5a).

With the advent of historical criticism, the historical Micah and his contribution began to recede into the background.[86] This new development was largely influenced by a methodological naturalism that reduced the preexilic prophets' role to preachers of doom. This resulted in the first three chapters being attributed to the historical Micah, whereas the more positive later chapters—"rose and lavender instead of blood and iron"—were from a later more optimistic time.[87] Thus the influence of Enlightenment thought in which the historical process was viewed as an "immanent frame" of fixed links between causes and effects subtly shaped scholars' assumptions.[88] Salvation oracles, whose predictions transcended the historical horizon of Micah, simply could not be attributed to him.[89] The practical outworking of this would mean that later disciples or tradents of the eighth-century prophet, possibly a Micah school, would have been responsible for these "predictive" oracles. Thus, for example, Ewald viewed chapters 1–5 as original to Micah and chapters 6–7 as being composed during the reign of Manasseh, which was notorious for rampant religious apostasy.[90] But it was not long before the acids of histori-

86. For a history of this process, see Knud Jeppesen, "How the Book of Micah Lost Its Integrity: Outline of the History of the Criticism of the Book of Micah with Emphasis on the 19th Century," *Studia Theologica* 33 (1979): 101–31.

87. For a concise description of the history of research on the book, see the two studies by Jacobs, *Conceptual Coherence of the Book of Micah* and "Bridging the Times: Trends in Micah Studies since 1985," *Currents in Biblical Research* 4 (2006): 314–15. The idea that the prophets could not be prophets of both judgment *and* salvation continues to be one of the essential assumptions of source analysis. In the classic words of Julius Wellhausen there can be no mixture of blood and iron with rose and lavender (in his comments about Amos 9:11–15). The entire passage is worth quoting for it shows how a priori commitments influence interpretation: "Rose and lavender instead of blood and iron. Amos means what he says. After he has just before surpassed all his earlier threats, he cannot suddenly blunt their sharpness, he cannot let milk and honey flow from the cup of Yahweh's wrath at the end. It is a later Jew who has appended this coda, and removed the genuine conclusion, because this sounded too harshly in his ears"; *Die Kleinen Propheten Übersetzt und Erklärt* (Berlin: de Gruyter, 1898), 96.

88. Charles Taylor, *A Secular Age* (Cambridge: Harvard University Press, 2009), 539–93.

89. For a convenient summary of the historical criticism of the book see Renaud, *Formation du Livre de Michée*, vi–xiv.

90. Heinrich Ewald, *Commentary on the Prophets of the Old Testament,* trans. J. Smith (London: Smith and Norgate, 1876), 2.293, 323–26.

cal criticism burned away other parts of the book from the historical Micah. Wellhausen observed similar themes in 7:8–20 and Isaiah 40–55 that pointed to their exilic provenance.[91] Then it was not long before Mic 4–5 was also dated to the period of the exile and restoration, for how could such messianic and even apocalyptic texts be dated to the eighth century BCE?[92] The critical consensus of scholarship that developed argued for nuanced variations of this view, marshaling more evidence. For example, Smith argues that while chapters 1–3 can be traced back to Micah, "nothing short of a complete reversal of current views of Hebrew eschatology . . . could make these chapters [4–5] intelligible for the age of Micah."[93] And as for chapters 6–7, they "seem to be a collection of miscellaneous fragments, coming from widely scattered periods from at least four different authors."[94] Thus it can be stated confidently that "not a word of Micah's is preserved for us concerning Israel's future."[95] Generations later, McKane comes to the same conclusions, arguing that to believe Micah spoke eschatological salvation oracles should "raise eyebrows," and thus it is essentially improbable that one can attribute "an eschatological messianic prophecy to an eighth century prophet."[96]

While certainly valuing the exegetical contributions of the above scholars, in my judgment they work with a methodology—to say it charitably—that limits predictive prophecy of a positive kind. In musical terms, the preexilic prophets had a greatly reduced repertoire of songs. Gordon describes the widespread use of this methodology with less nuanced language as "Procrustean commonplace."[97] Moreover, some scholars' conclusions betray an amazing ability to dissect the text into various literary layers.[98] To set up tensions within

---

91. Wellhausen, *Kleinen Propheten*, 144–47.

92. B. Stade, "Bemerkungen über das Buch Micha," *Zeitschrift für die alttestamentliche Wissenschaft* 1 (1881): 161–72.

93. Smith, *Micah, Zephaniah, and Nahum*, 12.

94. Ibid., 16.

95. Ibid., 25.

96. McKane is criticizing Artur Weiser's and Adam van der Woude's views of 5:1–5. Although he enlists other arguments he tips his historical-critical hand by his use of language; *Micah*, 156–57.

97. R. P. Gordon, "A Story of Two Paradigm Shifts," in *"The Place Is Too Small for Us": Israelite Prophets in Recent Scholarship*, ed. R. P. Gordon (Winona Lake: Eisenbrauns, 1995), 15.

98. The problem can best be illustrated by Smith's comments on the integrity of 6:9–16: "Tradition claims the passage for Micah and cannot be proved wrong; but on the other hand, the surrounding context, which is certainly not due to Micah, is likewise claimed for him by tradition; hence the question must remain open." It is only the content of this oracle that makes Smith demur and consider the reliability of tradition. But then he catches himself and realizes that tradition has not kept him from demurring about other passages. Tradition is only important as a criterion of

the material and on the basis of these tensions divide the content into sources is deeply problematic in my judgment. For example, one historical critic, who detects four redactional levels in Micah, harshly criticizes another for discerning seven![99]

This can become quite a subjective exercise in which basic assumptions predetermine the result. Who is to say that Micah could speak only blood and iron and not also lavender and rose? He probably would not do it at the same time to the same audience, but for someone who prophesied over a span of thirty years there would be many diverse occasions and audiences. As Kapelrud writes, there are many examples in other prophetic works of the integration of judgment and salvation.[100] In particular, Isaiah, Micah's contemporary, did not name his son Shear-jashub ("Remnant shall return") because he could play only the judgment tune on his prophetic harp. He certainly envisioned salvation after the judgment (Isa 8). Although it did not make much economic sense to him—and probably much less to us given his situation—Jeremiah purchased worthless land outside the besieged city of Jerusalem because he had been convinced it would be a great investment some day in the distant future (Jer 32). Did Micah think that judgment was the final word, even though the promises to Abraham seemed to be unconditional? To argue as some scholars do that speeches against social injustice imply a different speaker than speeches against cultic sins like idolatry misses the profound theological link between idolatry and social injustice.[101] Similar Western dichotomies between the cult and ethics lead other scholars to argue that Micah would never have mentioned the heathen diviner, Balaam (6:5), in his criticism of Israel:

> It is well nigh impossible to believe that Micah, whose moral sense was outraged by the greed of oppressive landlords . . . would have alluded with approval [to] such goings on as are attributed to Yahweh and Balaam. He would not have tolerated such coercion of a wonder-worker, such a cheapening of Yahweh.[102]

---

dating when content does not contradict it. By tradition, of course, Smith means the text itself—the superscription; *Micah, Zephaniah, and Nahum*, 130.

99. "Wolfe aboutit à une véritable pulvérisation des paroles prophétiques"; Renaud, *Formation du Livre de Michée*, xi; cf. 380–417. Renaud is commenting on R.-E. Wolfe, "The Editing of the Book of the Twelve," *Zeitschrift für die alttestamentliche Wissenschaft* 53 (1935): 90–130.

100. Arvid S. Kapelrud, "Eschatology in the Book of Micah," *Vetus Testamentum* 11 (1961): 392–405 at 393–94.

101. Mays, *Micah*, 25. On the inextricable connection between injustice, idolatry, and covetousness see the last section of this commentary.

102. McKane, *Micah*, 178.

Such a criticism reveals more about this scholar's beliefs than anything else.

It is interesting to see how much those beliefs enter into the discussion of certain texts. Thus one scholar can be surprised in the lament in 1:8–16 that "not one syllable speaks of the guilt of Judah or Jerusalem."[103] But for the surprise to happen 1:5 and 1:13b must be excised as interpolations. Similar emendations in the same text lead the same scholar to conclude that "the prophet Micah only now and then expressly points to Yahweh as the author of the imminent catastrophe."[104] But this ignores the elaborate introduction to the oracle in 1:2–4, which governs the entire text. Similarly the decision to attribute 7:1–7 to someone other than Micah ignores the literary strategy in the book in which the number of the guilty multiply from a few (2:1–11) to many (3:1–12) to the entire community (7:1–6).[105]

The final editor of the collection of the oracles clearly wanted his audience to understand that Micah was their human author. Presumably this editor was the person closest in time to the original Micah; and this needs to be taken seriously from a historical point of view. Perhaps the failure to give this serious consideration leads to a crisis in exegetical method that resulted in "the growing confusion over conflicting theories of composition [that] has increasingly buried the book in academic debris" and as a result "no general consensus of the book's form and function appears in sight."[106]

The philological commentary on Micah by Andersen and Freedman is not limited by the immanent critical frame of much scholarship. For example in commenting on the salvation oracle of 2:12–13, the authors make the point that "the possibility that Micah saw beyond the judgments of chapters 1–3 to some type of recovery . . . cannot be ruled out *a priori*."[107] This illustrates a willingness to consider the claims of the book itself.

While there are significant conservative evangelical alternatives to this critical position, which hold to substantial authorship by the prophet Micah, they are definitely a minority report. At the same time some critical scholars, without an explicit theological confession, claim that a background in the eighth century BCE supplies the historical horizon for most of the oracles in Micah. For example, Hillers argues that the assumption of a millenarian conceptual background can provide a rational explanation for both the judgment oracles and the messianic salvation oracles of Micah in the eighth century since

103. Wolff, *Micah*, 11.
104. Ibid., 15.
105. Ibid., 23. Wolff argues that the original Micah denounced only the leaders of Judah.
106. Brevard S. Childs, *Introduction to the Old Testament as Scripture* (Philadelphia: Fortress, 1979), 431.
107. Andersen and Freedman, *Micah*, 334.

the judgment oracles can be understood as an intense dissatisfaction for the present order, while the salvation oracles represent the future hope for a new age to replace the old one.[108] Similarly Shaw locates all the oracles before 720 BCE and the fall of Samaria. He claims that a detailed study of the speeches of Micah leads to this historical conclusion.[109] The advantage of these studies is that they attempt to understand the text on its own terms, although still within an immanent frame.

Finally, it needs to be borne in mind that some other factors lead scholars to argue for a later date for many of the oracles in the last half of the book (Mic 4–7). First, belief in the exaltation of Zion is a development found only in postexilic prophets. Second, some references seem to presuppose the Babylonian exile and deliverance from it. Third, the land is described in complete social and moral chaos. In my own judgment none of these considerations are absolutely crucial for deciding the proclamation of these oracles at a much later time than Micah. First, the exaltation of Zion was a very old belief in Israelite theology, being traced back to Davidic times or earlier (Ps 2, 46–48, 84, 87, 132).[110] Second, predictive prophecy could account for the one reference to Babylon in Mic 4:10.[111] Furthermore, there were many periods before the postexilic period when social and moral chaos could have been used to describe conditions in Judah and Israel. One has only to recall some of the prophecies of the other preexilic prophets (e.g., Hos 4:1–3). Finally, the comments of a theologian might help biblical scholars to consider other alternatives. In discussing a particular aspect of the Gospel of John, Volf's observations could be applied not only to Micah but to any other biblical book:

> Methodologically, the decision to treat the text as an integral whole is momentous. It makes the interpretive task possibly less involved, hopefully more profitable, but likely more difficult. Why more difficult? Obvious tensions in the Gospel [of John], and there are many, can be easily solved by multiplying authors and life situations in which they wrote and by explaining that these discrete parts were only later stitched together into the text we have presently. For instance, those who see a tension or even a contradiction between the universalistic claim that the word is "the true light,

108. Hillers, *Micah*, 4–8.

109. Shaw, *Speeches of Micah*, 221–25. Rudolph argues that the great majority of the speeches are those of Micah: the exceptions are 4:1–4; 5:6–8; 7:8–20, and the editorial sutures and glosses are 1:5bb, 7ab; 4:5; 5:4b–5a; 6:9ab; *Micha, Habakuk, Zephanja*, 136.

110. J. J. M. Roberts, "The Davidic Origin of the Zion Tradition," *Journal of Biblical Literature* 92 (1973): 329–44.

111. Unless of course Babylon is a cipher for an evil enemy the way Assyria is in Mic 5.

which enlightens everyone" (1:9) and a particularistic claim of Jesus that he "is the way, and the truth and the life (14:6), or between the affirmation that "God . . . loved the world" (3:16) and Jesus' statement that he "does not pray for the world" (17:9) can assign different statements to different authors and end up with neat positions. But quite apart from the procedure's being conjectural and circular, it is more or less, well, *boring*: The interpreter ends up with a smart book of historical reconstructions containing a string of flat positions. It is religiously and intellectually more profitable to explore the rich relief of the existent text, even if we occasionally have to build bridges across canyons and dig tunnels under impassable mountains.[112]

One can easily see the relevance for the book of Micah, where the basic tension between the judgment and salvation oracles is viewed as unbearable and therefore the tension is relieved by conveniently assigning the relevant texts to different authors. According to Volf, it is far better to live with the tension and let the text indicate what can and cannot be possible. Moreover, he argues that the common tendency to read works from the viewpoint of their unique characteristics confuses rather than clarifies meaning:

> The methodological decision to read the Gospel [of John] from the perspective of what is considered characteristic and unique has, on the whole, the same flattening effect. One construes the theology of John from what is deemed characteristic, and leaves behind other things as irrelevant—things that are said to trail along without being an organic part of John's theology—as though one were making a map of a mountainous region from an airplane on a cloudy day and noting only peaks but nothing below them. It is possible to chop off the peaks, so to speak, for apologetic reasons. . . . But it is no less problematic to disregard everything but peaks in a misplaced zeal for the unique. John can be understood adequately only by holding together the characteristic and the common even when there is a strong tension between them. It is the potentially tension-filled combination of both that gives the Gospel of John—and any other writing, indeed any other thing—its especially peculiar character.[113]

To change the metaphor, the book of Micah is often viewed from the rarefied elevation of the historical-critical airplane as a constellation of islands

---

112. Miroslav Volf, *Captive to the Word of God: Engaging the Scriptures for Contemporary Theological Reflection* (Grand Rapids: Eerdmans, 2010), 94.

113. Ibid., 94n4.

rather than a unified landmass because of the obstructing cloud cover. For example many scholars think of chapters 4–5 with their alternating messages of war and peace as contradictory, much like those of judgment and salvation, and thus a solution must be found in the recensional history of the book. The historical-critical airplane (transporting the scholar) needs to experience a kenotic descent, humbling itself below the clouds to be able to see if there is really a unified landscape to the book of Micah and to discern how these themes can be possibly integrated.[114] This means that the scholar must suspend judgment for a while about what is and is not possible for Mican authorship and try to understand the whole.

Structure

An outline of the book based on formal and semantic grounds is as follows:

Heading of the book: Micah, his message, his times, his audience (1:1)
    First movement—judgment and salvation I (1:2–2:13)
        A. Divine epiphany of judgment (1:2–2:11)
            1. Nations called to hear the Lord's voice and see his epiphany of judgment on Samaria and Jerusalem (1:2–5)
            2. Judgment of Samaria (1:6–7)
            3. Judgment of Jerusalem and exile (1:8–16)
            4. Reasons for judgment and exile (2:1–11)
                a. Judgment on wealthy oppressors (2:1–5)
                b. False prophets attacked (2:6–11)
        B. Divine epiphany of salvation (2:12–13)
            1. Gathering of the remnant (2:12)
            2. Breaker (2:13)
    Second movement—judgment and salvation II (3:1–5:15)
        A. Judgment on the present Jerusalem (3:1–12)
            1. Cannibalism of judicial officials judged (3:1–4)
            2. Corruption of prophets judged (3:5–8)
            3. Corruption of judges, prophets, priests judged with the destruction of temple (3:9–12)

---

114. Again Volf's comments border on understatement but they are accurate: "To be used fruitfully in a theological reading of the Bible, the historical-critical method must, at minimum shed its inherently secularizing bent and be redesigned to accommodate a worldview in which events are not adequately explained through reference to intra-mundane causalities"; ibid., 17.

    B. Future glory of Jerusalem and temple (4:1–5)
        1. Elevation of Zion and salvation of nations (4:1–4)
        2. Exhortation to follow Yahweh's ways in the present (4:5)
    C. Pathway to glory (4:6–5:15)
        1. Future: return of the exiles to form the kingdom (4:6–7)
        2. Present: vacuum of kingship, exile, and labor pains (4:8–5:1)
        3. Time in between: birth of king, remnant, and nations (5:2–9)
        4. Future: return of king, reform, and call to nations (5:10–15)
Third movement—judgment and salvation III (6:1–7:20)
    A. Yahweh's case against Israel (6:1–7:7)
        1. Need for true worship: justice, mercy, and walking with God (6:1–8)
        2. Judgment on injustice (6:9–16)
        3. Total corruption of the nation (7:1–7)
    B. Israel's hope in Yahweh's grace (7:8–20)
        1. Confession, hope, and triumph over the enemy (7:8–10)
        2. Ingathering of exiles and nations (7:11–13)
        3. Divine shepherd (7:14–15)
        4. Repentance of nations (7:16–17)
        5. Hymn of praise to the God of *ḥesed* (7:18–20)

The structure of the book is like a symphony with three major movements, which return to the same themes but increase their tempo and intensity, develop them further, and bring them to a resounding crescendo. These movements are indicated clearly by linguistic signals of prominence, calling the whole world to hear the word of Yahweh (1:2), the leadership of Israel to hear that word (3:1), and all of Israel to hear that word (6:1–2). Each section begins with the present and then gradually moves to the distant future. And each new movement is linked linguistically to the end of its predecessor. Thus as the first movement ends with a return from Babylonian exile and a focus on future leadership (2:12–13), the second movement signals a return to present-day Judah and Jerusalem with a focus on present leadership (3:1). As the second movement ends with a future call to the nations to repent (5:15), the third movement returns to the present with a call for Israel to repent (6:1). The message is loud and clear: in God's amazing grace and in Israel's renewal and obedience is found the hope for the world.

Composition

It is clear that oracles that once existed independently have been organized into a specific literary arrangement. The final editor who added the book's superscription (1:1) gives the impression of living well beyond the time of Micah. Since the superscription is similar to that used for Hosea and Isaiah, the editor probably worked on these prophetic books as well.[115] Whoever combined all of the individual prophetic books of the Twelve together did it at a period much later than the time of Micah and arranged them in an important sequence reflecting the threat of Assyria: Jonah, Micah, and Nahum. These books particularly focus on elements of the Israelite credo that stress God's compassion and judgment (Exod 34:6-7; cf. Jon 4:2; Mic 7:18-20; Nah 1:2-3). Editorial design also ensured that the oracles about the destruction and resurrection of the temple are found at the literary center of the book of the Twelve. This would have happened only when the Twelve was completed during the postexilic era.[116]

It is difficult to trace with certainty the evolution of *the book* of Micah but the following is clear: (1) The book in its final form is a unity, and this is particularly shown by the use of Micah's name at the beginning (1:1) and end (7:18). (2) The first two chapters are logically ordered, first focusing on judgment and then salvation. There is a call to the world to hear Yahweh's witness against it in the theophany of judgment against Samaria and Jerusalem, the two cities just mentioned in the introductory title. It can hardly be accidental that the first two oracles concerning judgment for these two cities occur in the same order: they serve to authenticate the prophet's witness. The second chapter then details the sins of the wealthy who have coveted and stolen land with the support of a corrupt prophetic institution. They will thus be banished from the land, while a purified remnant will return under the leadership of a divine king.

Similarly in Mic 3 there are three separate oracles originating from various contexts: judicial officials are attacked (3:1-4), prophets are castigated (3:5-8),[117] and finally the entire leadership of Judah is addressed (3:9-12). These speeches are all self-contained but each has been linked literarily by their content to emphasize a climactic theme of divine absence. Some attempt to explain this

---

115. There are grammatical similarities (e.g., the kings' names are not coordinated with a conjunction) and Hosea and Micah contain a rare spelling for Hezekiah's name. See Ben Zvi, *Micah*, 18.

116. Knud Jeppesen, "'Because of You': An Essay about the Centre of the Book of Twelve," in *In Search of True Wisdom*, ed. Edward Ball, Journal for the Study of the Old Testament Supplement 300 (Sheffield: Sheffield Academic Press, 1999), 196-210.

117. A good case could be made for arguing that 3:8 is another unit describing Micah's *apologia*. But I include it as part of 3:5-7 since it is probably dependent on this speech.

literary linkage as due to original composition either in speech[118] or writing,[119] but the clear demarcation of each oracle and the different addressees imply independence.

As these oracles culminate in the destruction of the temple, the next two chapters contain various oracles regarding the remnant, present judgment, exile, purification of Jerusalem, birth of a messianic king, and salvation and judgment of nations. These are arranged into four units comprising ten oracles. Again, each probably had an independent oral origin as is shown by one of them being found virtually verbatim in a totally separate context in another prophetic book (4:1-5, cf. Isa 2:1-5). But all the oracles are shaped around the following sequence: future (Mic 4:1-5), present (4:6–5:1), time in between (5:2-9), and future (5:10-15). The goal is first placed in sight, then the method by which that goal will be achieved.[120] This was done in order to juxtapose the resurrected temple and holy city next to the prophecy about their destruction.

The final section contains a number of independent oracles (6:1-5, 6-8, 9-16; 7:1-7, 8-20) designed with a present focus (6:1-16), culminating in a national lament and expectation of a just judgment (7:1-7). Each emphasizes a fundamental failure in meeting the basic requirements of the covenant. Each concludes with a turning from the sin of the nation to a hope in the living God (7:7) and faith that he will hear the liturgical song that follows (7:8-20). This song includes a lament with confession, acceptance of the judgment, and a hymn of hope beyond it.

Thus these independent speeches have been arranged in a strategic literary design. That the last unit (7:8-20) reflects on oracles from other parts of the book suggests that it is used as a conclusion to the book or may have even been composed for this purpose. All of this shows that oracles from each section of the book mutually interpret one another.

Theological Interpretation

This commentary is part of a series that is concerned with theological interpretation, which arises specifically out of a failure of the historical method to address theological issues, and thus it seeks somehow to bridge the gap between historical exegesis and theology, in order to "unite the two so long divided."[121]

---

118. Shaw, *Speeches of Micah*, 19-28.

119. Ben Zvi, *Micah*, 79.

120. See Jacobs, *Conceptual Coherence of the Book of Micah*, 148.

121. Joel B. Green and Max Turner, eds., *Between Two Horizons: Spanning New Testament Studies and Systematic Theology* (Grand Rapids: Eerdmans, 1999), 23.

The text of Micah is more than a piece of historical literature from the ancient world; it is Holy Scripture. Thus this commentary is an attempt to bring together the academy and the community of faith. In many ways this is simply to do what the church has always sought to do, to read the Bible as the words of the living God—not just as a text addressed to one particular historical situation but as a text addressed to all generations. With the rise of historical criticism a huge chasm was constructed between the text and theology. Exegetes were not interested in theology, and theologians practically had no time for the Bible. The current rise in theological interpretation is an attempt to try to build a bridge over the unfortunate divide so that exegesis and theology can dialogue with one another for mutual enrichment. Theology without exegesis is speculation and exegesis without theology is antiquarian.

This commentary will thus stress both exegesis and theology. Historical and literary considerations are the focus of the exegesis but with the ultimate intent of connecting the two horizons of the word of God then to the word of God now. That movement from one to the other will be aided by considering how the context of the canon contributes to the understanding of Micah's words today. Finally there will be a consideration of ten unifying themes of the book, the contribution of Micah to biblical theology, and how the book applies to key contemporary theological issues.

As far as the main commentary section dealing with exegesis and theology, context is imperative for understanding. But as with any hermeneutical method, there are problems. For example, determining the original historical context of an independent oracle is laden with difficulties when there are few clues available. For example, in Amos 7:10–17 it is clear where this judgment oracle originated—the historical context is described as a dispute between the prophet and the high priest while the prophet was predicting judgment at the temple in Bethel. But in Mic 2:1–5, for example, there are few such explicit indicators about location of this speech or its time. That it contains a prediction of judgment for social injustice probably indicates that it was presented before the invasion of Judah by Sennacherib in 701 BCE. Nevertheless there is no certainty about the location and the specific address of the message. There are, however, some clues. As an act of communication, it needed to address its recipients—the wealthy and greedy landowners—probably in a public place where their actions were being witnessed. Perhaps it was a speech in the temple precincts where worshippers gathered, or in the village of Moresheth where administrative state officials were seizing land from local farms.[122] More likely it was directed at the officials as they were actually involved in taking possession of estates, after

122. Wolff, *Micah the Prophet*, 17–26.

37

foreclosure and dispossession of the original owners. Consequently, conjecture is involved but it is the kind of necessary conjecture for understanding any historical evidence.[123]

At the same time there are definite parameters since these oracles are not free-floating timeless entities such as proverbs or maxims. The historical superscription (1:1) places the oracles within Micah's lifetime after he was called to be a prophet, and from historical evidence in various places, evidence can be gathered to help shed light on the original oral contexts of these sayings. Thus an original, historical context for this oracle (2:1–5) in the postexilic period is inappropriate. As the text is studied, certain signs point in a definite historical direction. For example the word "evil," which is used many times, resonates with other passages where evil is described going down to Jerusalem (1:12), and this is most likely in the context of the Assyrian judgment of 701 BCE where the land has been devastated. Assyrian records indicate that forty-six towns were taken, with Jerusalem alone surviving during this period. The context of the prediction of the fields and houses of the greedy wealthy being devastated suggests that such an oracle implies that such judgment was probably imminent.

It is not necessary to know the *exact* historical context in order to understand the words of this oracle, which clearly resonate across the centuries. While a general knowledge of that original historical context is important (cf. 1:1), the precise details are not as important. Some of these points can be illustrated with other literary works. Frye argues that if a person went to see the Shakespearean play *Macbeth* and came away with a greater knowledge of ancient Scotland, she would have missed the point entirely. But if she had learned what it was like for a man to gain a kingdom and lose his soul, she would be a successful interpreter.[124] Similarly, to know the precise historical context of the delivery of the oracle in 2:1 5 without coming away with a revulsion of the evil described is to lose one's exegetical and theological soul.

Some scholars argue that what is important is the *book* of Micah and not the original *oracles* of Micah. I have no problem with this claim as long as no wedge is drawn between the historical and canonical Micah. It is true that we no longer have access to the historical Micah, and surely he said much

---

123. Postmodernists sometimes use such examples to show the limited value of historical exegesis: there can be no certainty. But such contingency does not mean that thereby one glories in uncertainty and that any interpretation therefore is valid. This is patently absurd. For some helpful common sense in this regard, see James Barr, *History and Ideology in the Old Testament: Biblical Studies at the End of a Millennium* (Oxford University Press, 2005), 59–101.

124. Northrop Frye, *The Educated Imagination* (Toronto: Anansi, 1997), 24.

more than what is contained in his collection of prophecies. But we do have his prophecies, and the claim of the text—if the superscription or title of the book is taken seriously—is that these oracles reflect the speech of a person named Micah who lived during the reign of three kings in the late eighth century BCE.

Nevertheless, it is valid to make a distinction between the *Sitz im Leben* of an oracle—its historical context—and its *Sitz im Buch*—its literary context. There is clearly a difference. By juxtaposing oracles that were once independent in a new literary sequence, meaning is affected. For example, in almost all prophetic books oracles of judgment are balanced by oracles of salvation. Clearly this shows that judgment is not the last word of the prophet, nor is salvation something that is cheap. It is important to interpret the prophet's words in the historical context that is given for the oracles but also in the new literary context in which those oracles have been placed. In Micah this is extremely important because the different sections of the book help to mutually interpret one another. Thus references in the third section to a regathering of peoples from various nations (7:11–13) suggest gathering the Gentile nations rather than dispersed Jews, and the reference to the nations fearing Yahweh (7:17) suggests their worship. Consequently nations come to hear Yahweh (4:3) because the divine rule has been extended, that is, made distant (7:11). These texts are thus a further commentary on 4:1–5. Moreover the reference to the nations being instructed by Yahweh in the latter days (4:3) will happen best when Judah follows the same instruction (6:2).

Sitz im Buch needs to be extended also to *Sitz im Kanon*, the larger literary context of the canon, and for Christians that means also the New Testament. That is why in each section of exegesis there is a concern to locate the text in a broader theological context before considering contemporary implications.

Poetic Structure

The oracles of Micah provide excellent examples of Hebrew poetry virtually from the beginning of the book to the end.[125] There may be a few lines of

125. For an in-depth study of these poetic features, see Francis I. Andersen, "The Poetic Properties of Prophetic Discourse in the Book of Micah," in *Biblical Hebrew and Discourse Linguistics*, ed. Robert D. Bergen (Winona Lake: Eisenbrauns, 1994), 520–28. Some scholars argue that the idea of Hebrew verse is an illusion, and others that the entire Bible is written in verse. The truth lies in the middle between these two extremes. In my own studies of Hebrew verse the following grammatical facts separate it from narrative: the verb is usually fixed in first position in narrative (default) and rarely moves to second position for a number of discourse reasons:

prose here and there (e.g., 1:1; 3:1a; perhaps 2:5), but the main core of the book is verse. Much has been written about Hebrew poetry. Within the academy a consensus has emerged over the last few decades that the particular engine that drives Hebrew poetry is not meter or rhyme, nor even syntax, but a feature called intensification.[126] Thus the basic unit is two lines, the second line not just repeating the meaning of the first (parallelism) but intensifying its meaning. This can best be seen when numbers are used in poetic lines; the number in the second line is always higher than the number in the first line:

We will raise against them seven shepherds	הֲקֵמֹנוּ עָלָיו שִׁבְעָה רֹעִים	*hăqēmōnû ʿālāyw šibʿâ rōʿîm*
and eight installed as rulers. (5:4)	וּשְׁמֹנָה נְסִיכֵי אָדָם	*ûšəmōnâ nəsîkê ʾādām*

Will the LORD be pleased with thousands of rams,
with ten thousands of rivers of oil? (6:7)

Sometimes the basic unit transcends two lines for a point of special emphasis. A prime example of the intensification of meaning over three lines occurs at the end of a famous judgment speech in the book:

Zion shall be plowed as a field;
Jerusalem shall become a heap of ruins,
and the mountain of the house a wooded height. (3:12)

---

background information, beginning and ending of a paragraph, contrast, and so on. The verb is extremely rare in third position and never occurs in fourth. In poetry one cannot speak of a default position. The verb is apt to be in second position just as much as in first position, and it is found frequently in third position and sometimes in fourth. Thus it is clear that there is a fundamental difference between narrative and poetry. Clear differences can be shown by comparing the differences between a narrative and poetic retelling of the same event. I have done this in a popular article: "The Poetry of the Bible: Something Beautiful for God," *Gospel Witness* 92 (2013): 3–7.

126. For representative works, see Robert Alter, *The Art of Biblical Poetry* (New York: Basic Books, 2011); James L. Kugel, *The Idea of Biblical Poetry: Parallelism and Its History* (Baltimore: Johns Hopkins University Press, 1998); Wilfred G. E. Watson, *Classical Hebrew Poetry: A Guide to Its Techniques* (Sheffield: Sheffield Academic Press, 2009); Terence Collins, *Line-Forms in Hebrew Poetry: A Grammatical Approach to the Stylistic Study of the Hebrew Prophets*, Studia Pohl, series Maior (Rome: Biblical Institute Press, 1978); and Michael Patrick O'Connor, *Hebrew Verse Structure* (Winona Lake: Eisenbrauns, 1980).

Knowledge of the structures of intensification in poetry is an invaluable aid for understanding the message. The intensifying lines are not just saying the same thing as the previous lines, they are ratcheting up the meaning—amplifying the sound as it were—so that its overall message cannot be missed.

Other features like assonance—similarity of sound—and grammatical homogeneity are used to provide coherence and cohesion in the book. The following triad of lines display these features:

Her leaders for a bribe judge!	רָאשֶׁיהָ בְּשֹׁחַד יִשְׁפֹּטוּ	ro'šêhā bašōḥad yišpōṭû
Her priests for a price teach!	וְכֹהֲנֶיהָ בִּמְחִיר יוֹרוּ	wəkōhănêhā bimḥîr yôrû
Her prophets for silver prophesy! (3:11, my translation)	וּנְבִיאֶיהָ בְּכֶסֶף יִקְסֹמוּ	ûnəbî'êhā bəkesep yiqsōmû

The similar sounds contribute to a rhythmic effect producing phonological cohesion in the units. The similar syntactical pattern of subject-modifier-verb creates grammatical parallelism, and this abnormal word order suspends the appearance of the verb, creating a dissonance with its modifier: her leaders—for a bribe—judge / her priests—for a price—teach / her prophets—for silver—prophesy. This grammatical dissonance contributes to the sense of moral discord described by the text and emphasizes the venality behind the religious actions.

The book of Micah provides many examples of wordplay or punning in the Hebrew Bible, but this did not have the same poetic significance for ancient Hebrews as it does for modern Westerners. For the latter it is clever and witty, but for the Hebrews it was significant—even ominous—drawing an important connection between objects that would otherwise seem unrelated. Thus when Jeremiah sees an "almond tree," he knows that God will be "watching" over his prophetic word to ensure its fulfillment (Jer 1:11–12). There is no relation in English between "almond tree" and "watching" but in Hebrew the words have the same consonants and similar vowels (שָׁקֵד/šāqēd vs. שֹׁקֵד/šōqēd). God uses this pun to convince Jeremiah that his prophecies come with a divine guarantee. In Micah, there are many wordplays, but in one passage there is the equivalent of wordplay "overkill." In this passage, which is unique in the Bible because of its abundance of paronomasia, the meanings and sounds produced by the place name of Judean cities about to be destroyed by the Assyrian army function as omens of doom (1:10–16). Their names seal their fates. Thus the

Judean countryside southwest of the central mountain range is transformed from an idyllic setting to a topography of terror. Beth-leaphrah, probably originally named for its aridity (house of dust), becomes a place for mourners to roll in the dust (1:10). Zaanan probably was named because it provides a key exit for traffic moving from east to west in southwest Judah but it now becomes a place from which there will be no exit from coming judgment (1:11)! Achzib may have been so named because it was a charming and delightful place but its name sounds like the word for "lie" in Hebrew (אַכְזָב/'akzāb), and it will thus prove to be such a place to the kings of Israel in the face of the Assyrian judgment (1:14). It is important to note that more than mere information is being communicated with this paronomasia. The paronomasia paralyzes the hearer with fear. The sounds evoke doom and terror and assure the hearer of the certainty of doom.

While the book of Micah is mainly poetry, some prosaic lines serve the poetic function of closure, signaling abruptly the end of a poetic unit in a jarring manner. For example, the prosaic line in 2:5 terminates a poetic sequence beginning in 2:3:

> Therefore you will have no one to cast the line by lot
> in the assembly of the LORD. (2:5)

The prosaic closure of poetry signals the spiritual closure of final judgment.

Sometimes a change in the number of person, from third to second, indicates a climax in the poem. For example, in the hymn at the end of the book this change ends the poem:

> Who is a God like you,
> who forgives sin,
> who forgives the transgression of the remnant of his people,
> who is not angry forever?
> For he delights in mercy,
> he will have mercy on us again,
> he will trample all over our sins
> —*you* will cast all their sins into the depths of the sea!
> (7:18–19, my translation)

The shift from third-person to second-person marks a peak in the poem and also brings closure. Speaking *about* God now becomes address *to* God (for a similar example see Ps 23:4b).

But the question may be asked, Why was the poetic genre used by Micah and the prophets in general? In seventeenth-century England, one of the uses of the poetic genre was aesthetic delight. Thus George Herbert wrote poetry because

> A verse may finde him, who a sermon flies,
> And turn delight into a sacrifice.[127]

Thus culture can clearly dictate the use of poetic conventions. In the Sindhi language spoken in Pakistan, there is a type of poetry (*qawwali*) that is invested with hyperbole, repetition, vivid imagery, and lack of explanation that connects to cultural background, cultural responses, cultural actions, and expectations that are not obvious to an outsider. But "without [understanding] those links the impact and significance of the words cannot be retained."[128] Similarly in some African languages the lament genre has a special vocabulary and role. Moreover, in most cultures verse and music are naturally linked, constraining the use of language in certain contexts. Prose is normally used for the simple communication of information, while poetry has more than just the goal of the communication of information—it often aims at persuasion by using art, literary technique, and various forms to communicate, in order to register a powerful impact on the emotions and heart.[129] This accounts for the terseness of poetry, its vivid diction, and its surprising syntax. It is packed with feeling and emotion and involves the imagination in a way that breaks conventional linguistic stereotypes. It captures the passion of the prophet, who more often than not has "his life and soul . . . at stake in what he says and what is going to happen to what he says."[130] The form itself can hit the hearer like the pounding of a jackhammer on hard concrete, and like the latter, the poetic form can help punch through the hardness of—in this case—something much harder than concrete—a petrified heart. As a great commentator on the prophets once said,

127. George Herbert, *The Temple: The Poetry of George Herbert*, ed. Henry L. Carrigan (Brewster: Paraclete, 2001), 3.

128. Mark Naylor, "Qawwali: Can Biblical Poetry Be Translated?" Available online at nb.seminary.com/CCImpact/CCI_13.htm.

129. Language often is multidimensional. There are an informative mode, an expressive mode, a persuasive mode, an intimate mode. Sometimes the purpose of texts is not to convey accurate information but to express intimate presence. Contrast the difference between a news report and a love letter. For the discussion of this very point, see Alon Goshen-Gottstein, "Love as a Hermeneutic Principle in Rabbinic Literature," *Journal of Literature and Theology* 8 (1994): 247–67.

130. Heschel, *Prophets*, 7. For further considerations of the epistemology of poetry, see W. Brueggemann, *Finally Comes the Poet* (Minneapolis: Fortress, 1989).

The prophet seldom tells a story, but casts events. He rarely sings, but castigates. He does more than translate reality into a poetic key: he is a preacher whose purpose is not self-expression or the "purgation of emotions," but communication. His images must not shine, they must burn.[131]

The use of poetry to capture both the height and depth of emotions is described by Buechner when he writes about poetry being used by the prophets to articulate their wildest hope and their deepest despair:

At the level of words, what do they say, these prophet-preachers? They say this and they say that. They say things that are relevant, lacerating, profound, beautiful, spine chilling and more besides. They put words to both the wonder and the horror of the world, and the words can be looked up in the dictionary or the biblical commentary and can be interpreted, passed on, understood, but because these words are poetry, and symbol as well as meaning, are sound and rhythm, maybe above all are passion, they set echoes going the way a choir in a great cathedral does, only it is we who become the cathedral and in us that the words echo. . . . It is the experience that they stun us with, speaking it out in poetry which transcends all other language in its power to open the doors of the heart.[132]

Thus poetry is a genre that can be used to capture the heart by pressing language into service in a distinctive way. The ordinary becomes communicated in an extraordinary way because the conventional way of describing it has blinded people to its reality. It is no small wonder then that a major part of the Bible is written in verse. The main poetic form in the Hebrew language is uniquely shaped to convey the dynamic nature of the prophetic message. If intensity can be used to describe the prophetic personality, then the poetic structures of intensification are uniquely suited to help the prophet communicate as each line amplifies and enriches the meaning of its previous counterpart. Note how Micah describes the rapacious greed of the judicial leaders in Jerusalem. He could have simply described them as taking bribes from wealthy criminals, thereby becoming agents of corruption. What he does say is something far different. He uses provocative language to show a different side to the actions; the poetic quality intensifies the language, not only keeping the description of the activity before the eyes, but to mix the metaphor, amplifying its volume to an almost unbearable degree:

131. Heschel, *Prophets*, 8.
132. Frederick Buechner, *Telling the Truth: The Gospel as Tragedy, Comedy, and Fairy Tale* (New York: HarperOne, 2009), 21.

> Listen now, O heads of Jacob,
>> leaders of the house of Israel!
> Do you not know what justice means?
>> You haters of the good and lovers of evil!
> Rippers of the skin off people's back!
>> Even stripping the flesh from the bones!
> You who eat the flesh of my people,
>> while ripping their skin off,
>> crushing their bones,
> spreading them out like meat in the pot,
>> like flesh in the pan! (3:1–3, my translation)

The intensity of this poetic description of the activity of these judicial officials is unrelieved. With every line it gathers momentum, moving from a call for the leaders to listen, a reminder of their calling—to embrace justice—and then a summary description of the wholesale perversion of this calling, as they hate the good and love the evil. Then follows one of the most macabre descriptions in the Hebrew Bible of the activity of these so-called administrators of the Israelite legal system: two lines + three lines + two lines. They are cannibals! The bodies of the victims are torn apart for consumption, and nothing—absolutely nothing—is wasted! Every piece of flesh is thrown on the barbecue grill and every bone is thrown into the cooking pot. The poetry intensifies the horrifying activity, and the peculiar diction magnifies the monstrosity of the actions by providing images that will not easily be forgotten and that should stab even the most hardened conscience with unassuaged guilt.

If that macabre description using poetic language emphasizes the dark side of human life, what Buechner describes as the "horror of the world," the prophet has equally descriptive poetry to present God's dream for the future—"the wonder of the world":

> In days to come
>> the mountain of the Lord's house
> shall be established as the highest of the mountains,
>> and shall be raised up above the hills.
> Peoples shall stream to it,
>> and many nations shall come and say:
> "Come, let us go up to the mountain of the Lord,
>> to the house of the God of Jacob;
> that he may teach us his ways

and that we may walk in his paths."
For out of Zion shall go forth instruction,
    and the word of the LORD from Jerusalem.
He shall judge between many peoples,
    and shall arbitrate between strong nations far away;
they shall beat their swords into plowshares,
    and their spears into pruning hooks;
nation shall not lift up sword against nation,
    neither shall they learn war any more;
but they shall all sit under their own vines and under their own fig trees,
    and no one shall make them afraid;
    for the mouth of the LORD of hosts has spoken.
For all the peoples walk,
    each in the name of its god,
but we will walk in the name of the LORD our God
    forever and ever. (4:1-5)

There is probably no more stunning description of the triumph of Yahweh over evil than is found in this text. The prophet could have written in prose about the future emergence of the centrality of faith, resulting in the abolition of war and the subsequent peace and security, with a contemporary injunction to follow Yahweh despite present religious pluralism. But this particular poetic way of describing the future—the elevation of Zion, the decision of the nations to hear the Torah, their encounter with Yahweh, the return to their communities transforming their weapons into farm tools, and everyone sitting under their own vine without any fears whatsoever—is a far more powerful vision of the future. The poetic imagery and intensification is a particularly apt vehicle for expressing the longing of the human heart for peace and Yahweh's vision for the world.[133]

Discourse

Micah used a variety of genres to communicate his message:[134] lament (1:8-16; 2:1-5; 7:1-6), judgment speech (3:1-4, 5-8, 9-12; 6:9-16), salvation oracle (2:12-

133. Knut Heim, "How and Why We Should Read the Poetry of the Old Testament for Public Life Today," *Comment* (fall 2011).

134. For a complete list of genres, see Kenneth L. Barker, "A Literary Analysis of the Book of Micah," *Bibliotheca Sacra* 155 (1998): 437-48; and Timothy M. Pierce, "Micah as a Case Study for Preaching and Teaching the Prophets," *Southwestern Journal of Theology* 46 (2003): 77-94 at 82-85.

13; 4:1–5), disputation (2:6–11), covenant-lawsuit speech (6:1–5), entrance liturgy (6:6–7), futility curse (6:14–15), and hymn (7:18–20). As already discussed, most prophetic books existed in oral form first, and only later were they written down by the prophets themselves or by scribes.

We know little about the formation of prophetic books—with one exception, the book of Jeremiah. There it is clear that the original oracles given in a different time and place were transcribed by Jeremiah's scribe onto one scroll in order to have the entire text read to the people during a fast day so that they would be able to experience the comprehensive impact of the messages and perhaps repent (Jer 36). The key difficulty in interpretation is that many of these oracles or parts of them are linked to each other and often decontextualized historically so it is difficult to know sometimes where one begins and another ends. This is why Martin Luther observed famously about the prophets: "They have a queer way of talking, like people who instead of proceeding in an orderly manner, ramble off from one thing to the next, so that you cannot make head or tail of them or see what they are getting at."[135] In other words, the editor arranged these once disparate oracles into a literary sequence, and the result can be a type of literary disorientation. For example, does Mic 1:8 begin a new oracle, and is the prophet or God speaking? In a strictly grammatical interpretation it would seem that the speaker was God since he is the last person speaking in the text. But, most scholars argue that the context suggests that 1:8 begins a completely new unit with Micah as the new speaker.[136] It is not completely clear, however, and such a lack of clarity may even be employed for theological reasons. Perhaps there is no attempt to distinguish clearly the prophetic voice from the divine voice because the two were one and the same.[137]

Many scholars detect about thirty units in Micah that once existed independently as parts of speeches.[138] These were brought together by the prophet or a scribe and later reduced to writing. On the other hand, a recent monograph argues for six independent speeches that were later reduced to writing.[139] Some scholars even claim that the book was originally *written* by highly skilled scribes for a postexilic audience. Still others believe that it was

---

135. Cited in Gerhard Von Rad, *Old Testament Theology: The Theology of Israel's Prophetic Traditions* (Louisville: Westminster John Knox, 2001), 33.

136. Similar features are found in 1:15 and 2:7b.

137. Thus the editor sees no problem because the superscription equates the words of the prophet with the word of God. See, e.g., Samuel A. Meier, *Themes and Transformations in Old Testament Prophecy* (Downers Grove: InterVarsity, 2009), 71–77, esp. 72–73.

138. Mays, *Micah*, 1–12.

139. Shaw, *Speeches of Micah*, 221–25.

written as a dramatic performance. Wiklander makes the following observations in an important study on Isaiah that could just as easily be adapted
for Micah:

We are faced with a broad spectrum of opinions on the delimitation,
unity, and function of this text. Roughly speaking, these opinions may be classified as follows:

1. An original, coherent and well-formed discourse intended for reading
   and /or oral public performance.
2. A well-formed, redactional and literary unit consisting of originally self-
   contained speeches that were gradually shaped into a unified whole according to a fixed plan.
3. A loosely delimited, incoherent section of the book of Isaiah forming
   a collection of originally independent, poorly preserved sayings ema-
   nating from the prophet Isaiah and mingled with an abundance of later
   additions.
4. A series of originally independent units, speeches, or poems, which were
   collected and placed together without any overarching, organising plan—
   except for certain topical considerations and related key words—as parts
   of collections or extending beyond the limits of chs. 2–4.[140]

Wiklander observes that one of the main reasons for this diversity of opinion
is the conflicting views of coherence. Interestingly, in Micah studies a growing
number of scholars believe that the final form of the book reflects a real concern
for linguistic and conceptual coherence.[141] When all things are considered, the
most cogent explanation for the present form of Micah is that of self-contained
speech units that were gradually shaped according to a specific design.

In this commentary, I will seek to keep in view the historical and literary
context ("Micah's Word Then") and the theological trajectory of these words
within its canonical context to the present contemporary context ("Micah's
Word Now").

---

140. Bertil Wiklander, *Prophecy as Literature: A Text-Linguistic and Rhetorical Approach to
Isaiah 2–4*, rev. ed. (Malmö: Gleerup, 1984), 7.
141. Hagstrom, *Coherence of the Book of Micah*; Jacobs, *Conceptual Coherence of the Book
of Micah*; Cuffey, *Literary Coherence of the Book of Micah*.

Text

There are two extreme assessments of the text of Micah. As Rudolph states, some scholars assert that the text is extremely corrupt and that only the book of Hosea suffers from more textual corruption. Others claim that the text is in a relatively sound state of preservation. The truth, as Rudolph wisely observes, lies somewhere in the middle.[142] In some places (notably 1:10–16; 2:6–11; 7:1–6), the text seems to have suffered badly. The corruption of the text was due not only to the scribal errors that inevitably happen in the history of transmission but probably also because of the difficulties of understanding the challenging Hebrew at times. In the history of interpretation, scholars proposed many emendations, some of them more acceptable than others. The Septuagint provides help in certain instances, and some of its readings are valuable.[143] The other versions are less helpful. More often than not, the versions seek to explain the difficult Hebrew text, rather than reveal a better Hebrew *Vorlage*. Jeppesen's assessment of the problems is particularly apt:

> The question of the evolution of the Hebrew text of the book of Micah is probably a mystery which will never be unravelled. For the greater part of the work it seems as if the text has been well preserved; it is, after all, intelligible Hebrew. However, four or five times in the course of the work the text is so impenetrable that it is reasonable to suppose that it has been corrupted at an early stage of transmission. None of the classic translations contains the key to an explanation of how this has come about.[144]

Scholars often feel free to emend the text when the grammar and syntax do not seem to make sense. Elliger's radical theory postulates a damaged right edge of a manuscript for the listing of cities in 1:10–16, and as a result he proposes many emendations.[145] Others propose a theory of metrical constraints that then allows them to emend the text according to the required metrical pattern.[146] For example, Smith makes an emendation in 2:7b because to keep

142. Rudolph, *Micha, Habakuk, Zephanja*, 25–26.

143. E.g., the Septuagint provides the original reading of the Hebrew in 3:3b. Rudolph (*Micha, Habakuk, Zephanja*, 25–30) notes six improvements offered by the Septuagint: 1:11; 2:7; 3:3; 5:4; 6:13; and 6:16 (ibid., 26). I agree with 3:3; 6:13, 16.

144. Knud Jeppesen, "New Aspects of Micah Research," *Journal for the Study of the Old Testament* 8 (1978): 3–32 at 14.

145. Karl Elliger, "Die Heimat des Propheten Micha," *Zeitschrift des Deutschen Palästina-Vereins alttestamentlicher Wissenschaft* 57 (1934): 81–152.

146. Paul Haupt, cited in Andersen and Freedman, *Micah*, 203.

the Masoretic Text "constitutes very bad Hebrew for the last clause."[147] But what constitutes bad Hebrew may be a construct in the mind of the interpreter rather than in that of a native speaker. And sometimes genuine grammatical solecisms may also provide a clue to the emotional state of the speaker at the time. As Andersen and Freedman observe, the speaker may become grammatically incoherent because of the terrifying vision he has seen. If it is true from a general psycholinguistic perspective that speakers are prone to grammatical mistakes when suffering anxiety or severe stress,[148] then this could be the case for the prophets at times, particularly when the prophet witnessed a deeply troubling revelation. The prophet thus reverts to a more discourse-oriented, topicalized speech rather than one that is grammaticalized. A flood of words describing terrifying images leave his mouth with little concern for grammatical relationships. The revelation-induced panic leaves little time for grammatical precision. In fact Andersen shows that the more intense, emotional speeches of Micah have much shorter lines than, for example, his salvation oracles, and it is in some of these speeches that the text is very difficult to understand:

> The seven poems with the shortest cola are the most emotional in the book, and the poetic lines are short and jumpy—to the point of incoherence in the case of 1:10–16. They register profoundly disturbed states of mind: grief (1:10–16; 7:1–6), anguish (4:9–10; 4:14) indignation (2:6–11; 6:13–16), and in one case, jubilation (7:7–12). In contrast oracles of salvation achieve stately and serene effects through the use of longer cola. The calm deliberation of the judgment speech in 5:9–14 is awesome.[149]

For the most part, then, in this commentary I will use the Masoretic Text as my default text unless otherwise noted. There are definitely some places where I deem an emendation an improvement but these usually have some basis in the Septuagint.

The Hebrew text of Micah has different verse numbers throughout chapter 5. To aid readers of this commentary, I cite Micah according to English Bible verse numbers but the following chart of these differences is provided so readers can easily refer to verses in either Bible:

147. Smith, *Micah, Zephaniah, and Nahum*, 61.

148. David W. Carroll, *Psychology of Language* (Belmont: Thomson/Wadsworth, 2007), 194.

149. Francis I. Andersen, "The Poetic Properties of Prophetic Discourse in the Book of Micah," in *Biblical Hebrew and Discourse Linguistics*, ed. Robert D. Bergen (Winona Lake: Eisenbrauns, 1994), 520–28 at 525–26.

Hebrew Bible	English Bible
4:14	5:1
5:1	5:2
5:2	5:3
5:3	5:4
5:4	5:5
5:5	5:6
5:6	5:7
5:7	5:8
5:8	5:9
5:9	5:10
5:10	5:11
5:11	5:12
5:12	5:13
5:13	5:14
5:14	5:15

Micah's Place in the Minor Prophets (The Twelve)

In the history of interpretation, the historical and chronological location of the prophets was often the focus of attention. The prophets were often viewed in isolation, as lone figures who spoke the word of God to a decadent culture. Little attention was given to their canonical placement, and frequently a historical trajectory determined their presentation, with Amos being the first prophet followed by Hosea, Micah, Isaiah, and so on. Recent scholarship on the Minor Prophets looks beyond the individual prophet to see connections and associations between their prophetic books.[150] It should be borne in mind that the twelve "books" that constitute the Minor Prophets were originally written on one scroll, which was called "The Twelve" by its first Jewish audience. There is no textual evidence for the separate existence of the twelve books of prophetic speeches. Some scholars argue that the important literary dimension is now the book, and some even question whether the individual prophet's collections ever existed separately. That position strains credulity. It seems reasonable that

---

150. Paul R. House pioneered this new understanding of the Twelve from a strictly literary point of view, and his work has been followed by redaction critics and canonical critics; *The Unity of the Twelve* (New York: Bloomsbury, 1990); see also James Nogalski, *Literary Precursors to the Book of the Twelve* (Berlin: de Gruyter, 1993); and Christopher R. Seitz, *The Goodly Fellowship of the Prophets: The Achievement of Association in Canon Formation*, Acadia Studies in Bible and Theology (Grand Rapids: Baker, 2009).

twelve collections were combined onto one scroll and placed together in the early history of the canon in order to have four latter prophets (Jeremiah, Ezekiel, Isaiah, the Twelve) to combine with four former prophets (Joshua, Judges, Samuel, Kings).

Nonetheless, by combining the twelve separate collections of oracles, editing was necessarily done. Superscriptions were probably added by a common editor, and there may have been individual editorial work on the various works for literary presentation, a sort of fine-tuning of the literature. For example, a good number of scholars now believe that the final few verses of Malachi serve to close the entire prophetic corpus.[151] Moreover, the simple placement of twelve major units together creates a new literary context for each of the units, which itself creates new meanings. Thus, for example, the oracles about the death and resurrection of the temple are located in the exact center of the Twelve.[152] Could this be a literary accident? Hardly.

The end of the first book of the Twelve, Hosea, speaks about the importance of future repentance (Hos 14:2-4), and the next book, Joel, presents that repentance happening in the last days (Joel 2:14-17). Also the ending of Joel and the beginning of Amos link up with the same words (Joel 3:16; Amos 1:2), and Amos ends with an oracle about Edom (Amos 9:12) while Obadiah focuses on the same nation. The next three books all deal with Assyria, and each features the use of the divine name as it is classically used in its credo formulation in Exod 34:6-7. The subsequent two books, Habakkuk and Zephaniah, deal with the Babylonian judgment against Judah; and the last triad—Haggai, Zechariah, and Malachi—is postexilic. In addition to these literary links, many other catchphrases bind the books together.[153]

The final edition of the Twelve was produced in the postexilic period, during the Second Temple period, and it probably updated an exilic edition that consisted of earlier prophets. Some of the books probably circulated in

---

151. See, e.g., Joseph Blenkinsopp, *Prophecy and Canon: A Contribution to the Study of Jewish Origins* (Notre Dame: University of Notre Dame Press, 1977).

152. Mic 3:12 is the exact midpoint. It is part of an oracle that begins in 3:9; the next oracle that follows is the elevation of the temple (4:1-5).

153. Some of these are more convincing than others; see the list in Nogalski, *Literary Precursors to the Book of the Twelve*, 21-57. The literary links between the ending of Obadiah and the beginning of Micah seem incidental, as common words are used. But a good case can be made for some of these and for a more general literary framework for the Twelve. See John D. W. Watts, "A Frame for the Book of the Twelve: Hosea 1-3 and Malachi," in *Reading and Hearing the Book of the Twelve*, Society of Biblical Literature Symposium Series 15 (Atlanta: Scholars Press, 2000), 209-17; and Christopher R. Seitz, *Prophecy and Hermeneutics: Toward a New Introduction to the Prophets*, Studies in Theological Interpretation (Grand Rapids: Baker, 2007).

dependently earlier, as Micah is quoted word for word by Jeremiah about a century after his prophecy about Jerusalem (Jer 26:18; cf. Mic 3:12). Nonetheless, when the books were compiled and arranged by an editor(s), the number twelve was probably chosen to represent the twelve tribes, and this would accompany the three Major Prophets, whose number probably represented the three patriarchs.[154] In each of these four prophetic books, which are called the Latter Prophets, there are firm links that are probably due to editors. This is seen in the historical superscriptions (e.g., Isa 1:1; Hos 1:1–2; Mic 1:1).

There are other important general thematic similarities. For example, near the center of each book, there are judgment on the temple and salvation of the temple. This is clearest in the Twelve (Micah 3:9–12; 4:1–5), but it is also present in the other books. At the heart of Jeremiah is Micah's oracle about the destruction of the temple in a repeated speech of Jeremiah (Jer 26; cf. Jer 7). Similarly Ezekiel hears the news about the destruction of the temple and the death of his wife near the literary center of the book (Ezek 24). In Isaiah, despite a present announcement of salvation for Zion, there is a future announcement of judgment and exile (Isa 36–39). In each book the next sections after this judgment promise hope and restoration. Thus the larger literary design of each of the four Latter Prophets is a thematic sequence of judgment followed by hope. And in terms of the individual prophetic books of the Twelve, salvation oracles are frequently coupled with judgment oracles.[155] The result is that the prophets never leave the Israelites without hope, and particularly this would have been a great encouragement for the remnant that constituted the postexilic community for whom hope was often at a premium. This is how Ben Sira, writing shortly before the turn of the era, understood the Twelve and presumably the other prophetic books as well. They were not screeds of judgment: "Then, too, the Twelve Prophets—may their bones flourish with new life where they lie!—They gave new strength to Jacob and saved him with steadfast hope" (Sirach 49:10).

The Masoretic Text has a different order than the Septuagint.[156] The different orders are reflected below:

154. Gunnar Östborn, *Cult and Canon: A Study in the Canonization of the Old Testament* (Uppsala: Lundequistska, 1950), 44–45.

155. This is true even in Amos where one has to endure over eight chapters of "blood and iron" for the few verses of "roses and lavender."

156. There is possible evidence of an anomalous order which has Jonah following Malachi (see next footnote), but it is far from certain. See Hanne von Weissenberg, "The Twelve Minor Prophets at Qumran and the Canonical Process: Amos as a Case Study," *The Hebrew Bible in Light of the Dead Sea Scrolls*, ed. Nóra David, Armin Lange, et al. (Göttingen: Vandenhoeck & Ruprecht, 2013), 357–78 at 364–65.

Masoretic Text	Septuagint
Hosea	Hosea
Joel	Amos
Amos	Micah
Obadiah	Joel
Jonah	Obadiah
Micah	Jonah
Nahum	Nahum
Habakkuk	Habakkuk
Zephaniah	Zephaniah
Haggai	Haggai
Zechariah	Zechariah
Malachi	Malachi

Both sequences begin with the same first book and end with the same sequence of six. The Septuagint order for books 2–6 suggests decreasing order of size concluding with Jonah, a unique story about a prophet. This suggests a secondary order that altered an original order in which a prophet linked with the northern kingdom alternated with a prophet linked with the southern kingdom until the northern kingdom ceases.[157]

One striking feature of the Masoretic order is that of the Assyrian triad near the center of the Twelve: Jonah–Micah–Nahum. This small group highlights the revelation of the divine name in the Israelite credo (Exod 34:6–7) in critical places in each book. It is the basis for the salvation of Nineveh and supplies the reason that motivated Jonah to abandon his calling to preach to the sinful city. He understood only too well the theological implications of the credo: divine mercy could be expected for repentant sinners (Jon 4:2). In Micah an interpretation of the credo is probably the basis of the deluded

---

157. Hosea (north)–Joel (south)–Amos (north)–Obadiah (south)–Jonah (north)–Micah (south). The stronger literary links between the books in the Masoretic order argue that this is the original order. This order is confirmed by early evidence from Wadi Murabaat (100 CE) and the Nahal Hever Greek Minor Prophets scroll (100 BCE). The order is also followed by the Vulgate, while the earliest Septuagint order dates to manuscripts from the fourth–fifth centuries CE (Sinaiticus, Alexandrinus). For another perspective see Marvin A. Sweeney, "Synchronic Diachronic Concerns in Reading the Book of the Twelve Prophets," in *Perspectives in the Formation of the Book of the Twelve: Methodological Foundations—Redactional Processes—Historical Insights* (Berlin: de Gruyter, 2012), 21–34. The possibility of a sequence ending with Jonah is argued by Barry Jones but the evidence found in a manuscript at Qumran (4QXII) does not provide concrete proof for such a sequence; *The Formation of the Book of the Twelve: A Study in Text and Canon*, Society of Biblical Literature Dissertation Series 149 (Atlanta: Society of Biblical Literature, 1995).

assurance of the false prophets that God would never judge his people, and it is used at the end of the book to show that Yahweh will have mercy on the remnant of his people, after the judgment (Mic 2:7; 7:18–19). In Nahum the same credo explains the judgment of Nineveh generations later (Nah 1:2–4). An unrepentant sinful city experiences the certainty of divine judgment: God does not acquit the guilty who show no remorse. All three books deal not only with Assyria but they deal with the Israelite credo and how its theology is worked out in history.

There are also some other interesting links. Jonah is saved by being rescued by Yahweh from the depths of the waters in the belly of the whale (Jon 2:10), and Yahweh in Micah saves the remnant of his people by hurling their sins down to the depths of the waters (Mic 7:19)! In Micah, Yahweh declares to all nations who do not obey him that they will experience his judgment (Mic 5:15), and in Nahum that judgment is announced to Nineveh for its rebellion (Nah 1:2). In Micah the divine messenger lamenting throughout the land announces judgment to his people through the Assyrian army (Mic 1:8–16), but in Nahum the divine messenger delivers the good news of salvation to his people and judgment to the Assyrians (Nah 1:15).

That Micah, which is addressed to Israel and Judah, is sandwiched between two books dealing with the city of Nineveh shows that God's mercy does not come at the expense of his justice. Indeed the only two books in the Bible that end with questions are the books of Jonah and Nahum. But their questions show God's concern for mercy and justice and show that his justice is finally an example of his mercy. To a petulant Jonah brooding over his personal loss and lamenting the failure of God to judge the Ninevites, God says: "And should I not be concerned about Nineveh, that great city, in which there are more than a hundred and twenty thousand persons who do not know their right hand from their left, and also many animals?" (Jon 4:11). To the city of Nineveh and its king who have wreaked untold damage on the world, God says: "There is no assuaging your hurt, / your wound is mortal. / All who hear the news about you clap their hands over you. / For who has ever escaped / your endless cruelty?" (Nah 3:19). The same evil that went up before God in Jonah's time was not endless, as the people repented (Jon 3:5); but generations later in Nahum's time it can be described as endless; its continued existence is regarded as a calamity to the world (Nah 3:19). Thus God finally—mercifully—ends the existence of this calamity.

The unique position of Micah between these two books dealing with the nations shows the importance of the remnant for its ministry to the nations. In the salvation of the remnant lies the salvation of the world. When the remnant is brought back to Jerusalem and its final king comes to Zion to reform it, it will be exalted to the highest place and become a beacon to the nations. The nations that come and change will be saved—this is the message of Jonah (Mic 4:1–5). Those who do not will be judged—this is the message of Nahum (Mic 5:15).

Finally from a larger perspective, Micah is uniquely situated as a decisive turning point in the Twelve with a movement from judgment to salvation in which Jerusalem is critical.[158] The razed temple of judgment and destruction will become the raised temple of salvation and life for all the nations, as Yahweh regathers Israel and the nations and brings them all home (Nah 1:15; Hab 2:20–3:19; Zeph 3:14–20; Hag 2:7–9, 23; Zech 8:20–23; 14:1–21). "A nation that has been made pure and clean and from which God is no longer alienated, but has taken up his residence, becomes such a manifestation of the validity of the Torah that the nations come streaming to learn it and to conform their lives to it."[159]

158. Burkard M. Zapff, "The Book of Micah—The Theological Center of the Book of the Twelve?" in *Perspectives in the Formation of the Book of the Twelve: Methodological Foundations—Redactional Processes—Historical Insights*, ed. Rainer Albertz, James Nogalski, and Jakob Wöhrle (Berlin: de Gruyter, 2012), 143.

159. John N. Oswalt, "Isaiah 60–62: The Glory of the Lord," *Calvin Theological Journal* 40 (2005): 103.

Commentary

Prophetic Superscription (1:1)

This verse functions as the book's title and indicates important information about its content: divine source, human messenger, time of the message, and address. It is written in prose and has a clause length that far exceeds any other in the book. It is probably the only text that existed in written form from the beginning and was added to the collection of speeches within the book.[1] There may be a few other examples where oracles have been edited (rather than simply transcribed) to produce cohesion within the framework of the book. Because of its formulaic similarity with superscriptions of other prophetic books (exact parallels are found in Hos 1:1; Joel 1:1; and Zeph 1:1; similar expressions are found in Isa 1:1; Ezek 1:1; Jer 1:1–2; Amos 1:1; and Hab 1:1), the superscription was probably the work of the same editor of those books. It functions to frame the ensuing discourse, thereby providing crucial information necessary for understanding it and also creating "structures of expectation" for the audience.[2] The superscription supplies the essential information that the discourse is divine revelation expressed in a particular historical time. Knowledge of this history is important for understanding the collection of oracles that follow the superscription.[3]

---

1. The only exception being 3:1, which probably reflects Micah's editorial hand. But see Ben Zvi (*Micah*, 2–12) for a quite different understanding of the collection of oracles.

2. Deborah Tannen, ed., *Framing in Discourse* (Oxford: Oxford University Press, 1993), 5–6. For the use of this concept in the Bible under paratext features, see also Ched Spellman, *Toward a Canon-Conscious Reading of the Bible: Exploring the History and Hermeneutics of the Canon*, New Testament Monographs 34 (Sheffield: Sheffield Phoenix, 2014), 103–6. I am indebted to Spellman for the reference to Tannen's work.

3. Cf. Ben Zvi's statement: "Micah 1:1 and similar superscriptions are an integral—and most

Source. The grammatical subject of this lengthy introductory clause is "the word of Yahweh," and thus this subject identifies the source of information found in the book. This grammatical subject becomes the great subject of discourse in the book. Yes, this book is about Israel and Judah in the eighth century BCE but it is primarily about "the word of Yahweh." This subject supplies the book's raison d'être—why there is any book at all. The book owes its existence to Yahweh's transcendent speech. This phrase "the word of Yahweh" indicates prophetic discourse. It occurs 270 times in the Old Testament, virtually always in a prophetic context. In the two exceptions, it has a prophetic meaning, that is, it signals important divine revelation.[4] Thus by placing this expression at the beginning of Micah, the editor stamps the book with the divine imprimatur. It is not accidental that the expression "the word of Yahweh came to" or a similar phrase occurs at the head of every prophetic collection of oracles. "The title claims that the entire book is the result of the word of Yahweh."[5]

Thus the many words that follow this phrase are supremely important: they express the one word that is above all words. Hillers remarks that though

> in other contexts the phrase "the word of Yahweh" may express a rather specific conception of how communication from God to a prophet took place, in editorial superscriptions such as this it stands before collections of the most disparate materials, so that it is not to be taken as expressing anything about the means of communication, but only the idea that all that follows is somehow from God. For this editor, scripture is "the words of Yahweh."[6]

Some older commentators sought to psychologize Micah by stressing that he found his calling in the cry of oppression from the poor rather than in the voice of God.[7] But this superscription points to transcendence rather than immanence as the origin of his prophecies, as Micah himself testifies (3:8).

That the divine name "Yahweh" is chosen shows that this God is in cov-

---

significant—part of their respective books. Indeed they provide the rereaders with authoritative, interpretive keys, that to a large extent, govern the set of potential interpretations that the texts are allowed to carry"; *Micah*, 21.

4. In Gen 15:1 Abram receives a vision promising him descendants; in 1 Kgs 6:11 Solomon receives assurance of the divine presence if he obeys the Torah.

5. Mays, *Micah*, 37.

6. Hillers, *Micah*, 14. Wolff clearly sees the implications: "The 'religion of the book' is in the making. The book of Micah is to be read as the word of God"; *Micah*, 35. Clearly "the religion of the book" logically follows from the assumption of divine revelation.

7. E.g., "To this man of keen perception and sensitive soul, the voice of duty was the voice of God. As with Amos and Hosea, neither angel nor vision was necessary to rouse him in the prophetic spirit; he found his divine call in the cry of human need"; Smith, *Micah, Zephaniah, and Nahum*, 19.

enantal relationship with Israel, with a clear disclosure of his character and a clear expectation of character requirements on the part of his people. This is not a reference to divinity in general, but to a particular God in covenantal relationship to his people so much so that he can be known by his own personal name.[8]

Messenger. The second important piece of information in the title is the identity of the messenger: Micah the Morashite. His name is a short form of Micayahu (מִיכָיְהוּ/*mîkāyāhû*), found in Jer 26:18, which means "Who is like Yahweh?" It is a rhetorical question that emphasizes God's transcendence. Micah's humble origins stand in contrast to the rhetorical question that praises the greatness of God. He is from Moresheth, probably a town in southwestern Judah, also named Moresheth-gath, because it was near the Philistine city of Gath. That Micah was known by his hometown meant that his prophetic vocation was exercised elsewhere. He was "someone from away," and since we know that his prophesying registered a profound impact on Hezekiah in Jerusalem, it was in this city that he probably became known as Micah the Moreshite. Other prophets such as Amos (Tekoa; Amos 1:1)[9] and Nahum (Elkosh; Nah 1:1) were also identified by their location, but most prophets were distinguished by their family (e.g., "Isaiah son of Amoz"; Isa 1:1) or sometimes simply by a title ("the prophet Habakkuk"; Hab 1:1).

Micah's hometown, situated as it was in the lowlands between the Philistine plain on the west and the Central Mountain Range on the east, in the southwestern portion of Judah, served as the interface between two cultures— Philistine and Israelite.[10] Anyone growing up here would quickly become aware of developments in the capital city of Jerusalem to the east, which would have viewed this city as a key outpost on its southwestern border. Jerusalem would seek to guarantee the security of the nation by securing Moresheth, and thus the town would experience significant influence from the central government of the nation: economic, military, and cultural. Indeed, thirty-seven handles of storage jars with the words "belonging to the king" inscribed on them date from Micah's time.[11] At the same time, significant pressure exerted from the

---

8. See especially the revelation of the name at the exodus (Exod 3, 6).

9. Amos was also a prophet who exercised his prophetic role away from home.

10. Most identify the town with Tell el-Judeideh in the southwest part of Israel. It is clear that it is in the vicinity of Gath, and other locations that have been identified: Lachish, Mareshah, Adullam, and Achzib. Eusebius mentions a town near Eleutheropolis as the place where Micah the prophet lived. Jerome also mentions a church nearby the previous site that marks the prophet's tomb. For discussion and reassessment of all the evidence (plus a new proposal of Tell Harassim), see Yigal Levin, "The Search for Moresheth-gath: A New Proposal," *Palestine Exploration Quarterly* 134 (2002): 28–36.

11. Yosef Garfinkel, "2 Chr 11:5–10 Fortified Cities List and the *lmlk* Stamps—Reply to Nadav Naʾaman," *Bulletin of the American Schools of Oriental Research* 271 (1988): 69–73 at 70.

Philistine west would also have interests in gaining control. The reality of the Philistine influence is shown by the name Moresheth-gath, which identifies the town by its physical proximity to the Philistine center.[12]

The name of Micah's town means "inheritance," "possession," or "heritage" and thus suggests the importance of land and lineage and tradition.[13] This could not help but conjure up for anyone growing up in this town that the land was an inheritance from Yahweh. It was not a right. Israel was to be a steward of the land (Lev 25). This may be one reason why land is so central in the book of Micah. The ultimate punishment is to lose one's inheritance in the land (cf. Mic 2:5). That Micah's first oracle against Judah and Jerusalem is oriented toward the southwest shows his perspective. That part of the invasion was particularly relevant to him since he came from that area. The Assyrians destroyed forty-six cities in Judah, but Micah names the most relevant ones for him: neighboring towns with which he was familiar as well as the capital.[14]

As for Micah himself, little is known except that his prophecy in 3:12 was remembered verbatim a century later (Jer 26:18), and it inspired the repentance of King Hezekiah and the people over whom he reigned.[15] Anything else we know about Micah comes from his book.

Times. Micah delivered his message at a specific time, during the reigns of the kings of Judah named Jotham, Ahaz, and Hezekiah.[16] This reference shows the importance of history for understanding the biblical message: "The specific references to contemporary kings . . . [are] only one example of the constant

12. This town probably was founded by Canaanites. In the Amarna age the king of Gath complains to an Egyptian pharaoh that Lachish has stolen *mu'rašti'* (Moreshet), which was probably nearby Gath (Amarna Letters 335). Perhaps its close association with Gath becomes later reflected in its hyphenated name. This proximate association may also be reflected in a list in Chronicles where Gath surprisingly appears in a list of cities in southwestern Judah that Rehoboam refortified. It may well be that Moreshet-gath is meant (2 Chr 11:5–12).

13. Some try to derive the word from a Hebrew root meaning "to request" or "to plough"; see Levin, "Search for Moresheth-gath," 30.

14. Note Isa 10:28–32 for Isaiah's depiction of the Assyrian invasion. These were probably two phases of the same campaign. See Yohanan Aharoni, *The Land of the Bible: A Historical Geography* (Philadelphia: Westminster John Knox, 1979), 339–40. The text in Isaiah probably refers to a northern advance on Jerusalem instead of a southern approach, and thus is probably much more relevant to Isaiah's perspective.

15. The only difference is that the plural for "heap of ruins" in Micah ends with ן rather than the more standard ם: עִיִּין/'*iyyîn* (Mic 3:12) vs. עִיִּים/'*iyyîm* (Jer 26:18).

16. Some older scholars argue that this temporal reference contradicted Jer 26:18, which states that Micah prophesied during the reign of Hezekiah, but this demands a woodenly literal understanding of the passage in Jeremiah. Micah probably prophesied the judgment on the temple and city during Hezekiah's time, the point being made in the text of Jeremiah. See Smith, *Micah, Zephaniah, and Nahum*, 30; and Keil, *Minor Prophets*, 420–21.

biblical recognition that the religion of Israel is an 'historical religion.' Here is no revelation of a timeless truth to be contemplated—but the word of a Living God to be obeyed in concrete situations."[17] It is clear that the audience(s) of the book of Micah is constrained to hear and read the words of the prophet as spoken during this particular period.[18] There is certainly some latitude for determining the specific time for an oracle but within the general historical constraints indicated in the inscription.[19] This is a long period of time for his prophetic career, and the dating depends on a number of factors occurring at the beginning and the end of the ministry.

Do Jotham's dates refer to the last part of his father's Uzziah's reign, when he was reigning with his father, who was sick and therefore in seclusion during his last years (2 Chr 26:16–23)? And does the date of Hezekiah refer to his complete reign or just a portion, for example, the Assyrian crisis in 701 BCE? One standard set of dates is the beginning of Jotham's reign after the death of his father (742 BCE) to the end of Hezekiah's reign (687 BCE), a span of fifty-five years. This would be a maximum date for the prophetic mission of Micah. The minimum time would be in the last year of Jotham until the first year of Hezekiah's accession, a period of about twenty-two years, less than half the length of the maximum extent. At the same time it is clear from Jer 26 that Micah prophesied during the Assyrian crisis around 701 BCE when only the walls of Jerusalem stood between the Assyrians and the final collapse of Judah. According to this tradition recorded in Jeremiah, Micah's message of imminent judgment caused Hezekiah to repent, and the reform inspired by him saved the city from the Assyrians. This seems to be the natural context for many of Micah's judgment oracles (1:8–16; 3:9–12). Thus the period of Micah's prophecies most likely should extend until shortly after 701 BCE, constituting a period of about thirty-five years.

It is instructive that the editor of Micah's book does not include the northern kings of Israel in this chronological reference for Micah, even though Micah

17. Smith, "Book of Micah," 217.

18. This is even admitted by Ben Zvi, who sees the main audience as a postexilic one: "The readers are required by 1:1 to associate the speech that the implied author placed in the mouth of the godly voice with the monarchic—certainly not with their own postmonarchic—period, and even within the mentioned period, more particularly with the days that preceded Manasseh and a time in which other prophets (e.g., Isaiah) prophesied"; *Micah*, 52.

19. Thus while Ben Zvi (ibid., 80) is right to argue that the original audience of the book of Micah would not have heard the oracles in a way informed by modern historical-critical assumptions regarding original sayings to which accretions and redactions were made, nevertheless this superscription requires that they hear or read it in such a manner that is informed by historical considerations.

would have prophesied in the last decade of the nation of Israel. This omission of Menahem (745–737 BCE), Pekahiah (737–736 BCE), Pekah (736–732 BCE), and Hoshea (732–722 BCE) shows not only the southern perspective of the editor but probably also his belief that these last kings were royal pretenders. The prophetic editors usually omitted any mention of northern kings from the superscriptions, particularly for the prophets of the southern kingdom. For prophets to the northern kingdom, sometimes a northern king would be noted—especially if there was a long dynastic reign—but such a king would always be listed after the relevant kings of Judah (Hos 1:1; Amos 1:1).[20]

Micah lived in a time of crisis. There were in fact three relevant crises in the life of the nation during his prophetic tenure, one near the beginning of the prophetic call of Micah, one in the middle of his prophesying, and one near the end (for specific details see introduction).

Such critical political times coincided with religious and social crises into which Micah spoke. From his oracles and those of his contemporary, Isaiah, it is clear that a coterie of wealthy individuals in Jerusalem had accumulated large estates and vast resources for themselves. Their insatiable greed was sanctioned by a corrupt judicial and religious system. Variously described in the book, these profiteers dreamed and schemed of how they would pillage and pirate, robbing even the shirts from the backs of the poor, driving out farmers from house and home, and selling children into debt slavery (2:1–11). The judges and legal officials joined in the conspiracy by accepting bribes and turning blind eyes to criminal activity (3:1–4). The practice of cheating and dishonesty was rife in the business world, and the procurement of wealth by unjust means was the currency for "getting ahead" (6:11–14). The poor and those without many financial resources were the victims of this carnage, the human flesh consumed by the greed of the powerful (3:1–4). Not much archeological evidence testifies to the existence of the poor, but their memory is preserved in Micah's prophecies.[21] Probably one of the lowest points during this period was a complete disintegration of the moral fabric of society: there was no trust left, not even a modicum of decency. Judah was on the verge of becoming a failed state (7:1–6).

While it is common to speak of the root causes of crime today, it is clear for Micah, "the exegete of existence," that the root causes have to do with idolatry and a failure to honor the God of the covenant. From all reports in the book of Micah there was much religious activity and theological discussion

---

20. The only evidence of a northern king being mentioned is Jeroboam II, who essentially completes the dynasty of Jehu, which was divinely sanctioned by the prophets.

21. "Their voice was not heard, for they have always been ignored by human history. Only in the word of God, especially in Micah's book, are the poor considered for their true worth"; Alfaro, *Justice and Loyalty*, 6–7.

(6:6–7; 2:6–11). But like his predecessor in the north, Hosea, Micah viewed both as repugnant since they coincided with rampant social injustice. People were interested in performance and ritual and not spiritual transformation. Personal prosperity was more important than love of neighbor. Theological leaders stressed the love of God but never the judgment of God. Finally, the entire establishment cooperated with the wealthy elite in this hijacking of Israel's covenant.

Address. The address of Micah's message is succinctly stated: "Which he saw against Samaria and Jerusalem." These were the capital cities of the northern kingdom of Israel and the southern kingdom of Judah. As such they represent their respective countries, a good example of the literary device of synecdoche. But it is also true that these capital cities exerted considerable spiritual and political influence over their respective nations. Idolatry spread out from these important centers of influence as is shown in the first oracle, which stresses both the nations and their capitals (1:6).

It is difficult to say how many oracles were originally relevant to Samaria. The first major oracle directly deals with Samaria. And this is not an accident since it is in first position in the address (1:2–7). Other oracles within the book may also have been originally directed at the capital city of the northern kingdom, but it is difficult to be certain. Some scholars argue that 6:9–16 with its references to the statutes of Omri and the counsels of the house of Ahab was more relevant to the northern kingdom than to the southern, but by Micah's time the names of Omri and Ahab were notorious in Judah. Perhaps the reason why many oracles about Samaria were not preserved was due to Micah's (or the editor's) main interest—Judah and Jerusalem.[22] The presence of Samaria in the final form of the book serves as a powerful warning to Judah and to the nations.

The expression "which he saw" is an indicator that the following words came as a result of prophetic inspiration. Prophets at one time in Israel used to be called seers, but later were called prophets (1 Sam 9:9). Hebrew has many words for "see," but the term used here in Micah is rarely used for normal vision. It is more frequently employed for prophetic revelation. Thus it is used in the superscriptions of prophetic books or before major sections of oracles to describe vision as the method of inspiration (Isa 1:1; 2:1; 13:1; Amos 1:1; Hab 1:1). The preposition "against" suggests to some that the title is restricted to the *oracles of doom* that follow. But this simply depends on context.[23] It can simply mean "concerning" or "about."[24]

22. Renaud, *Formation du Livre de Michée*, 42.
23. Calvin, *Twelve Minor Prophets*, 153–54.
24. See, e.g., the very different meanings of the preposition in Isa 1:1 and 2:1. The disloca-

Judgment and Salvation I (1:2–2:13)

This first score of Micah's symphony of judgment and salvation consists of a variety of oracles that announce judgment on Samaria and Jerusalem and their respective kingdoms (1:2–16). This is followed by reasons for the judgment against Judah (2:1–5) and a dispute with false prophets who disagreed (2:6–11). The lengthy emphasis on judgment is relieved by a short oracle of salvation (2:12–13). The same God who appears in judgment devastating the land and leading the people into exile makes a final appearance leading a purified remnant from exile back home.

Topography of Terror: Impending Doom of Samaria and Jerusalem (1:2–16)

Structure. The first unit in Micah is a masterpiece of design and consists of two speeches probably first delivered at different times, the first an announcement of a theophany that calls the world to attention as the king of the universe leaves his throne room (1:2–4) to judge Samaria and Jerusalem (1:5). The first speech containing the judgment of Samaria (1:6–7) is followed by one on the judgment of Jerusalem (1:8–16). These two speeches would have been independent at one time, one announcing the doom of Samaria before 722 BCE and the impending doom of Judah, and the second proclaiming the destruction of Jerusalem in 701 BCE. Together they dramatize the impact of the terror of judgment coming to both the northern and southern kingdoms. Important linking phrases connect the units. After the theophany is described, its rationale is introduced: "*All this* is for the transgression of Jacob" (1:5). After the prediction of the judgment of Samaria, a similar phrase explains the wailing of Micah and his lament over the coming doom on Judah and Jerusalem: "*For this* I will lament and wail" (1:8). Thus the theophany in 1:2–4 is specifically linked to the judgment of the two cities in 1:5–7 and 1:8–16.

The first speech is strategically placed at the beginning of the book for a number of reasons: (1) It has a universal scope. The world of nations is called to witness the judgment against Israel because it has worldwide implications. (2) Samaria and Jerusalem were mentioned as the address of Micah's prophecies

---

tion of the relative phrase "which he saw" modifying "word of Yahweh" would more normally be expressed by a waw consecutive imperfect (preterite) emphasizing sequence. Here sequence is deemphasized in order to coordinate the source of the verbs and their addressees: "the word that was to" is nicely balanced by "the word that he saw against."

(1:1), and both cities are the target of his first prophecies. (3) The depiction of the awesome transcendence of God indicates that God is incomparable as the divine king, and he will not tolerate any rivals and any injustice in his world. As the one from whom all power is derived, he demands an accounting for how that power is used.[25]

All eyes and ears are thus directed to the divine king arising from the throne of his heavenly temple, descending to the earth to bring awesome judgment on Samaria, and then carving a path of judgment in southwestern Judah to the gates of Jerusalem. The elements of the structure portray this clearly: a call to attention to all the inhabitants of the world so that Yahweh can be a witness against them (1:2), a theophany (1:3–4), followed by a judgment oracle in which general reasons are presented for the judgments of Samaria and Jerusalem (1:5). Then the sentence of judgment on Samaria is introduced by the conjunction "therefore," which describes that judgment in detail (1:6–7), to which is attached a lament that mourns the imminent judgment of Jerusalem (1:8–16).

Literary Features. Words and phrases are pressed into service to communicate dynamically the theme of coming judgment. Imperatives are found at or near the beginnings of the two units, and imperfective verbs are frequent, emphasizing impending doom. The proliferation of imperatives in the second speech contributes to a mood of panic as one town after another is addressed.

Yahweh's actions are highlighted through key words. Yahweh emerges from his temple and "comes down" (וְיָרַד/*wəyārad*; 1:3) to tread on the high places of the earth. A swath of destruction begins with the mountains and valleys, then moves on to Samaria and southwestern Judah until finally "coming down" to Jerusalem (יָרַד/*yārad*; 1:12). The dissolution of the valleys into flowing water (מֻגָּרִים/*muggārîm*; 1:4) is echoed in the destruction of Samaria's fortifications (וְהִגַּרְתִּי/*wəhiggartî*; 1:6). The repetition of "all" in a triad of lines reinforces the comprehensive destruction of idolatrous Samaria in 1:7: these lines emphasize the *complete* obliteration of Samaria's idolatry.

The use of wordplay or paronomasia appears early and becomes a leitmotif through the entire text. The name "Samaria" (שֹׁמְרוֹן/*šōmərôn*; 1:5) sounds like "I will make destruction" (אָשִׂים שְׁמָמָה/*'āśîm šəmāmâ*; 1:7). Thus the name seals the city's fate. This becomes the dominant note in the second speech, as a virtual gazetteer of such names (1:10–15) is enveloped by the prophet's wailing (1:8–9) and the people's lamentation (1:16). The following chart illustrates this topography of terror, and when there is not a direct link between the town's name and its fate, an ironic twist is given to the meaning of the name (my translations):

25. W. J. Wessels, "Micah 1: An Apt Introduction to Power Talks," *Skrif en Kerk* 19 (1998): 438–47.

Name	Transliteration	English	Equivalent
Gath	*bəgat ʾal-taggîdû*	in Gath don't tell it	in Tell Town don't tell it
Beth-leaphrah	*bəbêt lĕʿaprâ ʿapār hitpallaštî*	in Beth-leaphrah roll in the dust	in Dust House roll in the dust
Shaphir	*ʿibrî lākem yôšebet šāpîr ʿeryâ-bōšet*	get yourselves out of there in nakedness and shame, residents of Shaphir	get yourselves out of there in nakedness and shame, residents of Beauty Town
Zaanan	*lōʾ yāṣěʾâ yôšebet ṣaʾănān*	the residents of Zaanan do not go out	no exit for Exit Town
Beth-ezel	*mispad bêt hāʾēṣel yiqqaḥ mikkem ʿemdātô*	the mourning of Beth-ezel means you will have no help	the mourning of Neighbor Town means no more neighbor
Maroth	*kî-ḥālâ lᵃṭôb yôšebet mārôt*	for the residents of Maroth hoped for good	for the residents of Bitterville hoped for better
Jerusalem	*kî-yārad rāʿ mēʾēt yhwh ləšaʿar yərûšālāyim*	for disaster has gone down from Yahweh to the gate of Jerusalem	for war has come down from Yahweh to the gate of the City of Peace
Lachish	*rĕtōm ham-merkābâ lārekeš yôšebet lākîš*	bind the chariot to the harness, residents of Lachish	bind the chariot to the harness, residents of Harness Town
Moresheth-gath	*lākēn tittĕni šillûḥîm ʿal môrešet gat*	therefore you will give parting gifts to Moresheth-gath	therefore you will give parting gifts to Inheritance of Gath
Achzib	*bāttê ʾakzîb lĕʾakzāb ləmalkê yiśrāʾēl*	the houses of Achzib will become deceptive to the kings of Israel	the houses of deception will prove deceptive to the kings of Israel
Mareshah	*ʿōd hayyōrēš ʾābî lāk yôšebet mārēšâ*	again I will bring a conqueror to the residents of Mareshah	I will bring a conqueror to Conquering Town
Adullam	*ʿad-ʿădullām yābôʾ kĕbôd yiśrāʾēl*	unto Adullam will come the glory of Israel	unto the land of the caves will flee the glory of Israel

For Westerners, this is a clever text because it abounds with wordplays and puns that could be conceived as "comic relief"[26] by "a man of letters." But for the ancient Israelite who linked names and destinies, this was ominous. Modern Westerners use names often simply based on personal preferences and popularity, but for the Hebrews names were important identity markers. For example, when Abram and Sarai received new names they also received new destinies (Gen 17). To discover the meaning of the name of an object or person is to discover destiny and identity. In this case, Micah chooses names with sounds or meanings that are virtual omens of disaster: *Nomen ist Omen.*[27] For example, Beth-leaphrah literally means "house of dust," and although the location of the town is unknown it was probably given its name because of its dry, desertlike climate. It was a "dust bowl." But Micah electrifies his audience with a different meaning. In the light of the approaching judgment of God he discerns the Hebrew mourning custom of rolling in the dust in pain and grief. He thus commands the residents of this town to experience their real destiny—to roll in the dust because of their coming grief. Similarly the town of Zaanan, a place named "going out" or "passageway," was probably a strategic location providing an exit from the lowlands of Israel to the Coastal Plain. But Micah announces that there will be no exit for "Exit Town" in the coming judgment. For those names for which there is no similarity of sound between the town and the word indicating its fate, the prophet plays on their meaning. Thus Shaphir, "Beautiful Town," becomes a place where the residents leave their homes stripped of any beauty because of the judgment of God. This is true especially for the one city that is in the center of the poem and that is the real target of the judgment—Jerusalem. This name sounds like the words "City of Peace," but its fate is the opposite—disaster.[28]

Finally, it should be pointed out that the text has some difficult grammatical problems such as a lack of concord with pronouns and verbs. For example the second-person feminine singular imperative is used with a second-person

26. E.g., Joyce Rilett Wood conceives of the text in such a way: "The wordplays focus attention on the cities and the actions that correspond to their names, but the prophet's witticisms also inject comic relief into the sequence of serious images"; "Speech and Action in Micah's Prophecy," *Catholic Biblical Quarterly* 62 (2000): 645–62 at 654. McKane wonders why there is a radical distinction between the "man of letters" in Mic 1 and the prophet of doom in Mic 2–3, but he partially answers his own question when he asks whether wordplay added pathos and power to the lament, in order "to magnify the dimensions of the catastrophe"; *Micah,* 57. Though a good number of these cities have not been identified by archaeologists and only occur here in the Bible (e.g., Beth-leaphrah, Shaphir, Beth-ezel, Maroth), their shock value assumes their historicity.

27. Renaud, *Formation du Livre de Michée,* 35.

28. Cf. the use of the word pair שָׁלוֹם/*šālôm* and רַע/*raʿ* in Isa 45:7. Mays, among others, also notes the allusion; *Micah,* 57–58. Ben Zvi fails to see this point, mainly because he fails to see Jerusalem as the structural center of the poem; *Micah,* 36–37.

masculine plural pronominal suffix in 1:11: "Pass by naked and in shame, you who live in Shaphir." The verb "pass by" lacks agreement with the pronoun "you." Similarly, the command issued to Lachish to bind the harness to the chariot is given in the second-person masculine singular imperative, even though Lachish is feminine (1:13). These grammatical problems may simply be due to corruption in the course of the textual history of the book but it is noteworthy that the text is not as problematic elsewhere. Moreover attempts to restore the grammar and meter to a more "correct" state—and there are many[29]—lack convincing authority and consensus. The question then may be legitimately asked as to why there is a major textual difficulty here in this text and not in other places. The clue to this puzzle may be supplied by the words that introduce the text. This is a wild lament by the prophet as he sees a swath of destruction with Samaria in its wake, stretching over southern Judah and threatening Jerusalem (1:8). If his words are "not the ravings of a lunatic,"[30] they are more like the uncontrolled grief of a person stunned by shock or grief. Andersen and Freedman are on the right track when they speak of how traumatic this vision is for the prophet. The prophets did not speak in serene detachment. When Amos saw visions of locust hordes and fiery judgment, he was no detached bystander (7:1-6)! Jeremiah describes the true prophet as broken to the bones, completely overcome by the words of Yahweh (Jer 23:9). Micah may have been so overwhelmed with his vision that he stutters and stops and makes grammatical mistakes. He is overcome by the doom of the words so much that he is totally disoriented, reflected in his grammatical confusion: "In a paroxysm of anguish, sharpened by a panoramic vision of desolation and ruin, the prophet points out his woe in fits and starts, in bits and pieces."[31] Micah reverts to a more topicalized discourse and abandons grammaticalization in so doing. His eye is startled by one appalling sight after another, and this cannot help but affect his grammatical precision. Conventional grammar cannot contain the explosive message.[32] He has been to the front where the battle is, and the sights that he has seen are still fresh in his memory and his words may seem like the ravings of the lunatic because people are totally unaware of their danger.[33]

29. See the standard commentaries. Most notable is the work of Karl Elliger, "Die Heimat des Propheten Micha," *Zeitschrift des Deutschen Palästina-Vereins alttestamentlicher Wissenschaft* 57 (1934): 81-152.

30. Andersen and Freedman, *Micah*, 247.

31. Ibid.

32. See, e.g., similar features in Hosea, where one scholar speaks of "artful incoherence"; John L. McKenzie, "Divine Passion in Osee," *Catholic Biblical Quarterly* 17 (April 1955): 287-99.

33. Elie Wiesel writes about a person from his hometown, Moishe the Beadle, who had escaped from Auschwitz and returned to warn his friends and family. He was written off as a

Key Words and Expressions. **Hear O peoples, All of them!** (my literal translation) is a direct quote from a forerunner of Micah, Micaiah ben Imlah, who first used this expression to arrest the attention of the people of Samaria, when there was doubt about the authenticity of his prophecy of the death of Ahab in battle and the defeat of Israel before the Arameans who were going to fight at Ramoth Gilead (1 Kgs 22:28). Although most scholars assume that the text in Micah originally was "all of you" instead of "all of them," an important literary allusion is missed. As Micaiah used these words to alert the people of Israel to the authenticity of his oracle, by using these words Micah is doing the same thing.[34] There are other important allusions to Ahab in Micah: the coveting of Ahab (2:1–2, cf. 1 Kgs 21), the house of Omri (6:16), and the death of Jezebel (7:10).[35] **Listen, Earth, and all who live in it** is a regular combination that describes the totality of the world and is thus more comprehensive than "all the peoples" (Deut 33:17; Ezek 19:7; 30:12; Ps 24:1). **Lord God . . .** Lord (Adonai Yahweh . . . Adonai) is the first use of the divine name in the speeches of Micah.[36] This use of the title Adonai with and without the divine name stresses the sovereign nature of Israel's God. He is a God who is Lord over creation—as the context indicates. **Be a witness against you:** some (including the Septuagint) translate this "is among you as a witness," but in similar contexts the idiom means "to be a witness against" (Num 5:13; Deut 31:21, 26, cf. 28; Jer 42:5; Ps 27:12).[37] Thus the sovereign Lord from his ultimate vantage point is the definitive witness of the crimes of humanity. Nothing escapes his notice. Yahweh bears witness first against the nations, indicating that they need to learn from the following scenario that Yahweh is also their judge.[38] **For lo, the Lord**

---

raving lunatic; *Night* (New York: Macmillan, 2012), 2–10. For the effect of psychological factors on grammar and syntax, see David W. Carroll, *Psychology of Language* (Belmont: Thomson/Wadsworth, 2007), 194.

34. Keil (*Minor Prophets*, 425) points out the importance of this literary allusion by showing that Micah had surely meditated on the story in 1 Kings, as indicated by other allusions in his oracles: his name, lying prophets (Mic 2:11; cf. 1 Kgs 22:22–23), horns of iron (Mic 4:13; cf. 1 Kgs 22:11), and the punch on the side of the face (Mic 5:1; cf. 1 Kgs 22:24).

35. I am indebted to Luke Nieuwsma for these references, as cited by P. Leithart, "Ahab in Micah," *First Things* 12 (2006): 11.

36. Names or titles of God occur forty-nine times in the book.

37. John T. Willis accurately reaches the conclusion: "There is no exception to this meaning in the Old Testament!"; "Some Suggestions on the Interpretation of Micah 1:2," *Vetus Testamentum* 18 (1968): 372–79 at 378.

38. "If God does not fail to judge his own, he will certainly judge those who do not belong to them"; McComiskey, *Micah*, 403. See also Willis, "Some Suggestions," 378. The reference to "you" must be traced back to its antecedent: the nations. "Yahweh through his punishment of Israel will testify against the nations"; Smith, *Micah, Zephaniah, and Nahum*, 35. Many scholars see "you" as having cataphoric value—pointing ahead to Israel since Israel is the subject of discourse in the

is coming out of his place: the Hebrew invites the reader to see through the prophet's own eyes as Yahweh emerges from his residence. There is an exact counterpart for this expression in Isa 26:21, which depicts Yahweh coming into the world to judge it for its sin. The same idea is present here. The idea of Yahweh's "going forth" is a standard description of a theophany that causes havoc in his enemies and creation.[39] **Will come down and tread upon the high places of the earth:** to tread upon the high places is to indicate ownership over the territory of someone: God is the owner of the earth because he treads upon its high places. No one else can do so.[40] The king of Assyria seeks to go up to the high places of the clouds and thus become like God (Isa 14:14). When God makes someone tread upon the high places, it is a sign of their dominion over their enemies (Deut 33:29; Ps 18:33; Isa 58:14). That Yahweh must *descend* to tread upon the high places is a picture of awesome transcendence and sovereignty over the earth.[41] **The mountains will melt under him and the valleys will burst open:** other texts indicate the same collapse of creation that occurs with the approach of God (cf. Ps 97:5). The verb "split apart" is used respectively for the rupture of wineskins (Josh 9:13), the tearing asunder of a city wall during a siege (2 Kgs 25:4), and the ripping apart of a body during a massacre (15:16). **Like wax near the fire, like waters pouring down a steep place:** the respective lines match their counterparts, the mountains melt like wax and the valleys liquefy. **The transgression of Jacob . . . sins of the house of Israel:** an important thematic pair in the book, as it appears again in the middle of the book and at the end. Micah's prophetic task is "to declare to Jacob his transgression, / and to Israel his sin" (3:8). Finally, Yahweh will forgive Israel's transgression and cast its sins into the depths of the ocean (7:18–19). "Transgression" has connotations of rebellion, and "sin" has associations of failure. As a word pair they describe the entire gamut of wrongdoing. **What is the transgression of Jacob? Is it not Samaria?** Literally "Who is Jacob's transgression?" That is, who is [responsible] for Jacob's transgression? Samaria is responsible, that is, the capital of the coun-

---

subsequent text and not the nations. Although the grammar allows this, it is not the most natural reading. See, e.g., Keil, *Minor Prophets*, 426–27.

39. J. Jeremias, *Die Geschichte einer Alttestamentliche Gattung*, Wissenschaftliche Monographien zum Alten und Neuen Testament 10 (Neukirchen-Vluyn: Neukirchener Verlag, 1965); and Stephen G. Dempster, "Mythology and History in the Song of Deborah," *Westminster Theological Journal* 41 (1978): 33–53.

40. In Job 9:8 God alone stretches out the heavens and treads upon the high places of the sea. Cf. Amos 4:13.

41. James L. Crenshaw, "wĕdōrēk ʿal bāmôtê ʾāreṣ," *Catholic Biblical Quarterly* 34 (1972): 39–53 at 53n45, shows that the metaphor is maintained in late Hebrew: Caleb conquered Palestine by taking its high places (Sirach 46:9), and youth should not let a woman tread on their high places and thus subjugate them (Sirach 9:1–2).

try has infected the rest of the country with its idolatry (cf. 1:7). **What is the high place of Judah? Is it not Jerusalem?** This shows that Judah is included in the previous reference to Israel, and thus the name Israel is not used exclusively for the northern kingdom. Instead of the expected "What are Judah's sins?" there is the shock of the substitute "high place" for "sins." Such high places were known as synonyms for pagan idolatry. The word is plural in Hebrew and thus links up with the previous theophany where Yahweh treads upon the high places (i.e., mountains). High places were used throughout Canaan as shrines to fertility gods erected on an elevated location in a village or a town. But through common association they became used for any idolatrous shrine. **A heap in the open country** is literally "a heap of the field." Samaria, the capital city complete with its ornate architecture, becomes a wasteland. This description of Samaria's fate anticipates the prophecy of Jerusalem and the temple's fate later in the book, when it will become a heap of rubble (3:12). The city will become decimated, from the stones of the buildings to their foundations. That Samaria was only partially destroyed in the destruction of 722 BCE and was rebuilt does not necessarily invalidate the prophecy, for that is to be woodenly literalistic.[42] **Wages,** literally a fee given to a prostitute for services rendered (cf. Deut 23:18; Isa 23:17; Ezek 16:31), are associated with idolatry and probably refer to the payment of temple harlots. Thus the NIV translates with "temple gifts." **For as the wages of a prostitute she gathered them, and as the wages of a prostitute they shall again be used:** there is a link in the Old Testament between idolatry and sexual promiscuity, which may have had its origin in the temple prostitution practiced in Canaanite cults. The prophet indicates that the money paid for the services of temple prostitutes and which had been converted to temple furniture and idols will be taken by a military enemy and used to pay prostitutes when the soldiers return to their homeland. Thus the wages of prostitution will again be used, but this time in an idolatrous land far from Israel.[43] Micah here presents an important principle of his prophesying in this lead oracle, that is, the correspondence between crime and punishment (2:1–5; 3:1–4, 5–7). **For this** may be editorial, and it links the preceding prediction of judg-

---

42. Thus, e.g., Walter Kaiser's dictum that in prophecy "the eventualities of what eventually happened had to fit perfectly what had been declared in word prior to its happening" needs to be modified; *The Messiah in the Old Testament* (Grand Rapids: Zondervan, 1995), 235.

43. See, e.g., Renaud, *Formation du Livre de Michée*, 15. Keil does not understand the text literally but more metaphorically: the wealth used for idolatry (spiritual whoredom) will be taken and used for the same purpose in the homeland of the enemy soldiers; *Minor Prophets*, 429. Similarly Wolff comments: "Samaria gave commercial goods and tribute to the great power Assyria and therefore 'gathered' 'whore's wages,' which made possible the splendid buildings of the royal residence"; *Micah*, 58.

ment to the cause of Micah's lament, for he sees in the destruction of Samaria the impending destruction of Jerusalem. **I will lament and wail** is a standard description of grief over great loss. Cf. David and his servants' behavior when fleeing Jerusalem after the treason of Absalom (2 Sam 15:30-32) and David's lament over the death of his son (19:1-7); expressions of anguish often resulted in people covering their heads, rolling in dust, and walking barefoot. Nakedness refers to captives and prisoners being led into exile. Here the woe is amplified as Micah howls like a wild animal and screeches like a wild bird. His grief is hysterical. **For her wound is incurable. It has come to Judah:** there are a number of grammatical problems here. The text literally says: "Its blows are incurable," and thus there is lack of grammatical agreement between the plural noun "blows" and the singular adjective "incurable." "Blows" could be a plural of intensity, thus functioning as a singular, and thus meaning "great blow," but used with this adjective it would take on the meaning of a great plague or wound that caused the judgment. On the other hand the Septuagint may preserve the original reading in the singular. Second, most translations assume that the referent of "its wound" is Samaria since the previous context suggests the judgment that has befallen the northern capital and that is therefore now coming to the southern kingdom. It is possible to understand the referent cataphorically pointing ahead to Jerusalem, but it is unnatural since the following text suggests the wound is contaminating Judah and advancing on Jerusalem. Third, some scholars understand "its wound" as "the plagues or blows of Yah(weh)." This means dividing the pronominal suffix from its noun (a radical measure) and changing the vocalization of the suffix (less radical). Both measures are unnecessary, and the use of the short form of Yahweh is very rare among the prophets (Isa 12:2; 38:11 [2x]). Thus it is best to see this text as referring to the previous judgment of Samaria, both in terms of its spiritual sickness, which spread to Judah, along with the consequent judgment. **Tell it not in Gath, weep not at all:** the subject of the two verbs probably refers to the people of Judah in general. But this first line is a deliberate echo of a popular lament composed by David after the deaths of Saul and Jonathan at Mount Gilboa, the "Waterloo" of ancient Israel (cf. 2 Sam 1:20). Here the quotation has been converted to head the list of a series of disasters coming to the south of Judah as the divine foot treads upon one town after another in an inexorable march of judgment. No Israelite could miss the allusion to the unspeakable grief that these words evoked. This is no ordinary judgment; it signals the end of an era! The command not to weep seems strange in a context of lament where the prophet is howling like an animal and commands people of the various towns to weep. But perhaps he is telling a general audience not to weep, because the judgment is so shocking that silence is a fitting emotional response at first (cf.

Job 2:12–13; Ezek 3:15–16). Perhaps also the contradiction shows incoherence produced by shock.[44] Or more likely the locative "there" is implied so the command not to publish the news in Gath is intensified with a command not to weep there (an Israelite telling this news would obviously weep).[45] **Yet disaster has come from the LORD to the gate of Jerusalem:** this is the central city of the twelve mentioned in 1:10–16. As Jerusalem is the "city of peace," it is fitting that it will experience disaster! This is probably the most severe judgment of all the towns, for the linkage in 1:3 is clear. The divine foot is about to claim the ultimate "high place" and center of idolatry in Judah—Jerusalem. **It was the beginning of sin to daughter Zion, for in you were found the transgressions of Israel:** this text alludes to 1:5, suggesting that the idolatry of the northern kingdom spread to the city of Lachish in the south and then to the rest of Judah. It is clear that Lachish was an extremely influential city that was well fortified. It was able to hold out longer against the Assyrians (and the Babylonians a century later) than all other cities in the south in 701 BCE except Jerusalem. Perhaps the focus on its military strength is the real point: it relied on military strength and this led to idolatry; trust in chariots—the rapid deployment forces in the ancient world—was an indicator of faith in superior military power (cf. Ps 20:7–8). **Parting gifts:** Lachish is viewed as giving a dowry to its daughter city, Moresheth-gath, who will soon depart to a new life as a "spouse" of the dreaded Assyrian army (cf. 1 Kgs 9:16)![46] **Moresheth-gath** is Micah's hometown, and the second name further identifies the place, near the major Philistine city of Gath. There are similar examples of names where the second member further identifies the first (e.g., Bethlehem of Judah in Judg 17:7–9; Abel of Maim in 2 Chr 16:4) lest it be confused with another location.[47] **The kings of Israel** no doubt refers to the kings of Judah, as the name "Israel" is still used of Judah (cf. Mic 1:5; 3:8–10). "Kings" likely refer to the house of David.[48] **The glory of Israel shall come to Adullam** is a reference to the king of Judah and his entourage (cf. Isa 5:13) fleeing to the cave of Adullam where David long before had to flee for his life from Saul. The coup de grâce of judgment is the departure of the

44. Waltke suggests that there should be no weeping at Gath, but Gath as a Philistine city would hardly be encouraged not to weep over the defeat of its perennial foes; "Micah," 61, 70–71.

45. See God's Word translation. Since most translations join this line with the first one, they assume the locative "there." Some reconstruct an original "Acco" from some of the Hebrew consonants for "weep," thus reading "Do not weep in Acco" (Young's Literal Translation; cf. International Standard Version). But this emendation remains conjectural.

46. Wolff, *Micah*, 62.

47. Keil, *Minor Prophets*, 436.

48. Ahaz can be referred to with either his name or the epithet "house of David" (Isa 7:10–13).

king from his throne, as "the glory of Israel . . . will again be hidden in obscurity,"[49] "reduced to a hole in the ground."[50] Calvin's suggestion that the town of Adullam represents the glory of Israel cannot be sustained by the grammar ("he shall come to Adullam, the glory of Israel").[51] **Make yourselves bald and cut off your hair . . . make yourselves as bald as the eagle:** it was a common custom among Israel's neighbors to shave their heads and mutilate their bodies in times of extreme grief. Israel as God's holy people was forbidden to engage in some of these customs (Deut 14:1). In ancient Israel, certain types of shaving were permitted as an act of intense mourning (cf. Isa 22:12), and the command to do it here makes clear that the Holy City, Jerusalem, will be in agony over the loss of its children. If the prophet has in mind pagan customs of mourning, he may be implying that the people have forfeited their status as the people of God![52] Mays regards a similar expression in 5:1 to be "an ironic taunt addressed to a people who reverted to pagan ways and perhaps wailed appeals to other gods in their hour of final distress."[53]

Interpretation—Micah's Word Then. This section would have consisted of two separate oracles, one given to Samaria before its destruction around 722 BCE and the other delivered in Judah before the invasion of Sennacherib in 701 BCE.[54] One consists of a legal genre, or covenant lawsuit, in which a complaint is presented, with Yahweh telling the nations that he is going to be a witness against them, and then surprisingly there comes a judgment oracle

49. D. K. Innes, "Some Notes on Micah, Chapter 1," *Evangelical Quarterly* 39 (1967): 225–27 at 227.

50. McKane, *Micah*, 53.

51. Calvin, *Twelve Minor Prophets*, 182. It is difficult to see "the glory of Israel" as an appositive phrase, since it is separated from its head, Adullam, by the verb.

52. On the other hand, some commentators argue that this shows that Micah's command is clearly prior to the Deuteronomic law! See Smith, *Micah, Zephaniah, and Nahum*, 50.

53. Mays, *Micah*, 114.

54. Mic 1:8–16 could have been delivered on two other occasions: shortly after 1:2–7 and the destruction of Samaria as a harbinger of the coming judgment to the south (Wolff, *Micah*, 40). But 1:8–16 suggests that an imminent catastrophe approaches. Similarly the oracle could have been spoken in 712 when the Assyrians conquered Ashdod and quashed a rebellion there in which Judah may have been involved. Thus the impending nature of the catastrophe, coupled with Hezekiah's rebellion when Sargon died in 705, indicates sometime before the 701 invasion. For a consideration of the possibilities, see Nadav Na'aman, "The House of No Shade Shall Take Its Tax from You: Micah 1:11," *Vetus Testamentum* 45 (1995): 516–27 at 525–27. Charles S. Shaw argues that the text should be dated to the Syro-Ephraimite crisis in 734 BCE, and the outlying towns are castigated for being involved in the anti-Assyrian coalition. But in my judgment there are no distinctions between the outlying towns and Jerusalem. The whole land is being swamped by the Assyrian enemy and all are called to lamentation; "Micah 1:10–16 Reconsidered," *Journal of Biblical Literature* 106 (1987): 223–29.

against Samaria. The second consists of a lament that functions like a judgment oracle as the towns of southwestern Judah are called to mourn over an impending invasion and consequent exile. The two units now function as an introduction to the entire book, stressing that the nations are called to listen in particular to what the divine judge is going to do to Israel and Judah for their violations of the covenant. The images are breathtaking as the divine judge descends to the heights of the earth and all creation rocks and reels before him as he comes first to Samaria and then to the towns of Judah. The announcement of Samaria's destruction leads to calls to lament in Judah as the prophet wails like a wild animal throughout the countryside, pronouncing one note of ominous doom after another and calling the population to join him in his grief.

It is also not accidental that the nations are introduced in this judgment scene at the beginning of the book, as they will reemerge again in the center of the book (4:1–5:15) and in the final scene of the book in a scene of salvation (7:11–13, 16–17). Micah's message is not just a narrow, nationalistic tract but has worldwide implications, because God's dealings with the people of Israel have universal import.[55]

Virtually all historical references dealing with the particulars of warfare have been blurred in this text except for the uprooting of foundations and the burning of objects in the oracle against Samaria and the reference to exile in the oracle against Jerusalem. Both oracles stress the awesome judgment of God and have been integrated together to show the continuity of that judgment in an unbroken thematic sequence as Yahweh steps down from the throne room of the universe to tread down on the high places of the earth, namely Samaria and Jerusalem, to claim ownership of them, since they have prostituted themselves to idols.

The link between the name of a city and its doom becomes a *cantus firmus* in a fugue as the topography of the country inspires terror. The names begin and end on a note of recollection of lament in Israel—David's lament for Saul and his own flight to a cave in Adullam.[56] "Do not tell the news in Gath!" immediately brings to mind the national disaster centuries before on Mount Gilboa when the Philistines won both a decisive victory and eliminated the dynasty of Saul in one fell swoop. Every Israelite would have understood the ominous import of these words as they would have become ingrained in them since early childhood when they learned "The Lament of the Bow" (2 Sam 1:19–20).

---

55. "It is the God of Israel . . . Who calls the nations of the world into judgment, and it is He Whom one day all nations shall worship in Zion"; Heschel, *Prophets*, 216.

56. McComiskey, *Micah*, 408.

Similarly, the reference to the "glory of Israel" going to Adullam recalls the true king of Israel hiding in a cave from sure death (1 Sam 22).

There is an unmistakable mood of panic as the text moves from Samaria to Judah. The vision is startling, stunning, shocking, and it is as if the prophet stammers and stutters through his speech because he is shuddering from sheer terror. The ominous tone struck by the opening words of the lament is continued by one wordplay after another in which the doom of a city is inextricably connected to its name and thus its fate is sealed. Some commentators try to convey the vision by using puns in English to translate the Hebrew wordplays. The following is an example from my own context in New Brunswick, Canada:[57]

> Give Anthrax to Halifax!
> A whack to Stewiacke!
> Provide a hearse for Amherst!
> Put on Sackcloth, residents of Sackville!
> People of Hillsborough, flee to the Hills!
> Rage because of the coming disaster, Gagetown!
> For a ton of disaster is coming to Fredericton!

The lament begins with the signal that the end has come for Judah just as it had come for the northern kingdom, and it ends with the dynastic ruler having to flee Jerusalem and hide in a cave like a common fugitive, while the people head off into exile. The language breathes pure panic.

That the book of Micah opens with these two oracles integrated into one text does not mean that these oracles were the first to be pronounced by Micah, neither does it mean that they were originally pronounced together since they represent historical events roughly two decades apart. These particular speeches were chosen to head the collection of oracles since they each target the cities mentioned in the superscription. They also establish the prophetic credentials of Micah. By the time the book was composed, Samaria was history, and so were many of the cities of Judah; Jerusalem survived by the skin of its teeth and this was due to a miracle. Were these events simply historical accidents? Were they the reflex of geopolitical movements in the region? This text supplies the answer in no uncertain terms. Both the destruction of Samaria and the escape of Jerusalem from certain death testify to Micah's authority as a prophet. On the one hand the ignoring of his message sealed the fate of the northern kingdom and much of the south in awesome judgment. But the heeding of his message

---

57. Peter C. Craigie imaginatively does the same for a context in Scotland; *The Twelve Prophets* (Edinburgh: Saint Andrews, 1985), 2.14.

of judgment spared Jerusalem from carnage in one of the most extraordinary miracles in all of history. Thus this opening text testifies powerfully to the truth of the prophetic words spoken through the lips of Micah of Moresheth. They tell the readers and hearers of the book about the events of the late eighth century BCE and point out that idolatry whether in gods of wood and stone or in military muscle is a sentence of death for the people of God and for creatures made in his image.

In the biblical text, this theophanic vision is part of a standard pattern. When God emerges from the throne room of the universe and into history, there is a profound shaking up of the cosmic order. Isaiah describes the same Assyrian terror from a perspective north of the city of Jerusalem rather than southwestern Judah. The Assyrian army causes panic in town after town until it stops at Jerusalem and waves its fist. Like Samaria, Jerusalem is to be judged for its idolatry (Isa 10:8–11, 28–34).

Interpretation—Micah's Word Now. This terrifying theophanic vision of judgment speaks powerfully to the people of God. Its places of worship can easily become coopted by the current idols of its times so that it is no different than the nations around it. Jerusalem, which was called to be a city of peace and light to the nations, had become one huge high place much like Samaria with its countless idols. Who were these prophets anyway, who seemed to "speak and act as if the sky were about to collapse because Israel has become unfaithful to God"?[58] Israel and Judah are not guilty of mere peccadillos but have fundamentally committed crimes against ultimate truth and crimes against love. For what is idolatry but making a substitute for God that is not God and cannot be God? Whether those idols are the actual fertility images of Baal and Asherah of the surrounding cultures or the militaristic might of places like Lachish, they fundamentally distort reality. Their worshipers look at the world through their lenses and see a very different world than that seen through the eyes of the justice and compassion of Yahweh. Yahweh cannot tolerate such lies that warp his world and the people in it, as injustice and lack of compassion run rampant in society. If the world would continue without his intervention, the sky actually would collapse.

But idolatry is not a crime only against truth, but finally a crime against love. Thus Micah announces the insight of an older, northern contemporary: idolatry is adultery (Hosea). The violation of the covenant is not just the breach of an impersonal code, but the offending of a person. Just as the adultery of a spouse cuts deep within the heart of his or her partner, so it is the same with Yahweh. And in this text, the rage and anger that is expressed in the judgment

---

58. Heschel, *Prophets*, 5.

suggests a deep wound in the heart of God. Micah's lamentations and screams in anticipation of the judgment of his cities and his people's lamentations of their children taken away from them are faint analogies for the deep pain that cuts through God's heart at his people's unfaithfulness and idolatry.

To speak of judgment in modern Western culture is to invite ridicule and laughter. For such a culture there is no sense of eschatology, no idea of an ultimate accounting. Time is viewed as an eternal "now." What is important is the present, not the past nor the future. People know more about the last sixty seconds than the last sixty years. This has been described as "presentism" or "simultaneity," or more colloquially the "CNN-ization of time": "The frenetic pursuit of breaking news . . . it simply records the onslaught of events."[59] But Scripture makes clear that history is moving to a goal and that an essential part of that goal is divine judgment. The judgment of Israel in Micah's time is a foretaste of judgment of the world. Without faithfulness to God every name can become an omen of disaster. As Samaria became fit for a burial and as the City of Peace became a City of War, so too all cities in the world can become the same: Rome can be reduced to loam, Seoul can become coal, Denver can become a viper's den, Shanghai can be shanghaied. Why? The answer is idolatry. Indeed as C. S. Lewis remarks: "All that we call human history—money, poverty, ambition, war, prostitution, classes, empires, slavery—is the long terrible story of man trying to find something other than God which will make him happy."[60] This is nothing else but idolatry, and the consequence, as Lewis describes, is radical injustice. Micah announces that the inhabitants of the earth are living a lie and that God finally will not tolerate such a lie. He will come one day to put the world to rights. The nations need to wake up and be prepared.

In the Christian church God has frequently been reduced to a manageable size, or domesticated. Is God not supposed to be a God of love and compassion, with limitless patience and infinite generosity? After all, does not love finally win?[61] But Micah's vision of God is like an atomic bomb that liquidates all attempts at divine management or domestication. God's love never comes at the expense of his justice.[62] This is just as important a New Testament truth

59. James K. A. Smith, *Desiring the Kingdom: Worship, Worldview, and Cultural Formation* (Grand Rapids: Baker, 2009), 159.

60. C. S. Lewis, *Mere Christianity* (New York: HarperCollins, 2001), 53–54.

61. See, e.g., Rob Bell, *Love Wins: A Book about Heaven, Hell, and the Fate of Every Person Who Ever Lived* (New York: HarperOne, 2011).

62. See the important study by Nicholas Wolterstorff, *Justice: Rights and Wrongs* (Princeton: Princeton University Press, 2008). J. P. Miranda puts an exclamation mark on Wolterstorff's study with his statement: "While not agreeing with [my] thesis he is indubitably right when he

as an Old Testament one. At the end of history a divine fire will consume all the enemies of God (2 Thess 1:7–8), melting not only all the idols but the very elements of the creation (2 Pet 3:12). As the creation disintegrates before the coming of God, people will call out for the rocks and caves to hide them from the searing judgment (Rev 6:14–17). Their question is *the* question: "For the great day of their wrath has come, Who is able to stand?" (6:17).

Micah will raise an answer to that question within his book again and again. It is *the* question—how does one relate to God? How can sinful humanity stand before a divine judge who is both just and holy and who has been a witness to all its deeds? Samaria is now history as Micah predicted. Judah was also judged, and Jerusalem was within a hair breadth of being destroyed. There is a lesson here for all who have ears to hear: "Hear, you peoples, all of you, listen!" The message that Micah 1 tells is a lesson of one society that ignored his word and another that woke up in time. The whole world is called to pay attention to its ultimately having to do with God, and he will come someday and tread down every high place and eliminate every idol, until the whole world will be filled with his presence as the waters cover the sea (cf. Isa 11:1–9). When he becomes one and his name one (Zech 14:9), every name will become a name of hope and salvation. Rome will become Home, Seoul will have a Soul, and the City of Disaster will become a City of Peace. In the meantime, as Calvin indicates, the text calls people to humble penitence: "Since God is said to melt the mountains with his presence, let us hence learn to rouse up all our feelings whenever God comes forth, not that we might flee to a distance from him, but that we might reverently receive his word, so that he may afterwards appear to us a kind and reconciled Father."[63]

Perhaps also ministers might learn to lament for their countries, for their towns, for their villages as Micah once did, and that empathy might become contagious. Micah's lamentation is a type of Jesus's lamentation over Jerusalem (Matt 23:37), and surely such grief should melt the hard hearts of believers and unbelievers alike, and induce them to wake up. David Hume, the seventeenth-century atheist, once arose early in the morning to travel to hear George Whitfield preach. After returning, he was asked if he was now a believer. "No," replied Hume, "but Whitfield sure is!" Micah believed; Whitfield believed. Do we?

---

writes: 'One of the most disastrous errors in the history of Christianity is to have tried—under the influence of Greek definitions—to differentiate between love and justice. The sense of justice is the only love that gets to the heart of the matter. . . . Love is not love without a passion for justice'"; cited in J. Du Preez, "Social Justice: Motive for the Mission of the Church," *Journal of Theology for Southern Africa* 53 (1985): 38.

63. Calvin, *Twelve Minor Prophets*, 161.

Dead Men Walking: Cause of Judgment and Exile (2:1–11)

Structure. Originally two individual oracles (2:1–5 and 2:6–11) were integrated into the second large unit in the book. The first major unit announced the judgment (1:2–16) but spoke little about its cause; this second unit specifically deals with the cause and reinforces the judgment (2:1–5) and then parries theological objections about the preaching of judgment (2:6–11). The first major speech mentioned imminent disaster and consequent lamentation (1:8–9, 16); this second main speech has the prophet announcing coming judgment for specific evil actions and telling particular sinners to begin lamenting their approaching doom (2:1, 4). The first major text ended with the impending exile of the people of Judah and their loss of land (1:16); this new unit announces this judgment of exile and loss of land (2:4, 10). Because people stole land, it will now be stolen from them. Those who drove the common people out of house and home will themselves be driven out.

The first oracle of this new unit (2:1–5) is a classic example of a woe oracle functioning as a judgment speech in which the reasons for the judgment are specified (2:1–2), followed by the divine judicial sentence (2:3–5) introduced by the logical conjunction "therefore" (לָכֵן/*lākēn*; 2:3). The conjunction is repeated to emphasize the judgment before the last statement (2:5), which disrupts the smooth poetic syntax with its prosaic style. This grammatical disruption signals a theological disruption: the oppressors are no longer the people of Yahweh! The entire oracle begins with a word used at a funeral to express grief and lamentation, "Woe" (1 Kgs 13:30), and concludes with the spiritual death of the criminals (Mic 2:5).

Linked to this judgment oracle is a text that functions as a disputation speech (2:6–11) in which Micah responds to the attempts of false prophets to silence him and his faithful prophetic colleagues.[64] He uses their own words in a sharp counterattack. Prophets often used the words of their opponents in order to refute them. For example, Amos 3 is a vigorous prophetic apology for a strident judgment speech.[65]

---

64. Adrian Graffy, *A Prophet Confronts His People: The Disputation Speech in the Prophets* (Rome: Gregorian Biblical Bookshop, 1984), 117–20. It is more likely that a disputation form would arise in daily life wherever opinions were contradicted, often in a legal milieu. Graffy cites H.-E. von Waldow's study ("Anlass und Hintergrund Propheten der Verkündigung des Deuterojesaja" [PhD dissertation, 1953], 28–36), which makes this commonsense opinion only to attempt to refute it.

65. Stephen G. Dempster, "Amos 3:1–15: Apologia of a Prophet," *Baptist Review of Theology* 5 (1995): 35–51; and Y. Gitay, "A Study of Amos's Art of Speech: A Rhetorical Analysis of Amos 3:1–15," *Catholic Biblical Quarterly* 42 (1980): 293–309.

The disputation speech is difficult to understand because of "the concise-ness of the expressions."[66] The problems are exacerbated by the overhearing of an ongoing debate in which it is not exactly clear who the debaters are, who is saying what, and what they are saying! This text was probably an originally in-dependent conversation that has been edited into its current place in the book.[67] The specific meaning and the reasons for interpretation will be presented below in the section "Key Words and Expressions." But the literal text is now shown to give an overview of some of the structural problems involved with interpre-tation (italic indicates uncertainty about the identity of the speaker):

> "*Do not* drip (prophesy)," *they* drip.
> "*They will* not drip (or *they will* not prophesy) about these things (or to
>   these people)."
> "*He will not remove disgrace.*"
> "Should it (i.e., disgrace) be said of the house of Jacob?"
> "Is the Spirit of Yahweh shortened?"
> "Does he do these things?"
> "*Do not my words do good to those who walk uprightly*?"

The differences in interpretation can easily be seen by comparing modern trans-lations of the text:

> [*Micah quoting false prophets:*] "Stop preaching!" they preach.
> "That's no way to preach; shame shall not overtake *us*.
> Is the house of Jacob condemned? Is the LORD's patience short? Is such
>   his practice?"
> [*Micah:*] To be sure, My words are friendly To those who walk in recti-
>   tude." (Tanakh, 1985 Jewish Publication Society translation)

> [*Micah quoting false prophets:*] "Do not preach"—thus they preach—
>   "One should not preach of such things;
>   disgrace will not overtake us."
> [*Micah:*] Should this be said, O house of Jacob?
>   Has the LORD grown impatient?
>   Are these his deeds?
> Do not my words do good
>   to him who walks uprightly? (English Standard Version)

---

66. Calvin, *Twelve Minor Prophets*, 193.
67. So, among others, Waltke, *Micah*, 110.

[*Micah:*] The people preach at me and say, [*False Prophets:*] "Don't preach at us. Don't preach about all that. God is not going to disgrace us. Do you think the people of Israel are under a curse? Has the LORD lost his patience? Would he really do such things? Doesn't he speak kindly to those who do right?" (Good News Translation)

While there are some significant differences, the general meaning is clear.[68] Micah counters the message of false prophets who are trying to silence him. It is just not certain exactly where Micah stops quoting his opponents. The Good News Translation understands both 2:6 and 2:7 to be the words of Micah's opponents. The 1985 Jewish Publication Society translation (Tanakh) presents the words of the opponents as 2:6–7a, while the English Standard Version limits their speech to 2:6. Moreover all these translations rely on a significant emendation as well: "Disgrace will not overtake us." But if due attention is given to the grammar and the poetic structure, it will be seen that the words of Micah's adversaries commence at the beginning of 2:6 with a command followed by Micah's comments, then their words are continued in 2:7 with three rhetorical questions implying a negative answer followed by Micah's comments again.

> [*Micah's opponents:*] "Do not drip (prophesy)," they drip (prophesy).
> [*Micah:*] "They will not drip (prophesy) about these (things or to these people)."
> He (Yahweh) will not remove disgrace.
> [*Micah's opponents:*] "Should it be said," O house of Jacob [*or* of the house of Jacob]?"
> "Is the Spirit of Yahweh shortened?"
> "Does he do these things?"
> [*Micah:*] "Do not my words do good to those who walk uprightly?"

But who are the opponents? Since these people use the vocabulary associated with a negative view of prophecy (the word "drip") at the beginning of the text, and Micah uses the same terminology to refer to them at the end of the text (2:11), it is most likely that they are false prophets who cannot accept Micah and his colleagues' messages of doom. The text begins and ends with a reference to Micah's prophetic opponents (2:6, 11). They challenge his message of doom (2:6–7a) with three statements, but Micah counters their attack (2:7b–9), which adduces further evidence of the rapacious behavior of the greedy Israelites. He

---

68. The differences in ancient translations are just as marked. For discussion, see Renaud, *Formation du Livre de Michée*, 82–83.

then continues his offensive by issuing commands to these covetous criminals
to leave the country (2:10), while sarcastically commenting on the false prophets' "prosperity gospel" (2:11). Thus from a literary point of view the return to
these deceivers and their message with which the unit begins provides closure
to the passage.

Literary Features. The first judgment oracle (2:1–5) is entirely poetic until
the last prosaic sentence (2:5). The sudden change from poetry to prose in 2:5
arrests the attention of the audience and simultaneously brings closure and
climax to the oracle.

In the first part of the judgment oracle, the reasons for the verdict, there
is considerable phonological cohesion. In the first four lines the second of alternating lines rhyme; in the next four lines each pair of lines rhyme:

הוֹי חֹשְׁבֵי־אָוֶן	*hôy ḥōšəbê-'āwen*
וּפֹעֲלֵי רָע עַל־מִשְׁכְּבוֹתָם	*ûpōʿălê rā ʿal-miškəbôtām*
בְּאוֹר הַבֹּקֶר יַעֲשׂוּהָ	*bəʾôr habbōqer yaʿăśûhā*
כִּי יֶשׁ־לְאֵל יָדָם	*kî yeš-lə'ēl yādām*
וְחָמְדוּ שָׂדוֹת וְגָזָלוּ	*wəḥāmədû śādôt wəgāzālû*
וּבָתִּים וְנָשָׂאוּ	*ûbāttîm wənāśā'û*
וְעָשְׁקוּ גֶּבֶר וּבֵיתוֹ	*wəʿāšəqû geber ûbêtô*
וְאִישׁ וְנַחֲלָתוֹ	*wə'îš wənaḥălātô*

The predictable patterns suggest that the criminal activity is working like
a smoothly oiled machine: everything is occurring according to plan. But one
factor has been left out of the picture: Yahweh. Thus comes the jolt of punishment in 2:3–5. "Therefore, thus says Yahweh" is a poetic anacrusis that interrupts
the predictable syntax. The poetic surprise makes a theological shock: suddenly
Yahweh shows up interrupting everyone's plans. The spoils of the robbers are
seized and divided up among enemies. The alliteration and assonance of five
statements is particularly powerful. The first one begins a lament with three
similar-sounding words:

They will taunt you with this mournful song	וְנָהָה נְהִי נִהְיָה	*wənāhâ nəhî nihyâ*

The remarkable threefold use of the Hebrew root *nāhâ* makes the statement a
superlative: "The saddest lamentation"![69] The content of their mournful song
is etched into the memory with inimitable sounds:

69. J. C. De Moor as cited in Andersen and Freedman, *Micah*, 283.

A	And say, "We are utterly ruined;	אָמַר שָׁדוֹד נְשַׁדֻּנוּ	'āmar šādôd nəšaddunû
B	my people's possession is divided up.	חֵלֶק עַמִּי יָמִיר	ḥēleq 'ammî yāmîr
B'	He removes it from me!	אֵיךְ יָמִישׁ לִי	'êk yāmîš lî
A'	He assigns our fields to traitors."	לְשׁוֹבֵב שָׂדֵינוּ יְחַלֵּק	ləšôbēb śādênû yəḥallēq

In all probability these were *the same words* of the victims that were exploited in the first place. Thus, in the shrieks of their victims the oppressors will hear their own cries. The symmetrical A-B-B'-A' structure suggests the completeness of destruction. If the poetry expressing the criminals' behavior represents the completeness of their plans, so does this poetry describe the totality of their punishment. But the irony is far from over: since the Israelite criminals planned and schemed evil on their beds (2:1), Yahweh schemes evil against this family (2:3), for it will be an evil time (רָעָה/rāʿâ). Moreover, whereas the criminals coveted and seized fields (2:2), they will be certainly destroyed (2:4)! Whereas they dispossessed people of their house and inheritance (2:2), they will have their land divided up among the enemy (2:4) and then be dispossessed from the congregation of Yahweh!

The attached disputation saying (2:6-11) begins and ends on the same note—the preaching of the false prophets. It is integrated into the previous unit by having a command delivered to Micah and some of his colleagues to cease their prophesying about "these things," which in the present context refers back to the judgment oracle (2:1-5).[70] Moreover the themes of dispossession from house and home are present in this text and link up with the greedy grabbing of land already described in the previous judgment oracle. Finally as the land-grabbers have no allotment (חֶבֶל/ḥebel) in the assembly of the LORD, it is because they have completely contaminated (תְּחַבֵּל וְחֶבֶל נִמְרָץ/təḥabbēl waḥebel nimrāṣ) the land!

The disputation speech uses repetition strategically to structure the unit and for ironic purposes. A rare word for prophesying that is repeated three times at the beginning of the unit and twice at the end functions to demarcate this section (נָטַף/nāṭap). Micah presents a direct citation of false prophets who forbid him to prophesy God's judgment (2:6) but he responds by mocking their "prosperity gospel." Obviously this is Micah's characterization of their discourse.

---

70. The command not to prophesy is in the second-person plural.

False prophets speak lies (וְשֶׁקֶר כִּזֵּב/*wāšeqer kizzēb*; 2:11) and seek to prevent Micah from prophesying God's judgment (2:6) while they prophesy of only wine and liquor (לַיַּיִן וְלַשֵּׁכָר/*layyayin wəlaššēkār*). One can hear the correspondence between their lies (שֶׁקֶר/*šeqer*) and their message-liquor (שֵׁכָר/*šēkār*).[71] Their words incapacitate their audiences!

Key Words and Expressions. **Alas:** an interjection virtually always associated with disaster and death (but cf. Isa 55:1). Six times it is used for mourning someone who is already dead (cf. 1 Kgs 13:30).[72] "The lament for the dead sounded across squares and through streets with the words, *hôy! hôy!*"[73] The criminals who plan to rob and pillage their fellow Israelites celebrate their actions but the divine perspective is very different. The thieves are the ones who are as good as dead! **For those who devise wickedness and evil deeds on their beds** literally says, "for those who devise wickedness and do evil deeds on their beds." Thus commentators wonder how the criminals can actually execute their plans from their beds. But this is to be woodenly literalistic, and the NIV substitutes "plot" while the NRSV avoids the problem altogether with the above translation.[74] The intensity of the Hebrew parallelism suggests that not only do the wicked thoughts take place at night, the intentions and the planning to execute those plans do also. **When the morning dawns:** what gets these people up in the morning is their desire to gain and grab. There is no delay! **Because it is in their power** literally says "for their hand is for a god," that is, they worship their own strength. Perhaps the original meaning of holding a literal idol in one's hand is suggested by Micah, but the expression has simply become an idiom in the language for having resources or strength at one's disposal. Thus these people actually commit evil because they have the ability whereas the true covenant keepers are to help others when they have the capability (Prov 3:27; cf. Gen 31:29; Deut 28:32; Job 12:6; Neh 5:5). **They covet fields, and seize them:** and thus a blatant violation of the tenth and eighth commands (Exod 20:17, 15), showing that the violation of other commands begins in the heart. "Seizing" is a more violent word than steal, more akin to the word "rob with force," and it is used to rip the skin off a person later in Micah (3:2; cf. Gen 21:25; Judg 9:25; Job 20:19). Brueggemann and Cheney argue that the command against "coveting" originally had to do with the misappropriation of land and was not to be understood as a matter of jealousy—a

---

71. Renaud, *Formation du Livre de Michée*, 102.

72. Some scholars suggest that this interjection derives from the social context of malediction or wisdom but it is clear it stems from the mourning rites of a funeral. For full discussion, see ibid., 61–64.

73. Wolff, *Micah the Prophet*, 137.

74. Note Ps 58:2, where the wicked "do" evil in their hearts.

matter of the heart. This text in particular is considered to be the most direct commentary on coveting in the Bible.[75] But such a view is reductionistic since the original command specifically addresses various objects, one of which is a person's estate (Exod 20:17).[76] To be sure, this text is a clear example of the coveting of fields and how it begins in the heart and is nurtured in the sleeping hours as the coveters gloat and scheme on their beds. King Ahab was a classic example of someone who "coveted" and "seized" Naboth's vineyard (1 Kgs 21). **Householder and house, people and their inheritance:** the Israelites were especially forbidden to covet houses since they represented much more than a physical structure but everything connected to it—household, family, land, and future (Exod 20:17). Thus "inheritance" "combines the notions of family and property with permanence."[77] The following chart reflects Israelite social structure and helps clarify this text:[78]

Family Structure	**Joshua 7**	**1 Samuel 9**
nation (גּוֹי/*gôy*)	Israel	Israel
tribe (שֵׁבֶט/*šēbeṭ*)	Judah	Benjamin
clan (מִשְׁפָּחָה/*mišpāḥâ*)	Zerahite	Matrite
house (בַּיִת/*bayit*): three generations	Zabdi/grandfather Carmi/father Achan/son	Abiel/grandfather Kish/father Saul/son

Thus what is envisioned is the crime of robbing persons of their "house and home," which basically consisted of the land and dwellings to sustain a three- or four-generation family. This was not done by the use of brute force, but as a result of legitimized violence in which loans would be called in against poor farmers who would be unable to pay and would consequently lose their estates, which would then enlarge the holdings of the rich creditors.[79] The loss of one's house had not only dire economic consequences but profound theological im-

---

75. Walter Brueggemann, *Finally Comes the Poet* (Minneapolis: Fortress, 1989), 100; and Marvin Cheney, "You Shall Not Covet Your Neighbor's House," *Pacific Theological Review* 15 (1982): 3–13.

76. The objects are sevenfold!

77. Waltke, "Micah," 96.

78. This analysis is based on Francis I. Andersen, "Israelite Kinship and Social Structure," *Bible Translator* 20 (1969): 29–39. See also Judg 18:18–20.

79. See Isa 5:8 for the same perspective through the eyes of Isaiah. For further discussion, see McKane, *Micah*, 61–64.

plications. The land was a gift from Yahweh, and as a result of his generosity, people could thrive and flourish in their own particular portion, enjoying divine blessing. Without land an Israelite would be economically and spiritually rootless, and certainly materially poor, probably reduced to debt slavery since there was frequently no other means of sustenance. To lose land and house meant to lose almost everything—almost to be desouled. There would also be no inheritance for future generations.[80] **Thus says the LORD** is a standard prophetic formula by which a prophet introduced his words, clearly indicating their source. *Thus says X* originally was used by a messenger to introduce the words of a third party.[81] It guarantees the words of the third party to the audience, and in an ideal world, the messenger was to be granted diplomatic immunity. This formula is used only twice in Micah, the second time being reserved for an attack against the prophets (3:5). **Among our captors he parcels out our fields:** the word "captors" is probably best translated "traitors" or "rebels" but who are they? Since there is considerable wordplay in this text and the two words are very similar in Hebrew (they differ in one letter; cf. Jer 49:4), "traitors" probably suggests the captors of an invading army. **Therefore you will have no one to cast the line by lot in the assembly of the LORD:** a second clause is added to the indictment and constitutes the only prose in the text describing solemnly the fate of the criminals. "You" is a second-person *singular* form of the pronoun whereas the previous pronouns are *plural*. This suggests a focus on the individual punishment of each criminal.[82] The reference to casting a line by lot translates a Hebrew idiom for determining a portion of land to assign boundaries for an estate. This was done when the Israelites first conquered the land (Josh 16:1; 17:1, 5, 14; 19:9, 39). Since these criminals seized the land of their neighbors, they will have their land seized from them. The "assembly of the LORD" is a rare phrase that means the worship community of Israel (Num 16:3; 20:4; Deut 23:1, 2 [2×], 3 [2×], 8; cf. 1 Chr 28:8; Neh 13:1). For example, some pagan neighbors of Israel were barred forever from worshipping with the Israelites (Deut 23:3–4). Thus this text means that these criminals will have no one to cast lots for land for them in a new, covenant community that will be reconstituted after the judgment of the exile because they will no longer be part of that community.[83]

---

80. Of course, this could be rectified for future generations in the year of Jubilee (Lev 25) but there is no evidence this was ever implemented in ancient Israel.

81. See, e.g., its secular usage in 2 Kgs 18:19 and also the insightful article by J. S. Holladay, "Assyrian Statecraft and the Prophets of Israel," *Harvard Theological Review* 63 (1970): 29–51.

82. Keil points out that a similar feature occurs at 3:10; *Minor Prophets*, 441.

83. This text probably assumes a future after the judgment of exile but a future in which these covetous Israelites and their families will have no part. Cf. Ehud Ben Zvi, "Wrongdoers, Wrongdoing, and Righting Wrongs in Micah 2," *Biblical Interpretation* 7 (1999): 87–100. Calvin

"Do not preach"—thus they preach: Micah is citing his opponents here. The word for "preach" is a relatively rare word usually associated with the dropping of liquid, whether raindrops (Judg 5:4; Ps 68:8), honey (Prov 5:3; Song 4:11), or ointment (Song 5:5), which leads some scholars to suggest that when applied to prophets it may mean that they preached passionately, sometimes spraying people with drops of saliva as they spoke.[84] It probably is a pejorative term since it is used in a similar context in Amos, when he is commanded to stop prophesying by a religious official in the northern kingdom (Amos 7:16; cf. Ezek 21:2, 7, from more than a century later). Some suggest that it may connote the idea of a speaker "dripping on" or nagging, or riding a hobbyhorse. It may connote both senses and if so it is used to censor Micah and his ilk—"these crazy prophets with a one-track mind!"[85] The imperative "do not preach" is in the second-person plural, which assumes that Micah and his prophetic colleagues are being addressed.[86] **One should not preach of such things:** most translations understand this statement like the NRSV as further words addressed to Micah and his colleagues, but they more likely represent Micah's counterattack. The text literally says, "They will not prophesy about [or to] these things."[87] He is saying that they refuse to preach a message of judgment. "These things" in its literary context clearly refers back to the announcement of judgment, but it can also mean "these people," that is, criminals in 2:1–2. Since the relevant word occurs in the next verse where it means the content of the judgment ("are not *such things* his doings?"), it is probably best to understand it in the same way here. The second part of the verse, **disgrace will not overtake us,** fits the context best if these are the words of the false prophets but it requires an emendation in the Hebrew text, and even with that emendation there is not agreement between the feminine plural subject and the masculine singular verb (reading *yassigēnû* for *yissag*). But if Micah is continuing his speech, which is most likely the case, this makes perfect sense as, "He [i.e., Yahweh] will not remove disgraces."[88]

---

understands this text to indicate the end of the land of Judah as a possession of the Jews. But this is to read too much into the pronoun, which refers only to the criminals; *Twelve Minor Prophets*, 193.

84. "The foam from the mouth of the ecstatic, epileptic *nebi'im*"; Smith, *Micah, Zephaniah, and Nahum*, 60.

85. Like the continuous drip of someone nagging away at a person (cf. Prov 19:13), or in more contemporary terms "like a broken record." See discussion of the ancient Jewish commentators Kimchi and Rashi in McKane, *Micah*, 75–79.

86. As Rudolph observes, one of the real mysteries of the prophetic books is why none of the prophets ever identifies his or her colleagues in mission. But it is clear from this plural verb form that Micah has such companions; *Micha, Habakuk, Zephanja*, 137.

87. See Waltke, "Micah," 112.

88. Cf. the Septuagint. In order for Yahweh to be subject in the Hebrew the verb must be revocalized slightly from *yissag* to *yassēg*.

Thus Micah is saying, "Since these prophets will not preach about judgment, Yahweh will not remove disgrace." He may have in mind the Assyrian crisis that is happening as he speaks![89] **Should this be said, O house of Jacob?** A slight change in the text reading "cursed" instead of "said" results in the meaning: "Is the house of Jacob cursed?" Even though this thought is implied, it is unnecessary to change the text. Micah has the false prophets continue their message with three rhetorical questions demanding a negative answer. In the first question the Israelites are addressed as the house (descendants) of Jacob, a term that focuses on their election. "Should this be said?" probably not only refers to the coming questions but also back to the preaching of judgment by the true prophets. Such things should never be said! Their next two questions firmly emphasize this point: "Will the Spirit of Yahweh lose patience? Are these things [Micah's words of judgment] his doings?" The answer is by all means assuredly "No!" This shows that the difference between Micah and his contemporary colleagues "in ministry" was theological. They disagreed over the reading of Israelite history. Micah's reading always leads to justice and holiness, and he will expand on this later (6:1–8). **Is the LORD's patience exhausted?** The phrase for the exhaustion of patience means literally "short of wrath" (Prov 14:17) and has its antonym the expression "length of wrath" in the classic characteristic description of God (Exod 34:6). The false prophets believe that Yahweh cannot contradict his own character as described in the Israelite credo (34:6–7). **Do not my words do good to one who walks uprightly?** Many scholars and translations assume that these words continue the words of the false prophets. But the switch to the first-person ("my words") signals that Micah and God have a rhetorical question of their own that assumes an affirmative answer rather than a negative one.[90] This rhetorical question indicates the ethical conditions of the covenant: to be sure, God has called Israel to be his people and to be blessed, but they must live responsibly to ensure that blessing. In other words, God "is still benevolent, but he has never been unconditionally benevolent."[91] In the immediate context "my words" refer back to "these things" whose antecedent is the words of doom in 2:3–5. In short, if the house of Jacob plunders the houses of its own people, it is not walking uprightly and cannot expect God's blessings; rather, it is indeed cursed, the Spirit of Yahweh will lose patience, and these words of judgment just announced are proof positive that God is going to act in this way! In the wider context "my words" could well be a shorthand state-

---

89. So Sweeney, *Twelve Prophets*, 363.

90. These scholars therefore read "his words" with the Septuagint instead of the Masoretic Text's "my words."

91. McKane, *Micah*, 76.

ment for "the words of the covenant," "the words of the Torah," or "the words of Yahweh," which all mean the same thing (Exod 24:3–4; Deut 4:10; 11:18; 28:58–29:1). **But you rise up against my people as an enemy:** the NIV translates more accurately here with "Lately my people have risen up like an enemy." The word "lately" literally means "yesterday" so Micah did not have to delve into history very far to select an example of the opposite of upright living and covenantal breach! Moreover, the shock is that God's people—his own people— have become an enemy, preying upon one another.[92] **You strip the robe** literally reads: "You strip off from the outside—a garment—glorious." This refers to the practice of reducing someone to destitution and leaving them naked by means of robbery of an especially cruel kind. Not content to deprive people of their estate, these thieves now strip them of whatever valuables they have left, taking even the shirt off their back! In many cultures clothing is a badge of glory, honor, and identity much the way it was in ancient Israel. Thus this robbery is a removal of whatever dignity the people have left. "References to the *śalmâ* (~*śimlâ*) or its equivalent in legal texts, in mourning customs, in folklore, show that this part of a person's dress has enormous social significance as a mark of social status and identity. To take away a person's 'cloak,' especially when it was their last possession, was a devastating indignity and an ultimate crime."[93] The outer garment in particular carried with it an important pragmatic function as it was used as a blanket for warmth at night (Exod 22:26–27; Deut 24:10–13). If it was taken in pledge as collateral for a loan, it was important that it be returned at night to the debtor for use as a blanket. Yahweh was particularly sensitive to this, and if the garment was not returned, the Israelite's only recourse was prayer, and Yahweh would hear because in his own inimitable words, "I am gracious" (Exod 22:27). To strip a person's garment from him or her was then to strip them of their basic identity—in a sense, their glory.[94] **From those who**

---

92. The intransitive meaning for the verb is due to a slight textual change, reading *qāmîm* instead of *yĕqômēm*.

93. Andersen and Freedman, *Micah*, 318.

94. Note a letter on a piece of clay dating about a century after Micah is written by a person trying to recover his garment that was taken in pledge: "Let my lord, the governor, hear the word of his servant! Your servant is a reaper. Your servant was in Hazar Asam, and your servant reaped, and finished, and he has stored (the grain) during these days before the Sabbath. When your servant had finished the harvest, and had stored (the grain) during these days, Hoshavyahu came, the son of Shobi, and he seized the garment of your servant, when I had finished my harvest. It (is already now some) days (since) he took the garment of your servant. And all my companions can bear witness for me—they who reaped with me in the heat of the harvest—yes, my companions can bear witness for me. Amen! I am innocent from guilt. And he stole my garment! It is for the governor to give back the garment of his servant. So grant him mercy in that you return the garment of your servant and do not be displeased"; available online at fowlerbiblecollection.com/yavneh-yam-ostracon.html.

pass by trustingly with no thought of war: the last phrase literally reads, "like those returning from battle." This probably refers to the peaceful return of soldiers from battle who have already fought—the war is over—and the last thing they expect is to be ambushed at home.[95] **The women of my people you drive out from their pleasant houses:** thus "my people" (2:8) are warring against "my people" (2:9). The women may be widows who have no means of physical sustenance any longer as their husbands have died, or they could simply be women whose debts were being recalled and who were exiled from their domiciles where they flourished (cf. Prov 31:10–31).[96] If the former case, then the prophets were concerned about the "quartet of the vulnerable": widows, orphans, refugees, and the poor.[97] The law made provision for them, indicating God's merciful compassion for the socially disadvantaged. The litmus test of good leadership was how it cared for these people (Ps 72:2–4, 12–14; Jer 22:15–16). By caring for "the least of these," a statement was being made about the value of all individuals. Their worth did not come from economic considerations, but from an "alien dignity." They were not "valuable"; they were off the scale of values![98] If this reference is simply to the wives of the debt-ridden husbands, it shows a poignant divine concern for the women who are robbed of the place where they flourished. "Pleasant houses" are literally "houses of her delight or luxury." This does not necessarily mean luxurious homes but luxurious to the women involved; it "brings out the value of the house for the occupant."[99] **From their young children you take away my glory forever:** the word that the NRSV translates "glory" is used frequently of God and his majesty and splendor particularly as he reveals himself in the temple and in creation (Ps 96:6; 104:1; 111:3; 145:5) but also it can be used for the king (21:5) and nobility and wealth (Lam 1:6; Prov 31:25). It is also used to describe humanity as God designed it to be, crowned with glory and honor in regal majesty (Ps 8:5).[100] Thus taking the

95. Note Waltke, "The last place they expected the enemy was in their own capitals"; *Micah*, 128.

96. It is remarkable that their husbands are not mentioned.

97. Nicholas Wolterstorff, *Justice: Rights and Wrongs* (Princeton: Princeton University Press, 2008).

98. "Rather than designating all human life as valuable, I would propose that all human beings are not valuable. They are invaluable. Our fellow human beings are not merely the most valuable things around. They are off the scale, truly incommensurable; not even to be introduced in to the rate of exchange whereby we convert the relative value of other things"; James Tunstead Burtchaell, *Rachel Weeping and Other Essays on Abortion* (Fort Collins: Life Cycle, 1991), 313.

99. Andersen and Freedman, *Micah*, 321.

100. Wolff mentions the importance of this passage as crucial for understanding this word since children are central in this psalm as those who praise God and who destroy the enemy; *Micah the Prophet*, 107–8.

children away from their homes is taking them away from the potential to be image bearers of God, flourishing in the land that he has given his people as a glorious inheritance. This is an especially egregious crime because not only have these miscreants stripped people of their clothing and homes, they have in a sense stripped God of his splendor in taking away the vulnerable and helpless children of Israel, the future of the nation, and robbing them of their destiny. **Arise and go; for this is no place to rest** most likely reflects Micah's frustration with the oppressors of the poor, and it might be loosely translated "Get the hell out!" They have "exiled" poor Israelites, and he tells them to go into exile themselves! The prophet has had enough, and he now explodes with anger with the use of these imperatives. If the false prophets have their imperatives (2:6) so does he! "For this is not your resting place" translates the literal Hebrew phrase "for not(!) this is your resting place," drawing attention to the fronted negative particle. In other words, this land that has been stolen to enlarge the estates of the rich, the inheritance Yahweh has given his people (Deut 12:9), is no longer "the rest" promised by God. This word "resting place" is a rich theological phrase that emphasizes all the blessings of the promised land to the people of God. Its verbal counterpart first occurs when God places Adam in the garden of Eden (Gen 2:15), thus indicating a place where all human needs are to be met, both physically with the abundant fruit of the garden and spiritually with the presence of God: it is a place of security, fulfilment, and peace. Micah later pictures peace abounding in the world with the rule of Messiah under an image that presents a vivid word picture of "rest": "Everyone will sit under their own vine and under their own fig tree, and no one will make them afraid, for the LORD Almighty has spoken" (4:4). But Judah in Micah's time is anything but such a place. **Because of uncleanness that destroys with a grievous destruction:** the words are carefully chosen to indicate the land has been totally polluted and cannot be a place of residence for the people of God anymore. It had become worse than a foreign, unclean land (cf. Amos 7:17). The word "uncleanness" is a highly charged religious word, used to indicate the pollution of the sacred in priestly texts. Here the entire land has become defiled by the *moral* contagion of the wealthy. **If someone were to go about uttering empty falsehoods** is literally, "If one walks [with] the wind and falsely has lied." "Wind" means emptiness (cf. Isa 41:29) and suggests an individual who has nothing substantial to say. He is nothing but a "windbag."[101] The two words "wind" (spirit) and "lying" occur together to describe the inspiration of false prophets in 1 Kgs 22:22. The allusion in which Micah's namesake is the true prophet

---

101. Theo Laetsch, *Bible Commentary: The Minor Prophets* (St. Louis: Concordia, 1956), 255.

among a myriad of imposters is probably not lost on his audience. Here the two words may function as hendiadys ("lying windbag"), and the point is that these prophets are the polar opposite of those whose ways are upright (2:8). **I will preach to you of wine and strong drink** is better translated "I will drip on about plenty of wine and beer." Micah is parodying these prophets as having a monotonous, predictable message. If they complain that his message is predictable, he says, "No wonder, all you harp on is 'Don't worry. Be happy!'" "Wine and beer" probably signify the content of the message rather than payment for services rendered. The words mean prosperity and pleasure or the good life as opposed to the words of Micah, who preached about "these things"—God's judgment (2:6). "Wine and beer" can denote a decadent lifestyle; they are viewed as the bane of kings since they cloud their judgment (Prov 31:4–7). Nazirites and priests on duty were forbidden to imbibe (Lev 10:9; Num 6:3; Judg 13:4, 7), and alcohol was often seen as a symbol of the good life. Alcoholic drinks were viewed as God's gifts but they could become ruthless taskmasters if one was not careful (cf. Ps 104:15 with Prov 31:4–7). Micah's contemporary, Isaiah, spoke about endless partying and no concern about the serious issues of life (Isa 5:11–12). **Such a one would be the preacher for this people:** the people are complicit in this dire state of affairs and are not innocent. Then as now endemic injustice requires an influential group of people that consents to the status quo. This is another reason why the false prophets have no words of judgment. Their audience dictates the message; no one wants to hear "bad news" (cf. Jer 5:30–31; 2 Tim 4:3).

Interpretation—Micah's Word Then. In the previous two oracles against Samaria and Judah, there was little in the way of specific reasons given for Yahweh's departure from his throne to tread a path of destruction through the cities of Israel. There is a general reference to idolatry but detail is lacking. One no longer has to wait for such specifics as they now become scandalous in their particularity: these sins were not accidental "slipups," but premeditated acts of theft of land and dignity, dispossessing men, women, and children from their "rest" on the land that God granted them (2:1–2).

The situation in life for the first oracle could have taken place at the courts where the wealthy landowners were having their robbery sanctioned by a corrupt court system, or Micah could have pronounced the oracle at one of the farms where the wealthy were coming to collect their "possessions" as the owners were evicted because of defaulted loan payments. There is a good precedent for the last example in Elijah's encounter with Ahab at Naboth's vineyard, when the Israelite king had come to collect his new "possession" (1 Kgs 21:16–20). Wolff thinks that Micah is speaking in his own hometown against the officials of the state who have been stationed there as part of a permanent occupation and who are grabbing up the land of the poor peasant farmers.[102] One thing is certain: Micah is confronting the rich oppressors of his people.

The whole way of life for these greedy Israelites has been geared toward insatiable consumption, and it has become so much of an obsession that not only are their daylight hours devoted to getting and grabbing more and more but so are their sleeping hours as they scheme and plan during the night on their beds. No time can be wasted for this mission of greed. Normally theft takes place during the night; here it takes place in broad daylight![103] What is more, these thieves do not drag their feet once their plans are hatched. They implement them immediately. Although this is not technically idolatry, which is the general reason for judgment in Mic 1, it is clearly a form of idolatry because covetousness reveals the god of one's heart (Eph 5:5). That god is Mammon, pure and simple.

Given the agrarian society of ancient Judah, this particular socioeconomic injustice would have been prevalent throughout its history. It "reflects the concentration of property through land foreclosure"[104] with its resultant evictions and confiscation (Deut 27:17; Prov 23:10–11). Though it was always regarded as reprehensible, in Micah's day it had become widespread, and it would have taken great courage to denounce it. But he rises to the challenge as the first word these schemers hear is "Alas!" It is a word of death, and a similar word is pronounced over the final description of the nation's lifestyle at the end of the book (Mic 7:1). From God's perspective these people are "dead men walking."[105] The coveters next hear the shocking judgment of the prophet: since they have schemed in the night and planned to grab and get, planning evil against their neighbors, Yahweh has also been awake in the night planning evil against them (2:3)! An evil time is coming when all their houses and fields will go to a fierce, merciless enemy who will drive *them* out of house and home, and in the coming reconstitution of Israel, these thieves will have no part whatsoever. The land-grabbers will be landless and homeless in the true sense of the word—they will have been expelled from the assembly of Yahweh! The evil they planned will return on their own head.[106]

The disputation oracle (2:6–11) placed alongside this oracle was probably

102. Wolff, *Micah*, 74–75.

103. I owe this insight to Alfaro, *Justice and Loyalty*, 25.

104. Ben Zvi, *Micah*, 44.

105. Harry P. Nasuti, "The Once and Future Lament: Micah 2:1–5 and the Prophetic Persona," in *Inspired Speech: Prophecy in the Ancient Near East: Essays in Honor of Herbert B. Huffmon*, ed. John Kaltner and Louis Stulman (New York: Bloomsbury, 2004), 143–60 at 145.

106. Terence E. Fretheim, "'I Was Only a Little Angry': Divine Violence in the Prophets," *Interpretation* 58 (2004): 371.

originally independent, as it is directed toward Micah and his prophetic colleagues who were preaching a negative message of judgment by prophets who
had a more upbeat and positive message.[107] It was delivered in a similar social
context but probably not on the same occasion.[108] The language is cryptic but
the sense is clear. The demonstrative pronouns ("these things") refer to the
message of Micah and his comrades. They are told to cease and desist from their
unwelcome and unpalatable message. Such "judgment" is totally unacceptable
since in the eyes of these false prophets God could never bring disgrace upon
his own people and curse them. This shows the struggle that Micah faced. Corruption and crime were being justified by a different reading of Israel's narrative
by its theological leaders.[109] This essentially gave Israel a free pass—a license
to sin—as it was believed that God would never judge his own people. After all
was not God a God of love to Israel and were not such judgments against his
covenant people contrary to his character?[110] How could Jacob ever be cursed?
Had not Balaam tried to curse him (Num 22–24)? Had not God told Abraham
that whoever tried to curse him would be cursed (Gen 12:3)? Could God ever
become impatient with his people (Exod 34:6)? Of course not! Thus in the eyes
of such theological authorities all "these things" that Micah was announcing
were outrageous! For God to do "these things" would violate his character.

Not only did Micah not accept this one-sided theological narrative that
was being spun by his colleagues in the prophetic profession, neither did he
"roll over and die" in the face of strong opposition. He returned to the ethical foundation of the Hebrew faith and defended the Lord's announcement of
"these things" (words of judgment). "Do not my words do well to the one whose
ways are upright?" Was not this the word that came to Abraham who was called
to teach his children the way of Yahweh, justice, and righteousness, so that

107. Note the plural reference of the imperative to cease prophesying in 2:6a. Many assume
it was exactly the same context and that the detractors are not prophets but those who have been
condemned; see Wolff, *Micah*, 80–81. However, pejorative terminology for prophecy used frequently in the text suggests that *preachers* of judgment are being criticized by prosperity prophets.
Moreover the plural command for Micah and his comrades to stop prophesying suggests another
venue, which is probably similar. Isaiah may have also been targeted by these false prophets.

108. Rudolph, *Micha, Habakuk, Zephanja*, 60.

109. Ibid. Rudolph makes the telling point that these leaders defended themselves so to
speak with the Bible in their hands! What texts were at stake? Rudolph suggests Exod 34:6 but
certainly Gen 12:3; Num 23:7–10, 19–23; 24:9, 17 need to be considered as well as Ps 77:12. I am
indebted to Wolff (*Micah*, 82) for the last important reference.

110. "Those to whom he addressed the announcement of Yʜwʜ's judgment found his
message, not only personally offensive but theologically inconceivable. The confrontation between
prophet and audience concerned ultimately the question of their understanding of God"; Mays,
Micah, 67.

God could fulfill the promises made to him (Gen 18:19)? Was not this message also clearly identified with "the words of the covenant"? Was not a plethora of curses attached to the failure to act righteously and justly (Lev 26; Deut 28)?[111] To be sure, the theological narrative of his opponents could be supported by the doctrine of election, but it was a distorted narrative of cheap grace without ethical praxis, an election without responsibility. Micah's prophetic predecessor in the north, Amos, had to attack with great ferocity the same heretical view (Amos 3:1–2).[112] As Rudolph observes perceptively, this false view does not hold together both sides of the election equation: the equation is not only promise ("I will be your God") but also obligation ("you will be my people").[113] The tragedy of omitting the second side is that election divinely sanctioned the continued pillaging, exploitation, and disenfranchisement of the common people in the southern kingdom. If the religious institutions would not speak up for the people—and even had a hand in their oppression—what hope could they ever have?

Micah fought this distorted theology of "hypergrace" with all his intellectual and rhetorical might.[114] How could the eviction of men, women, and children from their ancestral homes be pleasing to Yahweh, the God who had delivered his people from slavery? How could robbing shirts from the back of the poor be acceptable, or the banishment of women from their homes, or the despoiling of children, who represented Yahweh's glory? Exile—not rest in the land—was the punishment for this crime as the land itself could not tolerate such evil. Moreover the theological support for this distorted view of election was nothing but hot air. Those who preached such heresy may have been popular in the eyes of the establishment, but God was not impressed. These prophets who preached "an optimistic gospel of infinite grace [believed that] no matter what Israel did or did not do, Yahweh was the great Forgiver, able to save and keep."[115] They were soon to learn that God was also the great judge.

Interpretation—Micah's Word Now. The violation of the command not to covet is the major sin that Micah deals with in this text, as is the theological truth that God will some day judge. Coveting leads to an insatiable desire for

111. In both texts, blessings and curses are comprehensively listed, and the curses far outnumber the blessings!

112. See Stephen G. Dempster, "Amos 3:1–15: Apologia of a Prophet," *Baptist Review of Theology* 5 (1995): 35–51.

113. Rudolph, *Micha, Habakuk, Zephanja,* 138.

114. "In their pseudo-orthodoxy they claim that grace will triumph while at the same time they are keeping it from having any worth in their own lives"; Wolff, *Micah the Prophet,* 11.

115. Leslie C. Allen, "Micah's Social Concern," *Vox Evangelica* 8 (1973): 22–32 at 25.

more and therefore results in oppression, and the oppression is legitimized by a corrupt religious establishment whose message essentially caters to the desire for more by prophesying only about how religion leads to "the good life." Theologian Sally Brown provides a contemporary expression of Mic 2:

> Imagine [prosperous landholders] gathered at a benefit gala. Bursts of laughter ripple through the room; their mood is buoyant. Their common bond, in addition to an elite social standing, is a knack for finding the upside in a volatile land market. But just as they are lifting their glasses to congratulate themselves, the party is interrupted by a messenger. Drinks are poised mid-air; all are strained to listen. The messenger bears a funeral announcement? Whose? Theirs.[116]

She captures well the idea of the funeral announcement for this wealthy group of exploiters who are celebrating their new acquisitions of real estate.

Modern Western culture needs to hear a text like Mic 2 and ask, When is enough enough? There is something wrong when a minority of the population on the planet supports a billion-dollar diet industry and the rest scrape by to survive. At the end of World War I an influenza epidemic killed millions of people; at the turn of the third millennium an affluenza epidemic is killing millions of people. Western advertising helps spread the contagion as the dreaming and scheming never stop. Everything is up for sale.[117] People even have their bodies inscribed with tattoos to advertise. They sell their life insurance policies to acquire more money; they mortgage away their future. They put advertisements on their houses and cars—all for a price. Is nothing sacred?[118] Such an attitude of consumerism and affluenza should be anathema to the covenant community and is a sign of the *idolatry* of the marketplace in Western culture. The poet Christian Wiman paints a picture of this idolatrous beast in his description of the morning crowd of train commuters as they "cram and curse and contort into one creature, all claws and eyes, tunneling, tunneling, tunneling toward money."[119]

The reality is that the economy of Western culture is largely based on covetousness. It is an "easy sell" if an idol has displaced the living God. George Herbert said it well when writing about how to raise children:

116. Sally A. Brown, "Micah 2:1–11," *Interpretation* 57 (2003): 417–19 at 417.
117. Naomi Klein, *No Logo*, 10th anniversary ed. (New York: Picador, 2009).
118. Michael J. Sandel, *What Money Can't Buy: The Moral Limits of Markets* (New York: Farrar, Strauss & Giroux, 2012).
119. Christian Wiman, *My Bright Abyss: Meditation of a Modern Believer* (New York: Farrar, Strauss & Giroux, 2013), 88.

The way to make thy sonne rich, is to fill
> His minde with rest, before his trunk with riches:
> For wealth without contentment, climbes a hill
> To feel those tempests, which fly over ditches.

But if thy sonne can make ten pound his measure,
Then all thou addest may be call'd his treasure.[120]

Above all, children need this rest of God since they represent in a unique way the glory of God. Billy Joel's perceptive song "No Man's Land" describes the situation in many big cities of Western culture—spiritual wastelands where children have been systematically "desouled" as the divine glory has been stripped away from them:

> I've seen those big machines come rolling through the quiet pines
> Blue suits and bankers with their Volvos and their Ballantines
> Give us this day our daily discount outlet merchandise
> Raise up a multiplex and we will make a sacrifice
> Now we're gonna get the big business. . . .[121]

Many cities in the West want to build casinos to stimulate their economies, and casinos simply operate on the basis of covetousness and greed and exploitation. The bankrupt city of Detroit can find over half a billion dollars to build a new arena for its revered hockey team while its city infrastructure, including its schools for the education of the young, is in dire need. Nearby Flint is a national scandal for its tainted water caused by government corruption and greed.

Over such a culture should be pronounced the word "alas," and the religious professionals and preachers who shore up and encourage such a state of affairs only hasten the death of this culture. All they care about is prosperity and wealth, and some of them fly off in their private jets preaching a gospel of "wine and beer" instead of calling people to account before a holy God. To fail to censure such false prophets is a failure of nerve.[122] It is true that God is merciful but he is also just and holy, a truth which has been lost on many ministers.

The attitude of the Christian church in this society should be for its pastors to speak the truth in love presenting Christ as the answer to such covetous-

120. George Herbert, *The Temple* (Cambridge: Buck & Daniel, 1633), 14.

121. Billy Joel, "No Man's Land," *River of Dreams* (New York: Columbia Records, 1993).

122. This has nothing to do with demonization of the opposition; this has everything to do with calling a spade a spade. Cf. Jennifer K. Berenson Maclean, "Micah 3:5–12," *Interpretation* 56 (2002): 413–16.

ness, criticizing injustice, and rebuking evil, while the members of the church dream and scheme of ways to bless their neighbors. As Limburg remarks:

> This prophetic saying places a special responsibility on those persons within the people of God who have been given much. It would call us to lie awake at night once in a while devising plans to help the hungry, the hurting, the homeless in our neighborhoods and our world. It also points us to the parable about the faithful steward, which concludes, "Every one to whom much is given, of him will much be required."[123]

After all, this text shows clearly that what possesses our thoughts in our private bedrooms determines the public nature of our society. Covetous thoughts lead to injustice and oppression and no future. "Thoughts of God and neighbor are the first lines of defense against such desires: the word of God and the response of prayer are what we must have constantly at our side; that is the loaded pistol we keep ready against the surprise attacks of covetous thoughts."[124]

Breakthrough: A New Theophany (2:12–13)

Structure. This is a salvation oracle based on the simple mercy of God. One of the key differences between a judgment oracle and one proclaiming salvation is the lack of an explicit reason for the action of God, which in the case of the latter is grounded in God's mercy. The oracle here consists of nine lines, and it is the shortest unit thus far. At the end of lengthy speeches of judgment there is finally some relief! God will gather the scattered remnant of his people into one place, this remnant that has experienced the judgment of exile; and as the good shepherd, God will decisively and forcefully collect his "flock" within the walls of the enclosure of exile. Then he will break open the walls of their prison, leading his people into a new exodus. He is their true king, and a true leader is not interested in exploiting them; he wishes to liberate them!

Literary Features. This poem begins and ends with repetition. God announces decisive action in the first-person at the beginning and is the subject of a stupendous announcement at the end. The poetry of intensification presents this announcement with growing suspense, concluding with a divine epiphany.

---

123. James Limburg, *Hosea–Micah* (Louisville: Westminster John Knox, 2011), 174. See also Calvin's wise comments: "It behooves carefully to consider how greatly displeasing to God are frauds and plunders, so that each of us may keep himself from doing any wrong, and be ruled by a desire of what is right"; *Twelve Minor Prophets*, 187.

124. Wolff, *Micah the Prophet*, 53.

The oracle begins with an astonishing announcement in the first-person. The unique double use of an infinitive absolute form with a finite verb form emphatically signals a new departure for Judah. This is the only time this emphatic construction occurs in all of Micah's prophesying, and it indicates a decisive announcement "to save" in contrast to the previous judgment. To be sure, those who are saved constitute a "remnant" but one of considerable size. The repetition stresses Yahweh's gathering of Jacob and the remnant of Israel, and it highlights the certainty of the action of salvation. In contrast to previous leaders who have pillaged and prophesied falsely, here is a decisive action of God gathering his people finally to save them from their fate in exile. The gathering is compared to the gathering of sheep in a pen, but it is such a large gathering that the noise is deafening. This is presented chiastically:

A	together	יַחַד	*yaḥad*
B	I will make it	אֲשִׂימֶנּוּ	*'ăśîmennû*
C	like a flock of sheep of the fold	כְּצֹאן בָּצְרָה	*kəṣō'n boṣrâ*
C'	like a flock in its pen	כְּעֵדֶר בְּתוֹךְ הַדָּבְרוֹ	*kə'ēder bətôk haddobrô*
B'	they will be noisy	תְּהִימֶנָה	*təhîmenâ*
A'	from the amount of people	מֵאָדָם	*mē'ādām*

Yahweh, the great shepherd, gathered his flock in an enclosure; and then someone smashes the walls of the enclosure leading the remnant out of their confinement. Another chiasm is used to present the symmetry of the action. *A breaker* who smashes down the walls of the enclosure goes before the people, and the people *break out*; then they *pass through* the breach as the king *passes through* before them:

A	breaker	עָלָה הַפֹּרֵץ לִפְנֵיהֶם	*'ālâ happōrēṣ lipnêhem*
B	people break out	פָּרְצוּ	*pārəṣû*
B'	people pass through	וַיַּעֲבֹרוּ שַׁעַר וַיֵּצְאוּ בוֹ	*wayya'ăbōrû ša'ar wayyēṣə'û bô*
A'	the king passes through	וַיַּעֲבֹר מַלְכָּם לִפְנֵיהֶם	*wayya'ăbōr malkām lipnêhem*
	[breaker's identity:] Yahweh is at their head!	וַיהוָה בְּרֹאשָׁם	*wayhwh bərō'šām*

The king is thus the "Breaker," and the last line breaks the chiastic pattern by revealing the identity of the Breaker: Yahweh is at their head!

Key Words and Expressions. **I will surely gather all of you, O Jacob, I will gather the survivors of Israel:** the emphatic construction and the first-person singular verbal form announce hope for the exiles; the emphatic construction used also in the next line shows that this is an announcement of prophetic hope against a dire background of judgment but it assumes the judgment has happened. This is also the first reference to Jacob being addressed as "you" in the text, drawing attention to the intimate relation between Yahweh and his people. God is once again on personal terms with them. The reference to the "survivors" of Israel further specifies Jacob. This term literally means "remnant" and has a history that can be traced back to the early period of Israel and does not automatically imply a postexilic date. It refers to the survivors of an ordeal, those who are left after severe disaster and/or judgment.[125] Here it most likely refers to the remaining ones who will be gathered in exile long after the judgment of Samaria and Jerusalem. Similar expressions are used in other prophetic books with a clear implication of return from exile (cf. Jer 23:3; Zeph 3:19). **I will set them together like sheep in a fold, like a flock in its pasture:** the remnant theme is continued by a shepherd theme, and the two are found together in other prophetic texts. The idea of a shepherd leading his flock as a metaphor for Yahweh's leading of his people is first found in the blessing of Joseph when Jacob describes God with a number of epithets: Mighty One, Rock of Israel, Shepherd, God of your father, and Shaddai (Gen 49:24; cf. 48:15). Exodus 3 has an allusion to the divine shepherd as Moses leads the flock of Jethro, his father-in-law, and is called to lead God's flock, the people of Israel, out of Egypt. Thus Yahweh was regarded as the Good Shepherd since the shepherd was a popular symbol of kingship in the ancient world (Ps 23).[126] **It will resound with people** liter-

---

125. Gerhard F. Hasel, *The Remnant: The History and Theology of the Remnant Idea from Genesis to Isaiah* (Berrien Springs: Andrews University Press, 1972); and Stephen G. Dempster, "The Prophetic Invocation of the Ban as Covenant Curse: A Historical Analysis of a Prophetic Theme" (ThM thesis, Westminster Theological Seminary, 1978).

126. E.g., the Egyptian pharaoh is often depicted carrying a shepherd's staff. In a building inscription Sesostris I says: "He begat me to do what should be done for him, to accomplish what he commands to do, he appointed me shepherd of this land, knowing him who would herd it for him"; Miriam Lichtheim, *Ancient Egyptian Literature*, vol. 1: *The Old and Middle Kingdoms*, 2nd ed. (Berkeley: University of California Press, 2006), 116. The prologue to the Code of Hammurabi portrays the king as a shepherd of his people: "I am the salvation-bearing shepherd, whose staff is straight, the good shadow that is spread over my city; on my breast I cherish the inhabitants of the land of Sumer and Akkad; in my shelter I have let them repose in peace; in my deep wisdom have I enclosed them"; James B. Pritchard, *Ancient Near Eastern Texts Relating to the Old Testament with Supplement*, 3d ed. (Princeton: Princeton University Press, 1969), 163.

ally reads "they [the gathered sheep] will be noisy from man." The preposition "from" can mean separation, that is, far away from human beings, but this does not make much sense in the context since presumably there are many humans around. The preposition can also have a causal meaning, for which there are two possible meanings. The sheep's bleating is due to fear from human beings, which would make sense in the context since they would be afraid of harm.[127] But it can also mean that the very loud uproar is due to a large number of people. This is the more likely meaning, given the situation; thus the metaphor has changed from sheep to people. The sheep are in fact Judah's exiles who have become a large number as a result of their being gathered into one place by a shepherd. **The one who breaks out will go up before them:** the so-called prophetic perfect is used here to indicate the certainty of the future event, thus "*will* go up." In the prophet's mind the event has already happened.[128] The word "to break out" is used in a variety of contexts and has the notion of "breaking through" or "breaching." Thus a baby can be called Perez (Breacher) because it has broken out from the womb before its twin (Gen 38:29). Servants who escape (break away) from their masters can be described with this verb (1 Sam 25:10). A city wall that provides safety from the enemy can be breached during war (2 Kgs 14:13; 2 Chr 26:6; 32:5). Amos had predicted that the enemy would breach the walls of the Israelite cities and lead out people through the gaps (Amos 4:3). This leads Driver to suggest that "a breaker" was a sapper or a military unit that was responsible for breaching walls.[129] In the present context, the Israelites are crammed like sheep behind the walls of the city that imprisons them, and God appears among them as "the breaker," smashing breaches through the walls and leading the people through the openings to freedom and to their homeland. In Israelite history, particularly during the time of David, there were two famous incidents in close historical proximity where God "broke out" and destroyed the enemy. They were so memorable that the name "breach" was given to the places where they happened. In a remarkable incident God decisively "broke out" against the Philistine armies in their attempt to thwart David's rise to power (2 Sam 5:20). The place was called Baal-perazim (Lord of the Breaches) and became a symbol of God's power over Israel's enemies (Isa 28:21). On a negative note, when David was trying to consolidate his kingship by returning the ark to Jerusalem, God's wrath broke out against Uzzah for defiling the ark, and the place became known as Perez-uzzah (2 Sam 6:8). In the present context,

---

127. Leslie C. Allen, *The Books of Joel, Obadiah, Jonah, and Micah* (Grand Rapids: Eerdmans, 1976), 300.

128. Thus this is also called "the perfect of certitude"; G. L. Klein, "The Prophetic Perfect," *Journal of the Northwest Semitic Languages* 16 (1990): 45-60.

129. Samuel R. Driver, "Notes on Difficult Texts," *Expositor* 5 (1887): 266-67.

Micah envisions a future when God's grace will break through any barrier no matter how insurmountable and lead his people to freedom. The name will not be given to a geographical place but to a royal person, who will break Israel out of the womb of exile, when he himself is born (cf. Mic 4:9–10; 5:3). **Their king will pass on before them, the Lord at their head:** the intensification suggests that "king" and "Lord" are the same individual, the second line amplifying the drama of the identification (cf. Isa 33:22; Zeph 3:15). This is not just any king but *the* king! Thus this image suits the context as Yahweh is viewed as a shepherd-king, a common symbol in the ancient world. Israel has had plenty of leaders, but they have been abysmal failures. Political and economic leaders pillaged and pounded them into the ground, and spiritual leaders justified it in the name of God, but this eventually led the nation to the dead end of exile. These leaders were terrible shepherds who not only neglected their flocks, but became parasites, leeches, and (as will soon be discovered) even cannibals. Now Yahweh finally addresses this situation and becomes their Good Shepherd who tenderly gathers his people and then sets them free from their prison of exile (cf. Isa 40:11).

Interpretation—Micah's Word Then. This new announcement in light of what has been happening is concise but electrifying. The exile predicted in the previous announcements of judgment is now an assumed fact and is coming to an end (1:16; 2:4–5, 10). The glory of Israel, who had been sent off to a cave in Adullam (1:15), has returned but it is a different king who has come to gather into an enclosure his people who have survived the judgment. There he waits with them. He no longer descends from his throne to tread down their cities in judgment and justice (1:2–16) but rather he arises within them to break down the walls of their prison, leading them out in glorious triumph! Such powerful ideas are presented in the beautiful poetry of intensification as growing suspense builds and Yahweh's name is finally announced as the leader of and the main reason for their liberation.

As an independent oracle this text is best viewed as an announcement of salvation, given either in the time of Micah or much later by someone else who is prophesying about a liberation from Babylonian captivity during the exilic period. The reasons why the second option is preferred by many scholars are primarily twofold: (a) Micah was only a preacher of judgment; and (b) since the assumption is that the text speaks of a much later time, it is highly improbable that Micah would address such a temporally distant audience. However, there is no reason to assume that this oracle was not delivered by Micah. To assume that he had the vocabulary of only judgment in his prophetic lexicon is to place a narrow restriction on his speech. And to limit his powers of prophetic vision to the immediate future is a naturalistic assumption. Micah could easily have given this note of hope to a group of his disciples or a group who were forlorn because of the coming judgment. Perhaps the Assyrians were surrounding the walls of Jerusalem at that very moment, and Micah gave this group hope. Judgment and future exile would not be the last word. This passage clearly looks beyond judgment and considers a situation in which a remnant of people need rescue. Where the rescue takes place is not indicated, but it is suggestive of a location in exile, given the circumstances of Micah's preaching about exile in the Assyrian crisis. Perhaps it was somewhere in the Assyrian Empire since the Assyrians were known to deport populations to other conquered areas in order to dampen the fires of nationalism.[130] That the location could have been Jerusalem, where the surrounding population has found refuge during the Assyrian invasion of 701, is an intriguing possibility. In this case "the breaker" would lead the people out of their "prison" into freedom when the Assyrians are defeated.[131] But this is not a natural reading of the text, and the walls of Jerusalem would hardly have been viewed as confining walls during a siege.

That this prophecy was the words of a false prophet (since it was believed that Micah preached only judgment) is improbable since the false prophets never assumed there was going to be a judgment, which is implied by the remnant terminology and the circumstances implied by the oracle.[132] Finally, the view that this is actually a message of judgment by Micah, who is stating that "the breaker" is going to lead them out of Jerusalem into exile is also highly improbable given the remnant terminology. In such an unlikely scenario, the people would be brought to a foreign land as a "climactic statement that the fall of the city and the capture of its population is indeed the work of Yнwн."[133]

The general terminology of the oracle and its similarity to other salvation oracles in other prophets shows that it partakes of their themes and motifs and is clearly associated with deliverance from exile (Isa 11:11–12; Jer 23:4–5; 31:8–10; Zeph 3:19–20). Other similar passages in Micah suggest the same (4:6–7, 10; 7:12–13). Thus it relieves the overwhelming darkness of the judgment with a ray of light. Exile is not the final word. Garments (אֶדֶר/*'eder*) have been robbed as the houses of *Jacob* have been plundered and Yahweh's glory (הֲדָר/*hādār*)—the children— have been taken away. Judgment has come because the land has been defiled. But Yahweh is a good shepherd-leader, not like their past leadership. He gathers his

---

130. It could have even been Babylon, which was under Assyrian hegemony for a long period of time.

131. Leslie C. Allen, *The Books of Joel, Obadiah, Jonah, and Micah*, 2nd ed. (Grand Rapids: Eerdmans, 1994), 301. See also Smith, *Hosea, Amos, Micah*, 483n9.

132. The false-prophet view is argued by A. S. van der Woude, "Micah in Dispute with the Pseudo-Prophets," *Vetus Testamentum* 19 (1969): 244–60.

133. Mays, *Micah*, 76.

flock (עֵדֶר/'ēder) together in their prison house of exile and smashes down the prison walls, leading his people, *Jacob*, out to freedom. Whereas the former leaders used their position of power to oppress and imprison, Yahweh uses his to liberate and empower. Whereas false prophets were interested only in a prosperity gospel of the good life for personal gain and had no interest in telling the real truth, Yahweh decisively and emphatically speaks words of truth that judgment is not the final word. Thus, at the end of Micah's first major section there is a vision of salvation after the scathing judgment, a vision of restoration and true leadership with Yahweh appearing as the final focus at the head of the people.[134]

The theme sketched in skeletal form in a mere two verses here is resumed and developed in the next section, where Yahweh gathers his exiles and suffering remnant (4:6–7) and returns them from Babylon (4:10). He will send a shepherd-king to save them, and he will extend his rule to the ends of the earth (5:2–5). And finally the remnant coming home from exile will be a signal for the nations to do the same and return to their real home, Jerusalem (7:12–13; cf. Ps 87). The picture that brings into focus Yahweh the king at the end of this first section of Micah is thus brought into sharper focus at the end of each of the next sections: Yahweh brings his people home, breaking down their walls of imprisonment (2:12–13), smashing down every idol and everything that might capture their trust (5:10–15), and finally removing any and every obstacle between him and his love for them (7:18–20).

Interpretation—Micah's Word Now. The themes of remnant, a good shepherd gathering a scattered flock, salvation from exile, and divine kingship find expression in the other prophets (Amos 9:11–15; Hos 1:11; 3:1–5). But Micah's contemporary to the south develops more fully this sketch of Micah. Following a description of a new Davidic king who is a peace-bringer, there is the following prophecy:

> In that day the Lord will reach out his hand [יוֹסִיף/*yôsîp*] a second time to reclaim the remnant that is left of his people from Assyria, from Lower Egypt, from Upper Egypt, from Cush, from Elam, from Babylonia, from Hamath and from the islands of the [Mediterranean] sea.

> He will raise a banner for the nations
>   and gather [וְאָסַף/*wǝ'āsap*] the exiles of Israel;

---

134. Many scholars cannot evade the force of the content of this oracle as a salvation oracle but cannot account for its placement, where it seems to interrupt judgment speeches. It seems more congruent in between 4:6–7 and 4:8–10 and thus is viewed as out of place in the present arrangement of Micah. See Jacobs, *Conceptual Coherence of the Book of Micah*, 84; cf. Renaud, *Formation du Livre de Michée*, 115–17.

he will assemble [יְקַבֵּץ/*yəqabbēṣ*] the scattered people of Judah
from the four quarters of the earth. (Isa 11:11–12 NIV)

These themes are developed with greater intensity in the second part of
Isaiah, which could really function as an expanded sermon or treatise on Mic
2:12–13. The divine shepherd-king is one who brings his little lambs home with
tenderness; his sovereign strength guarantees the fulfillment of the promises.
One of the first acts of such a king is the rupture of the walls and gates of
Babylon to save his people (Isa 45:2). Later prophets seem to follow a similar
blueprint for the future. Jeremiah and Zephaniah use the same terminology to
describe the future under the rule of the new king (Jer 23:4–5; 31:8–10; Zeph
3:19–20). Ezekiel points to the failure of leadership as causing the demise of the
nation—the people were led by corrupt shepherds who killed and ate the sheep
rather than feeding and guiding them. All these shepherds will be replaced by a
true shepherd-king—a new David, a king after God's own heart (Ezek 34:23–24;
cf. Zech 10:2).

The New Testament amplifies these themes: Jesus prays for shepherds to
seek the lost sheep of the house of Israel (Matt 9:35–36). He himself is the Good
Shepherd who lays down his life for the flock (John 10:14–15). He is the ultimate
breaker of the prison house of death. It is because he breaches the walls of his
own tomb that he can breach the walls of the tomb imprisoning humanity. As
Zimmerli remarks, "The event of resurrection breaks open the world of death."[135]
And in the final book of Revelation these themes finally "break out" in all their
power. The saints are released from Babylon as its walls come crumbling down.
And they will be led home where they will enjoy eternal bliss: "For the Lamb at
the center of the throne will be their shepherd, / and he will guide them to springs
of the water of life, / and God will wipe away every tear from their eyes" (7:17).

In the history of the church there have been many times when the church
has been in a form of exile, needing to hear these words of hope. No matter
the seeming distance from God, no matter the seeming barriers to him, the
church will be triumphant breaching the gates of hell itself[136] because its Good
Shepherd is also the breaker, the king, Yahweh! It is important to observe the
contrast between Yahweh as the true model of leadership and those who are
oppressive and covetous. The church may have suffered so much and its future
can seem very bleak, but a text like this makes it clear that the last word is not

---

135. W. Zimmerli, *Man and His Hope in the Old Testament*, Studies in Biblical Theology
(Naperville: Allenson, 1968), 148. I am indebted to Mitchell Chase for this citation: *Resurrection
Hope in Daniel 12:2* (PhD dissertation, Southern Baptist Theological Seminary, 2013), 64.

136. Theo Laetsch, *Bible Commentary: The Minor Prophets* (St. Louis: Concordia, 1956), 258.

brokenness but blessing. The decisive word here is clearly the divine action. The remnant does little but survive. The contemporary church can certainly be considered a community in exile, living in a world where covetousness rules and economic exploitation is pervasive, surrounded by the prison walls of a new Babylon, which celebrates a value system of strength and power, success and achievement. As the words of Emmylou Harris, a contemporary songwriter indicate, that sense of exile is only too real for many people:

> Five lane highway danger zone
> SUV and a speaker phone
> You need that chrome to get you home
> Doin' time in Babylon
> Cluster mansion on the hill
> Another day in Pleasantville
> You don't like it take a pill
> Doin' time in Babylon.[137]

The church itself is too often captivated by Babylon as it sees its numbers dwindle in the West. Yet it must continue to trust in its breaker for a breakthrough. Though judgment must be taken seriously, the last word is not judgment and imprisonment but freedom! After the storm the sun breaks through the clouds.

The contrast between the corruption of the previous leaders and Yahweh's concern for liberation and empowerment is sharp. Contemporary leaders need to ask themselves if their leadership is oppressive or empowering, leading people into bondage or liberation. They need to live in the light of the past liberation from the prison house of sin because of the death and resurrection of Christ and in the light of the future liberation of the planet from death that will happen at the second coming of Christ. Christ provides the model of leadership. The contrast between good and evil leadership will become even sharper in the next section of Micah.

Judgment and Salvation II (3:1–5:15)

The second section amplifies and intensifies the notes already struck in the first major division. It begins with the sins of the present corrupt Jerusalem

---

137. Emmylou Harris, "Time in Babylon," *Stumble into Grace* (Burbank: Nonesuch Records, 2003). This song inspired Walter Brueggemann, *Out of Babylon* (Nashville: Abingdon, 2010).

and its judgment but then moves to a stunning vision of a future Jerusalem that is just and peaceable and in which resides the salvation for the remnant of the people and the nations. Before this vision of Jerusalem can be achieved, however, Israel must go through a period of refinement and judgment that is considered to be like the birth pangs of Daughter Zion. This labor will eventually result in the birth of a king who will gather the remnant, reform Zion, and issue a call to the nations to come to Zion and give up their practices of war. The centerpiece of the section is 4:1–5, which is clearly linked by way of contrast to the previous section on judgment (3:1–12), and yet it is also inextricably linked to the subsequent section in which it is the end result of a process described there.

A. Judgment on present Jerusalem (3:1–12)
   1. Cannibalism of judicial officials judged (3:1–4)
   2. Corruption of prophets judged (3:5–8)
   3. Corruption of judges, prophets, priests judged with the destruction of temple (3:9–12)
B. Future glory of Jerusalem and temple (4:1–5)
   1. Elevation of Zion and salvation of nations (4:1–4)
   2. Exhortation to live faithfully in light of the future (4:5)
C. Pathway to glory (4:6–5:15)
   1. Return of exiles to the kingdom (4:6–7)
   2. Vacuum of kingship, exile, and labor pains (4:8–5:1)
   3. Birth of king, remnant, and nations (5:2–9)
   4. Return of king, reform, and call to nations (5:10–15)

Judgment on the Present Jerusalem (3:1–12)

Structure. The structure in Mic 3 is straightforward, as a series of three judgment oracles focus on a dominant theme—the absence of God. Corrupt officials who do not dispense justice will not experience divine help when they are in trouble. Corrupt prophets will receive no more divine revelations. Finally, corrupt leadership in Jerusalem will result in the destruction of the temple, the supreme sign of the presence of God.

The first oracle is a judgment speech in which the present judicial leadership is as different from Yahweh's leadership as night is from day; the second is a judgment speech against corrupt prophets who care more for profits than anything else; and the third is a final judgment oracle aimed at all the leaders in Jerusalem including the priests. Each judgment oracle focuses on the specifics of the indictment (3:1-3, 5, 9-11) followed by the sentence of the punishment (3:4, 6-8, 12). These two parts in each oracle are clearly separated by formal markers indicating the transition from indictment to sentence (אָז/*’āz* ["then"] in 3:4; לָכֵן/*lākēn* ["therefore"] in 3:6, 12).

Literary Features. The previous section concluded with a graphic picture of a righteous leader, the divine king at the head of his people (בְּרֹאשָׁם/ *bərō’šām*), liberating them in the future as he and they break through (הַפֹּרֵץ פָּרְצוּ . . ./*happōrēṣ . . . pārəṣû*) the closed gate (שַׁעַר/*ša‘ar*) of their exilic prison. The scene shifts now to the present leaders of Jerusalem as the heads of their people (רָאשֵׁי יַעֲקֹב/*rā’šê ya‘ăqōb*), who spread out the flesh (שְׁאֵר/*šə’ēr*) of their people in a pot to cook (פָּרְשׂוּ כַּאֲשֶׁר בַּסִּיר/*pārəśû ka’ăšer bassîr*) and pulverize their bones to produce soup (פִּצֵּחוּ/*piṣṣēḥû*).

As for the three judgment speeches, the first one (3:1-4) is heavy on the details of the indictment and light on the sentence. The second (3:5-8) consists of more balance between accusation and sentence, but there is an additional speech contrasting Micah with the false prophets (3:8). The final oracle (3:9-12) has a lengthy indictment building to a climactic punishment (3:12). The three judgment speeches are linked by a number of literary features, and they are presented in an escalating development in which God's absence is gradually removed until the destruction of the temple graphically demonstrates his complete departure.

Close analysis of the text reveals a more intricate unity to these three judgment speeches. The first oracle ends with a judgment in which judicial leaders who are constantly giving unjust answers to plaintiffs can expect no answers from God when they are in a crisis (וְלֹא יַעֲנֶה אוֹתָם/*wəlō’ ya‘ăneh ’ôtām*). The judgment of the false prophets in the second oracle is the same—the sun of their inspiration will darken and they will no longer receive an answer from God (כִּי אֵין מַעֲנֶה אֱלֹהִים/*kî ’ên ma‘ăneh ’ĕlōhîm*). Then Micah speaks in the first-person, forcefully contrasting his message with those of the false prophets, which links nicely back to the way the first oracle opens ("then, I said"). In addition to binding the first two oracles together this second occurrence of a first-person verbal form also provides an effective segue to the final oracle of judgment, which is the most damning one in the entire book. Thus 3:8 is what literary scholars term a Janus construction—looking back to and concluding the previous oracles while it also looks ahead and introduces the climactic oracle, serving a pivotal function:[138]

---

138. Ben Zvi (*Micah*, 76-77) notes that C. J. Dempsey points out clearly the integral role of 3:8 in this text; see C. J. Dempsey, "The Interplay between Literary Form and Technique and Ethics in Micah 1-3" (PhD dissertation, Catholic University of America, 1994).

First-person—"Then I said"
> Indictment of judicial officials—"Hear! O leaders of Jacob"
> Sentence—no answer from God
> Indictment of prophets
> Sentence—no answer from God

First-person—"But I am filled with the Spirit"
> Indictment of all leaders—"Hear this! O leaders of Jacob"
> Sentence—destruction of temple and absence of God

Finally, the entire text begins with a poetic anacrusis ("then I said"; 3:1) and ends with one ("therefore because of you"; 3:12).

Key Words and Expressions. **And I said** may be evidence that Micah has been involved in editing his own oracles. Wolff thinks that it originally contrasts with the false prophets' message in 2:11 and thus represents an earlier form of the book, which has been obscured by a later insertion (2:12–13), much like the ending of the third book of the Psalter.[139] This may well be the case but there is no textual evidence.[140] Others assume that 2:12–13 is part of a false prophecy but this reading is counterintuitive.[141] False prophets never even imagined that there would be an exile. It is probably best to simply understand "and I said" as Micah redacting his oracles and assuring that this new section is connected to his present and not the future (2:12–13). **Know justice:** the Hebrew verb "to know" is used not just for intellectual discernment but to indicate a preferred choice, and often is used for "to love." Thus Yahweh says about Israel in Amos: "You only have I known among all the nations of the earth" (3:2). He clearly means something more than mere cognition since he also knows all the nations, but he has set his special affection on Israel and chosen them to be his people. Similarly Adam "knew" Eve and she became pregnant (Gen 4:1). This is a special type of affectionate knowing. Judicial leaders should be intimately aware of issues of justice but here they are woefully ignorant! **You who hate the good and love the evil:** to love good and to hate evil is a way of stating what it means to be a true member of the covenant, since good and evil are not philosophical abstractions but relate to what Yahweh commands and forbids. Yahweh loves the good and hates evil (Ps. 45:7). Sometimes "good" itself can be a synonym for Yahweh. Micah's northern contemporary, Amos, uses the same words in the context of judicial leadership when he says, "Seek Yahweh and live" (Amos 5:4);

---

139. Wolff does not use this example but it is a good parallel.
140. Wolff, *Micah*, 95.
141. A. S. van der Woude, "Micah in Dispute with the Pseudo-Prophets," *Vetus Testamentum* 19 (1969): 244–60.

and, "Seek good and not evil in order that you may live. . . . Establish justice in the gate" (5:14–15). The people of the covenant who love Yahweh must hate evil (Ps 97:10). Thus "the good" is a shorthand description for the requirements of the covenant (cf. Mic 6:8). These judicial leaders define the good as the objects of their lusts and the evil as the obstacle that prevents their fulfillment.[142] **Who tear the skin off my people, and the flesh off their bones** is literally "who rob the skin from my people." This is a shocking image. When Micah first attacked the greedy landowners, he accused them of robbing the houses of their people (2:2) and ripping their shirts from their backs (2:8), now he accuses the leaders of robbing people of their flesh! The prophet may also be alluding to the Assyrian practice of flaying captured enemies as a means of inspiring terror and discouraging resistance. Perhaps if there is an allusion to this practice, Micah is clarifying the identity of the *real* enemy. **Who eat the flesh of my people, flay their skin off them, break their bones in pieces** is a graphic description indicating escalating intensity and probably to be translated: "who eat my people's flesh by stripping off their skin and breaking their bones in pieces." Those who ought to be engaged in justice (מִשְׁפָּט/*mišpāṭ*) practice the worst form of robbery (הִפְשִׁיטוּ/*hipšîṭû*) imaginable. **And chop them up like meat in a kettle, like flesh in a caldron:** the people have been treated like meat to be devoured by greedy judicial officials. These texts are surely metaphorical, although some commentators think that this practice may have been taken literally.[143] But cannibalism was practiced in antiquity only in times of dire distress like siege conditions that produced starvation (Deut 28:52–57; 2 Kgs 6:24–30). Thus the strategy of the prophet is to shock and evoke revulsion. This is a desperate tactic to get his audience to wake up and face reality by facing themselves! **Then they will cry to the Lord:** the word "cry" connotes the idea of deep distress, and therefore is an urgent petition for help. Tamar cries out after she has been raped (2 Sam 13:19). David cries out when he hears about the death of his son, Absalom (2 Sam 19:4). When Jehoshaphat's life is threatened, he cries out (1 Kgs 22:32). The outcry of Sodom's victims is horrific (Gen 18:20). Presumably the people coming to court were in deep distress, seeking justice and they "were thrown to the wolves." The same fate awaits the judicial officials when their time of deep distress comes. They will cry out and silence will be their only answer. **Who cry "Peace" when they have something to eat, but declare war against those who put nothing into their mouths:** although this is a colorful way of saying that these prophets are mercenaries, the use of this language sustains the cannibalistic metaphor. In Hebrew the last word of the previous clause is "my

142. Rudolph, *Micha, Habakuk, Zephanja*, 70.
143. Anderson and Freedman, *Micah*, 354, 553.

people" and the first two words of the new clause are "who bite with their teeth." Thus there is the suggestion that these prophets not only "cause my people to go astray, they chew them up with their teeth." The word "bite" has a noun form meaning "interest," since interest on a loan was often exorbitant and was the equivalent of a huge economic "bite." These prophets, however, do not just work for money. They are far more malicious. They declare war on those who will not pay them. In addition to slandering reputations, humiliating people, and spiritually abusing the poor, this also meant cursing them. In non-Western cultures this still happens today in traditional religions, as powers are unleashed against the targeted victim. "Probably the prophets produced oracles of misfortune against those who did not support them."[144] For example, when Jeremiah contradicted the words of Hananiah, the latter publicly humiliated him (Jer 28). This is nothing less than spiritual bribery. In many countries, a bribe smooths the way for any favor (peace) but a failure to offer a bribe means nothing but trouble (war).[145] **Without vision:** one of the main media of revelation for prophets was the vision, which would show them what God was going to do or what he desired. It was similar to an inspired dream (Isa 29:7; see Num 12:6–8), and it was often used as a technical term to describe the contents of a prophetic book in its superscription.[146] Here Micah says that such visions will cease. Times in Israel when the prophetic word ceased were often viewed as times of judgment (1 Sam 3:1; Amos 8:11–14; Prov 29:18; Lam 2:9). **Without revelation:** the word for revelation often indicates seeking to ascertain the divine will through illicit means (Deut 18:10, 14). In a few cases it has a more neutral meaning (Prov 16:10; Isa 3:2). Micah probably uses it here in a pejorative way to attack the false prophets, classifying their activity as a form of divination. **They shall all cover their lips** is literally "cover their mustache." This was a sign of humiliation. Lepers had to cover their faces as a sign of disgrace and mourning (Lev 13:45), and this was the normal practice for mourning the dead (Ezek 24:22, 27). Thus these greedy prophets will probably become social lepers. **Who abhor justice and pervert all equity** is literally who "abominate or loathe jus-

---

144. Mays, *Micah*, 83.

145. In many evangelical churches leaders in power can marginalize critics within their churches by verbal attacks and personal slander. Examples are legion. See, e.g., David Johnson and Jeff VanVonderen, *The Subtle Power of Spiritual Abuse: Recognizing and Escaping Spiritual Manipulation and False Spiritual Authority within the Church* (repr. Minneapolis: Bethany, 2005).

146. One way to describe the contents of a prophetic book is with this particular noun or its cognate verb. Both noun and verb are used in Isa 1:1; the verb is used in Amos 1:1; Mic 1:1; and Hab 1:1; the noun is used in Obad 1 and Nah 1:1. The rest of the prophetic inscriptions use the term "word of Yahweh" (Jer 1:2; Ezek 1:3; Hos 1:1; Joel 1:1; Jonah 1:1; Zeph 1:1; Hag 1:1; Zech 1:1; Mal 1:1). The term "burden" also seems significant (cf. Nah 1:1; Mal 1:1).

tice." This points to the unnatural perversity in the leaders and their moral devolution. Earlier the leaders were scolded with the rhetorical question, "Should you judicial leaders not embrace justice?" (Mic 3:1). Now the prophet does not even bother with such an appeal. These people are not just indifferent to justice; it makes them sick. **Who build Zion with blood and Jerusalem with wrong** is literally "who builds Zion in bloods." The use of the singular participle ("build") indicates individual responsibility, while the plural reference to bloodshed (literally "bloods") probably stands for multiple killings. A clear illustration of the abomination of justice is the building of Zion and Jerusalem—the city of Shalom—with the shedding of blood! The city has been built as a result of social oppression and murder. A parallel text is found in Habakkuk: "Woe to the one who builds a city in blood(s), who founds a town in violence" (Hab 2:12). Jeremiah chastises Jehoiachin for building his house without justice and righteousness and cheating his employees of their wages (Jer 22:13–15). It is instructive to see the antonym of this expression. Jeremiah provides Jehoiachin with the example of his father, who knew Yahweh by looking after the cause of the poor and the needy (22:16). Micah's oracle is thick with irony describing a tragedy. The city that was to be a beacon of hope and peace to the nations has become the opposite—a place of assault and murder! **Its prophets give oracles for money** is another pejorative reference to the prophesying of the false prophets. Their oracles have degenerated into crass predictions as the word for "divination" is used again for prophesying. Monetary gain is their only interest. **Zion shall be plowed as a field; Jerusalem shall become a heap of ruins, and the mountain of the house a wooded height:** the text gradually expands with great intensity from Zion, which was the name for the Canaanite fortress, to the entire city, Jerusalem, and finally to the hill where the temple was located. The center of holiness now becomes an ordinary hill overgrown with trees.[147] It is extraordinary that the divine name is not mentioned in the destruction of the temple. The "mountain of the house" is just that—not the "temple hill of Yahweh." Yahweh has long since departed.[148]

Interpretation—Micah's Word Then. Each of these three oracles was probably delivered at various times to various audiences in Jerusalem, the capital of Judah. The first one was addressed to court officials, so it would have been

---

147. This is probably not a veiled reference to the cultic site of Kiriath-yearim. The suggestion is based on the "mound overgrown with thicket" (literally "highplaces of the forest"). Kiriath-yearim means "City of the Forest," and it was a high place (cultic center). According to one scholar, the passage is a double entendre, indicating a critique of the city temple by farmer Micah and Hezekiah's cultic reforms; Mark Leuchter, "The Cult at Kiriath-yearim: Implications of the Biblical Record," *Vetus Testamentum* 58 (2008): 526–43.

148. Wolff, *Micah*, 120.

spoken wherever they were gathered, most likely in the city gate where cases were heard. The second speech to the prophets was probably delivered wherever they were giving oracles for services rendered, whether in the marketplace or the temple. Micah's apology (3:8) was probably elicited in such a context, as he specifically contrasted his own understanding of his vocation with those of these crass profiteers. The context for the third speech was certainly the temple during a time of worship when all the addressees would have been present, particularly the priests,[149] and perhaps during the Assyrian crisis of 701 BCE, with the Assyrian armies outside the walls of Jerusalem and threatening certain destruction. The false prophets were prophesying salvation confidently, relying on Yahweh, but Micah did not mince words, with offers of cheap grace.[150]

The individual speeches suggest a genuine personal confrontation with these corrupt leaders. The language is highly charged, and the original situation must have been intense. It would have required formidable courage to face down these "power brokers" of the political and religious establishment and call them out on their corrupt practices. In particular the comprehensive condemnation of all the leaders during worship at the temple and the unpredictable, unthinkable, even inconceivable, prediction of the destruction of the

149. A similar situation is found in Jeremiah's famous temple sermon (Jer 7, 26; cf. 36).

150. The same event is presented differently in Isaiah, and neither Micah nor his preaching is mentioned. Hezekiah is told by Isaiah the prophet that God heard his prayer on behalf of the remnant that remained and would save the city and the temple on account of David (Isa 36–37). Were therefore Micah and Isaiah at odds? Not at all. Isaiah had the same message about social injustice and in some ways a much harsher message than Micah. But Isaiah saw the repentance of Hezekiah and was able to promise salvation from the Lord. One memory of the event had Hezekiah listening to the message of Micah and repenting and thus averting the calamity (Jer 26). This raises the question in the minds of some whether Micah was a false prophet since his prophecy did not occur. But similar questions can be raised for Jonah. The biblical prophetic message was never fixed in stone like oracles in other religions. There was openness to history in which human agency played a genuine role (cf. Jer 18). Prophesying was aimed at evoking repentance, which would then avert the disaster. Thus Micah saying the unthinkable shocked the people into doing the unthinkable (repentance) and averting the unthinkable (destruction of the holy city). Other religions sought to change the situation by making substitutes to experience the judgment. Thus if a king learned of his fate through divination, he would select a substitute who would then be killed in his place; Jack Newton Lawson, *The Concept of Fate in Ancient Mesopotamia of the First Millennium: Toward an Understanding of Šīmtu* (Wiesbaden: Harrassowitz, 1994), 110–21. Ahab tries to do something like this when he hears about his fate from Micaiah the prophet (1 Kgs 22:30). He disguises himself as an ordinary soldier in the battle while Jehoshaphat dons the royal robes of the northern king. But it all fails when a randomly shot arrow pierces Ahab's armour. Does this mean that Ahab's fate was sealed? Only if he did not repent. Without repentance it was impossible to avert the disaster. God would find a way to judge him, even if it meant an arrow shot at random by an anonymous archer.

temple would have invited a death sentence for Micah as it did for Jeremiah a century later (Jer 26).

In the first speech directed to the judicial officials, Micah uses macabre imagery to shock them back into reality. These were individuals whose job it was to be concerned for justice, who were supposed to have a concern for that which was right and equitable and to ensure that the poor were not oppressed by the powerful. But Micah says that the courts have been taken over by the criminals and that vice has become virtue! They hate the good and love the evil, and a gross example of their practices is even provided: they have become cannibals, flaying the bodies of the oppressed, consuming their flesh, and even pulverizing their bones to make soup from the marrow. Instead of serving people, they serve them up for human consumption. "What the farmer in the Shephelah routinely does to his cattle, the leaders in the capital city do to human beings."[151] The drawn-out description of the horrific practices of these officials is an attempt to strike their conscience, even though it may be too late. Nonetheless, Micah shines a light on their outrageous evil. When these corrupt officials need help for their future plight, there will be none. Yahweh will hide his face and ignore their cries.

In the second example that targets the prophets, Micah lambasts them for perverting their calling. Instead of providing guidance for their people, they lead them astray. They are prophets only for hire, and their mercenary behavior is disgusting. Instead of speaking the truth with their mouth because they are filled with God's Spirit, they speak lies because their concern is to fill their mouth with food. Their appetites and audiences determine their message, not God: those who can pay hear the words of shalom; those who do not hear the words of holy war! "What comes out of the mouth of these prophets depends on what has been put into it."[152] The prophets no doubt invoked curses upon those who did not pay them. The verdict on these prophets is much longer than their indictment, which shows the strength of Micah's opposition. He states that these prophets will experience a total eclipse of inspiration, using the key word "darkness." They have not been true to their calling to lead people into light, and now they themselves will walk in darkness. They will experience shame and ignominy, and their mouths will utter groans and cries for their lamentable condition. When they go to God for any inspiration, there is nothing—just intolerable silence. "Those who refuse to listen to the voice of Yahweh because money is making better music will soon not hear his voice at all."[153] Micah then contrasts his calling

---

151. Wolff, *Micah*, 9.

152. Ibid., 102.

153. Hans Walter Wolff, "Prophets and Institutions in the Old Testament," *Currents in Theology and Mission* 13 (1986): 10.

with these spiritual profiteers.[154] Unlike these mercenaries, he is filled with four elements that are presented chiastically. The first and last elements emphasize him being filled with power and strength, which means in this context courage in the face of opposition. Courage "must be possessed by those who would speak unpopular things."[155] The second and third qualities emphasize the Spirit of God and justice, which are essentially inextricable—God's concern for the oppressed and victims and right order in society, the very things loathed by the leaders of Israel.[156] This is the only place in the book of Micah that describes the call of the prophet, and it is clear that God—not his audience—determined his message.

In the third oracle, Micah probably spoke in the temple attacking the three basic institutions in his society necessary for its social and spiritual health: the political system (courts and government), the prophetic establishment, and the temple complex with the priesthood. His lengthy indictment focuses on the political leaders first and the prophets last, while briefly mentioning the priesthood for the first time. He attacks the political and judicial leaders for considering justice abominable. Harsher words could not be found: justice, necessary for the basic order of society, makes these people wretch! They thus pervert the good and the true into their opposite. The city of Zion has therefore been built by means of oppression and evil. The city walls, the palaces, the stones used to make opulent buildings have been erected at a great human cost. Major building projects occurred during the reign of Hezekiah in order to prepare for an Assyrian invasion. His Broad Wall, his tunnel to provide water to another part of the city, and his fortifications would have required "thousands of man-hours of hard physical labor to cut and move tons of rock" (2 Chr 32:1–6).[157] Who knows how many people died during such massive construction projects?

Moreover, the personnel of the judicial, political, and religious institutions are singled out for being sold out to money. Micah then mocks the last group, the prophets, with their own words, which are presented as famous last words: "Is not the LORD among us? No disaster will come upon us." The whole system is propped up on a rotten theological foundation. Micah pronounces judgment in climactic form: "It is precisely because God is no longer among you that you

154. This text is surely an allusion to Micah's prophetic call. Wolff's denial of this by stating that the word "filled" is never used for an account of a prophet's call is a correct observation but not a necessary conclusion. In texts like Jer 1 and Ezek 1–3 the prophet becomes infilled with the words of Yahweh. The words are placed in the prophet's mouth in the first instance, and a book is ingested in the second!

155. Wolff, *Micah*, 105.

156. Ibid., 106.

157. Smith, *Hosea, Amos, Micah*, 493.

will experience disaster! The city will be destroyed and ploughed like a field, no one will know where the temple once was because of an overgrown thicket. It will be a place of curse—an abode for the wild animals of the forest." These words would have sounded like "an exploding bomb"[158] in the ears of everyone in the temple—an outrageous blasphemy.[159]

Many of the prophets' words often fell on deaf ears, but the preaching of Micah in this case was different. Historical references during a later period indicate that the preaching of Micah brought about repentance in the king and people, and Jerusalem and the temple were spared from destruction. The elders in Jeremiah's time remembered this repentance and used it as a precedent not to persecute Jeremiah who was speaking a similar message of judgment (Jer 26:18–19).

This shows the importance of speaking inconvenient truths. Judgment was averted because of repentance. Micah changed the course of history for Judah for a century.

Interpretation—Micah's Word Now. Micah's words in this chapter cry out against modern consumerism, false prophets, and a corrupt religious establishment. Though one rarely hears of literal cannibalism in the contemporary world, metaphorical cannibalism is rampant. A consumer society often consumes its own. Canadian philosopher George Grant decries the underlying viewpoint behind that ubiquitous phrase in Western culture: "human resources."[160] His life's work was a protest against the commodification of humanity. Eugene Peterson laments the same point:

> "Resource" identifies a person as something to be used. There is nothing personal to a resource—it is a thing, stuff, a function. Use the word long enough and it begins to change the way we view a person. It started out harmlessly enough as a metaphor and as such was found useful, I guess. But when it becomes habitual, it erodes our sense of the person as a soul—relational at the core and God-dimensioned.[161]

The media frequently portrays women as so many consumer products in a multibillion dollar advertising industry where the female body is enlisted to sell goods.[162] The sexualization of young girls starts early, well before adoles-

---

158. Wolff, *Micah*, 108.

159. Rudolph, *Micha, Habakuk, Zephanja*, 74.

160. George Grant, *Technology and Justice* (Toronto: Anansi, 2011).

161. Eugene Peterson, *Christ Plays in Ten Thousand Places: A Conversation in Spiritual Theology* (London: Hodder & Stoughton, 2011), 38.

162. Linda LeMoncheck, *Dehumanizing Women: Treating Persons as Sex Objects* (Totowa: Rowman & Littlefield, 1985).

cence, through provocative dolls and clothing, and the psychological and social implications are staggering.[163] The proliferation of a multibillion pornography "industry" results from consumer demand; the aim of this business is the depiction of human beings as objects "to satisfy sexual desire through its sexual consumption or other sexual use."[164] The widespread practice of human trafficking that nets over one hundred billion dollars a year staggers the imagination.[165] The Western media "consumes" its celebrities as quickly as it produces them, and there may be no greater brothel in the West than Hollywood;[166] even professional athletes have become consumer products sacrificing their bodies for money and fame. Whether through abortion in the West, which often targets ethnic minorities and the poor, or mass gendercide in the East, which views females as disposable objects, the "consumption" of human beings by others still continues in different forms than it did in the ancient world. Where is the judicial leadership that can be counted on to stop such practices? Often, like Israel and Judah in Micah's times, it is complicit and sometimes has to be shamed into doing something.[167] This text is a vivid reminder to the nations since they are overhearing (1:2), as well as to the believing community: there is a supreme leader who will not stand idly by at the violation of his moral order. The maxim "what goes around comes around" is not the result of an impersonal force running history. It is found in the words, "Then, they will call out and I will not answer them, because of their evil deeds."

Second, even in the contemporary church, there are many examples of leaders who have abused their privileges, becoming rich off the backs of their people, whether through financial means or sexual exploitation. One leader

163. Margaret Talbot, "Little Hotties," *New Yorker* 82 (2006): 74–83.

164. The complete quote: "Any object that has been manufactured to satisfy sexual desire through its sexual consumption or other sexual use as a woman or child, or as a man, or transsexual, or as part or parts or combinations of these, or variations of these"; Melinda Vadas, "The Manufacture-for-Use of Pornography and Women's Inequality," *Journal of Political Philosophy* 13 (2005): 177. In more philosophical language, pornography creates "an ontological divide between the category of woman and the category of person" (192).

165. Andrew Barr, "Forced Sex Trade Profits Highest in Asia, But Traffickers Earn More Per Victim in Developed Nations: UN Report," *National Post* (May 21, 2014); available online at news.nationalpost.com/2014/05/21/profits-from-sex-trade-highest-in-asia-but-traffickers-make -more-money-per-victim-in-developed-countries-un-report/.

166. Cf. actor John Cusack's remarks on his life in Hollywood in particular: "I have actress friends who are being put out to pasture at 29. They just want to open up another can of hot 22. It's becoming almost like kiddie porn." See theguardian.com/film/2014/sep/25/john -cusack-hollywood-maps-to-the-stars-interview.

167. Gary Haugen, *Good News about Injustice: A Witness of Courage in a Hurting World*, 10th anniversary ed. (Downers Grove: IVP, 2009).

has a last name that says it all: Dollar. Venality is rampant among spiritual leadership in the evangelical church, as is the sexual consumption of women and children in other parts of the church. One leader glamorizes the present life with a message that the best life for the believer is not off somewhere in the distant future—pie in the sky—but now. "You can have it all now!" His 17,000-square-foot home as well as his private jet show that he "walks the talk." Many spiritual leaders have been scandalized in affairs. The paramour of one of them said that he threw her aside "like a piece of hamburger somebody threw out in the street."[168] "Ripping God's people apart rather than leading them will not be tolerated for long."[169] The words of Jesus Christ carry the same electrifying message to such contemporary leaders at the final judgment as those that Micah once delivered: "I never knew you; go away from me, you evildoers" (Matt 7:23).

Micah, like other true prophets, pointed to his spiritual qualifications as being of the utmost importance. Those qualifications resulted in the infusion of the Holy Spirit to declare the sins of his people. This was not an easy task for him to do but the Holy Spirit gave him courage. Paul said similar things to Timothy that he should not worry about his youth because God had given him not a spirit of fear and timidity but a spirit of courage: "For the Spirit God gave us does not make us timid, but gives us power, love, and self-discipline" (2 Tim 1:7). Pastors and ministers need to receive their agenda from God and his concern for justice rather than from their audiences. As Rudolph remarks, "While those [false prophets] scurry for wealth and possession, he [Micah] had strength and courage to announce warnings and accusations."[170] From where did he get the strength? The example of C. H. Spurgeon expresses it best. Every time he ascended to the pulpit he reminded himself: "I believe in the Holy Ghost. I believe in the Holy Ghost. I believe in the Holy Ghost." For the false prophets "God is merely the fifth wheel on the wagon, whereas in the case of the true prophet God is the wheel that drives all wheels."[171]

One of the worst judgments possible is the spiritual disaster of divine silence. The reason is due to either the people's lack of desire to hear the word of God or the prophetic refusal to declare the word of God because of greed or fear. One wonders about the current self-imposed famine of the word of God in North America; churches hire pastors who tell them what they want to hear, not what they need to hear. Their pastors have become spiritual prostitutes, giving

---

168. Leslie Berkman and Peter King, "Felt like Discarded 'Hamburger': Woman's Story of Bakker Tryst Told for First Time," *Los Angeles Times* (March 27, 1987).

169. Smith, *Hosea, Amos, Micah*, 496.

170. Rudolph, *Micha, Habakuk, Zephanja*, 73 (my translation).

171. Wolff, *Micah the Prophet*, 72.

the customers what they desire for a price.[172] Many pastors have been trained to be administrators and CEOs, and they have plenty of motivational speeches "to rally the troops" but almost nothing in terms of a word from God.[173] One commentator writing about this passage but also about the contemporary church says: "Silence is a worse form of judgment. . . . But even worse are preachers who preach only that God is love and will not judge sinners."[174]

The charismatic church speaks much about being filled with the Spirit but little about the Spirit of justice. When Michael Cassidy changed his message at a charismatic conference in South Africa after he heard that Stephen Biko had died "accidentally," he was reprimanded by the conference officials because he had meddled in politics. Cassidy remarked that a conference on the Holy Spirit should have something to say about holiness and therefore justice.[175] Bonhoeffer lamented that the churches in Germany did not cry for the Jews in their worship services during the years of the Holocaust.[176]

And as James Limburg incisively points out, professional theologians are not left "off the hook" by this text:

> Once again the antennas may be up, the receivers tuned in, the switches thrown. To put it in other words, the lexicons have been consulted, the commentaries and concordances lie strewn around the desk. Yet even with the mastery of the techniques of form and redaction criticism, not to mention the sophistications of the word processor, it is possible that the theologian may sit alone at night gazing into the darkness with no vision, no word from God. . . . Micah's diagnosis warns that it is still possible for a theologian to become more concerned about fees than faith, about honoraria than honor. The response of God may then be the same: silence. The theologian experiences a burn-out or a flame-out, with no more fire, no more steam, no more passion for justice or for God. Then the theo-logian has broken with his or her vocation. There is no contact with *theos*, and thus no longer an authentic *logos*, and the preacher is left with nothing to preach.[177]

172. I owe this analysis of the situation to a personal conversation with longtime pastor and biblical scholar Byron Wheaton.

173. Eugene H. Peterson, *Working the Angles: The Shape of Pastoral Integrity* (Grand Rapids: Eerdmans, 1987).

174. Waltke, "Micah," 2.

175. Michael Cassidy, *Bursting the Wineskins: The Holy Spirit's Transforming Work in a Peacemaker and His World* (Wheaton: Shaw, 1983), 193.

176. Eric Metaxas, *Bonhoeffer: Pastor, Martyr, Prophet, Spy* (Nashville: Nelson, 2011), 281.

177. James Limburg, *Hosea–Micah* (Louisville: Westminster John Knox, 2011), 177.

Where are the Micahs who are full of the Holy Spirit and who will call sin for what it is wherever it is, and who do not care for the approval of people, nor for their money because they serve a higher master?

Third, the texts about the destruction of the temple point to the futility in relying on structures and institutions and buildings in the absence of true worship that promotes justice and righteousness and shalom. When the city of peace is built on bloodshed, it is just a matter of time before it becomes history. The same is true for denominations, churches, Christian organizations. No one can rely on the Lord without a commensurate concern for justice and righteousness. The widespread phenomenon in Western culture of what Bonhoeffer named "cheap grace" is a disastrous theology.[178] Such a theology leads to an antinomianism and the contemporary heresies associated with having Jesus Christ as Savior and not as Lord, a sort of "barcode" Christianity.[179] But the whole point of the faith is to get heaven into people and to get the hell out. Without justice and righteousness, there is no point to faith. Moberly writes about the "demoralization of God" in the modern world: "We rightly proclaim and celebrate God's love and grace yet we wrongly fail to understand the inescapably moral and demanding nature of that love and grace. . . . We have forgotten the nexus between knowing God and doing his will."[180]

History does tell us, though, that this radical message of judgment helped avert divine judgment in Micah's time. It was this oracle in particular that was remembered as the turning point, in causing the king and people to repent. The preaching of judgment can affect change. Thielicke reflects on the lost opportunity for such preaching in his own time under the Third Reich in Germany:

> The church was the one voice that could make the cry of the tormented to be heard and furnish it with the commentary of the preaching of judgment. There were some brave men of both confessions—I am speaking of Bishop Wurm of Wurttemberg and Count von Galen, the Catholic Bishop of Munster—who did raise their voices. Certainly it would have been well,

---

178. "Cheap grace means the justification of sin without the justification of the sinner. Grace alone does everything, they say, and so everything can remain as it was before. 'All for sin could not atone.' The world goes on in the same old way and we are still sinners. . . . Well, then let the Christian live like the rest of the world"; Dietrich Bonhoeffer, *The Cost of Discipleship* (New York: Touchstone, 1995), 43–44.

179. See in particular the works of Dallas Willard, e.g., *The Divine Conspiracy* (New York: HarperCollins, 2009), 36–37.

180. R. W. L. Moberly, "In God We Trust? The Challenge of the Prophets," *Ex Auditu* 24 (2008): 31.

and surely it was called for, if Christianity in Germany had spoken with one determined, unanimous voice in this situation.[181]

Would to God that he would raise up courageous messengers of the truth today.

Future Glory of Jerusalem and Temple (4:1–5)

Structure. This oracle is central to the section, a Janus-like structure, looking back to the present corrupt Jerusalem in Mic 3 and looking ahead to the future Jerusalem and how this grand vision will be achieved (4:6–5:15). This text is a centerpiece for the entirety of Micah's second major section as it illustrates dramatically that judgment is not God's final word, as the temple— the supreme signal of God's presence with his people—is resurrected and in contrast to the ancient Tower of Babel in distant history now dominates the landscape, towering over everything as a sign, beckoning the nations to come and transform their instruments of war and waste into those of peace and productivity. This new salvation oracle presents a new Jerusalem, whose center is the temple, the source of world peace, and it is the antithesis of the old Jerusalem, the source of bloodshed and war. It is also the exact opposite of Babylon and its notorious tower.[182] This text is a simple oracle of salvation (4:1–4), to which an exhortation for living in the present is attached (4:5). Micah 4:1–5 is linked to the previous section on judgment as God's final answer to corrupt leadership and worship and provides the goal for the process of purification and renewal in the subsequent oracles. It contains temporal phrases at beginning and end (4:1, 5) that link the text to the distant future and signal a commitment to serve God forever. The announcement of salvation is stunning, given its present literary setting. It announces that the place of blood and violence has become the center of world peace and the catalyst for a new United Nations; the place where false leadership, false prophecy, and false teaching were institutionalized will one day become the place where true leadership, true prophecy, and true teaching will be installed since Yahweh in person will teach his ways.

The text is simple in its structure, and it is placed here to open a new chapter of God's dealings with Jerusalem in order to contrast dramatically with the past. He has not given up on Jerusalem, the temple, and his people and intends

181. Helmut Thielicke, *Between Heaven and Earth: Conversations with American Christians*, trans. John Doberstein (New York: Harper & Row, 1965), 143.

182. Renaud, *Formation du Livre de Michée*, 172–73.

to resurrect them from death in order to accomplish his mission. It is the centerpiece of his design for the world. This is reflected in the following structure:

> Failure of present leadership, death and resurrection of the temple, new
>   leadership
> A. The corruption of Israelite leadership and the departure of God (3:1–12)
> B. Resurrection of the temple (4:1–5)
> A'. Gradual emergence of new Israelite leadership and the presence of God
>   (4:6–5:15)

As three units which highlight the corruption of Judah's leadership led up to 4:1–5, four major units follow it and indicate the transformation of Judah and its leadership preparing the way for the events described in 4:1–5. Micah 4–5 also initiates a new literary structure that is explicitly signaled by clear stanza markers:

> the latter days . . . in that day, the word of the LORD
>   goal (4:1–5)
>   process (4:6–5:15)
> A   in that day, the word of the LORD (4:6–7)
> B   and you, Tower of the Flock (4:8)
>   and now . . . (4:9–10)
>   now . . . (4:11–13)
>   and now . . . (5:1)
> B' and you, Bethlehem Ephrathah (5:2–4)
>   he will be the one of peace (5:5–6)
>   the remnant of Jacob will be (5:7)
>   the remnant of Jacob will be (5:8–9)
> A' it will be in that day, the word of the LORD (5:10–15)

In this structure the goal is Zion, which will be exalted in the last days, but the subsequent units function as the process by which this goal will be achieved.[183] There is a movement from the ideal, future Zion to which the nations will come, to the way in which this will happen through a purified, refined, and renewed Zion, which issues an edict to the nations (5:15). The exiles will be brought home in the distant future (4:6–7) but in the present time "you, Daughter Zion" to whom the kingdom will come will experience a difficult and painful process (three "now" sayings). It is likened to a time of childbirth

---

183. For a similar analysis, see Jacobs, *Conceptual Coherence of the Book of Micah*, 141–56.

in which Zion experiences labor pains and groans. The theme of Daughter Zion pervades this entire section (4:7, 8, 10, 11, 13; 5:1; cf. 5:3). A new section parallel to Zion begins in 5:2 with Bethlehem Ephrathah addressed (5:2–4), and Bethlehem gives birth to a universal king, whose birth has powerful implications (three "will be" sayings): hope in him will sustain Israel against enemies (5:4–6), enable the remnant in exile not only to survive but to thrive (5:7–9), and finally when the exiles return, the process will almost be complete. The king will purify the nation "on that day" (5:10; cf. 4:6) before announcing peace to the nations (5:10–15). The nations that respond will be transformed (4:4); those that do not will experience judgment (5:15). This structure is remarkably similar to the structure of Isa 2–4, where the same vision begins the chapter as the ideal Jerusalem of the future (2:1–5), which is followed by a description of the present Jerusalem that will purified through judgment and the day of Yahweh (2:6–4:1), until the ideal Jerusalem is pictured again as a purified and holy city (4:2–4).[184]

Literary Features. Two key words are used throughout the text. The first word is "walk": "Many nations shall *come* and say: 'Come, let us go up to the mountain of the LORD, to the house of the God of Jacob; . . . that we may *walk* in his paths.'" "For all the peoples *walk*, each in the name of its god, but we will *walk* in the name of the LORD our God forever and ever." Five times the word "walk" occurs, and the *middle* occurrence tells the purpose of this walking. The nations walk toward Jerusalem so "that they can walk in the paths of the LORD." And what are the paths of the LORD? They are the paths of peace and prosperity. The second word is "nations" or "peoples." This word occurs seven times, and its striking repetition frequently with the adjective "many, mighty, all" suggests a massive, universal pilgrimage to Zion. It as if the nations have had enough of war and suffering and now want the ways of peace. And finally, what is Israel in the present to learn from this vision of the future? Despite the nations currently walking in the ways of their gods in the present, Israel must resolve to walk in the name of its God forever and ever (4:5)! It must be a sign of the future in the present!

The text has a good number of artistic devices using wordplay and assonance. At the end of the days (בְּאַחֲרִית הַיָּמִים/*bəʾaḥărît hayyāmîm*), the temple will be the top (first) of the mountains (בְּרֹאשׁ הֶהָרִים/*bərōʾš hehārîm*). In the first five lines, four rhyming lines center a nonrhyming line, accentuating its prominence and therefore the height of the temple. The rhyming words are presented below:

184. John N. Oswalt, *The Book of Isaiah, Chapters 1–39* (Grand Rapids: Eerdmans, 1986), 113.

הַיָּמִים	*hayyāmîm*	days
הֶהָרִים	*hehārîm*	mountains
מִגְּבָעוֹת	*miggəbāʿôt*	hills
עַמִּים	*ʿammîm*	peoples
רַבִּים	*rabbim*	many

Key Words and Expressions. **In days to come** is probably a technical term in the Old Testament for the end of history. It occurs fourteen times, in many cases with an eschatological meaning. Sometimes it may simply suggest an indefinite period in the future, but particularly when used in the prophets it suggests the time period near the end of history, when God's kingdom will be established in the world. This is clearly the case here.[185] Thus this is a long-range prophecy that is the final goal of the oracles in this section. **As the highest of the mountains:** the meaning "as" is signaled by the use of the Hebrew preposition בְּ/*bə*, indicating in this case identity (*beth essentiae*), meaning that the mountain of the house of Yahweh is the highest of the mountains.[186] Although some translations indicate that this means importance, this is a consequence of its elevation. The elevation is probably to be understood metaphorically because of the prominence of the Torah. But this picture suggests that "God's heavenly dwelling place and his earthly temple are joined as one."[187] In the ancient world, kings celebrated the building of temples with similar language: "He built his master's house exactly as he had been told to. The true shepherd Gudea made it grow so high as to fill the space between heaven and earth, had it wear a tiara shaped like the new moon, and had its fame spread as far as the heart of the highlands."[188] **Peoples shall stream to it:** the use of this metaphor is striking. Streams will flow up the mountain! Babylon in its heyday was regarded as the place to which the nations streamed for commerce and political influence (Jer 51:44), but in the last days Jerusalem will be the source of peace and life. **Far away** is not found in the parallel passage in Isa 2:1–5. It emphasizes

185. Gen 49:1; Num 24:14; Deut 4:30; 31:29; Isa 2:2 = Mic 4:1; Jer 23:20; 30:24; 48:47; 49:39; Ezek 38:16; Dan 10:14; Hos 3:5. The phrase also occurs in Aramaic in Dan 2:28. For further study of this phrase, see Stephen G. Dempster, "'At the End of the Days'—An Eschatological Technical Term: The Intersection of Context, Linguistics, and Theology," in *Festschrift for George Klein*, ed. Paul Wolfe (Nashville: Broadman & Holman, forthcoming).

186. Bruce K. Waltke and Michael O'Connor, *An Introduction to Biblical Hebrew Syntax* (Winona Lake: Eisenbrauns, 1990), 198.

187. Smith, *Hosea, Amos, Micah*, 508.

188. Gudea Cylinder A and B: c.2.1.7. I am indebted to Wolff (*Micah*, 120) for this reference.

Yahweh's worldwide influence and the magnetic attraction of his Torah.[189] **But they shall all sit under their own vines and under their own fig trees:** these words are also not found in Isaiah, and they emphasize a further consequence of Yahweh's worldwide rule: lasting peace, prosperity, and contentment. Covetousness and fear are absent. Micah does not contradict Isaiah's universal vision by describing an isolationism where people dwell securely on their own private property.[190] Micah's vision is just as universal! Moreover, not only does Micah predict "a royal dream of disarmament" but also "a personal agrarian dream of well being."[191] Solomon's early rule spawned such a dream (1 Kgs 4:25), and it would be a mark of forgiveness and healing of the land in the future (Zech 3:10). **For all the peoples walk, each in the name of its god, but we will walk in the name of the LORD our God forever and ever:** to walk in the name of a god was to be identified with that god. It was to manifest the character of that god and to receive its help and strength (Zech 10:12). Goliath came to David with the sword, spear, and javelin, but David came to him in the name of the LORD (1 Sam 17:45). But there is a significant exegetical question here: does this text continue the future reference in which even though the nations have heard the word of Yahweh and transformed their lives, they will then return to their locales and resume the worship of each of their gods (which would necessarily mean that they will resume their old habits of war)? Or does this text return the audience to Micah's present in a world of war, insecurity, and idolatry and encourage Micah's contemporaries to resolve to be faithful, that is, he means to say, in the light of the exaltation of Zion in the future, live in such a way so as to model the future to the nations in spite of their idolatry?[192] The conjunction כִּי/*kî*, which is translated "for" by the NRSV (and left untranslated by the NIV), should probably be best understood with concessive force here as "although" or "even if" (cf. Isa 54:10).[193] This makes the first meaning improbable. But it is dubious for other reasons as well. In fact, a future acceptance of religious

189. Mays, *Micah*, 97.

190. Mark E. Biddle, "Obadiah-Jonah-Micah in Canonical Context: The Nature of Prophetic Literature and Hermeneutics," *Interpretation* 61 (2007): 154–66 at 156.

191. Walter Brueggemann, "'Vine and Fig Tree': A Case Study in Imagination and Criticism," *Catholic Biblical Quarterly* 43 (1981): 193.

192. See also a third one, which does not take the unity of the text seriously because it views 4:5 as the work of a later skeptic who flatly contradicts the utopian vision of 4:1–4. "Verse 5 . . . is a rejoinder to Mic 4:1–4 by someone who was skeptical about the description of the ideal future which it contained or even viewed it with hostility, and who contrasted the Utopian portrayal with the realities of the present which contradicted it"; McKane, *Micah*, 126.

193. See Hans Walter Wolff, "Swords into Ploughshares: Misuse of a Word of Prophecy?" *Currents in Theology and Mission* 12 (1985): 143.

pluralism strains credulity,[194] for texts like this one argue for the supremacy of Yahweh and consequently the delegitimation of all forms of idolatry. It would be absurd to expect the nations to resume idol worship once they have seen its folly and have heard from Yahweh. This would essentially nullify the authority of Yahweh's word in that final day. This statement, then, functions as a resolute exhortation for the people of Israel to be faithful in the present time, much like its companion piece in Isa 2:5.[195] Also by using the first-person plural pronoun ("*we* will . . ."), Micah is identifying personally with his audience.

Interpretation—Micah's Word Then. Many scholars assume that this speech must have been presented anonymously generations after the pronouncement of judgment on the temple.[196] In other words, it could not have been presented during the same time period by the historical Micah since it is a clear contradiction of his words. He would have taken hope away and then given it back, thus defeating the purpose of his judgment oracle.[197] For example, Mays states categorically that "the message has no place in the mission of Micah as defined by these oracles and his own mission (3:8), and it is clearly a contradiction of 3:12, the prophecy for which he was remembered a century later after it was uttered."[198] Thus a historical context for this oracle is reconstructed for the period of the exile when the temple lay in ruins or for the postexilic period when the people needed encouragement to rebuild the temple (or if it had been rebuilt, to realize its cosmic significance). Van der Woude agrees with Mays that the speech contradicts Micah but he argues that

194. E.g., see Ben Zvi, *Micah*, 101–2. Cf. Mark E. Biddle, "Obadiah-Jonah-Micah in Canonical Context: The Nature of Prophetic Literature and Hermeneutics," *Interpretation* 61 (2007): 154–66 at 156–57, who argues that Micah retracts the hope for universal Yahwism.

195. Smith, *Micah, Zephaniah, and Nahum*, 88; similarly Marvin A. Sweeney, "Micah's Debate with Isaiah," *Journal for the Study of the Old Testament* 93 (2001): 111–24. Calvin suggests that this text returns the audience to Micah's present, and in light of the demolition of city and temple, and the triumphalistic idolatry of the nations, the remnant in exile will faithfully serve Yahweh because of the hope in 4:1–4; *Twelve Minor Prophets*, 270–71.

196. The vexed question as to whether this prophecy was original with Micah or Isaiah (cf. 2:1–5) leads to the following proposals: (1) Isaiah is original (e.g., Wildberger); (2) Micah is original (Calvin); (3) they have a common source (Snaith); (4) an editor takes the same poem and adapts it to each book (Stade); and (5) Yahweh independently gives the same revelation to each prophet (Archer). For a list of the differences, see Marvin A. Sweeney, "Micah's Debate with Isaiah," *Journal for the Study of the Old Testament* 93 (2001): 111–24 at 113–15. For a discussion of the various interpreters and their conclusions, see E. Cannawurf, "Authenticity of Micah 4:1–4," *Vetus Testamentum* 13 (1963): 26–33, who argues for the fourth view and seems unaware of Archer's view.

197. Thus, e.g., Micah would have canceled the impact of 3:12 with the comforting words of 4:1–5; Smith, *Micah, Zephaniah, and Nahum*, 84.

198. Mays, *Micah*, 95.

it came from a false prophet during Micah's time.[199] But both of these options are non sequiturs. As mentioned before, Micah's prophetic repertoire was not limited to judgment, and there is no indication in the text that this speech comes from a false prophet. It is notable, though, that this prophecy and its virtual duplicate in Isa 2:1-5 putatively stem from the eighth century BCE. In their present literary contexts they provide striking contrasts with the Jerusalem and temple of that day. And they each present the future establishment of Zion and its throne—the temple—as the locus of world rule and world peace, and this is preceded in each by the corruption of the present Zion, followed by the process by which Zion will be transformed by Yahweh to fulfill his purpose for the nations.[200] Micah probably used this message and adapted it for his own purposes. He could easily have taken some of his own disciples aside sometime after the pronouncement of judgment on the temple to tell them that this did not mean the end of the sanctuary but the clearing away of the old sinful place, for a new purified holy building with universal significance. He would have delivered the oracle in the temple precincts to enable his audience to experience in some tangible measure the significance of what he said. Or he may have preached this sermon to a repentant audience after the reform of Hezekiah, to show them the far-reaching significance of their repentance and to encourage them to pursue the living God and not the dead idols of the nations.[201] But the real key to the historical context of the oracle is the exhortation appended to the end of the speech: "Even though all the nations may walk in the names of their gods, we will walk in the name of the LORD our God forever and ever" (Mic 4:5). Despite ubiquitous idolatry among the pagan nations, and the terrible blight of war, the people must continue to be faithful, realizing that some day their temple will bring healing and peace to the nations and even the abolition of war. Thus the people would be encouraged to show the way to the nations in their own lifestyle in the present. As they went up to the temple to hear the

199. A. S. van der Woude, "Micah in Dispute with the Pseudo-Prophets," *Vetus Testamentum* 19 (1969): 244–60.

200. Marvin A. Sweeney, "Micah's Debate with Isaiah," *Journal for the Study of the Old Testament* 93 (2001): 111–24 at 118.

201. Calvin argues that different audiences could easily explain the different oracles. The first judgment oracle was delivered to the main population and the salvation oracle to the remnant of believers within it. Jesus gave messages in a similar way, speaking to a larger audience and then later giving his disciples a fuller explanation (Matt 13). John T. Willis argues that Micah could well have had two audiences: the general population and a smaller group "away from the madding crowd." The unfaithful, first group he afflicted and the second, faithful group he comforted; "Fundamental Issues in Contemporary Micah Studies," *Restoration Quarterly* 13 (1970): 77–90 at 85. Smith argues that such an oracle as the above was given "to strengthen the righteous in their resolve to trust God in difficult times"; *Hosea, Amos, Micah*, 430.

Torah, they were challenged to change in such a way so much that their hearts of hate and envy would be changed to hearts of love and gratitude. And this would in some small way point the way to the nations. Thus this oracle links together three important themes: the exaltation of Zion, the pilgrimage of the nations to Zion, and universal peace.[202]

In the context of the book, the razing of the temple to the ground (3:12) thus provides a deliberate foil to the raising of the temple to the sky. The heap of ruins will someday become the highest mountain! The two temples thus become a study in deliberate contrast. The house that has become an ordinary high place in the forest (וְהַר הַבַּיִת לְבָמוֹת יָעַר/*wəhar habbayit ləbāmôt yā'ar*) now is the highest mountain (הַר בֵּית־יְהוָה נָכוֹן בְּרֹאשׁ הֶהָרִים/*har bêt-yhwh nākôn bərō'š hehārîm*). The religious and political leaders have made Zion a travesty of justice, selling their services to the highest bidder. But now the Lord himself who has led the exiles home (2:13) produces real justice in Zion and Jerusalem, and his priestly Torah and prophetic word are proclaimed from Zion's holy hill, free of charge. In Micah's time Zion was built on bloodshed and violence; one day it will become a place of peace for the entire world, as the nations will migrate to Zion and return home, transforming their instruments of violence and war into the technology of peace. In Micah's time, the famous last words of the prophets comforted sinful people telling them not to worry but be happy so that they could continue living unholy lives because God was in their midst—although he had long ago abandoned them. In the future the nations will exhort one another to go to Zion because they genuinely want to know how to live in peace. In Micah's time Judah viewed itself and its temple as an exclusive religious and political club, confident that God was with them, insulating and protecting itself from the rest of the world and the judgment of God. In the future the nations will be all important, as Israel will be a magnetic hill to bring divine blessing to the world. Zion will be a beacon to the nations and the dispenser of world peace. It will be the center of a true United Nations. "Strikingly, Yahweh sits exalted in the royal city, but it is his Torah, not the royal scepter, that casts the dominant shadow over the landscape."[203] At this position in the book, this prophecy assumes the destruction of Jerusalem but looks far beyond it.

This text is the beginning of an entire section that develops the true place and role of Zion, Jerusalem, and the temple among the nations of the world. In some ways this announcement of salvation is the end goal of a process that began

202. See Renaud, *Formation du Livre de Michée*, 165.
203. Rick R. Marrs, "'Back to the Future': Zion in the Book of Micah," in *David and Zion: Biblical Studies in Honor of J. J. M. Roberts*, ed. Bernard Frank Batto and Kathryn L. Roberts (Winona Lake: Eisenbrauns, 2004), 77-96 at 94.

as an appeal to the nations in 1:2 and is further developed in the rest of Mic 4–5 and in the final chapter of the book. Thus the prophet placed the end result of the process of regathering, renewal, and resurrection at the beginning of the section in order that it may sharply contrast with the destruction, devastation, and death of the present Zion, Jerusalem, and the temple. In its present context in the book of Micah it is deliberately placed as a dramatic foil to 3:9–12.[204] Thus the idea of "walking" comes to the center of the book. Whereas the wicked wealthy walk proudly (2:3), false prophets walk and deliver oracles that are nothing but wind and lies (2:11), the nations currently walk in the name of their gods (4:5), and Jerusalem walks in the statutes of Omri and Ahab (6:16), nonetheless the people of Judah are urged to walk uprightly (2:7), walk in the name of Yahweh (4:5), and walk humbly with their God (6:8). Thus when the people of Judah change their gait, the nations will eventually come to walk in Yahweh's paths (4:2).[205]

This text teaches that "arms cannot be given up without abandoning swollen appetites as well."[206] But swollen appetites are not the problem. The human appetite is infinitely large but cannot be satisfied by anything except God. And it is only when all idolatry has come to an end and Yahweh and his temple alone are exalted in the world that such a day will finally be achieved for the world. "What to us seems inconceivable, to Micah was a certainty: War will be abolished. They shall not learn war any more because they shall seek knowledge of the word of God. Passion for war will be subdued by a greater passion: the passion to discover God's ways."[207]

Interpretation—Micah's Word Now. The key interpretive question is whether this text will be fulfilled in a literal fashion at the end of history in a millennium, or if it is to be understood as being fulfilled in the temple of the Christian church, as it seeks to bring the gospel of peace to the nations. In the Sermon on the Mount, Jesus suggests the latter when he calls his disciples to be like a city set on a hill, to be the light of the world as they reveal their Father through their good works (Matt 5:14–16). The church is the body of Christ, which is the new temple inhabited by the Spirit of God, which has been given at Pentecost. There Babel was reversed, and the new reality is a temple of life that beckons the nations to hear the Torah and to be changed, exchanging

---

204. "In its present literary context . . . it stands in startling contrast to 3:9–12 where the utter destruction of Zion and the transformation of the mount of Y H W H into a wooded hill is announced"; Mays, *Micah*, 94.

205. This paragraph is greatly indebted to the chart in Hagstrom, *Coherence of the Book of Micah*, 119.

206. Walter Brueggemann, "'Vine and Fig Tree': A Case Study in Imagination and Criticism," *Catholic Biblical Quarterly* 43 (1981): 193.

207. Heschel, *Prophets*, 235.

their arms for instruments of reconciliation and peace. There are numerous examples of how the church has been an instrument of peace in its past. In the early church, serving in the military was viewed as incompatible with serving Christ because among other considerations a Christ follower could not use the sword to shed blood.[208]

According to an early Christian historian, Theodoret, a monk named Telemachus helped bring an end to the gladiatorial games when he was horrified at the spectacle and climbed down into the arena to try to separate the combatants. The bloodthirsty crowd stoned him to death but his death caused the emperor to abolish these gory spectacles.[209] In more recent times, an Anglican Bishop, Dom Dinis Sengulane, was at the forefront of bringing to an end a violent nineteen-year civil war in Mozambique. Inspired by the prophet Micah, he began the Transforming Arms into Tools Project, which advocated the return of weapons—tools of death—in exchange for tools, sewing machines, and building materials—tools of life. In one example a village turned over all of its weapons for a tractor! Over the course of a decade nearly one million weapons have been exchanged. The armaments have been incorporated into bed frames, chairs, tables, or various works of art. A tree of life made from AK-47s, pistols, and rocket-propelled grenade launchers became the new symbol of peace.[210] But perhaps the most powerful modern illustration of transformation comes from an example during World War II when a Baptist chaplain in the United States Army, Lieutenant Leon Maltby, made a set of communion cups from the cases of machine gun bullets from which the lead was extracted. He served a Japanese Christian with these after the war. Instruments made for destruction were transformed into receptacles carrying the healing blood of Jesus Christ. It had a profound impact on the recipient.[211] The cross—an instrument of curse and destruction—had become the basis for a meal. In the words of George Herbert:

> Who know not love, let him assay
> And taste that juice which on the cross a pike
> Did set again abroach; then let him say
> If ever did he taste the like.

---

208. Adolf von Harnack, *Militia Christi: The Christian Religion and the Military in the First Three Centuries* (Philadelphia: Fortress, 1981); Cecil John Cadoux, *The Early Christian Attitude to War: A Contribution to the History of Christian Ethics* (London: Headley, 1919); and John Howard Yoder, *Christian Attitudes to War, Peace, and Revolution* (Grand Rapids: Brazos, 2009), 42–56.

209. Theodoret, *Ecclesiastical History* (London: Bagster, 1844), 326–27 §5.26.

210. See almalink.org/transtool.htm.

211. Don A. Sandford, "Bullets into Communion Cups," *Sabbath Recorder* 44 (1991): 11–12.

> Love is the liquor sweet and most divine,
> Which my God sees as blood; but I as wine.[212]

Pathway to Glory (4:6–5:15)

Structure. This final section consists of four balanced units that link up with each other in a chiastic fashion and show the means by which the glory will be achieved. It will be a pathway marked by great suffering, indicating a future return from exile, a present groaning in labor pains, which will finally give birth to a leader from Bethlehem, whose prophecy will inspire the remnant in exile, and reform at home and that inspires a call to the nations to obey or be judged. Thus the link to the nations to obey (5:15) returns to the previous unit (4:1–5), which indicates the nations will come and obey the word of Yahweh from Jerusalem.

This sequence of salvation oracles is linked by key words, as the first and last oracles are united by the expression "in that day, declares the LORD" (4:6; 5:10) orienting their time to the distant future in the general time slot of "the latter days" in 4:1. The oracles in between begin with a reference to "you" (4:8; 5:2) and are followed by a sequence of three units each dealing with the present time ("now" in 4:9, 11; 5:1) and the time between the present and the future ("then" in 5:5, 7, 8). That this integrated unit is meant to be understood as a response to the previous oracle about the elevation of the temple (4:1–5) is clearly shown by the temporal references and the ending of the first oracle of the new series with language that echoes the ending of the central salvation unit: "We will walk in the name of our God forever and ever" (4:5); "in that day . . . the LORD will rule . . . from that day and forever" (4:7). Moreover the focus on the nations and Jerusalem throughout shows the clear connection to 4:1–5. Thus the events described in this large unit indicate the method by which Jerusalem's and the temple's glory will be achieved. In terms of strict chronology the present crisis will lead to present salvation but eventual exile and suffering, resulting in a preservation of the remnant and a return to Judah, followed by reform and a call to the nations to hear the word of the Lord. The chiastic nature of the text can be shown as follows:

A   return of the remnant to the kingdom of God's rule (4:6–7)
B   present vacuum of kingship and birth pains of exile (4:8–5:1)
B'   birth of a king and the remnant among the nations (5:2–9)
A'   reform of the remnant to the kingdom of God's rule (5:10–15)

---

212. George Herbert, *The English Poems of George Herbert: Together with His Collection of Proverbs Entitled Jacula Prudentum* (London: Rivingtons, 1871), 32.

The Hebrew structure is lucid:

A	4:6–7	בַּיּוֹם הַהוּא נְאֻם־יְהוָה	bayyôm hahû' nə'ûm-yhwh
B	4:8	וְאַתָּה מִגְדַּל־עֵדֶר עֹפֶל	wə'attâ migdal-ʿēder ʿōpel
		בַּת־צִיּוֹן	bat-ṣiyyôn
	4:9–10	עַתָּה לָמָּה תָרִיעִי רֵעַ	ʿattâ lāmmâ tārîʿî rēaʿ
	4:11–13	וְעַתָּה נֶאֶסְפוּ עָלַיִךְ	wəʿattâ ne'espû ʿālayik
	5:1	עַתָּה תִּתְגֹּדְדִי בַת־גְּדוּד	ʿattâ titgōdədî bat-gədûd
B'	5:2	וְאַתָּה בֵּית־לֶחֶם אֶפְרָתָה	wə'attâ bêt-leḥem 'eprātâ
	5:5	וְהָיָה זֶה שָׁלוֹם	wəhāyâ zeh šālôm
	5:7	וְהָיָה שְׁאֵרִית יַעֲקֹב בְּקֶרֶב	wəhāyâ šə'ērît yaʿăqōb bəqereb
		בְּקֶרֶב עַמִּים רַבִּים	ʿammîm rabbîm
	5:8	וְהָיָה שְׁאֵרִית יַעֲקֹב בַּגּוֹיִם	wəhāyâ šə'ērît yaʿăqōb baggôyim
		בַּגּוֹיִם בְּקֶרֶב עַמִּים רַבִּים	bəqereb ʿammîm rabbîm
A'	5:10	וְהָיָה בַיּוֹם־הַהוּא	wəhāyâ bayyôm-hahû'
		נְאֻם־יְהוָה	nə'ûm-yhwh

Literary Features. The first unit (4:6–7) is compact, consisting of an introduction followed by five lines in which Yahweh imposes his will on his people, a will calculated to save and heal, a will expressed in five first-person verbs that transform Israel from a broken people into a strong nation. A concluding pair of lines describe the result: Yahweh's dominion over his people in Mount Zion.

The repetition of the similar sounds for the lame (הַצֹּלֵעָה/haṣṣōlēʿâ [twice]), the exiles (הַנִּדָּחָה/hanniddāḥâ), and those driven away (הַנַּהֲלָאָה/hannahălā'â) underlines the weakness of this community and its restoration by Yahweh.

In the next unit (4:8–5:1) repetition is used throughout the text as a structuring device to link the various subunits. The metaphor of Zion or Jerusalem personified as a female and used implicitly in 1:16 is resumed explicitly and pervasively (4:8 [2×], 9–10 [15×], 11–13 [6×], 5:1 [2×]) so much so that Daughter Zion dominates this section. Feminine forms of the verb and pronouns indicate her cries (4:9), her birth pangs (4:10), her departure from the city, exile and deliverance (4:10), an assault or attempted rape by the nations (4:11), her obliteration of her enemies (4:13), and the command for her to marshal troops (5:1). Also repetition is used to emphasize deliverance in 4:10 where the locus of Judah's exile is mentioned three times: Babylon, there, there!

Moreover many wordplays help communicate the power of the message: thus although there will be a kingdom (מַמְלֶכֶת/mamleket, הַמֶּמְשָׁלָה/ham-memšālâ) in the future, there is no king (מֶלֶךְ/melek) now. Although there is no counselor (יוֹעֵץ/yōʿēṣ) now, God's counsel (עֵצָה/ʿēṣâ) will save Jerusalem.

The Daughter of the Troop is commanded to marshal her troops (תִּתְגֹּדְדִי בַת־גְּדוּד/titgōdədî bat-gədûd), and the judge of Israel (שֹׁפֵט/šōpēṭ) is struck with a rod (שֵׁבֶט/šēbeṭ) by his captors. The divine rule (הַמֶּמְשָׁלָה/hammemšālâ) will emanate from the city of peace, Jerusalem (יְרוּשָׁלַם/yərûšālayim)! Clearly these themes are developing 4:1–5, which focuses on Jerusalem being the center of world peace. World peace (שָׁלוֹם/šālôm) will not come from Babylon (שָׁם/šām) but will eventually come from a divine ruler (מוֹשֵׁל/môšēl; cf. 5:2), and his kingdom will have its capital in Jerusalem (יְרוּשָׁלַם/yərûšālayim).

The third unit (5:2–9) describes Bethlehem as a small player (צָעִיר/ṣā'îr) among the clans of Judah, but from this small town will go forth (יֵצֵא/yēṣē') a ruler (מוֹשֵׁל/môšēl). There is a fine example of an anagram, as this ruler will be exalted to the ends of the earth and bring peace (שָׁלוֹם/šālôm).[213]

The theme of the remnant (שְׁאֵרִית/šə'ērît) and Ashur (אַשּׁוּר/'aššûr) are given prominence through word association. Assyria's power will be to no avail:

> This one will be our peace
> When Assyria enters our land
> When it enters our land,
> When it treads in our borders.

Similarly the last activity described in this major unit becomes the main one in the final section (5:10–15) in a tail-head linkage: the remnant's conquest of all its enemies becomes the theme of the renewal of Zion when God will purge it of all his enemies:

All your enemies will be cut off	וְכָל־אֹיְבֶיךָ יִכָּרֵתוּ	wəkol-'ōyəbêkā yikkārētû
In that day	וְהָיָה בַיּוֹם־הַהוּא . . .	wəhāyâ bayyôm-hahû' . . .
I will cut off	וְהִכְרַתִּי	wəhikrattî
	וְהִכְרַתִּי סוּסֶיךָ מִקִּרְבֶּךָ	wəhikrattî sûsêkā miqqirbekā
	וְהַאֲבַדְתִּי מַרְכְּבֹתֶיךָ	wəha'ăbadtî markəbōtêkā
	וְהִכְרַתִּי עָרֵי אַרְצֶךָ	wəhikrattî 'ārê 'arṣekā
	וְהָרַסְתִּי כָּל־מִבְצָרֶיךָ	wəhārastî kol-mibṣārêkā
	וְהִכְרַתִּי כְשָׁפִים מִיָּדֶךָ	wəhikrattî kəšāpîm miyyādekā
	וּמְעוֹנְנִים לֹא יִהְיוּ־לָךְ	ûmə'ōnənîm lō' yihyû-lāk
	וְהִכְרַתִּי פְסִילֶיךָ וּמַצֵּ־	wəhikrattî pəsîlêkā
	בוֹתֶיךָ מִקִּרְבֶּךָ	ûmaṣṣēbôtêkā miqqirbekā

213. James T. Dennison Jr., "Micah's Bethlehem and Matthew's," *Kerux* 22 (2007): 4–11 at 6.

וְלֹא־תִשְׁתַּחֲוֶה עוֹד   *wəlō'-tištaḥăweh 'ôd*
לְמַעֲשֵׂה יָדֶיךָ   *ləma'ăśēh yādêkā*
וְנָתַשְׁתִּי אֲשֵׁירֶיךָ   *wənātaštî 'ăšêrêkā miqqirbekā*
מִקִּרְבֶּךָ
וְהִשְׁמַדְתִּי עָרֶיךָ   *wəhišmadtî 'ārêkā*

The repetition of this last verb in a staccato series of actions along with the repetition of the possessive pronoun at the end of each line shows the comprehensive nature of Yahweh's reform. It destroys all false objects of trust until Yahweh is left alone. The threefold repetition of the prepositional expression "from your midst" emphasizes the removal of these idols.

Key Words and Expressions. **In that day** is a temporal reference indicating that the events described will happen in the general period of the days to come (4:1), so it must be regarded as the distant future.[214] **Those whom I have afflicted** suggests the punitive nature of the exile and the admission of guilt by those so punished.[215] **O Tower of the Flock** could also be a place name (cf. Gen 35:21), "the Tower of Eder," which would have been located near Bethlehem. Rachel died just before arriving here when she was giving birth to Benjamin (35:19–21), and the associations with Bethlehem suggest the renewal of the Davidic Empire. They also trigger the idea of birth pangs of an expectant mother, which becomes a dominant theme later. But used as it is here for Jerusalem, "Tower of the Flock" suggests that Jerusalem has been reduced to a little watchtower in a field, perhaps as a result of the Assyrian invasion (cf. Isa 1:8).[216] **Hill of daughter Zion:** the Hebrew word translated "hill" refers to the spur of the eastern hill of Jerusalem, which was originally the stronghold of Zion, captured by David (2 Sam 5:7). Again the Davidic associations help contribute to the renewal of the kingdom of Israel. **Is there no king in you?** is a rhetorical question understood either as sarcasm ("Where is your king who is supposed to help you?") or as a call to hope ("Look at your divine king who can help in the midst of crisis"). Given the context, the former meaning is more appropriate.[217] It suggests that although Hezekiah is physically present in Jerusalem he is not providing real leadership in the light of the current crisis—probably the invasion of Sennacherib in 701. In the present (in contrast to the future) the people need real leadership, and such leadership is absent. **To Babylon:** this prediction

214. For further discussion, see Simon John DeVries, *Yesterday, Today, and Tomorrow: Time and History in the Old Testament* (Grand Rapids: Eerdmans, 1975).

215. Renaud also cites Zech 8:14, which is likewise applied to "the catastrophe of the exile"; *Formation du Livre de Michée,* 186.

216. See ibid., 190–91.

217. But cf. ibid., 205.

suggests that Micah was a prophet of the distant future, as Babylon was not a major power during Micah's lifetime. Nevertheless, Babylon was a constant thorn in the side of Assyria during Micah's own lifetime. Isaiah, Micah's contemporary, predicted a similar fate for Judah when Hezekiah showed Babylonian emissaries treasures in Jerusalem (Isa 39). These representatives were seeking to garner support for a rebellion against Assyria. Most scholars argue that these passages are later additions that reflect the later Babylonian period of captivity but such an argument is unnecessary.[218] **There the LORD will redeem you:** the word "redeem" suggests purchasing back a lost object. For example, it was the duty of the next of kin to help purchase family property that had been sold because of an economic exigency (Lev 25:25–30). Similarly, in early Israel it was the duty of the next of kin to avenge the blood of a relative who had been murdered (Num 35:10–34). Moreover, if a married man left his wife a childless widow, his brother (or next of kin) had the obligation to marry her in order to provide an heir (Deut 25:5–10). **Now many nations are assembled against you:** this ancient idea of the nations gathered against Zion to destroy it is found in a number of psalms (Ps 2, 46–48, 110, 125) as well as other prophetic texts.[219] In this text the time seems to be clearly the present ("but now"), and thus the reference to many nations is probably poetic license for the Assyrian attack on Jerusalem in 701 BCE.[220] **Let her be profaned, and let our**

218. "The prediction . . . [Judah should] be carried away to Babylon, and that at a time when Assyria was in the field as the chief enemy of Israel and the representative of imperial power, goes so far beyond the bounds of the political horizon of Micah's time, that it cannot be accounted for from any natural presentiment"; Keil, *Minor Prophets*, 466. On the other hand, it may be that Babylon is referred to as the place of departure and not as a major power. Peter Craigie notes that the Assyrians deported Babylonians to Israel after its conquest (cf. 2 Kgs 17:24) and could easily exile the people of Judah to Babylon; *Twelve Prophets*, 2.36. This Assyrian policy of mass deportation of captives to other locations (including Babylon) to dampen the fires of nationalism was well known in the ancient world, and two examples take place under Sargon; see Bustenay Oded, *Mass Deportations and Deportees in the Neo-Assyrian Empire* (Wiesbaden: Reichert, 1979), 63–64. For a thorough study of all the evidence with a conclusion that this prophecy would not have been that strange to an eighth-century BCE audience in Judah, see James B. Diggs, "Implications from Ancient Near Eastern Deportation Practices for an Understanding of the Authorship of [ʿaḏ Bāḇel] in Micah 4:10" (PhD dissertation, Southern Baptist Theological Seminary, 1988). For further discussion see Rick R. Marrs, "'Back to the Future': Zion in the Book of Micah," in *David and Zion: Biblical Studies in Honor of J. J. M. Roberts*, ed. Bernard Frank Batto and Kathryn L. Roberts (Winona Lake: Eisenbrauns, 2004), 77–96 at 87n29; Arvid S. Kapelrud, "Eschatology in the Book of Micah," *Vetus Testamentum* 11 (1961): 392–405 at 398–99; and Rudolph, *Micha, Habakuk, Zephanja*, 87.

219. Ezek 38–39 and Zeph 3:16–20 imply that Israel has returned from exile. See Keil, *Minor Prophets*, 471–73.

220. It is clear that the Assyrian army also had mercenaries from various nations. Stephanie

eyes gaze upon Zion suggests the thought of assault and rape of Jerusalem by the enemy hordes: as one translation puts it, "Let our eye obscenely gaze on Zion" (Tanakh, 1985 Jewish Publication Society translation). The word "defile" is used of harlotry when a woman defiles herself (Jer 3:2, 9). **Arise and thresh, O daughter Zion, for I will make your horn iron and your hoofs bronze:** cattle would often thresh the corn and wheat in ancient society, and the practice continues in different parts of the world.[221] In ancient Near Eastern iconography bulls are frequently represented trampling enemies.[222] Daughter Jerusalem now becomes like a bull, and its enemies are wheat to be trampled, showing the divine empowerment of Jerusalem; it is able to pulverize its enemies. **You . . . shall devote their gain to the LORD** is usually the last act of the ancient military rite of holy war, in which the wealth was dedicated to Yahweh.[223] The wealth did not belong to the victorious army but to the Lord. **Now you are walled around with a wall . . . with a rod they strike the ruler of Israel upon the cheek:** the first part of this sentence is more accurately translated "marshal your troops, O city of troops!" since the NRSV translation above depends on a slight emendation in the Hebrew. But no such change to the text is necessary. Hebrew wordplays help convey the dramatic nature of the actions. It is the fate of the ruler to be struck with a ruler (i.e., rod)! To strike a person on the cheek or side of the face was a sign of stark humiliation (1 Kgs 22:24; Job 16:10; Ps 3:7; Isa 50:6; Lam 3:30).[224] The king as the supreme judge of the nation has been humiliated. This would have been the case during the Assyrian siege of Jerusalem, when Hezekiah was ruthlessly mocked by the Assyrian spokesman (2 Kgs 18:17–19:14). **But you, O Bethlehem of Ephrathah:** the mention of this location is significant more for genealogy than geography.[225] Bethlehem was in the district of Ephrathah (Ruth 4:11), much as a town in modern Western countries is part of a county, which is in turn a part of a province or state. The location of Ephrathah

---

Dalley notes that the Assyrian army in the late eighth/seventh century BCE employed Samarian and Urartian cavalry; "Foreign Chariotry and Cavalry in the Armies of Tiglath-pileser III and Sargon II," *Iraq* 47 (1985): 31–48.

221. E.g., in Ethiopia; see youtube.com/watch?v=ytiMHAHnGcw.

222. William Matthew Flinders Petrie, *Flinders Petrie Centenary, 1953: Ceremonial Slate Palettes: Corpus of Proto-Dynastic Pottery* (London: British School of Egyptian Archaeology, 1953), 15. For discussion of the ancient iconography, I am indebted to James B. Diggs, "Implications from Ancient Near Eastern Deportation Practices [*'ad Bābel*] in Micah 4:10," (PhD dissertation, Southern Baptist Theological Seminary, 1988), 48–50.

223. Gerhard von Rad, *Der heilige Krieg im Alten Israel* (Göttingen: Vandenhoeck & Ruprecht, 1951); and Philip D. Stern, *The Biblical Herem: A Window on Israel's Religious Experience*, Brown Judaic Studies (Providence: Scholars Press, 1991).

224. See Mays, *Micah*, 115.

225. Smith, "Book of Micah," 223.

distinguishes this Bethlehem from the village in northern Galilee (Josh 19:15; Judg 12:8). Thus, the choice of these names indicates that this is a reference to David, for this Bethlehem was the birthplace of Israel's greatest king. This is the only time in the Old Testament that the birthplace of the coming ruler is mentioned. **One of the little clans of Judah:** the clan was a large group of families, which combined with other such groups to form a tribe. It is here used poetically for the town of Bethlehem, probably to stress the issue of lineage from families because the focus in the text is on a famous person from Bethlehem— David! Judah is important since an ancient prophecy linked the tribe with the emergence of a world ruler (Gen 49:8–10). Bethlehem was so small and insignificant that it does not appear in the list of forty-six cities in the tribe of Judah in Josh 15:20–63. **From you shall come forth for me one who is to rule in Israel:** there is the clear allusion to Nathan's oracle (2 Sam 7:12), which guaranteed that a Davidic descendant would always occupy the throne of Israel. The Hebrew reads "from you will come forth for me" (מִמְּךָ לִי יֵצֵא/*mimməkā lî yēṣēʾ*) and as such it echoes Nathan's words "who will come out of your loins" (יֵצֵא מִמֵּעֶיךָ/*yēṣēʾ mimmēʿêkā*), referring to the succession of a Davidic king. There is also a reference to the emergence of a Davidic ruler in Isa 11:1 (וְיָצָא חֹטֶר מִגֵּזַע יִשָׁי/*wəyāṣāʾ ḥōṭer miggēzaʿ yišāy*). Over time this would take on messianic significance as the expectation for the emergence of a great ruler for Israel grew. The same verbal root is in the next word in Hebrew, "origin," and thus this double use of the root raises the messianic temperature.[226] **Whose origin is from of old, from ancient days** recalls the Davidic Empire. Similar phraseology looks back to Asaph and David (Neh 12:46), the exodus (Ps 77:11), and Moses (Isa 63:11). Micah himself uses a similar expression to refer to patriarchal times (7:20). But the time frame can conceivably be stretched back to the beginning of time (Ps 74:12–17).[227] **Therefore he shall give them up ... then the rest of his kindred shall return to the people of Israel:** the prophet predicts a time when Israel will be given up, perhaps to a foreign power or enemy,[228] until the birth of this king with Davidic ancestry, and then his brothers—the people of Judah—will join the people of Israel—the northern kingdom—and a reunification will occur. This resumes the theme of 4:8b, where the reference to the

226. Renaud, *Formation du Livre de Michée*, 225.

227. Note Calvin's wise comments: "Some maintain ... that the prophet speaks of the eternal existence of Christ; and as for myself, I willingly own that the divinity of Christ is here proved to us; but as this will never be allowed by the Jews, I simply prefer taking the words simply as they are—that Christ will not come forth unexpectedly from Bethlehem, as though God had previously determined nothing respecting him"; *Twelve Minor Prophets*, 299.

228. Similar linguistic examples stressing captivity or being given over to the power of the enemy are in Num 21:3, 29; Judg 20:13; 1 Sam 11:12; 2 Sam 14:7; 20:21; 1 Kgs 14:16; Hos 11:8; Ps 118:18.

"former kingdom," that is, the united kingdom, appears. The one who gives birth could be a number of figures: Daughter Jerusalem/Daughter Zion who has been addressed consistently in the text (4:8–11, 13; 5:1) or the nation, but it could also be someone within the city, representing the people. Isaiah has a similar prediction of a woman who would bear a king named Emmanuel (Isa 7:14).[229] This text may even be a further interpretation of the birth of a king from the house of David.[230] Shepherd imagery is even used as he stands and shepherds his flock in the strength of Yahweh. In the ancient world shepherd imagery was often used for kings, and the Davidic king will be a shepherd just like David but his flock will be the people of Israel from the very beginning of his rule. The idea that Yahweh could be the subject of the verbs ("Yahweh will stand and shepherd his flock with strength") though grammatically possible is unnatural and counterintuitive.[231] **And they shall live secure:** this meaning is supplied by a single Hebrew verb, which thus depends on 4:4 for completion: "They will dwell each person under his fig tree . . . without fear." The ruler of peace will have brought about the kingdom of peace. **For now he shall be great to the ends of the earth:** a description of the worldwide nature of his rule and the expression "to the ends of the earth" is virtually a technical term for the universal scope of the Messiah's rule (Ps 72:8; Zech 9:10; cf. 1 Sam 2:10; Ps 2:8).[232] **And he shall be the one of peace:** does this mean "he will be the one of peace" or "he will be peace" (NIV translates "he will be our peace" or simply "this state of affairs will be the peace"). In the first two examples the phrase refers to the Messiah, whereas in the third, the reference is to the new political reality wrought by the Messiah. Given the focus on the Messiah in the context, the phrase indicates the Messiah. As for the two possible meanings ("he will be the one of peace" versus "he will be peace"), the first is a title used to identify an agent of peace, and there is ancient Near Eastern precedent for its use.[233] There

---

229. Note the similar expressions יוֹלֵדָה יָלָדָה/*yôlēdâ yālādâ* (Mic 5:3) and וַיֹּלֶדֶת/*wayōledet* (Isa 7:14). See Theo Laetsch, *Bible Commentary: The Minor Prophets* (St. Louis: Concordia, 1956), 270.

230. Mark E. Biddle, "Obadiah-Jonah-Micah in Canonical Context: The Nature of Prophetic Literature and Hermeneutics," *Interpretation* 61 (2007): 154–66 at 162–63, who cites Renaud as arguing that this text is a much later midrash on the Isaiah text. The evidence for its lateness is not compelling.

231. See Ben Zvi, *Micah*, 126–27. The word order would be unusual in this context (verb-modifier-subject), and even granted its possibility here it would be highly unlikely that Yahweh would be the subject of "will stand."

232. Rudolph argues that it just means "world famous," but in this context it suggests worldwide rule; *Micha, Habakuk, Zephanja*, 98.

233. Kevin J. Cathcart, "Notes on Micah 5:4–5," *Biblica* 49 (1968): 511–14. See further Norman W. Porteous, "The Prophets and the Problem of Continuity," in *Israel's Prophetic Heritage:*

is little difference in meaning between the two statements but the first suggests a formal title of the Messiah. The Messiah is described in a similar way by Micah's contemporary, Isaiah, as being the Prince of Peace, whose domain has no limit (Isa 9:5–7). **We will raise against them seven shepherds, and eight installed as rulers:** the expression seven/eight emphasizes that "the supply of leaders will be equal to the demands that may be made."[234] These are rulers whom the people will raise up over the Assyrians in their own land, suggesting hegemony over Assyria. If this reference to Assyria is understood literally, there is no example of such an event ever taking place, although perhaps Micah might be thinking of ruling Assyria through Babylonian rebels. Perhaps a clue to the meaning of this text is found in the subsequent oracles that describe the remnant. Though the remnant is weak and suffering in exile, they have become like shepherds with a supernatural strength that they do not realize. By being faithful to Yahweh and trusting in the coming shepherd, they can defeat Assyria from within. Thus the Assyrian Empire—standing for the enemies of God—will meet its demise. **The land of Nimrod** suggests that the language of typology is being used to characterize Assyria. This would be like calling Germany the land of Hitler during the 1930s and 1940s. Nimrod was regarded as the founder of the Tower of Babel, a place of titanic defiance, and his name suggests rebellion (Gen 10:8–10).[235] Perhaps Micah means to say that the land—any land that is characterized by rebellion against Yahweh—will be subdued. Thus even the name Assyria has taken on symbolic value for a mighty nation that defies Yahweh. It is a place of rebellion, a code word for a hostile power.[236] **They shall rescue us from the Assyrians:** the Hebrew is better translated "he shall rescue us," thus probably referring to the coming ruler in 5:2–4. **Then the remnant of Jacob, surrounded by many peoples** could be interpreted that the remnant is in its own land surrounded by many peoples or that it is scattered abroad among the peoples. It probably means the latter since in the parallel expression in 5:8, the phrase "among the nations" is added. Thus this is probably a reference to exilic Israel. **Like dew from the Lord, like showers on the grass, which do not depend upon people or wait for any mortal:** these metaphors always have a positive meaning in the Bible, and in a similar context the coming messianic king is regarded as being as refreshing as showers upon the grass (Ps 72:6).

Essays in Honor of James Muilenburg, ed. Bernhard W. Anderson and Walter Harrelson (New York: Harper & Brothers, 1962), 21.

234. Smith, *Micah, Zephaniah, and Nahum*, 108–9.

235. The name can mean "Let us rebel!" Later Jewish interpretation stressed this meaning. See K. van der Toorn and P.W. van der Horst, "Nimrod before and after the Bible," *Harvard Theological Review* 83 (1990): 1–29.

236. Mays, *Micah*, 119.

Similarly an early promise in the patriarchal period describes Jacob as receiving dew from heaven as a divine gift so that he can be a blessing to the nations (Gen 27:28). Now Jacob's descendants are in exile awaiting his coming and having a similar function to the nations. Moreover, they do not depend on their own resources for doing this. The dew and showers simply appear as if from heaven without any human help whatsoever. They are regular and independent of any human effort. This salubrious impact on the nations comes from God and not from the remnant's innate ability. **Like a lion among the animals of the forest:** the remnant will rise to meet the challenge of its enemies in exile. Just as a lion needs no defense, neither will the remnant. In early Egyptian iconography the king is depicted as a lion ravaging his enemies.[237] Just as the Messiah and his people are likened to dew in early texts and thus the remnant, so the Messiah is likened to a lion in early blessing texts (Gen 49:9; Num 24:9), and here his people are described in the same way. Even though the remnant is weak in exile, it will function in a similar way to the coming Messiah and in fact anticipates his coming. This coming king will bring dew to the nations if they submit (Ps 72:6; 2 Sam 23:4; cf. Ps 110:3) and be a conquering lion if they do not (Gen 49:9; Num 24:9). **In that day, says the LORD, I will destroy your horses . . . chariots . . . cities of your land . . . all your strongholds:** horses and chariots represent the military hardware used for the rapid deployment of forces for offensive purposes in battle. A nation that had many would be virtually invincible. Cities and strongholds represented the lines of defense for a nation. Normally they were heavily fortified for protection. Thus Micah says that God will remove the people's trust in their offense and defense—their trust in military power and security. Earlier Micah had spoken about this trust in military strength as the beginning of Judah's sin (1:13b). **I will cut off sorceries . . . and you shall have no more soothsayers; and I will cut off your images and your pillars . . . your sacred poles . . . your towns:** this represents the people's trust in the spiritual forces behind their faith in military offense and defense. Witchcraft and those who cast spells represent the cultic personnel responsible for encouraging idolatry, and the idols themselves were represented by male gods and their consorts. The male god would be represented by an upright stone (a phallic symbol) and the female god by a wooden pole or tree (representing fertility). "Sacred pole" translates the Hebrew word Asherah, which was the actual name of a female fertility goddess. Recent archeological evidence documents these practices from Micah's time, and these idolatrous customs are particularly linked with

237. See the Two Gazelle Palette in William Matthew Flinders Petrie, *Flinders Petrie Centenary, 1953: Ceremonial Slate Palettes: Corpus of Proto-Dynastic Pottery* (London: British School of Egyptian Archaeology, 1953), 14.

cities.[238] **I will execute vengeance:** the word "vengeance" is best understood as God's vindication of his holiness and justice in the world. Only God can really exercise this since he is the supreme judge of the world. The classic theological and sociological study of "vengeance" was written by Mendenhall.[239] Mays essentially sums up Mendenhall's research in the following words: the vengeance of Yahweh "is not irrational personal revenge to satisfy wounded ego, but the exercise of legitimate sovereignty in a punishment that must occur if the rule of God is to be maintained against the self-seeking power and lusts of men."[240] Thus in order for there to be peace there must be force exercised to establish it, but it is a force that is motivated finally by justice and love.

Interpretation—Micah's Word Then. Many of these texts would have had an independent historical origin, and they originated in Judah's present crisis with the Assyrian armies outside the walls of Jerusalem ravaging their land, but they have been worked into a larger text that is oriented to the future, when the temple and God's rule will dominate the world. Thus the first unit links up to "that day" and speaks of a return for exiles in the distant future who are crippled, lame, broken and judged, and feeling hopeless and powerless. There is no sign of any future whatsoever for these no-things![241] But the truth is "the real constituency of Yhwh's reign will be the crippled flock transformed into a strong nation."[242] This is what is necessary before Zion can be completely restored (4:1–5). "Through Yahweh's transformative action, this ragtag remnant, beaten and crippled and judged becomes a strong nation."[243]

The use of the female metaphor "Daughter Zion" more fully develops a motif from Mic 1. This stresses the note of protection, beauty, intimacy, and glory in this text but most of all that of a mother in labor. Daughter Zion is shown simply as the Tower of the Flock yet that modest and humble picture will give way to that of a great kingdom (4:8). Exile will finally lead to glory, and the nations will be defeated. In the "now" sayings the text shifts back to the present

238. E.g., the burial inscription from Qirbet el-Qom in Judah refers to a blessing invoked by Yahweh of Samaria and his Asherah. See Knud Jeppesen, "Micah 5:13 in the Light of a Recent Archaeological Discovery," *Vetus Testamentum* 34 (1984): 462–66.

239. George Mendenhall, *The Tenth Generation: The Origins of the Biblical Tradition* (Baltimore: Johns Hopkins University Press, 1974).

240. Mays, *Micah*, 127.

241. Wolff, *Micah the Prophet*, 163.

242. Ibid.

243. Rick R. Marrs, "'Back to the Future': Zion in the Book of Micah," in *David and Zion: Biblical Studies in Honor of J. J. M. Roberts*, ed. Bernard Frank Batto and Kathryn L. Roberts (Winona Lake: Eisenbrauns, 2004), 77–96 at 88.

and how this glory will be achieved. There is thus a temporal movement from the humble beginnings (Tower of the Flock) to hope beyond the crisis, to a humiliation of the king for which relief does not seem in sight. If this process is not understood one could easily conclude that there are blatant contradictions in the text.[244] For example, on the one hand the nations make a pilgrimage to Zion to learn Yahweh's ways, and on the other they gather together to attack the holy city.[245]

But this kaleidoscope of images has an inner logic. It represents a message of hope for the people despite the current situation. Before the latter days—the then and there—there is the here and now. This crisis in which there are so much pain and humiliation and suffering will not last forever. In the same way, before a child is born, there are the excruciating labor pains.

From the picture of intense urgency and suffering sketched in the previous four-unit poem of Israel among the nations (4:8–5:1), a new four-unit poem (5:2–9) describes how salvation will happen only after a delay. The powerless judge (5:2) will give way to a powerful ruler after a long interval of time.[246] Thus this section constitutes an explanation "for the present delay in the accomplishment of salvation."[247] The address now to Bethlehem of Ephrathah recalls the beginning section in which Jerusalem is addressed as the Tower of the Flock (Migdal Eder; 4:8). The lowly nature of Bethlehem among the various villages of Judah is fitting given the present crisis in which the capital city of Jerusalem and its king have been humiliated. The passage drips with irony:

> Assyria comes to lay waste the cities of Israel and Judah—to level, burn, destroy, Samaria in 722/21 B.C.—to besiege, to terrify, to shut up Hezekiah in Jerusalem in 701 B.C. What is insignificant Bethlehem against such an onslaught? Of what use is this inconsequential little village—once upon a time birthplace of Israel's king, now superseded in Jerusalem with Samaria

244. E.g., some scholars view the text as completely convoluted; e.g., Smith, *Micah, Zephaniah, Nahum,* 9–11. Others see some of the oracles as basically contradicting Micah, the word of false prophets of salvation; e.g., Rudolph, *Micha, Habakuk, Zephanja,* 92–93 (comments on 4:11–13).

245. See, e.g., Mark E. Biddle, "Obadiah-Jonah-Micah in Canonical Context: The Nature of Prophetic Literature and Hermeneutics," *Interpretation* 61 (2007): 154–66 at 157. He understands these two themes (conversion and conflict) as presenting competing ideologies. That two series of texts throughout prophetic literature present these two themes (conversion in Isa 2:1–5; Jer 4:1–3; Mic 4:1–5; Zech 2:11; 8:22–23; 9:10; 14:16–19; conflict in Ezek 38–39; Mic 4:11–5:1; Joel 3:9–17 [Heb 4:9–17]; Zeph 3:8; Zech 12:2–9; 14:1–3) does not imply contradiction or competing ideologies. It simply implies different stages in the one process.

246. Hagstrom, *Coherence of the Book of Micah,* 63.

247. Ibid., 76.

smoldering from Assyrian torches and Jerusalem surrounded by Assyrian muscle? What is Bethlehem Ephrathah among the clans of Judah—among the sons of Israel?[248]

The reference to Bethlehem shows that this future ruler had an ancient pedigree, one that could be traced back to the nation's beginnings under David, and before that to the time of the patriarchs and perhaps even earlier: "The text is clear that the mentioned Davidide is not a regular king but an ideal king whose time has not yet come and whose actions, power and dominion actually originate with YHWH."[249] Thus a new David would be born, but this will not happen until "when he gives them up until the time when she who will give birth gives birth." The syntax is difficult but the subject of the first verb is certainly God, the object "them" probably refers to Judah and its people, and the mother probably refers to a future mother of the king or, more figuratively, Daughter Zion. The point is that Judah will emerge from its crisis only when this new eschatological David is born. The consequences of the birth of this new king will be the unification of the north and the south: The rest of his brothers (Judah) will return to the sons of Israel. Then this person will emerge ("stand") and shepherd his people in the strength of Yahweh and in the majesty of his name, which will produce security for his people and eventually worldwide rule.

Complementing the temple's elevation to the highest point in the landscape, the new king will be exalted to the ends of the earth. This king will be someone who will eventually come to Zion, purify it, and make it ready to be a beacon to the nations.[250] Before that distant future can be realized, however, there is the problem of the present Assyrian crisis. The announcement of the coming one of peace buoys up hope and will help the people deal with the Assyrian enemy. He may enter Judah's borders but in the end his own borders will not be secure. The king of peace will ultimately triumph over Nimrod; Bethlehem is greater than Babel. Thus the Tower of the Flock (4:8) and the Hill of Daughter Zion (4:8) will give much more hope than the Tower of Babel, associated with Nimrod and Assyria in ancient times (Gen 10:8–11). There will be more than enough leaders appointed to defeat the enemy in its own territory, and ultimately the messianic king will provide final deliverance: The shepherd will send forth conquering shepherds. Second, in

248. James T. Dennison Jr., "Micah's Bethlehem and Matthew's," *Kerux* 22 (2007): 4–11 at 5.

249. Ben Zvi, *Micah*, 129.

250. "The description of his power goes perfectly with the description of universal peace seen earlier (4:1–4) and complements it by affirming that the peace described there will be effected by the Ruler born in the insignificant town of Bethlehem"; McComiskey, *Micah*, 428.

the ensuing interim period the remnant will be not just preserved but will be a refreshing blessing to the nations in which it finds itself. It will be like dew on the grass and showers on the field. Israel will thus be a blessing in the midst of the world, despite its apparent weakness and decimation. But for those nations and countries that oppose it, it will be like a lion, destroying with an almost supernatural force all its enemies that are opposed to God's plan to save the world.

The reference to the lion introduces the final section showing that Yahweh will make war against war (5:10–15) and completely reform the land of Judah. By the placement of this oracle at the end of a series that all begin with the same verb (5:5, 7, 8) and that flow from the sequence of events promising the exaltation of the temple (4:1–5) and a ruler (5:2–4), the final link in the chain of this promise (4:1–5) is put firmly in place. Universal peace will come when Yahweh declares war on war and his people trust fully and only in him. This will be the peaceable kingdom. The "I" repeated nine times fittingly shows the divine monergism at work. Humans must respond by not worshiping idols (5:13b) and by obeying (5:15b):

> Only through God's activity of destruction within his own community does the community become the place of peace where all defensive and offensive concentrations of power have been destroyed along with all means of carrying on occult religious practices which are to guarantee its independence and security. Precisely by being stripped of its power Zion is equipped for trusting its God-given call to promote peace. The nations will be overcome only by an Israel that has been purged.[251]

Micah 5:10–15 links up immediately with 4:6 and 4:1 with its temporal reference and also with the three previous subunits. With its *violent* and *militaristic* imagery it ironically signals the final step to the path of universal peace. It first of all clarifies that Jerusalem and Judah must be purged of all idolatry and likewise that the idolatrous nations must also submit to the divine rule. If they submit to the divine rule the result will be 4:1–4 and if they do not the result will be 5:15. This unit's linkage to 4:6 indicates that this event signifies the return of the kingdom, and its linkage with 5:5, 7, 8 suggests that the exile is now over and that the new king has emerged from Israel and has returned to set up the kingdom.

Moreover, the last verse of the previous unit (5:8–9) becomes the theme of 5:10–15 in a nice example of tail-head linkage:

251. Wolff, *Micah the Prophet*, 97.

145

Your hand will be lifted up in triumph over *your* enemies,
and all *your* foes will be *destroyed*.
"I will *destroy your* horses from among *you*
and demolish *your* chariots.
I will *destroy* the cities of *your* land
and tear down all *your* strongholds.
I will *destroy your* witchcraft.

Here "your enemies" is not the nations but the idols within Israel. The new
king's manifesto becomes "destruction" but the destruction of all the things
that make for war and destruction: all offensive and defensive armaments and
all false religion. These are the "hardware and software" of war and must all be
destroyed if there is to be peace finally in the world. Demilitarization means
de-idolization! As Fretheim points out, "God's use of violence, inevitable in
a violent world, is intended to subvert human violence in order to bring the
creation along to a point where violence is no more."[252] Thus this text (and this
whole section in which it is embedded) stresses the importance of complete
trust in Yahweh. Salvation will come only through Yahweh. It is complete folly
to trust in anything or anyone else.[253]

Finally the last two lines provide a caesura for the entire unit with sharply
jarring syntax, rhythm, and content. The turn to the nations also means that
the reform must go beyond Judah and extend to the world. They are called to
hear and obey the divine word or experience judgment:

וְעָשִׂיתִי בְּאַף וּבְחֵמָה נָקָם	*wəʿāśîtî bəʾap ûbəḥēmâ nāqām*
אֶת־הַגּוֹיִם אֲשֶׁר לֹא שָׁמֵעוּ	*ʾet-haggôyim ʾăšer lōʾ šāmēʿû*

The nations have been issued an ultimatum—they have witnessed the
renovation that happened in Judah, and they too must submit to the rule of
the new worldwide king (cf. Ps 2:7). The ones that hear the word of Yahweh
will migrate to Jerusalem and create a world of peace (Mic 4:1–5); those who
do not will eventually be judged (5:15). Thus the ending of the second section
(Mic 3–5) echoes the beginning address to the nations in 1:2 to hear the word
of Yahweh:

252. Terence E. Fretheim, "'I Was Only a Little Angry': Divine Violence in the Prophets,"
Interpretation 58 (2004): 371.
253. Cf. David J. Bryant, "Micah 4:14–5:14: An Exegesis," *Restoration Quarterly* 21 (1978):
210–30 at 230.

Hear, you peoples [שִׁמְעוּ עַמִּים כֻּלָּם/*šimʿû ʿammîm kullām*], all of you;
   listen, O earth, and all who live in it,
let the Lord GOD be a witness against you,
   the Lord from his holy temple.

Interpretation—Micah's Word Now. The Christian church needs to consider its mission in the light of the work of God in these verses. Not many wise are called, not many wealthy, but God uses the weak things of this world to build his impregnable kingdom (1 Cor 1:26–29). In the contemporary church the concern for status, prestige, and size, as well as the "right type" of people continues to mark many congregations, but these qualities are plainly at odds with what God is doing in the building of his kingdom. The lame, the exiles, the blind, the no-things of this world constitute the stuff of which the kingdom is made. When Martin Luther was teaching a doctrine of creation from Gen 1:1 he once remarked: "God created the world out of nothing. As long as you are not yet nothing, God cannot make something out of you."[254] The church must never forget its roots. It constitutes not just the community of the crippled but the community of the crucified. Living out of its weakness it then becomes strong, a mighty nation, over whom the crucified God rules.

   The woman in labor during crisis times resulting in much suffering and finally birth is an important metaphor that goes back to the beginning of the Bible, with the idea of curse and blessing. The first woman was to have pain in childbirth but this pain would eventually give birth to a seed that would destroy the serpent (Gen 3:14–16). Although this Protoevangelium has been so overlaid with Christian interpretation, it should not be cavalierly dismissed. That descendants are extremely important in the subsequent biblical storyline and that there is a focus on genealogical lists after Gen 3 should make the reader pause and reflect.[255] Similarly the focus on a Davidic descendant after the time of David is important. Throughout Israelite history, the various attempts to destroy the Israelite males in Egypt (Exod 1–2), the destruction of the Davidic descendants by Athaliah (2 Kgs 11:1–3), and the plan to slaughter the infant Jesus (Matt 2:1–18) all suggest the importance of a Davidic descendant for a universal kingship. But in Micah the suffering associated with such a king is first and foremost represented in the mother with labor pains and the humiliation of Zi-

---

254. Helmut Thielicke, *How the World Began* (Cambridge: Clarke, 1964), 25.
255. Walter R. Wifall, "Gen 3:15: A Protevangelium?" *Catholic Biblical Quarterly* 36 (1974): 361–65; T. Desmond Alexander, "Genealogies, Seed, and the Compositional Unity of Genesis," *Tyndale Bulletin* 44 (1993): 255–70; and Stephen G. Dempster, *Dominion and Dynasty: A Biblical Theology of the Hebrew Bible* (Downers Grove: InterVarsity, 2003).

on's king. The idea here is that a new birth for the people of God is represented partially in return from exile, victory over enemies, and relief from their king.

In some sense, the church needs to consider times of sufferings as productive as labor pains in birth. It needs to develop a theology of suffering, for it is through the crucible of suffering that its character is being shaped. Too often in the contemporary church, suffering is viewed as a terrible evil to be avoided at all costs. Thus the church in the West buys into the therapeutic culture that is virtually omnipresent. For such a culture, pain is avoided, medicated, and even denied.[256] With the advent of the euthanasia movement, death is even used as a means to eliminate it in the wider culture. This means that for such believers the songs of lament are absent, and they have to keep their private pains absent in order to be thought spiritual and successful in a "feel-good" and "happy" church. But such a passage as this one in Micah reminds us that suffering can have a redemptive purpose. It is an old truth, harking back to the beginning in Gen 3:15–16. The groaning in labor is a sign, a sign of the future, that the child will be born, that glory is to follow suffering. Eve becomes the mother of life!

Isaiah in particular sees the birth of a ruler, named Emmanuel, as being the scion of a kingdom that will bring universal peace. The links between the woman who gives birth in Isa 7:14 and the one in Mic 5:3 are particularly striking,[257] as are the feats of their progeny.[258] Some of the later prophets develop the idea of redemption from Babylon as being a key in the program of Israel for this future rule. Oftentimes the present kingship and the failure of the house of David will contrast with a future ruler who will do all things well (cf. Isa 7; 9; 11).

The New Testament sees the birth of Jesus in Bethlehem as proof of his divine Messiahship, as the king who will have universal relevance (Matt 2:1–18). The journey of the Magi from the east to see him indicates this worldwide significance of Zion and the nations starting their pilgrimage to Zion.[259] The use of Micah by the rabbis to indicate the birthplace of the Messiah shows how this passage was understood in the first century. Although the Greek text of

---

256. Philip Rieff, *The Triumph of the Therapeutic; Uses of Faith after Freud* (Harmondsworth: Harper & Row, 1968); and George Rawlyk, *Wrapped Up in God: A Study of Several Canadian Revivals and Revivalists* (Burlington: McGill-Queen's University Press, 1988), 135–40.

257. "The verse [in Micah] is reminiscent of Isaiah 7:14 and 9:6. Yahweh is preparing a child to be born to an unnamed woman of Israel"; Walter Harrelson, "Nonroyal Motifs in the Royal Eschatology," in *Israel's Prophetic Heritage: Essays in Honor of James Muilenburg*, ed. Bernhard W. Anderson and Walter Harrelson (New York: Harper & Brothers, 1962), 158.

258. See, e.g., Renaud, *Formation du Livre de Michée*, 248, who links these themes back to Gen 3:15!

259. Note particularly the gifts the Magi bring to Jesus in Matt 2:11 (gold, frankincense, and myrrh) and the riches of the nations that are brought to Zion in Isa 60:6 (gold, frankincense).

Matthew shows significant differences with that of the Masoretic Text and the Septuagint, generally it represents a concise abridgement of the Hebrew and Greek texts:

Masoretic Text	Septuagint	New Testament
But you Bethlehem-ephrathah, [are] little to be among the chiefs/thousands of Judah. From you for me he will go forth to be a ruler in Israel. And his goings forth are from the past, from ancient times.	And you Bethlehem, *house of* Ephrathah, little to be among the thousands of Judah. From you for me he will come out to be for a ruler in Israel. And his goings forth are from the beginning, from ancient days.	And you Bethlehem *the land of Judah, by no means* are you little among the leaders of Judah. *For* from you will go forth a leader *who will shepherd my people* Israel.

Some of the differences highlight the idea of leadership,[260] and it is clear that Matthew's addition "who will shepherd my people Israel" is summarizing the thrust of the passage.[261] However, there seems to be a major difference between Micah and Matthew, when Micah says that Bethlehem is insignificant among the thousands/chiefs of Judah, while Matthew declares in his citation that Bethlehem is by no means least among the rulers of Judah. Matthew's loose "translation" appears like a blatant contradiction. Nonetheless, this is probably a dynamic-equivalence translation bringing out the spirit of the Micah passage in which insignificant Bethlehem becomes important because it is the birthplace of the Messiah.[262] Clearly Matthew sees the birth of Jesus in Bethlehem as the fulfillment of this prophecy. Moreover, Herod's order to massacre every infant in the vicinity of Bethlehem is analogous to Pharaoh's destruction of Hebrew baby boys during the oppression preceding the exodus (Exod 1:15–2:10). The murder of these children is viewed as further fulfillment of a prophecy that stressed the exile and destruction of the northern kingdom (Jer 31:15). That the mother of these children, Rachel, died in childbirth weeping for her children near Bethlehem probably triggered this association in Matthew's mind (Gen 35:16–20).

In Matthew Jesus is viewed in many ways. He is the blessing of Abraham

260. For a detailed study of the differences, see Craig L. Blomberg, "Matthew," in *Commentary on the New Testament Use of the Old Testament*, ed. G. K. Beale and D. A. Carson (Grand Rapids: Baker, 2007), 5–7.

261. As well as perhaps alluding to Davidic kingship with a reference to 2 Sam 5:2.

262. See, e.g., D. A. Carson, "Gundry on Matthew: A Critical Review," *Trinity Journal* ns 3 (1982): 86–87.

to the world (1:1–17), the Savior of his people from their sins (1:21), Emmanuel ("God with us"; 1:23), Balaam's star rising over Israel (2:1–2), the new Moses proclaiming a new law from a new mountain (Matt 5–7), the healer of every disease (Matt 8–10), and the Good Shepherd who sends his disciples to the lost sheep of the house of Israel (9:35–38; cf. 25:32; 26:31). But he is particularly a shepherd who suffers a deathblow so that the lost sheep can be found (26:31). The deathblow is absorbed by his great power of life, and by the end of the book all authority has been given to him, as he sends out his disciples to the ends of the earth to proclaim his rule and proclaim peace to all nations (28:20).

Meanwhile his disciples are shepherded in the strength of the Lord and bring his message to the nations. They hear the announcement that when this is done, the end will come, and the Messiah as the Good Shepherd will divide the sheep from the goats (25:31–46). Even in the present, although it is true that salvation has been accomplished for the Christian, there is a very real sense that salvation is also in the future, when the church will be redeemed from the Babylon of a world system (the entire book of Revelation). Although Mother Zion has given birth to a child who will rule the nations, that rule has not yet been completely established (Rev 12). Meanwhile "nearer is our salvation than when we first believed" (Rom 13:11). Now is the time of the conversion of the nations. The Messiah has broken down the barriers that divide people and nations—"he is our peace," says Paul (Eph 2:14).[263] Moreover, Paul says the message of the cross is foolishness to those who are lost and the power of God to those who are saved (1 Cor 1:18)—an aroma of death to those who reject it and an aroma of life to those who accept it (2 Cor 2:16).

The church has a double duty, as it waits during the period of the birth of the one of peace and his final coming: to be a refreshing blessing among the nations bringing healing and life and also to be a ruthless opposition to evil, wherever it is found. Despite its checkered history it has been on the vanguard of improving the lot of society. Thus the establishments of hospitals, schools, social agencies, literacy programs, and economic empowerment have been its legacy wherever it has gone.[264] When it has been at its best, it has often been implacably fierce in its opposition to evil and injustice, using its peaceful methods to end oppression and violence. The names of Wilberforce, Dunant, Barth, Bonhoeffer, King, Tutu, and Haugen reveal the difference Christians have made with their implacable opposition to evil.

---

263. Hans Walter Wolff, "Swords into Ploughshares: Misuse of a Word of Prophecy?" *Currents in Theology and Mission* 12 (1985): 139.

264. Rodney Stark, *The Rise of Christianity: A Sociologist Reconsiders History* (Princeton: Princeton University Press, 1996); and Jonathan Hill, *What Has Christianity Ever Done for Us? How It Shaped the Modern World* (Downers Grove: InterVarsity, 2005).

Finally, it is instructive to compare the larger unit in Micah with its conclusion of Yahweh's war on war and his final appeal to the nations with other texts that have strikingly similar themes. For example, Isa 2 contains the exaltation of Zion as the ideal Jerusalem, and the present Jerusalem is described in Micah as containing all the objects in Judah that God will destroy. In Isaiah, as in Micah, all these entities need to be abased before Zion as the ideal is raised (cf. Isa 4:2–4):

> You, LORD, have abandoned your people,
> the descendants of Jacob.
> They are full of superstitions from the East;
> they practice *divination* like the Philistines
> and embrace *pagan customs*.
> Their land is full of silver and gold;
> there is no end to their treasures.
> Their land is full of *horses*;
> there is no end to their *chariots*.
> Their land is full of *idols*;
> they *bow down to the work of their hands*,
> to what their fingers have made. (Isa 2:6–8)

Such practices characterize the present Jerusalem, and they must come to an end before the temple will be exalted. Thus Yahweh—in the day of Yahweh—will purge the land and humble everything proud and tall so that only the temple and Yahweh will be exalted (Isa 2:9–22).

But the most conspicuous parallels are found in Zechariah. A coming king will put an end to war with his universal reign:

> Rejoice greatly, Daughter Zion!
> Shout, Daughter Jerusalem!
> See, your king comes to you,
> righteous and victorious,
> lowly and riding on a donkey,
> on a colt, the foal of a donkey.
> I will take away the chariots from Ephraim
> and the warhorses from Jerusalem,
> and the battle bow will be broken.
> He will proclaim peace to the nations.
> His rule will extend from sea to sea
> and from the River to the ends of the earth. (Zech 9:9–10)

Here the king comes to Zion on a donkey instead of a war horse, indicating that he is coming as an emissary of peace. Daughter Zion can shout now—not because its king is absent—but because he is present! The first action of the king is to destroy the horses and chariots in the northern kingdom and in Jerusalem. This suggests also that he unites north and south. After eliminating military hardware from the land, he then proclaims peace to the nations; he presents them with the opportunity for amnesty. Zechariah presents the same concept as Micah but not in such comprehensive terms. Micah's king from Bethlehem is the agent of cleansing in Jerusalem and in the land, and he must accomplish this first in order to proclaim peace to the nations. Zion's king is coming to prepare the world for the exaltation of Zion and universal peace.

Some of these texts in Micah mark the "bookends" of the life of Jesus Christ. His birth occurs in Bethlehem and is marked by royalty and destiny, and his death is presaged by a regal funeral anointing before he entered Jerusalem during his final week. When he comes to Zion, he arrives as its king to prepare for the exaltation of his temple for universal rule. The Gospel writers do not miss the chance to emphasize this (Matt 21:1–14). When Jesus comes into Zion, he is returning as Jerusalem's rightful king, and he is on a universal mission of peace. But in order for him to accomplish this, he must eliminate the instruments of violence and war and idolatry. How will he accomplish such an act? He first enters the temple and purges it. The house of God that was made to be a place of prayer for all nations had become a den of violence and robbery. Thus Jesus drives out the merchants with his whip. And afterward he heals the crippled and blind with his healing touch. The temple is becoming a place of shalom again. Then Jesus prophetically rebukes the religious leaders for telling him to silence the children's praises.

But Jesus does more. As the righteous and powerful king, he renounces all violence and becomes subject to a kangaroo court and suffers a cruel death. He could have called legions of angels to destroy the forces of wickedness but he must purge his people finally, and so he goes the way of the cross, thereby taking all the violence upon himself that was due to the people's sins because of all their idolatry. This brings an end to the true temple of God—God fully resident in him—and by completely submitting his life to God he becomes victorious in experiencing resurrection. As one of the signs of his victorious reign, this new king announces peace to the nations. They can come to him and bow and be forgiven and experience healing. Or they can delay and be judged. The choice is theirs. Thus in the last days, "the nations . . . stand before a choice. Either they hear Yahweh's voice and advance with the people of God toward peace (4:1–5b), or they refuse (4:5a; 5:15b) and become liable to the wrath of Yahweh (5:15a)."[265]

265. Wolff, *Micah*, 162.

The new Israel consisting of Jew and Gentile—God's new temple—lives now in the moment between Christ's first and second coming. To live true to its mission it must renounce all violence and idolatry and trust in God alone. But it now lives to call the nations to peace, and in the meantime, before the second coming, it is called to obey and be reconciled to God. A general amnesty has been declared: the nations must lay down their weapons and accept the terms of peace. If not, they await an awesome judgment to come. In his sermon on Mars Hill—the heart of the nations—Paul announces both peace now and an appointed day of judgment in the future (Acts 17:26–31).

Tempted constantly to take up arms and trust in various forms of idols, the church must realize that it is called to an absolute trust in Yahweh, and this means that it must take the path of peace pioneered by its master. It calls people to repentance and to be transformed so that they become fashioners of the tools of peace from the armaments of war. Thus as the new temple in which God dwells they embody the beatitude of their master: "Blessed are the peacemakers, for they will be called the children of God" (Matt 5:9).

Judgment and Salvation III (6:1–7:20)

The third movement in the book of Micah amplifies and intensifies the previous two sections while stressing a call to repentance and renewal, so that the grand picture of the temple in the previous section might become imminent. In terms of the macroliterary structure of the book, the call to hear is heard again. Its opening imperatives to listen echo forcefully the beginning lines of the previous two major movements in striking head-to-head linkage (1:2; 3:1). Like the first section, which called the entire *world* to attention, and the second, which called the *leaders* to attention, this text calls the *people of Israel* to attention. Thus, much of the same ground in the previous sections is covered but this text increases the intensity by focusing on the people. Israel has failed in the very basics of the covenant, and these facts are emphasized: a failure in *ḥesed, mišpāṭ,* and walking with God. These lead to judgment, but beyond this is hope and salvation if there is true penitence, a salvation that strikes the notes of hope in other parts of the book and blends them into a virtual crescendo, stressing triumph over enemies, an ingathering of the nations, divine guidance, and a hymnic meditation on the divine name—the God of *ḥesed*. The larger macrostructure of the passage is as follows:

A   Yahweh's case against Israel (6:1–7:7)
    1. need for true worship: justice, mercy, and walking with God (6:1–8)
    2. judgment on injustice (6:9–16)

  3. total corruption of the nation (7:1–7)

 B Israel's hope in Yahweh's grace (7:8–20)

  1. confession, hope, and triumph over enemy (7:8–10)

  2. ingathering of nations (7:11–13)

  3. divine shepherd (7:14–15)

  4. repentance of the nations (7:16–17)

  5. hymn of praise to the God of *ḥesed* (7:18–20)

True Worship: Justice, Mercy, and Walking with God (6:1–8)

Structure. The text is divided into three subunits (6:1–5, 6–7, 8) that deal with Yahweh's requirements of his people. In an initial disputation speech Yahweh presents a case against his people and calls the elements of creation to be witnesses (6:1–5). A set of questions then seek to present the proper requirements of worship (6:6a), and a series of three sets of negative answers are given in the form of rhetorical questions (6:6b–7). Finally the question of true worship is resumed (6:8) with the correct reply in the form of three positive counterresponses to the earlier rhetorical questions. There is a balanced poetic symmetry in this structure as the entire text consists of pairs of lines that indicate intensification and amplification, and these are brought to an end by a triplicate of lines expressing justice, mercy, and humble companionship with God as the essence of Israelite faith.

  Literary Features. The call to the mountains and hills to be the inanimate witnesses of Israel's actions is part of a particular genre of speech but expressed in a monotheistic context. The many gods of polytheism are not called to be witnesses of the terrible things that Israel has done because they do not exist. Thus mountains and hills have been around from time immemorial so they would have been present when covenant violations took place. But the mountains and hills also serve to remind Israel of what will happen to them. When God will emerge from his throne—the ultimate high place—he will tread upon the other high places and the mountains will melt and the hills will collapse in his path (1:3–4).

  The use of wordplay stresses the significance of the meaning in this first oracle of this third section. For example, God complains to Israel, "How have I wearied you [הֶלְאֵתִיךָ/*hel'ētîkā*] since I brought you up [הֶעֱלִתִיךָ/*heʽĕlitîkā*] from Egypt?" Just as it is easy to change the meaning of a word profoundly with a slight change in form, Israel has done the same with its religion. In fact Yahweh provided liberation rather than bondage, but Israel turned its faith back into bondage.

This legal procedure is continued with further interrogation: "My people, what have I done to you? How have I burdened you? . . . With what shall I come before the LORD. . . . What is the good? Has he not told you?" There are a series of twelve questions in this short section. The questions are mainly instructional since they are rhetorical, that is, reminding the people of information that they already know.

The use of the two queries asking about the requirements of true worship in the oracle lead to the use of three sets of rhetorical questions, each presented in escalating intensity. These questions with their expected negative answers invalidate current Israelite practices in the cult. The questions of true worship are then resumed with three correct answers matching the escalation of the three previous rhetorical questions.

Initial questions (6:3)
O my people, what have I done to you?
　　In what have I wearied you? Answer me!
Questions pertaining to true worship (6:6a)
With what shall I come before the LORD,
　　and bow myself before God on high?
Questions in escalating importance exemplifying Israel's distorted theology
　　of worship (6:6b–7)
Shall I come before him with burnt offerings,
　　with calves a year old?
Will the LORD be pleased with thousands of rams,
　　with ten thousands of rivers of olive oil?
Shall I give my firstborn for my transgression,
　　the fruit of my body for the sin of my soul?
Questions about true worship resumed (6:8a)
He has shown you, O mortal:
　　What is good?
　　And what does the LORD require of you?
Three answers presented in escalating importance (6:8b)
To act justly
and to love kindness
and to walk humbly with your God.

That intensification/amplification is one of the main features of Hebrew poetry is crystal clear in both the questions and the answers. The pairs of lines move from individual sacrifices to thousands of offerings to the ultimate sacrifice of a human life, which is off the scale of values. Within the pairs of lines there is also graduation. Burnt offerings in the first line are increased to yearling calves in the second, which provided the most tender and sumptuous meat. The next pair of lines moves from thousands of rams to ten thousands of rivers of oil. Olive oil was a prized possession in the ancient world, being used for cooking, lighting, cosmetics, and medicine. It was also used for consecration in religious rituals, and its value and longevity made it ideal for a commodity of exchange. Because of its value it would often be used in sacrificial rites. Sacrificing thousands of rams is credible for a person of wealth or a king (1 Kgs 8:63), but ten thousands of rivers of oil is not. Thus the last material offering is greatly exaggerated. The final pair of lines uses assonance and rhyme to emphasize the offerings, and the second member of this set intensifies the first, by deepening the personal element:

Will I give my first-born for my rebellion	הַאֶתֵּן בְּכוֹרִי פִּשְׁעִי	ha'ettēn bəkôrî pišʿî
the fruit of my womb for the sin of my soul?	פְּרִי בִטְנִי חַטַּאת נַפְשִׁי	pərî biṭnî ḥaṭṭaʾt napšî

The reference to "fruit of my womb" intensifies the word "firstborn," making it more intimate and personal; and "rebellion" is made more personal by the phrase "sin of my soul." Thus the human being made in the image of God is envisioned as being offered as the ultimate sacrifice to God for atonement for sins. There could be no greater sacrifice envisioned than one's own flesh and blood.

Similarly there is increasing amplification of significance in the positive answers. To do justice is the basic requirement of the covenant—stressing action—and *ḥesed* is also an obligation of the covenant, but by stressing the love of *ḥesed*, the motives of the heart come into focus. Both of these requirements emphasize a life of helping the poor and defenseless in society; the first highlights the necessary action, the second accentuates the inner attitude of solidarity and loyalty that inspires and motivates the action, and the third stresses the wellspring from which both come—a humble walk with God.

Key Words and Expressions. **Rise, plead your case before the mountains:** the mountains and hills and everlasting foundations of the earth are addressed as worldwide *and* enduring witnesses in the court case that Yahweh has against his people. Thus they describe the scope of the audience—worldwide—and the history of the audience—virtually timeless.[266] In the ancient world, a multitude of gods would be invoked as witnesses for treaties and legal proceedings, but for Israel monotheism made this problematic, so other enduring witnesses such as

---

266. Rudolph, *Micha, Habakuk, Zephanja*, 109.

the various elements of creation would be enlisted. For example, when Joshua renews the covenant with Israel he places the covenant document under a large stone and then declares that the stone will serve as a witness to the proceedings of the covenant (Josh 24:26–27). The person being addressed here is probably the prophet instead of Israel. **For the LORD has a controversy with his people:** the word "controversy" translates a key Hebrew term that signifies that there has been a breach against the covenant and that the prophet is engaged in a covenant lawsuit.[267] The prophet is acting like a crown prosecutor bringing Yahweh's lawsuit against his people. Yahweh will one day bring his case against the nations and instruct and chastise them (Mic 4:4) but here he must first do it to his people before that great day. **O my people, what have I done to you? In what have I wearied you?** The tone is surprisingly not accusatory but rather conciliatory, as Yahweh expresses exasperation at his people's failure to be changed by the covenant. The placing of "my people" at the front of the sentence highlights God's concern for Israel. **I brought you up from the land of Egypt:** this statement not only expresses the key moment of Israel's salvation as a nation indicating a release from backbreaking oppression, but it is also Yahweh's own personal signature, how he wishes to be known: I am Yahweh—the one who brought you up from Egypt! **I sent . . . Moses, Aaron, and Miriam:** God did not liberate his people and leave them to fend for themselves, he led them through the wilderness and provided important leadership: political (Moses), priestly (Aaron), and prophetic (Miriam).[268] This important triad of leaders led Israel through its forty-year sojourn in the wilderness before they all died. **Remember now what King Balak of Moab devised, what Balaam son of Beor**

267. For the key studies see Herbert B. Huffmon, "The Covenant Lawsuit in the Prophets," *Journal of Biblical Literature* 78 (1959): 285–95; G. Ernest Wright and David Noel Freedman, "The Lawsuit of God: A Form-Critical Study of Deuteronomy 32," in *Israel's Prophetic Heritage: Essays in Honor of James Muilenburg*, ed. Bernard Anderson and Walter Harrelson (London: SCM, 1962), 26–67; Julien Harvey, "Le 'Rîb'-Pattern, Requisitoire Prophétique sur la Rupture de L'alliance," *Biblica* 43 (1962): 172–96; and James Limburg, "Root Rîb and the Prophetic Lawsuit Speeches," *Journal of Biblical Literature* 88 (1969): 291–304. For a more popular presentation of this phenomenon, see Delbert R. Hillers, *Covenant: The History of a Biblical Idea* (Baltimore: Johns Hopkins University Press, 1969). The category that scholars use to describe this speech form is "covenant lawsuit." Here Yahweh is the plaintiff with his prophet, the mountains and hills are the witnesses, and the defendant is Judah. That Yahweh frequently also has to be the judge does not invalidate this form as a legal procedure. In the nature of the case, Yahweh must usually be both plaintiff and judge. Michel de Roche believes that the term "lawsuit" is not an accurate enough term to describe this practice; "Yahweh's Rîb against Israel: A Reassessment of the So-called 'Prophetic Lawsuit' in the Preexilic Prophets," *Journal of Biblical Literature* 102 (1983): 563–74. In my judgment his study is an overreaction.

268. Targum Jonathan on Mic 6:4 mentions that Miriam was to be a teacher of only women, while Moses is a teacher of the law, and Aaron a teacher of atonement.

answered: at the end of the wilderness journey Israel experienced a formidable threat when Balak hired a famous prophet to curse Israel. Micah does not need to provide the answers, as even any Israelite child would know that the curse was turned into a blessing in Balaam's mouth because of the intervention of Yahweh (Num 22–24; Deut 23:5–6). Thus an ultimate spiritual threat was conquered by Yahweh's help for his people. **[Remember] what happened from Shittim to Gilgal:** Shittim represented the last stop on the eastern side of the Jordan before Israel crossed into the promised land (Josh 2:1; 3:1), and Gilgal was the first stop in Canaan after crossing the Jordan (5:1–10). But these names signified much more. It was at Shittim that many Israelites broke the covenant and succumbed to the temptation of Moabite idolatry (Num 25:1). Nevertheless, Yahweh was faithful and successfully brought his people into the promised land. This transition from Shittim to Gilgal, then, is not only a "summary of sacred history, lead[ing] from exodus to conquest, from promise to fulfillment,"[269] but a last exodus from near damnation at the edge of the promised land to "a military consolidation of Israel's possession of the land."[270] **That you may know the saving acts of the Lord:** "saving acts" (literally "righteous deeds") of the Lord are the victories Yahweh has accomplished for his people, and in this context they represent all the previous deeds of Yahweh for his people: liberation from Egypt, guidance in the wilderness, deliverance from Balak, and crossing the Jordan into the land of promise. In 1 Sam 12:7 the same word stands at the head of a list of divine acts on behalf of Israel: the exodus and the raising up of judges. Clearly these righteous deeds are deeds of salvation, and the entire intent of these acts is to effect change in the people that have been delivered.[271] There may be a hint of judgment by the use of this term in order to show how Yahweh has acted faithfully for Israel, and by implication this faithfulness has not been reciprocated.[272] Israel has been the recipient of Yahweh's faithfulness in these mighty acts so that they might reflect Yahweh's image to the world, that they might be Yahweh's agents of peace to each other and thus broker a peace with the world and end all war. **And bow myself before God on high?** The picture of prostration and exaltation is striking in the same verse. The word "bow down" in other contexts suggests those bent over because of dis-

---

269. Hillers, *Micah*, 78.

270. Rodney R. Hutton, "What Happened from Shittim to Gilgal? Law and Gospel in Micah 6:5," *Currents in Theology and Mission* 26 (1999): 94–103 at 98.

271. Cf. the comments of Wolff: "The object of the remembrance and knowledge is always the great saving acts of Yahweh; the goal of this remembrance and knowledge, however . . . is new obedience, new love, and walking in the ways of Yahweh"; *Micah*, 170.

272. Rodney R. Hutton, "What Happened from Shittim to Gilgal? Law and Gospel in Micah 6:5," *Currents in Theology and Mission* 26 (1999): 94–103 at 101.

tress and oppression (Ps 57:6; 145:14; 146:8). The unique form of the Hebrew verb form suggests a reflexive meaning, captured by the NRSV: "bow myself down." **Shall I give my firstborn for my transgression?** clearly indicates human sacrifice. There is a debate whether human sacrifice was practiced in ancient Israel. Although there is no material extrabiblical evidence of child sacrifice in Canaan (aside from a possibility on the Merneptah relief of Ashkelon), there is evidence of such child sacrifices at Carthage in North Africa, a colony founded by the Phoenicians, who shared the religion of their Canaanite neighbors in Israel. Many urns containing the ashes of children have been discovered in a cemetery there and point to child sacrifice despite claims to the contrary that emerge periodically.[273] Other biblical texts indicate that the Israelites during various periods succumbed to the worldview of their neighbors and engaged in similar practices (Lev 20:2–5; Judg 11:30–40; 2 Kgs 16:3; 17:17; 23:10; Jer 7:31; 19:5; 32:35; Isa 30:27–33). In particular the people of Judah during Micah's time had a notorious—and certainly influential—example in King Ahaz, who sacrificed his son when he first became king (2 Kgs 16:3). His sacrifice of his son was apparently performed to demonstrate ultimate commitment to the deity, to influence the future, and to guarantee prosperity. Micah may be not so subtly critiquing a current practice in Israel by suggesting that it should be unthinkable, particularly for atonement. **He has told you, O mortal, what is good** is literally "he has told you, O Man: What is good?" The Hebrew word for "what?" is an interrogative and probably not an object.[274] Perhaps a better translation in English is to turn the entire statement into a rhetorical question: "Has he not told you, O Man, what is good?" This ensures that the statement retains its interrogative force. "O Mortal" is the generic Hebrew term for humanity and the name given to the first man (Adam). Mays suggests it probably refers to any person in Israel.[275] But it can be used for any human being as well. It is as inclusive as possible. This seems to indicate that not only are the most basic terms of the covenant clear to Israel but also to humanity at large. The meaning

273. Susanna Shelby Brown, *Late Carthaginian Child Sacrifice and Sacrificial Monuments in Their Mediterranean Context* (Ann Arbor: University Microfilms, 1989); John Day, *Molech: A God of Human Sacrifice in the Old Testament* (Cambridge: Cambridge University Press, 1989); and Jon D. Levenson, *The Death and Resurrection of the Beloved Son: The Transformation of Child Sacrifice in Judaism and Christianity* (New Haven: Yale University Press, 1995). Many scholars suggest that child sacrifice was a normal part of orthodox Israelite faith in the early years but was disallowed in the late preexilic period. It is much more probable that it was practiced in Israelite religion from an early period but this was the result of Canaanite influence.

274. Although it is used indefinitely as an object in a number of passages, notably Gen 2:19; 37:20; 1 Sam 20:4.

275. Mays, *Micah*, 141.

of the term "good" is defined by context—it is further defined narrowly as what God requires of human beings. Israel has heard this word before in the Torah with a remarkably similar answer, an answer requiring walking with God, justice, love, and the good:

> And now, Israel,
> what is Yahweh your God asking from you?
> But only to fear Yahweh your God,
> to *walk* in all his ways,
> to *love* him,
> to serve Yahweh your God
> with all your heart and with all your soul
> and to keep the commandments of Yahweh your God, and his decrees
> that I am giving you today for your own *good*? (Deut 10:12–13, my translation)

Thus "the good" is what the Lord requires—the right and true way to live—and this means that it will surely benefit a person. Yahweh is not telling his people one thing and doing another. As this text proceeds, Yahweh distinguishes himself as someone who does justice and who loves helping the weak:

> For Yahweh your God is God of gods and LORD of lords, the great and mighty and awesome God, who shows no partiality and will not take a bribe. He defends the cause [literally "does the justice"] of the orphan and the widow and *loves* the foreigner, giving them food and clothing. (Deut 10:17–18, my translation)

Thus to walk with Yahweh is to do what he does, which is the good![276] **To do justice** means "to act justly." The same expression occurs in Prov 21:15: "The doing of justice is a joy for the righteous but for those who practice evil it is grief." A similar phrase is found in Prov 21:7: "The violence of the wicked will drag them away, because they refuse to do justice." Sometimes the verb occurs with the related word "righteousness": Abraham will teach his children "to keep the way of Yahweh, in order to do righteousness and justice" (Gen 18:19). In particular the context in this passage suggests helping people in distress. Sodom is a place of injustice in which the cries of victims of injustice demand a divine answer. Abraham will teach his children a different way of life. To do justice is

---

276. At a later time in Israelite history there will be skepticism about whether it is possible to know the good (Eccl 6:12).

often to help someone in need, that is, to be an advocate for someone whose rights are being violated. Thus God is the ultimate just one as he champions the cause of the widow and orphan and all who are oppressed (Deut 10:18; Ps 146:7). Abraham thus holds God accountable to a standard of justice when he argues that God will maintain the rights of the righteous in Sodom by not destroying them with the wicked. Thus the judge of all the earth does justice (Gen 18:25). Solomon practiced justice by vindicating the rights of a prostitute, by returning her stolen child (1 Kgs 3:28). Thus justice is something that one primarily *does*. The word "justice" is often collocated with the word "righteousness," and together they mean social justice.[277] **And to love kindness:** this combination of verb and noun is unique in the Old Testament since one usually *does* kindness.[278] The Hebrew word חֶסֶד/*ḥesed*, here "kindness," is a difficult word to translate, as it connotes a combination of concepts such as "loyalty," "mercy," "fidelity," and "steadfast love." It usually signifies help provided by a stronger to a weaker partner in a covenant relationship, the covenant relationship not always being necessary. It most often is collocated with the word "faithfulness" to the point that these two words can often be regarded as a hendiadys meaning "faithful love." The combination "to love kindness" suggests that this idea of helping someone in need should occupy a central place in one's heart and affections. Practicing justice is something that one does, but loving *ḥesed* is something that one is; and being the latter will surely result in the former. One does not help others simply because of a sense of duty but because of a genuine desire to help. **To walk humbly** is the third and last component in the trilogy of answers to the question of the good that God requires. One must walk with God in a certain manner. The adverb "humbly" can also be translated "circumspectly" and "carefully." The Hebrew word occurs in Prov 11:2: "When pride comes, then comes disgrace; but wisdom is with the humble [צְנוּעִים/*ṣᵊnûʿîm*]." Since this is a case of antithetic parallelism the word "humble" (as in NRSV) suggests a more suitable alternative than "circumspectly" or "carefully," which the versions and later Hebrew might suggest.[279] The form of the adverb in Hebrew is that of a causative verb, which suggests "to make oneself humble." The idea of walking with God is an important metaphor for Israel, and it will contrast later with

277. Moshe Weinfeld, *Social Justice in Ancient Israel and in the Ancient Near East* (Jerusalem: Magnes, 1995); and Nicholas Wolterstorff, *Justice: Rights and Wrongs* (Princeton: Princeton University Press, 2008).

278. It occurs only once in the Bible but five times in the Dead Sea Scrolls, where it means "neighborly love" (Community Rule 2.24; 5.4, 25; 8.2; 10.26). See Renaud, *Formation du Livre de Michée*, 299.

279. James Philip Hyatt, "On the Meaning and Origin of Micah 6:8," *Anglican Theological Review* 34 (1952): 236–39. But for a more balanced discussion, see McKane, *Micah*, 187–91.

walking in the statutes of the house of Omri (6:16). The most common human daily activity is walking, and thus to walk with someone is to be in fellowship with them, sharing a common set of values (cf. Amos 3:3). It is a metaphor for being in fellowship with God. Abraham is a good example in the Old Testament of living the good life as he walked in the way of Yahweh and taught that way to his children, a way particularly marked by justice and righteousness (Gen 18:19). This was the essence of the covenant and the means by which the nations would be blessed.

Interpretation—Micah's Word Then. This third movement in the book of Micah recalls the previous two movements and will later build to a crescendo. The themes struck in the preceding sections will be struck again but this time the music is louder. And one of the striking features of this text is that this section no longer seems to involve just the cities of Samaria and Jerusalem and some of their leaders (Mic 1-2) or all the leaders of Judah (Mic 3) but rather the people as a whole, as well as the nations. As the leadership has become faithless, so have the people. The negative parts of this section indicate that it is the people themselves who are addressed from the beginning. They have become totally corrupt, bereft of the most important requirements for living: justice, mercy, and fellowship with Yahweh. They are more concerned with religious performance than a quality of being.

This speech was probably first delivered at the temple where a larger number of people were gathered, since it is an indictment of them, not specific leaders. The teaching of the Torah with its sacred history, the pronouncements of the priests, the smell of the sacrifices, and the call to an ethical life all make it likely that the prophet is presenting his oracle in the sanctuary at Jerusalem. Perhaps it was during the crisis of 701 BCE while the people were trying to do penance for their wrongdoings.[280] But Micah speaks in no uncertain terms that Israel has totally missed the whole point of its election, saving history, and cult. God is more exasperated than angry: "God's sorrow and disappointment are set forth before the people."[281] The vocatives, the imperative, and the sketch of history followed by rhetorical questions contribute to a sense of divine frustration with Israel. Here the reader or hearer gets a real window into God's troubled heart as to what to do with his people. He has done everything, and they now perceive him as a wearisome burden!

The text begins with imperatives urging the people to listen to the word of Yahweh and then to defend themselves before the enduring elements of

280. J. T. Willis cited in Renaud, *Formation du Livre de Michée*, 315. See also Sweeney, *Twelve Prophets*, 394–95.
281. Heschel, *Prophets*, 126.

creation that bear witness against them. These elements are addressed and called to take their place in a universal court to hear Yahweh's case against his people. That case is presented in 6:3–5 and is really a history of redemption in which Yahweh presents his righteous acts from the liberation of the exodus, the guidance through the wilderness, the deliverance from Balaam's curse, and the gift of the promised land. The point is that Israel needs to learn a lesson from Yahweh's incredible salvation and provision. It is not as if he has given birth to them and left them without aid; he has provided for them all along the way. His goal has been that his people might know his righteous acts and somehow connect all the historical dots in their minds and reach certain conclusions. Those connections should lead them to the conclusion that they must know Yahweh, and as a result they might follow Yahweh and become like him. The provisions in the Torah were that Abraham was to be blessed because he would teach his children to walk in the way of Yahweh, which means the way of justice and righteousness. Similarly the Torah can be summed up in this way: when it is given it is clear that Israel is to image Yahweh to the nations, to be holy as he is holy, to be a nation of priests to the nations (Exod 19:5–6).[282]

In Mic 6:6–8 we see two fundamental answers to the question of how to connect the historical dots: that is, how should the individual approach God, particularly after having wronged him? A first set of questions basically poses this dilemma of how people should worship God. Then three sets of rhetorical questions that stress what the individual should bring before God are offered. Each set builds on the previous one in escalating intensity as the gifts brought to God as worship offerings increase in value until they finally become the fruit of one's own body. The point is that these sacrifices suggest not only extraordinary outward performance but also the exhausting of one's own personal resources, including one's own family—the ultimate sacrifice. Second, each gift, particularly as it increases in value, is a one-time event. But the answer that the rhetorical question expects is negative for each one. In light of all the historical dots being connected, Israel must know that Yahweh does not want more and more of the outward aspects of religion that can be found in any society and surely were also being practiced in the late eighth century in Judah. He does not want the gifts of people—no matter how extraordinary, how ornate, how sacrificial. What then does he want? How should we approach Yahweh? This again is no mystery to Israel, and the prophet presents it to humanity in general, to make sure that these requirements are not enigmatic.

What is the good that God wishes? What does God require? If the three

282. See John A. Davies, *A Royal Priesthood: Literary and Intertextual Perspectives on an Image of Israel in Exodus 19.6* (London: Continuum, 2004).

sets of wrong answers were graduated in terms of the increasing value of gifts, the three correct answers are presented in the same way, as Calvin points out, from a movement from the second table of the law emphasizing love of neighbor to the first table of the law accentuating love of God.[283] There is in this answer a "liberating simplicity."[284] Instead of burnt offerings and year-old calves, Yahweh wants people *to do justice*. That is, he wants them to be advocates for those whose rights are being denied or violated. He wants them to practice equity and fairness in their dealings so that they do not themselves violate the rights of their neighbors who are made in God's image. There is a horizontal dimension of loving one's neighbor in this command. Yahweh does justice and wants his people to do justice. Second, he wants them not just to practice *ḥesed* but to love *ḥesed*. This is remarkable, for throughout Israel's law there is the concern for practicing *ḥesed*, which means being a person of loyalty and faithfulness and someone who *helps* people particularly in their need. Thus *ḥesed* is something that a person *does*, and it often translates into providing practical help for someone in need. A human being who embodied *ḥesed* in the Bible was Ruth who helped her bereft widowed mother-in-law, going beyond the call of duty in returning with her to Israel to help her, while also helping her own dead husband obtain an heir for the family.[285]

The person who most embodies *ḥesed* in the Old Testament is Yahweh, who is described as being full of *ḥesed* and who maintains *ḥesed* for thousands of generations. In other words there is no end to his *ḥesed*—it cannot be confined to the boundaries of space and time (Ps 136). If one characteristic defines Yahweh, it is *ḥesed*. Yahweh's anger lasts a moment compared to his *ḥesed* lasting a lifetime (Ps 30:5). In the great autobiographical statement of God in the Old Testament, *ḥesed* is the only quality that is mentioned twice, and it is the means by which God maintains love for thousands of generations (Exod 34:6-7). In order for him to do this he must forgive all manner of sin, and when he does punish sin, he limits its temporal scope to three—at most—four generations! There is a short statute of limitations on his anger but none on his *ḥesed*! Thus *ḥesed* is like justice, a relational term preeminently, but it is more than advocating rights and ensuring fairness and equity, it is more a mode of being where there is a fundamental connection with another person, who is often weaker and who is crying out for help. Forgiveness and mercy are of its essence—*help* that can be depended upon in time of need.

283. Calvin, *Twelve Minor Prophets*, 343.

284. Krister Stendahl, "Central Committee WCC: Four Bible Studies," ed. Emilio Castro, *Ecumenical Review* 37 (1985): 489.

285. Note in particular Ruth 3:10. Her first *ḥesed* was to help Naomi; her last *ḥesed* was to help her deceased husband by marrying Boaz.

The third answer is the privilege of walking with God. The first question was, How should I bow myself down to come before the most high God? The final answer is to walk in a humble manner with God. The amazing truth is that it is possible to walk with the most high God—who is now called "your God"! How can that be done? Not by bringing some outlandish gift in a one-off manner but in an ongoing relationship. Practicing justice, loving *ḥesed*, and walking humbly with God are not one-off events but are characteristics of a life.

This is the final, proper response to knowing the righteous acts of Yahweh. The personal performance of one-time sacrifices totally misses the point.[286] What is necessary is the change from a life that is concerned for personal performance and what a person can offer to Yahweh, to a life in which a person gives his or her own life to Yahweh, to join him in the divine cause in the world in doing *mišpāṭ* from a *ḥesed*-filled heart.[287] This is what it means to walk with Yahweh: to engage in the things that he does. Thus Mays is right when he sees the organic connection between all of these actions: "The specific requirement is to do justice which is a way of loving mercy, which in turn is a manifestation of walking with God."[288] Moreover, this is clearly linked to Yahweh's great desire for his people, that they imitate the divine nature and behavior. Thus the whole call of Israel is to image Yahweh, to have the image of Yahweh restored in humanity. Other biblical texts speak of the importance of proper worship since it leads to becoming like God and therefore to true life. Idolatry leads to becoming like the idols and therefore the consequence is death. Brueggemann discerns insightfully that theological anthropology is at stake: "Perhaps we have no more important theological investigation than to discern in whose image we have been made."[289]

Isaiah, Micah's contemporary in Judah, had similar words expressing the need of doing justice and being an advocate of the oppressed and downtrodden. He totally rejects the cult and rituals and sacrifices if they are not congruent with a life of faithfulness with God (Isa 1:10–17). In Isaiah's critique the cult can never be a substitute for justice and righteousness. Yahweh sought "justice and mercy not oxen and sheep."[290]

---

286. Ronald T. Hyman, "Questions and Response in Micah 6:6–8," *Jewish Bible Quarterly* 33 (2005): 157–65 at 163.

287. "You offer all possibilities from your own possessions down to your own child, but one thing only you forget to offer—namely yourself!"; Rudolph, *Micha, Habakuk, Zephanja*, 112 (my translation).

288. Mays, *Micah*, 142. "I have no greater joy than to hear that my children are walking in the truth" (3 John 4 NIV).

289. W. Brueggemann, *The Prophetic Imagination* (Minneapolis: Fortress, 2001), 17.

290. Smith, *Micah, Zephaniah, and Nahum*, 24.

Earlier in the northern kingdom two prophets, Amos and Hosea, preached on the same theme, but Hosea is closer in thought to Micah when he emphasizes *ḥesed* more than *mišpāṭ*. He critiques a desire of the people to repent because he sees it as fleeting as a passing cloud or the morning dew. What God desires is a more durable and permanent attitude rather than a passing fancy:

> Your love is like a morning cloud,
> like the dew that goes away. . . .
> For I desire steadfast love and not sacrifice,
> the knowledge of God rather than burnt offerings. (Hos 6:4–6; cf. Amos
>   5:21–24)

The social consequences of the people's covenantal failure detailed earlier by Hosea are due to lack of faithfulness, *ḥesed*, and knowledge of God in the land (Hos 4:1–3). The blatant violation of the Torah in trampling the rights of people to such an extent that blood flowed in the streets of the cities of Israel is traced back to the failure of long-term commitments of faithfulness, *ḥesed*, and companionship with God in the land. Indeed Micah's idea of fellowship and walking with God is not that different from knowing God, which is connected to his expression "that you might know the saving acts of God." Like Micah, Hosea contrasts *ḥesed* and knowledge of God with sacrifice and burnt offerings.

Jesus stood firmly within the same tradition. He remarked to the religious leaders that they were more concerned with tithing the smallest herbs in their possession—dill, mint, and cumin—but in their zeal to ensure that their sacrificial offerings were presented they had omitted to do the weightier matters of the Torah, which are likewise viewed in a tripartite formula like Micah's: justice, mercy, and faith (Matt 23:23). Jesus cited Hos 6:6 twice in criticism of religious people who were zealous about matters of cult but neglectful of their brothers and sisters (Matt 9:9–13; 12:1–8).

Interpretation—Micah's Word Now. Like ancient Judah, the contemporary church oftentimes forgets the ultimate sacrifice of God and thus supplies all the wrong answers to the questions regarding true religion. The largest donors receive the most recognition in churches. Church leaders are frequently chosen for their success in the corporate world. German theologian Dietrich Bonhoeffer lamented the cheap grace that had been preached across the land in Germany in the 1930s making it ripe for the bursting of the dam of justice by the Nazi Storm Troopers.[291]

---

291. Dietrich Bonhoeffer, *The Cost of Discipleship* (New York: Touchstone, 1995), 43–44.

Churches may be concerned with fine performances of music, eloquent homilies by distinguished orators, the magnificent art captured in stained glass displays—a sort of high cultured church—or in the more popular movements, the concerns might be centered on quality praise and worship, large numbers in attendance, the ministry of the Spirit, and the hip pastor/speaker with a glass lectern and a bottle of Sierra Springs. If anyone would challenge congregations with a concern for social justice and the poor, they might well hear the reply, "Stick to religious topics! Don't talk about everyday matters! Remain in the sacred realm where God's name is adored!"[292] Micah would vehemently disagree.[293]

The quest of ancient philosophers was to seek the good life or the *summum bonum*, the foremost goal of ultimate importance or the highest end or good for human beings. The requirements of God in 6:8 do not go against the grain of human nature but contain the most fundamental insights of what it means to be human. Human beings flourish when they seek justice, love *ḥesed*, and walk with God. Another way to put this is to cite a proverb from the wisdom literature: "A person of *ḥesed* nourishes his own life; but the cruel person troubles his own nature" (Prov 11:17, my translation).

Judgment on Injustice (6:9–16)

Structure. While some commentators believe that this text "defies all attempts to trace any logical continuity,"[294] the overall structure in its general outlines can be understood as a judgment speech. The inhabitants of a city are addressed and commanded to pay attention. They are already experiencing punishment but it has not resulted in changing their ways (6:9). Then their sins are listed and described as crimes of injustice in the marketplace and violence in society—in action and word (6:10–13). The sins of injustice are listed first (6:10–12) followed by the fruits of injustice (6:13). Punishment in the form of futility curses is pronounced upon them (6:14–15), and this is followed by a brief summary of their crimes (6:16a) and the resumption of their punishment (6:16b).[295] The

---

292. Wolff, *Micah the Prophet*, 141.

293. An Asian observer makes the following relevant point: "We have freedom in many Asian countries to preach the gospel, to speak in tongues, to conduct healing ministries as long as the gospel does not disturb, the tongues do not make sense (and) the healing does not extend to the diseases of the body politic"; T. Thomas cited in J. Du Preez, "Social Justice: Motive for the Mission of the Church," *Journal of Theology for Southern Africa* 53 (1985): 44.

294. Smith, *Micah, Zephaniah, and Nahum*, 129.

295. Delbert R. Hillers, *Treaty-Curses and the Old Testament Prophets* (Rome: Pontifical Biblical Institute, 1964), 28–29.

opening imperative in the address, followed by the use of rhetorical questions to describe the sins of the people, and an emphatic particle and pronoun to indicate the transition from sin to judgment (6:14) all function as signals of the logical structure.

Literary Features. The use of rhetorical questions continues a literary theme of the previous unit. Moreover, the list of the sins of the people all end with a similar sound, and the concatenation of words shows their less than desirable practices:

עוֹד הַאֵשׁ בֵּית רָשָׁע אֹצְרוֹת רֶשַׁע	*ʿôd haʾiš bêt rāšāʿ ʾōṣərôt rešaʿ*
וְאֵיפַת רָזוֹן זְעוּמָה	*wəʾêpat rāzôn zəʿûmâ*
הַאֶזְכֶּה בְּמֹאזְנֵי רֶשַׁע	*haʾezkê bəmōʾzənê rešaʿ*
וּבְכִיס אַבְנֵי מִרְמָה	*ûbəkîs ʾabnê mirmâ*

Similarly God begins to smite the people (הַכּוֹתֶךָ/*hakkôtekā*) because of their sins (חַטֹּאתֶךָ/*haṭṭōʾtekā*), and the linguistic link emphasizes the conceptual link between punishment and sin. Moreover, as Leithart points out, Judah has been walking in the way of Ahab (אַחְאָב/*ʾaḥʾāb*; 6:16) while they are called to "Ahab" *ḥesed* (אַהֲבַת/*ʾahăbat*; 6:8).[296]

Key Words and Expressions. **It is sound wisdom to fear your name** is literally "he who sees your name is wise," or "wisdom sees your name." A slight change in the vocalization of the Hebrew produces the more natural "to fear your name is wisdom." This is a slight interjection to indicate that true religion, "the fear of Yahweh," should result in wisdom, and when it does not, the rod of discipline must be used. This is an important theme in wisdom literature (Prov 13:24; 22:15; 23:13-14; cf. Ps 89:32). **The scant measure that is accursed:** "scant measure" is a translation of the Hebrew word for "ephah," a dry measure estimated to be anywhere from 3/8 to 2/3 of a bushel, used to measure flour, barley, or other grains. The text suggests that a "short" ephah was being used, which resulted in less grain being measured out to potential buyers, who thought they were acquiring the standard measurement. Such a practice is regarded as despicable (Deut 25:14; Amos 8:5). Keil mentions the German equivalent of "a hungry purse."[297] **Wicked scales and a bag of dishonest weights:** again this is the opposite of justice and equity. False weights are kept alongside true weights in order to decrease the ephah (the grain being sold) and to increase the shekel (the money being received). An earlier prophet to the northern kingdom, Amos, had already described this criminal practice (Amos 8:5). In the Torah

---

296. Peter J. Leithart, "Doing Ahab," *First Things* (January 9, 2008).
297. Keil, *Minor Prophets*, 499.

and wisdom literature there is the constant prohibition of such injustice (Deut 25:13–16; Prov 11:1; 16:11; 20:10, 23). **Your wealthy are full of violence**: violence (חָמָס/*ḥāmās*) is the polar opposite of *ḥesed*, which results in *mišpāṭ*. The word suggests aggressive, physical attacks on people, including murder, which resulted in wealth and property taken by "naked force."[298] Its first appearance in the Bible is in the rampant destruction wreaked by humanity before the great flood. God could not sit idly by and watch his creation violated.[299] In Ezekiel the clause "the city is filled with violence" is virtually synonymous with "the land is filled with murder" (7:23). **There shall be a gnawing hunger within you:** the word for "gnawing hunger" occurs only once in the Hebrew Bible, and its meaning must be conjectured from the context. It may be from a Hebrew root (שחח/*šḥḥ*) that means "bowed over," which in turn may be related to a word in Syriac connoting "dysentery," and thus would graphically color the meaning of these futility curses.[300] **The statutes of Omri:** a similar expression is found in Jer 10:3, where idolatry is one of the "customs" of the nations ("statutes of the peoples"; cf. Lev 20:23; 2 Kgs 17:19). The "statutes of Omri" may refer to "rules" that Omri devised for the cult of Baal that the people of Israel were obligated to follow[301] or economic practices of the northern kings, "a law-code of the individualistic commercialism which was now displacing the ancient community economy of Israel's past."[302] More likely it is a general term referring to the firmly established customs and practices of the dynasty established by Omri, one of which was idolatry. Omri was the king who led Israel further into sin as a result of moving the capital from Tirzah to Samaria and thereby opening up trade with the Phoenicians on the coast (1 Kgs 16:16–24). This led to the spread of ideas, particularly when he married his son to Jezebel, a Phoenician princess who brought an entourage of Canaanite prophets with her to Israel (1 Kgs 16:31). Omri's political influence lasted long after his death since even after his dynasty had ended the Assyrians referred to an Israelite king as "son of Omri"[303] on the Black Obelisk and the Israelite nation as the *bît Ḥumrî* ("the house of Omri") in other Assyrian texts.[304] Also the Mesha Stele erected by a Moabite king refers to

---

298. Wolff, *Micah*, 194.

299. In Gen 6:6 God's "heart was deeply troubled." The only other use of the Hebrew verb in this form describes Dinah's brothers' reaction to the news of her rape (Gen 34:7)!

300. A. Ehrman, "A Note on Micah vi 14," *Vetus Testamentum* 23 (1973): 103–4.

301. W. Shaw Caldecott, "Jotham," in *International Standard Bible Encyclopedia* 3.1754.

302. R. B. Y. Scott, cited in Leslie C. Allen, "Micah's Social Concern," *Vox Evangelica* 8 (1973): 22–32 at 30.

303. James B. Pritchard, *Ancient Near Eastern Texts Relating to the Old Testament with Supplement*, 3rd ed. (Princeton: Princeton University Press, 1969), 281–82.

304. Ibid., 283–84.

King Omri's conquest of Moab.[305] "The statutes of Omri" in which the people of Judah walked were diametrically opposed to the statutes of Yahweh by which Israel was supposed to walk (cf. Mic 6:8c). The idolatry they propagated led to outrageous crimes (1 Kgs 21). Omri and his son Ahab were notorious idolaters.

Interpretation—Micah's Word Then. The second oracle in Mic 6 clearly speaks about coming judgment upon the people for their failure to practice justice, to love mercy, and to walk humbly with their God.[306] This second oracle makes a smooth transition from the cult to the culture, from the temple to the marketplace, and the divorce between Yahweh's desire and the people's desire is complete. Most commercial trade took place in the marketplace; in the course of a day most of a town's population would visit here to make purchases or to socialize. This economic hub has become a nightmare, according to Micah, as neighbors cheat each other instead of practicing *ḥesed*. Rather than walking humbly with Yahweh, the merchants walk in the statutes of Omri and Ahab. The form of the verb "to keep" (the ways of these kings) suggests a careful, intentional practice of their ways.[307] Consequently, Micah announces that Yahweh has finished arguing with his people and calling them to listen (6:1-8); he will now begin to punish them by applying the rod of discipline to show them the futility of sin (6:9-16). Those people who are interested only in profits will experience profound dissatisfaction. Whatever they try to do in the area of acquiring goods to satisfy their senses will not work: eating will not satisfy; saving will be impossible; planting seed will not return a harvest; the olive press will not yield oil; nor will the vat produce wine. All of these staples in ancient Judah will disappear at the beginning of the punishment, and the end will be exile.

By virtue of this oracle's position as the second unit in this section of the book, it provides a smooth segue from the temple and worship to the marketplace and work. There Yahweh had a dispute with his people, but it never reached resolution in judgment. Now it does. His people are called to hear again (שִׁמְעוּ/*šimʿû*; cf. 6:1, 2) Yahweh's voice (קוֹל/*qôl*; cf. 6:1c).[308] Their actions show that there has been a complete disconnect between the demands of Yahweh (6:8) and their behavior (6:10-12).[309] Moreover the people experienced a salva-

---

305. Ibid., 320–21.

306. "Both [6:9–16 and 7:1–6] in turn lay bare the absence of justice and loyalty in the life of the people"; Mays, *Micah*, 10.

307. The only other time this verb form appears is Ps 18:23 (= 2 Sam 22:24) where it suggests care in keeping oneself from sin.

308. The argument is that of John T. Willis, "The Structure, Setting, and Interrelationship of the Pericopes in the Book of Micah" (PhD dissertation, Vanderbilt University, 1966), 259–64.

309. Cf. the comments of Wolff: "After 6:8, vv. 9ff. at first appear to be a concrete and de-

tion history so that they might know the mighty acts of Yahweh; now because of their behavior they will know Yahweh giving them over to ruin. Finally Yahweh had begun their history by bringing up his people out of Egypt; now he will end it by giving them over to ruin.

Such blatantly unjust practices on the part of the Israelites, which lead to their houses being treasure troves of wealth, is a false picture of reality. In reality such homes are havens of wickedness. The wealth is all stained by the violence and dishonesty that acquired it. The wealth has curses attached to it—the curses of the covenant! In the various curse lists in the Bible there are similar futility maledictions, whether in Leviticus (26:16b, 20) or Deuteronomy (28:30–31). Other prophets seem to major on futility curses, and the theological idea is simply the pointlessness of sin. It does not deliver on its promises (cf. Amos 5:11–12; Zeph 1:13). The prophet Jeremiah remarks, "My people have committed two sins: They have forsaken me, the spring of living water, and have dug their own cisterns, broken cisterns that cannot hold water" (Jer 2:13 NIV). Similarly Haggai's words to the beleaguered postexilic community major on the same theme (Hag 1:5–6).

But it is the wisdom book of Ecclesiastes that strikes most sharply this note of futility apart from the fear of God. The eye is never satisfied with seeing nor the ear with hearing (1:8), nor is the purse ever satisfied with enough money (5:10), nor the mouth with food (6:7). In the New Testament the same feature of wisdom teaching occurs when Jesus speaks of those who perish while saving their lives and those whose lives are saved while losing them (Matt 16:25). The pursuit of life leads to death, and the pursuit of death results in life. The quest for self-fulfillment leads to endless dissatisfaction. When Jesus speaks to the woman from Samaria at the well of Jacob, he points out to her that going back to the same well again and again will never relieve her thirst. It is only when she drinks from the living water that her thirst will be quenched (John 4). James makes similar statements about the wicked. Their lust is never satisfied (James 4:2–3; 5:2–3).

Interpretation—Micah's Word Now. It was Augustine who formulated the statement "you have made us for yourself, and we will not find rest until we find rest in you" (*Confessions* 1.1). This is a short prayer that concisely expresses the truth of Micah's oracle. When people put their trust in material considerations, they are never fully satisfied. Nevertheless this idol drives them to cheat in the marketplace and to fill their homes with the treasures of violence. But the God of Micah was "no Olympian, remote from everyday living. He is the Lord of

tailed exposition of that verse"; *Micah*, 198. See also Sweeney (*Twelve Prophets*, 394) who sees the seamless connection between this unit and the previous one.

the shopping center, whose claim over his people extends to the most mundane of life's duties."[310] One of the judgments in Western culture for the vast network of sweatshops and slave industries that supply the Western world with its goods and luxuries is the profound dissatisfaction that can be seen in the vacant faces of those walking the halls of the supermalls, zombielike, listening to the omnipresent Muzak. The truth of this point is seen in the ubiquitous tabloids, talk shows, newspapers, and various media outlets in Western society. Lance Armstrong has to keep racing to prove himself and must return to competition to do it again even when much older. He sits in his room with all of his titles and championships staring him in the face and still it is not enough. Michael Jordan's life is over because basketball is over. He states, "I like reminiscing. I do it now watching basketball more than anything. Man, I wish I was playing right now . . . I would give up everything now to go back and play the game of basketball."[311] But at the age of fifty it is impossible. The central theme in the novels of American writer Walker Percy is, "Why does man feel so sad in the twentieth century? Why does man feel so sad in the very age when, more than any other age, he has succeeded in satisfying his needs and making the world over for his own use?"[312] Why in spite of so many things and so much plenty are people so sad in the modern world? Calvin argued that the human mind is a factory of idols, and the chief problem with an idol is that it is not God and therefore cannot ultimately satisfy the human heart.[313]

The celebrity culture in the Western world is one whole failure to satisfy the desires of the human heart. Perhaps the reason why there has been such a failure in marriage and other institutions in the West is that they have been given the dubious responsibility of becoming the bearers of ultimate meaning. It is interesting that the songs and the poems of the modern world are haunting. From the pop culture icons who glory in the satiation of every sensual desire, we hear the words ringing perhaps prophetically, "I can't get no satisfaction." Or, "I still haven't found what I have been looking for." The words of these modern visionaries are "written on the subway walls," and they are faint echoes of the book of Micah. When a people abandons God, the prophet comes and says, "You will eat but not be satisfied."

310. Leslie C. Allen, "Micah's Social Concern," *Vox Evangelica* 8 (1973): 22-32 at 29.

311. Wright Thompson, "Michael Jordan Has Not Left the Building"; available online at espn.go.com/espn/story/_/page/Michael-Jordan/michael-jordan-not-left-building.

312. See, e.g., the essay "The Delta Factor" in Walker Percy, *The Message in the Bottle: How Queer Man Is, How Queer Language Is, and What One Has to Do with the Other* (New York: Open Road Media, 2011), first published in *Southern Review* (Winter 1975): 29-64 at 29.

313. John Calvin, *Institutes of Christian Religion,* ed. John T. McNeil, trans. Ford Lewis Battles (Philadelpha: Westminster, 1960), 1.108.

Meanwhile in Africa as the message of faith has caught fire on this continent, there are now 360 million Christians—a growth percentage of incredible proportions given that there were 10 million Christians on the entire continent in 1900. There are many reasons for the growth of Christianity, but one of the main ones is given by an African author describing the new faith of an Igbo man:

> It was not the mad logic of the Trinity that captivated him. He did not understand it. It was the poetry of the new religion, something felt in the marrow. . . . He felt relief within as the hymn poured into his parched soul, The words of the hymn were like drops of frozen rain melting on the dry palate of the panting earth.[314]

Total Corruption of the Nation (7:1–7)

Structure. This lament is similar to the mournful dirge with which the book begins (1:8–16), and from the point of view of its placement in the book, it is an intentional echo of that earlier text. As the first lament stressed the grief poured out because of the coming judgment in 701 BCE, this lament stresses the total corruption of society, which will result in a coming judgment necessary to purge and renew Israel to prepare it to take up its role to be a light to the nations. The lament begins with a rare interjection, and it is followed by agricultural metaphors describing the sorry state of society: a vineyard bereft of grapes and a barren fig tree. To reinforce the metaphor that righteous people in Judah "are no more to be found than ripe fruit,"[315] eight descriptions of people follow: the initial two classes are the kinds of people absent from Judah—the righteous and the faithful—and the next six groups are the types of persons present in Judah—the incorrigible and the corrupt. A further agrarian metaphor (a brier) describes the remaining population. Then a warning of coming judgment follows, with an exhortation not to trust anyone in such tumultuous times. Finally, against this dark background the prophet looks to God in hope.

Literary Features. The text begins and ends with a first-person reference. In the first case the prophet is lamenting on behalf of the people who need to confess their sin over what has happened in their nation. Interestingly, in Mic 1 the people cry over the judgment they will experience, and here in Mic 7 they cry over their moral condition. The wider literary context suggests that the

---

314. Philip Jenkins, *The Next Christendom: The Coming of Global Christianity* (New York: Oxford University Press, 2011), 57.

315. Hagstrom, *Coherence of the Book of Micah*, 96.

prophet is also speaking on behalf of the city of Jerusalem since the "I" is later determined to be feminine ("Where is the LORD *your* God?"; 7:10b),[316] and in the previous context the judgment oracle was aimed at the city.

There are a number of significant wordplays in the text. The third line ends a description of barren vines (אֵין־אֶשְׁכּוֹל/*'ên-'eškôl*), and the beginning of the next line has the verb "to eat" (לֶאֱכוֹל/*le'ĕkôl*). This rhyme emphasizes the connection between grapes and eating, stressing that this natural act did not occur because of the *absence* of fruit. Similarly there are no righteous human beings (בָּאָדָם/*bā'ādām*) in the land; instead, people prey upon human blood (לְדָמִים/*lədāmîm*). Now that the righteous (יָשָׁר/*yāšār*) are gone, the righteousness of those who are left (יָשָׁר/*yāšār*) is like a thorn hedge (מִמְּסוּכָה/*mimməsûkâ*). As a result the day of their appointed judgment (פְּקֻדָּתְךָ/*pəquddātəkā*) comes, the time of their confusion (מְבוּכָתָם/*məbûkātām*). God is the one who watches to gather the fruit of the vine (הָיִיתִי כְּאָסְפֵּי־קַיִץ/*hāyîtî kə'ospê-qayiṣ*), and when there is none, his people are to watch for the day of judgment (מְצַפֶּיךָ/*məṣap-pêkā*), but Micah and the remnant will look beyond that day and watch (אֲצַפֶּה/*'ăṣappeh*) for Yahweh, who is the light in the darkness. Powerful onomatopoeic alliteration is delivered to the ear with the slithering and slimy procurement of bribes by corrupt leaders: הַשַּׂר שֹׁאֵל וְהַשֹּׁפֵט בַּשִׁלּוּם/*haśśar šō'ēl wəhaššōpēṭ baššillûm*. The use of similar alliterative patterns in the description of the family members indicates linguistically the natural bonds between members of the family and hence the unnatural treachery: כִּי־בֵן מְנַבֵּל אָב/*kî-bēn mənabbēl 'āb*.

Finally, it is God's great desire to find אִוְּתָה נַפְשִׁי/*'iwwətâ napšî* "good fruit"—that is, *ḥesed ûmišpāṭ*—in the life of his people to satisfy his hunger for righteousness, but the desire for the great person in Judah, the leadership, is simply to find personal profit to satiate greed (הַוַּת נַפְשׁוֹ הוּא/*hawwat napšô hû'*).

The literary structure of the text is generally limited to the use of pairs of complementary lines but at key points there is a triplicate set of clauses to accentuate an activity. This occurs near the end of the unit to produce a penultimate climax (printed in NRSV on four lines):

> Put no trust in a friend,
>> have no confidence in a loved one;
> guard the doors of your mouth
>> from her who lies in your embrace.

Then a set of four clauses builds to a summative climax indicating the moral morass in Judah:

---

316. The pronoun is second-person feminine singular.

For the son treats the father with contempt,
>   the daughter rises up against her mother,
>   the daughter-in-law against her mother-in-law;
>   your enemies are members of his own household.

A final triplicate reveals the only one who can be trusted:

> But as for me, I will look to the LORD,
> I will wait for the God of my salvation;
> my God will hear me.

Key Words and Expressions. **The vintage** is an important image used to describe Israel. God was the one who planted his people as a vineyard, his people, so that it would bless the world with their vintage—the best grapes—and bring joy to the world with its wine (Ps 80; Isa 5:1–7; Jer 2:21; Ezek 17; Hos 10). The resulting grapes and wine were to be in fact justice and righteousness but as Isaiah remarked, they were bitter (Isa 5:1–7), and as far as Micah was concerned, they were nonexistent. **The faithful have disappeared:** this word is from the same root as the quality that above all God desires: loving-kindness. It can either mean the one whose chief characteristic is *ḥesed* or one who is the object of God's *ḥesed*. It probably means the former in this context since it is the one indispensable quality necessary for the flourishing of human life, and this kind of person is missing from the land: a person who is faithful in love.[317] **They hunt each other with nets:** the use of a net for hunting and fishing for humans has a long history, being first traced back to 2400 BCE to Eannatum of Lagash, in the famous Stele of the Vultures. Eannatum's victory over the neighboring city of Umma depicts his god, Ningirsu, carrying the enemy away in a hunting net.[318] Micah is saying people are hunted down like animals in Judah. **Their hands are skilled to do evil** is literally "two hands upon evil to do well (diligently)." Usually it takes practice to learn how to become right-handed or left-handed, and it is rare for people to be ambidextrous, but here in Judah the people have learned to become ambidextrous in doing evil.[319] **They pervert justice** is a *hapax le-*

---

317. "The *ḥāsîd* is someone who has entered the *ḥesed* relationship and who demonstrates his obedience by loyalty to the requirements of the covenant"; Thomas E. McComiskey, "Exegetical Notes: Micah 7," *Trinity Journal* 2 (1981): 63.

318. Harriet Crawford, *Sumer and the Sumerians* (Cambridge: Cambridge University Press, 1991), 165.

319. There is evidence of ambidextrous soldiers in the Nubian army from Micah's time. See Nadav Na'aman, *Ancient Israel and Its Neighbors: Interaction and Counteraction* (Winona Lake: Eisenbrauns, 2005), 104–5.

gomenon but its cognate noun means "rope" or "cord." Thus all of these leaders are viewed as complicit with each other, all "bound" together, in a conspiracy of crime. Sweeney pertinently finds a connection with the following description of thorns: "Goodness and righteousness are so interwoven or tangled up with evil that they have become like thornbushes that are impossible to untangle."[320] **The day of their sentinels, of their punishment, has come:** "the day" is a day of judgment. There may be an allusion to "the day of visitation" (punishment) portended in Exod 32:34 for the rebellious golden calf generation.[321] Sentinels on the walls of fortified cities would sound an alarm if an enemy approached. Prophets sometimes described themselves as religious sentinels who sounded spiritual alarms to warn the people of imminent danger (Ezek 3:17; 33:2, 6, 7; Hos 9:8). **Put no trust in a friend:** the new chain of imperatives presupposes the crisis of judgment. There is evidence in both the prophets and ancient Near Eastern literature that such a total breakdown in community was eschatological, portending the end of an era.[322] Jesus used this text in the Gospel of Matthew when he was thinking of a coming eschatological crisis of judgment, and he warned that the most intimate family members could not be trusted (Matt 10:34–38). One could have faith only in God. **But as for me, I will look to the LORD:** the word "look" is the intensive form of a verb and is used for someone who observes carefully and expectantly watches for a sign. It is the same word for "watchmen" used above (cf. Isa 21:6). "In a world where even neighbor and family are not to be trusted (vv. 5f.), only God is left. But *he* is there."[323]

Interpretation—Micah's Word Then. Micah places in the mouth of his beloved city a national lament because it had lost its true spiritual identity and thus was no longer a witness *to* the nations. This lament was probably delivered at a social gathering where the general population and its leaders congregated, perhaps on a national festive holiday at the temple or in the gate of the city. Historically it may have been given before 701 BCE since there is the expectation of judgment in the text, and the social and moral conditions are absolutely abysmal. Perhaps the Assyrian army was ravaging the countryside—even outside the walls of Jerusalem as the oracle was being given. As the people were praying, Micah stands up and laments and gives them a type of confession: to recognize "the decadence, malevolence and domestic disorder"[324] of their society, their complete corruption, and the total breakdown in community life that has hap-

---

320. Sweeney, *Twelve Prophets*, 408.

321. I am indebted for this reference to Bo Ivar Reicke, "Liturgical Traditions in Mic. 7," *Harvard Theological Review* 60 (1967): 349–67 at 357.

322. Ibid., 357–61.

323. Mays, *Micah*, 156.

324. McKane, *Micah*, 214.

pened, and to look not to any human being for any hope but to Yahweh, their only hope in this crisis. They thus had to fully accept their condition.

It is probably no accident that the lack of fruit in this metaphor directly follows the previous oracle where the people futilely attempted to produce crops, while walking in the statutes of Omri. The oracle amplifies the volume of the previous oracle (6:9–16), in which there was no *mišpāṭ*, no *ḥesed*, but only walking in the paths of Omri and Ahab. In this text the themes are continued: now the harvester, Yahweh, laments when he finds no fruit for all his labors. This is because no one practices *ḥesed* in the land, the judicial officials are corrupt, and instead of walking with God, people are hunting each other in an ancient parody of *The Hunger Games*.

It is also no accident that this lamentation is placed at the end of the book as the last description of the people of Judah before the eschatological judgment of refining and renewal. This is not only a darker description than that of the previous oracle,[325] it is the darkest in the book. If any reader of the book had doubts about the moral wasteland of ancient Judah, those doubts are now put completely to rest. In particular the qualities that Yahweh desired in 6:8 have vanished: *ḥesed* and *mišpāṭ* and fellowship with God.[326] No more damning description of the people could be presented.

Here there is no "community with a common focus on the God of Zion but fragmented by appetite and self-interest. It is a community that feeds off suffering brought about by injustice . . . marked by loss, grief and the ruin of its land and life within it."[327] The society has degenerated over a period of time to the point that no redeeming qualities are left. In the story of the judgment of Sodom and Gomorrah, Abraham interceded for the city, arguing with God not to destroy the city if there were ten righteous people left. Such intercession would not have worked in Micah's time. Thus in the coming judgment the prophet urges distrust of any individual and even the members of the most trusted and stable institution in society—the household. There is no sanctuary anywhere. Except Yahweh.

Just as Yahweh has looked for fruit on the empty vine, and Judah could expect nothing but judgment because of the presence of evil in the land, the prophet envisions himself as the nation and looks beyond and above the moral morass to Yahweh to locate hope. The transition to 7:7 signals a watershed moment in the third section of Micah and in the book as a whole.[328] When the

---

325. As Rudolph correctly notes; *Micha, Habakuk, Zephanja*, 126.

326. Ibid., 123.

327. David J. Reimer, "The Prophet Micah and Political Society," in *Thus Speaks Ishtar of Arbela: Prophecy in Israel, Assyria, and Egypt in the Neo-Assyrian Period*, ed. R. P. Gordon and H. M. Barstad (Winona Lake: Eisenbrauns, 2013), 203–24 at 224.

328. Hagstrom, *Coherence of the Book of Micah*, 103.

last vestige of human confidence has been taken away, Judah finds that God is still there. He is the one who can inspire hope. And he will eventually hear the cries of the nation that will come to him. And so the last speech of the book is not Judah's lament for its condition (7:1-7) but what it needs to cry to Yahweh in order for him to hear its prayer (7:8-20).

Throughout the book there has been the address from Yahweh to Israel to hear (1:2; 3:1; 6:1), and now Yahweh provides Judah words to speak to him so that he will hear (7:7, 8-20)! Why would he do this when it has been so unfaithful? Because a heart that is truly penitent will always find a listening ear with God. Because behind the thick curtain of divine wrath is a God whose tender mercies are great![329]

Throughout the prophets there is the growing lament that although the nation had auspicious beginnings it had become corrupt with little hope. If Micah could not find a faithful person in Judah, Hosea experienced the same futile search in the northern kingdom a few decades earlier: "There is no faithfulness, no love, no acknowledgment of God in the land" (4:1-2). Isaiah, Micah's contemporary, also used the metaphor of a vineyard to describe the sorry state of affairs that was the nation of Judah. Yahweh had done everything possible to produce a fruitful vineyard to bless the nations but it had yielded bitter grapes. In a poignant wordplay, Isaiah said that Yahweh had hoped for right (מִשְׁפָּט/mišpāṭ) but obtained instead blight (מִשְׂפָּח/mišpāḥ), had expected the good (צְדָקָה/ṣədāqâ) but got instead blood (צְעָקָה/ṣəʿāqâ) (5:1-7, esp. 5:7). Jeremiah, like Diogenes in Greece, began a search for an honest man and could not find one in the entire city of Jerusalem: "Go up and down the streets of Jerusalem, look around and consider, search through her squares. If you can find but one person who deals honestly and seeks the truth, I will forgive this city" (5:1 NIV; see also 9:2-5).

Jesus applies this text in a different way as he fortified his disciples for coming persecution. They will experience difficult times because the gospel will be divisive, even dividing intimate family members from one another:

> Do not suppose that I have come to bring peace to the earth. I did not come to bring peace, but a sword. For I have come to turn
>
> > a man against his father,
> > > a daughter against her mother,
> > a daughter-in-law against her mother-in-law—
> > > a man's enemies will be the members of his own household.

---

329. Cf. Gerhard von Rad, *Old Testament Theology: The Theology of Israel's Historical Traditions*, trans. D. M. G. Stalker (Louisville: Westminster John Knox, 2001), 1.318.

> Anyone who loves his father or mother more than me is not worthy of me;
> anyone who loves his son or daughter more than me is not worthy of me;
> and anyone who does not take up his cross and follow me is not worthy of
> me. (Matt 10:34–38 NIV)

This text is used differently by Jesus but it also portends an eschatological crisis. The coming of Jesus forced people to make ultimate decisions that cause inevitable divisions. When individuals make the decision to follow Jesus, they encounter intense opposition.

Paul uses similar passages from the Hebrew Scriptures to show that what was true for Israel at this particular time is also true for the entire human race—everyone has been infected by the sin virus (Rom 3:10–18). Nevertheless, Paul is able to move beyond this diagnosis to the cure that God provided in Jesus Christ, the righteous sin bearer, who bore God's judgment for humanity's redemption (3:20–26).

Interpretation—Micah's Word Now. While Micah is not specifically teaching a doctrine of original sin, it is clear that cultures can degenerate as a result of corruption and moral decay. One scholar writes about the tenth generation being the end point for a decaying culture.[330] When there were no longer ten righteous people in Sodom, the judge of all the earth did justice (Gen 18:16–33). The Israelites had to wait four hundred years before conquering Canaan until the sins of the Amorites cried out for justice (15:13).[331] Wolff believed that God was judging Germany with Allied bombs because of the horrific sin of his country. He once used the story of Sodom and Gomorrah to urge righteous Germans to leave or be struck with fire from heaven, in this case, from the Allied Bombers.[332] Western media plays a significant role in the pollution of society. It hunts for stars to turn into celebrities, to use them and abuse them, all the while turning them into agents of destructive influence on vulnerable youth. And it accepts absolutely no responsibility for the moral pollution it pumps into society from the effluent of its sewers. A few years ago a premier screening of the *Dark Knight Rises* was shown in a theater in Aurora, Colorado. In the theatre a young man dressed up as The Joker massacred twelve people and wounded dozens more with a high-powered rifle in an act of horrific violence that simply mirrored the violence on the screen. Out of respect for the victims, the production company suspended the publishing of its earnings for a few days. The actors who starred

330. George Mendenhall, *The Tenth Generation: The Origins of the Biblical Tradition* (Baltimore: Johns Hopkins University Press, 1974).

331. The four hundred years can equate to ten generations of forty years each.

332. Hans Walter Wolff, *The Old Testament and Christian Preaching,* trans. Margaret Kohl (Philadelphia: Fortress, 1986), 18–22.

in the movie even visited some of the victims to express their sympathies, with absolutely no sense of shame or personal responsibility. If gratuitous violence in Western culture is a disease, it is an epidemic and the media accepts precious little responsibility for the contagion.

In 1965, the great Canadian philosopher George Grant wrote a landmark book on Canadian politics entitled *Lament for a Nation*, in which he lamented Canada's loss of true nationalism as it had been swallowed up by the liberal capitalism of the United States.[333] Here, Micah places in the mouth of his beloved city a national lament, not for it being assimilated into the global influence of other nations, but rather because it had lost its true spiritual identity and thus was no longer a witness to the nations. Perhaps the problem lies at the door of the church itself, which has not been the salt and light it was called to be. But Micah's last word in this lament points to the ultimate solution: thank God for God, that in the midst of such corruption, human beings can look to the Lord to hear their cry. "This precipitous pessimism, in spite of everything, drives our prophet not to despair but into the arms of God."[334] That is the perfect segue into the final section of Micah.

Israel's Hope in Yahweh's Grace (7:8-20)

Structure. The last unit consists of five stanzas (7:8–10, 11–13, 14–15, 16–17, 18–20) and it is in the form of a hymn that seeks to recall major elements of the book of Micah and use them in a liturgical format to address Yahweh in order to obtain a response. Each stanza is clearly demarcated structurally. Two of them begin with urgent imperatival forms: 7:8–10, 14–15. One begins with nominal clauses (7:11–13), another with prefixed verb forms indicating a future action yet to be accomplished (7:16–17), and the final unit begins with a rhetorical question that echoes the name of Micah from the beginning of the book (7:18–20). The structure is artistically organized into a chiastic pattern as follows:

A   anger of Yahweh, trampling of enemy, and rhetorical question (7:8–10)
B   Yahweh rebuilds Jerusalem and gathers nations (7:11–13)
C   Yahweh shepherds Israel into luxurious land (7:14–15)
B'   Yahweh humbles nations and they believe (7:16–17)
A'   rhetorical question, anger of Yahweh, trampling of enemy (7:18–20)

---

333. George Grant, *Lament for a Nation: The Defeat of Canadian Nationalism*, 40th anniversary ed. (Montreal: McGill-Queen's University Press, 2005).

334. Wolff, *Micah*, 210.

The final stanza concludes with a description of seven characteristics of Yahweh that provide the final answer of the book to any and every question about Yahweh's identity. Within the text then there is a steady progression from punishment and defeat to rebuilding and restoration to a salvific influence on the nations and finally a focus on a magnificent picture of God! Thus the question that is asked by the enemy and is understood to be a rhetorical question by the enemy in the first stanza is answered in the last stanza by a rhetorical question, which actually provides an answer. Thus the question of the enemy—"Where is Yahweh your God?"—is answered by Micah with the question: "Who is like Yahweh?" Then this question is answered with seven distinguishing divine characteristics: pardon, forgiveness, temperance, *ḥesed*, mercy, conquest of sin, and its complete abolition.

In this final speech of the book, there is a conscious echoing of earlier speeches, thus making this section a fitting conclusion. The first unit recalls the judgment sections that are increasingly amplified in the book (1:2–2:11; 3:1–12; 6:1–7:7), the second stanza the regathering of the exiles and the rebuilding of Jerusalem (2:12–13; 4:6–7; 5:1–15), the third stanza the shepherding motif and the exodus (2:12–13; 4:6–7; 5:1–15; 6:1–5), the fourth stanza the humbling of the nations and their salvation (4:1–5; 5:15), and the fifth stanza the God of transcendence (1:1, 2–16) and the God of *mišpāṭ* and *ḥesed* (6:6–8).

Literary Features. In a book rife with wordplays and various poetic techniques, it would be natural to assume that this last text would be a study in the use of such techniques. Thus it is no accident that such a piece of poetry was chosen to conclude the book. It is anchored firmly in place by a tight chiasm in its first line, which links it to the last statement of the previous unit. Thus it is clearly the response to the statement "my God will hear me." Consequently the structure is apparent:

my God will hear me	יִשְׁמָעֵנִי אֱלֹהָי	*yišmāʿēnî ʾĕlōhāy*
do not rejoice over me, My Enemy!	אַל־תִּשְׂמְחִי אֹיַבְתִּי לִי	*ʾal-tiśməḥî ʾōyabtî lî*

The statement "my God will hear me" is the reason why Israel can now begin its speech with the words: "Do not rejoice over me, My Enemy!" Because of faith in God the previous futility curses are turned into the opposite—irrevocable blessings: though I fall, then I rise; though I sit in darkness, Yahweh will be my light! Thus Yahweh is walking with Israel in the darkness, and he will put it to rights and vindicate its cause.

There is a gradual progression from sitting in the darkness of judgment where the key word is darkness to "the day of building your walls and the day of extending your boundaries" and then to the wonders of the divine acts in the past "as in the days when you came out of Egypt." This is followed by a day when Israel will be vindicated by the nations who will finally fear Yahweh "in the latter days." This time will be concluded by the cessation of judgment and the complete revelation of Yahweh's character as displayed in the promises made to the patriarchs "in days long ago" (מִימֵי קֶדֶם/*mîmê qedem*). These closing words resoundingly echo a key phrase in the middle of the book that was a promise of salvation. The messianic ruler had "goings forth from of old, from ancient days" (מִקֶּדֶם מִימֵי עוֹלָם/*miqqedem mîmê ʿôlām*). This is the eschatological shepherd who is the one who will rule in the latter days unto the ends of the earth, guaranteeing that his people will no longer sit in the darkness but rather under their own fig trees and vines (cf. 5:4; 4:4; 7:8).

There is also a focus on "seeing" in the text and similar-sounding words like "shepherd" and "fear." In the first stanza, though Israel cannot see in the darkness, Yahweh will be a light, and this will eventually lead to Yahweh bringing the nation out of the darkness into the light and Israel seeing (אֶרְאֶה/*ʾerʾeh*) Yahweh's salvation. Consequently Israel's enemy will see (וְתֵרֶא/*watēʾreʾ*) its shame, and Israel will then see its enemy's demise (עֵינַי תִּרְאֶינָה בָּהּ/*ʿênay tirʾennâ bâh*). In the future God will cause Israel to see (אַרְאֶנּוּ/*ʾarʾennû*) wonders as in the days of Egypt, and two of those wonders will be to experience (אַרְאֶנּוּ/*ʾarʾennû*) the divine shepherd's care that leads to his flock feeding (יִרְעוּ/*yirʿû*) in green pastures. In turn the nations will see (יִרְאוּ/*yirʾû*) Israel's salvation and be ashamed but they will end up fearing (וְיִרְאוּ/*wayirāʾû*) Yahweh and worshiping him. The text concludes with a grand vision for everyone to see Yahweh and his seven qualities, the central one of which is his *ḥesed*:

> who pardons sin
>> forgives the transgression of the remnant of his inheritance
>>> he does not stay angry forever
>>>> but delights to show *ḥesed*
>>> he will again have compassion on us
>> he will tread our sins under our feet
> you will throw all our iniquities into the depths of the sea

The essential qualities that God requires of humanity are qualities that essentially define his nature. He requires that human beings do justice (עֲשׂוֹת מִשְׁפָּט/*ʿăśôt mišpāṭ*) and love *ḥesed* (אַהֲבַת חֶסֶד/*ʾahăbat ḥesed*). Thus in the first stanza God will do justice for Israel (וְעָשָׂה מִשְׁפָּטִי/*waʿāśâ mišpāṭî*), and in the last he will forgive Israel and save the nation because he loves *ḥesed* (כִּי־חָפֵץ חֶסֶד הוּא/*kî-ḥāpēṣ ḥesed hûʾ*).

Key Words and Expressions. **Do not rejoice over me, my enemy:** the key interpretive questions are: Who are the referents in this passage? Who is the "I"? And who is the "enemy"? The identity of the "I" is probably identical to the referent in 7:7, where it was established that it was the prophet as a representative of the nation. It is Mother Israel or Daughter Jerusalem experiencing a period of intense labor and pain before giving birth. As for the enemy, there are possible references within Micah to enemies: wealthy landowners (2:2), others within the society (7:5), foreign nations (5:8). Since, however, the form is a unique feminine form, it is most likely a reference to a conquering city such as Nineveh or Babylon. In 4:10 during a time of crisis in the future, the prophet compares Israel's exile in Babylon to the labor of a woman giving birth to a child:

> Writhe and groan, O daughter Zion,
>   like a woman in labor;
> for now you shall go forth from the city
>   and camp in the open country;
>   you shall go to Babylon.
> There you shall be rescued,
>   there the LORD will redeem you
>   from the hands of your enemies.

Here Babylon is identified by the prophet as being part of the enemies of Israel. In Isaiah, Babylon is called similarly a virgin daughter, who has enslaved the world with her beauty and promise (Isa 47). Babylon was the prominent enemy of Judah, having captured it, destroying its capital city and its temple, and imprisoning its people in Israel. It had become a virtual type of evil as representing everything that was at cross purposes with the kingdom of God. But the enemy could also be Assyria viewed as a symbol of evil as well (cf. 5:5–6). Thus the enemy probably is a typological figure representing the opposite of Daughter Jerusalem. **I must bear the indignation of the LORD, because I have sinned against him:** Judah now has become aware of all its sin, which has been cataloged in the book, and confesses that it will suffer the just judgment of God. **Until he takes my side and executes judgment for me:** ironically God had a case against Judah but there will come a time when he will take up its case and execute judgment for it (literally "do my justice"). The remnant of Judah realizes the promise of God, and though it has suffered precisely because the people had not done justice, or upheld God's cause in the world, God will still fulfill his ultimate purposes for the remnant of his people. **I will see his vindication** means "I will experience his salvation." When a list of saving acts for Israel was rehearsed, the people were told that these were done so that they might know

183

the righteous acts of the Lord, or his saving victories (6:5). **Then my enemy will see, and shame will cover her:** the enemy will see the salvation of God's people. Later the nations will have the same vision and the same experience (7:16), and their shame is described further: impotence, speechlessness, deafness, crawling upon the ground. It is a picture of total abasement. **Where is the Lord your God?** This rhetorical question is often asked by foreign oppressors who wish to place the absence of Israel's God right in the nation's face so to speak (Ps 42:3, 10; 115:2; Joel 2:17).[335] Reworded in the indicative the statement reads, "Your God is powerless!" Similarly Rabshakeh, the emissary of Assyria, presented Jerusalem with the ultimatum to surrender. He attempted to persuade Hezekiah and his people by providing a "hit list" of peoples that Assyria had already conquered and asking rhetorical questions that emphasized the impotence of the gods of these nations (2 Kgs 18:33–35). The enemy in this stanza was doing exactly the same thing, stressing the impotence of Judah's God. The remainder of the stanza and the poem answers this very question. **Now she will be trodden down like the mire of the streets:** Israelite history provided a perfect precedent of an evil queen, an enemy of the people of God, who suffered this very fate. After asking a rhetorical question to Jehu, Jezebel was hurled down to the ground in the street below and trampled by the horses of Jehu's chariot (2 Kgs 9:30–37). **The boundary shall be far extended** is literally "that is a day a rule is extended." Many translations like the NRSV understand the word translated "rule" as boundary, suggesting that the boundaries of Jerusalem will be enlarged. Normally the word is used to indicate the defining of a limit such as a statute or law, and sometimes it means a spatial or temporal boundary.[336] But in a similar passage in 4:3 the word "extend" refers to royal decisions that have affected distant nations, who have been brought under the ambit of Yahweh's instruction. The people mentioned here can be either the Jewish exiles returning home and coming from different lands[337] or the nations in fulfillment of the promise in 4:1–4. Calvin remarks that Jerusalem "would become the metropolis of the world."[338] The language of Assyria—from the far east—and

335. Elijah does essentially the same thing to the prophets of Baal (1 Kgs 18:27).

336. Spatial in Isa 5:14; Jer 5:22; Prov 8:29; Job 26:10; 38:10; and Ps 148:6; temporal in Job 14:5, 13. I follow Sweeney (*Twelve Prophets*, 410–11) here, who argues for the extension of the royal rule. Calvin understands the text to mean the "decree [of foreign nations] shall be made far" and thus far removed; *Twelve Minor Prophets*, 384. Consideration of 4:3 suggests the implausibility of this reading.

337. Smith, *Micah, Zephaniah, and Nahum*, 149–50.

338. Calvin, *Twelve Minor Prophets*, 387. Some commentators suggest that a temporal reference is indicated: "that day—distant is the date." But the context suggests otherwise. See Smith, *Micah, Zephaniah, and Nahum*, 149–50.

Egypt—from the far west—and from "sea to sea" and "mountain to mountain" suggests that what is envisioned is the nations coming to Jerusalem in fulfillment of 4:1-4. But this need not exclude the regathering of exiles (cf. 4:6-7). The mention of Egypt and Assyria bears a remarkable similarity to their inclusion among the people of God in Isa 19:23-25 and Ps 87. **The earth will be desolate because of its inhabitants, for the fruit of its doings** echoes a truth found in other passages of Scripture: morality affects ecology. Thus the earth is cursed as a result of the first sin (Gen 3:17-19; 4:10-12), and the ground will not cover Abel's blood (4:10). For the prophets the same truth is found (Hos 4:1-3; Jer 12:4) as in other biblical writings (Ps 107:34). Micah is probably mentioning the consequences of the nations not submitting to Jerusalem.[339] **Shepherd your people with your staff, the flock that belongs to you, which lives alone in a forest in the midst of a garden land; let them feed in Bashan and Gilead as in the days of old:** this is a tender image of Moses leading his sheep in the wilderness, and thus a touching metaphor for God and his people. God was described earlier in the book as the one who would gather his people like sheep in a fold and lead them home from exile (2:12-13; 4:6-8). A similar theme is prophesied by Isaiah: "He gathers the lambs in his arms and carries them close to his heart; he gently leads those that have young" (Isa 40:11 NIV). But here in Micah the shepherd-king born from Bethlehem is probably implied.[340] He will bring his sheep into a new land with rich pasture. The last time the word "forest'" occurred was when the temple mount was turned into a forest land (Mic 3:12). The tide has now turned! Now the word is being used to describe the rich fertile soil of Israel. The flock of God's people are led to the green pastures of Bashan and Gilead, two locations noted for their luxuriant grasslands and prize cattle (Amos 4:1-3). **As in the days when you came out of the land of Egypt:** the exodus was the major salvific event for Israel in the Old Testament, and it will be repeated! This language is used to show the significance of Israel's future hope. **The nations shall see and be ashamed of all their might; they shall lay their hands on their mouths:** the language in this text consists of stock phrases for humiliation and defeat in the ancient Near East.[341] The nations will be ashamed of all their power. In the end it will be nothing compared to the power that brings Israel back from exile. The nations stand dumbfounded by what is happening to Israel, and they thus will realize the true emptiness of force and

---

339. Keil, *Minor Prophets*, 511.

340. Ibid., 512.

341. E.g., Amarna Letters 100-103. I am indebted to Michael L. Barré for these parallels; "A Cuneiform Parallel to Ps 86:16-17 and Mic 7:16-17," *Journal of Biblical Literature* 101 (1982): 271-75.

strength and come abjectly abased to give honor to God and his people. To put the hands over the mouth is to be silenced into submission, astonished with awe (cf. Job 21:5; 40:4; Isa 52:15). They will thus march up to the temple mount and transform their instruments of war into ones of peace (Mic 4:1–4).[342] **They shall turn in dread to the LORD our God:** the same expression is used by Hosea to describe the conversion of Israel in eschatological times (3:5). The word probably refers to the final part in the drama of Micah—the conversion of the nations (Mic 4:1–5). **Who is a God like you?** A rhetorical question placed at the end of this unit mirrors the rhetorical question that began the poem: "Where is the LORD your God?" This question is now answered with seven qualities by which God wants to be remembered above all (7:18–19). The question also serves to provide a clear echo of the beginning of the book, where Micah's name is found ("Who is like Yahweh?"), thus clamping the beginning and the ending of the book together. This book has been all about Micah's God. **Pardoning iniquity:** the first phrase in a significant sequence of God's attributes in Exod 34:7, which function to define the divine name. It suggests the lifting up of sin from someone and thus the bearing of it by another party. In Isaiah, the suffering servant is someone who bears the sin of many (Isa 53:4, 11). The word suggests suffering love. **Passing over the transgression of the remnant of your possession:** the idea signified is that of someone who overlooks a fault. Proverbs 19:11 says that a man's wisdom is to have patience rather than anger, and his glory is to overlook a fault. "Remnant of your possession" refers to God's people as the possession that he inherits, that is, his inheritance. They are those who have survived the judgment. **Because he delights in showing clemency:** the word "clemency" translates *ḥesed*, a meaning that suits well the context of pardon and forgiveness. It is not just that God practices *ḥesed* or shows it, but that he *delights* in it. It is what gets him excited! Calvin aptly remarks: "For the only prop or support that can raise us up to God, when we desire to be reconciled to him is this—that he loves mercy."[343] **He will again have compassion upon us; he will tread our iniquities under foot. You will cast all our sins into the depths of the sea:** these are the divine attributes found in the great exegesis of God's name in Exod 34:6–7. God is compassionate much like a woman whose instincts yearn for her offspring. The sins that God treads under foot is the third reference to sin in the text, matching the threefold forgiveness of God in Exod 34:7 and in the same order. This treading down of sin suggests that God is not

---

342. See Wolff, *Micah the Prophet*, 207. Calvin sees this as having salvific import as well: the nations will close their mouth, "thus being silent, they may become his disciples"; *Twelve Minor Prophets*, 396.

343. Calvin, *Twelve Minor Prophets*, 403.

just forgiving or overlooking it; sin is personified here as an enemy that God actively destroys. Where once it was formidable, now it is vanquished. Before Cain murdered Abel, God warned him about the necessity of mastering sin (Gen 4:7). Now that can finally happen, but only with God's help. Moreover, not only will sin be overcome, it will be forever removed from sight—thrown into the depths of the ocean. Just as Yahweh cast all Pharaoh's army into the depths of the sea drowning them forever (Exod 15:2, 19), he will do the same to Israel's sins. **You will show faithfulness to Jacob and unswerving loyalty to Abraham, as you have sworn to our ancestors, from the days of old:** the words "faithfulness" and "unswerving loyalty" translate the Hebrew words *'emet* and *ḥesed*. The order of this word pair is almost always *ḥesed* and *'emet*, but here they are strikingly reversed to end on a final note of *ḥesed*. This shows also the importance of the patriarchal promises. God is faithful to the promises he made to Abraham so that he would be a blessing to the entire world.

Interpretation—Micah's Word Then. This final prayer seems to be deliberately composed for worship, and it may have been part of a confession ritual in worship for the people of Judah as they are about to go through the experience of judgment or are going through it. If Micah is the composer and this is dated to his period, the historical context may have been the period of 701 BCE. The enemy would have been the taunting Assyrians, perhaps represented by Rabshakeh their ambassador, who was heaping insults on the leaders of Judah. The reference to the regathering of exiles would therefore be a prophecy of what soon would be—the exiles who Micah predicted would leave are to be regathered. Or it could be a reference to the return of the Israelite exiles of 722 BCE. Many scholars view this text as dated to the exilic period as a way of coping with this time, acknowledging the people's sins and looking forward in hope to what God is going to accomplish because of his promises in the rest of the book of Micah. Thus in this view, a later editor added this poem to the book to provide it with appropriate closure: But as one scholar notes: "Whether this liturgy was composed by Micah or has come into his collection by some inexplicable reason is a question which higher criticism will never be able to answer without a good portion of arbitrariness."[344] In my judgment, this text was probably added to the book by the same editor who added the superscription in order to provide a fitting conclusion, in which there is a play on the personal name of Micah at the beginning and at the end. It probably contained material used by Micah to inspire Hezekiah and the people to repent during the Assyrian crisis of 701.

As a final prayer given to Judah to pray on its own behalf, this poem

---

344. Bo Ivar Reicke, "Liturgical Traditions in Mic. 7," *Harvard Theological Review* 60 (1967): 349–67 at 366.

picks up major themes throughout the book and develops them almost to a crescendo pitch. The book begins with the darkness and judgment of exile and divine wrath and moves through a time of return and reconstruction and ingathering of the nations, to a final great vision of God that features seven of his incomparable characteristics: pardon, forgiveness, cessation of anger, *hesed*, compassion, subjugation of sin, and its complete and utter removal.

If the previous unit ended on a note that God would hear Judah (7:7), this one begins the prayer that God will hear. And it is a prayer of confession and acceptance of the punishment of judgment with an awareness of the darkness and pain. In the midst of this judgment there is the awareness of the taunts of the enemy (cf. Ps 137). But the enemy will not triumph, and even Israel has confidence in the midst of judgment that it is not the final word. This section specifically picks up the themes of judgment throughout the book and makes the point that it is not final but will be borne and that Israel will get out to the other side. In the first stanza, Israel will rise from being laid low by all the judgment predicted in the book (1:8–16; 2:1–5; 3:1–12) when it confesses its sin, which it never did before (cf. 1:5; 3:8). Before, Yahweh has contended with the nation (1:2–5; 6:1–2) and called the people to do justice (6:8), but after confession and penitence he will contend for the nation and do justice for it!

The second stanza functions like an announcement to the people of their glorious future. Emerging from the darkness of exile is an announcement that there will be a day of rebuilding and restoration of the exiles and the conversion of the nations. Three important events are described: the rebuilding of Judah, a universal migration of peoples there, and the desolation of the rest of the earth.[345] The exiles and nations will come from the far northeast (Assyria) and from the far southwest (Egypt) and from sea to sea and mountain to mountain. There will be a great return and ingathering, and this resumes themes found in each section of the book (2:12–13; 4:1–4, 6–8).

The third section is a prayer to God to lead his people personally through the wilderness as Moses did years before and to bring them to a plentiful land. With the expression "which lives by itself in a forest," there may be an allusion to the terrible judgment of the temple mount being turned into a forest[346] and the call of God to begin the transformation of the land and mount. The theme of the divine shepherd is used here as a critical factor in the restoration. Again this develops similar themes in the book in which there has been a promise of an eschatological shepherd-king who will lead his people and finally rule unto the ends of the earth (2:12–13; 4:1–4, 6–7; 5:2–5).

---

345. Smith, *Hosea, Amos, Micah*, 574.
346. Wolff, *Micah*, 226.

A fourth section continues the prayer by focusing on the nations and their self-abasement as a result of the work that God has been doing in Israel. They are completely stupefied and will finally worship God and honor Israel. Even though there is a triumphalist depiction of the nation of Israel, this does not contradict "the universalist vision that the nations will embrace Yahwism."[347]

Finally there is a resounding conclusion with a grand vision of Yahweh in the form of a hymn. A breathtaking spectacle of Yahweh coming in judgment began the book, and a much grander vision of Yahweh coming in salvation ends the book. "Who is like Yahweh?" is the question with which the book began, and "Who is like Yahweh?" is the question with which the book ends. This question is the question that Exod 15 asks at the beginning of Israel's saving history and answers—that Yahweh is the incomparable God because he throws Israel's powerful enemies down to the bottom of the sea. The same thing happens in this final vision of Micah. When the question is asked here, it is answered with seven characteristics of God, the last one of which sends Israel's enemies—its own sins—down to the bottom of the sea. "Sin is given death blows."[348]

This hymn in its depiction of the transcendence of Israel's God is incomparable in the ancient world and even within the Bible.[349] This last hymn is basically a further reflection on the relevance of the meaning of the divine name expounded in Exod 34:6–7 and occurred in the context of Israel's outrageous apostasy. The hope for Israel and thus the nations is born "out of Yahweh's character and not the presumption of the innocence of the accused."[350] That the book ends with a specific echo of the king who will come and emerge from Bethlehem is of no small importance. It is this king who will rule unto the ends of the earth and shepherd the peoples in his glory. He is testimony to the glory of God revealed in this passage and, as Calvin reminds us, that glory "principally shines in this—that he is reconcilable and that he forgives our sins."[351]

In this text, then, there is the prophet representing the nation, who acknowledges his sin, bears the wrath of God, endures the darkness, is resurrected from this death on a particular day to be a beacon to the nations and to experience divine blessing and kingship once again in Zion.[352]

---

347. Rudolph as cited by McKane, *Micah*, 233.

348. Paul Schrieber, "Fourth Sunday after Pentecost: Micah 7:18–20," *Concordia Journal* 10 (1984): 103.

349. "Here as nowhere else—especially not in the pagan world, as far as I can determine—the incomparability of Yahweh's forgiveness of sins is celebrated in song"; Wolff, *Micah*, 229.

350. Jacobs, *Conceptual Coherence of the Book of Micah*, 75.

351. Calvin, *Twelve Minor Prophets*, 401.

352. "Seeing that the country and nation are destroyed by internal corruption and external aggression, the prophet confesses his own sins and the sins of the people. He must bear the Lord's

The elements of judgment and darkness, defeat of an enemy, followed by exile and return and restoration of Israel, the return of divine kingship to Zion, and the conversion of the nations are major and minor themes in virtually all of the prophets, for example, Hosea, Amos, Joel, Isaiah, Ezekiel, Jeremiah, and Zechariah. The sequence of events may not all be duplicated in the above order but these prophets all see an eschatological future with Zion at the center of Yahweh's reign over the world.

The development of these themes is expressed most comprehensively and clearly in Isa 40–66. These are the themes of the coming exile of judgment, the forgiveness of sins, the return of Yahweh as king and his people to Zion, the rebuilding of Zion, Zion becoming a beacon to the nations, the temple being elevated to the highest place, the renewal of nature and the world, and the messianic king/servant who will rule over the world that is filled with the knowledge of Yahweh as the waters cover the sea. Ezekiel stresses the return from exile as a resurrection from death, the restoration of Israel led by a new Davidic shepherd-king, and a coming battle against the nations, followed by the exaltation of the temple whose waters will bring healing to the nations (Ezek 33–48). Zechariah is more esoteric but the main lines of his thinking are clear: a return from exile, forgiveness and atonement for the people in one day, a Davidic king coming to Jerusalem and announcing peace to the nations, great turmoil and suffering in Israel, a battle with the nations in which Israel emerges victorious, Jerusalem and its temple having a central place in the new world order, and God's holiness emerging from the epicenter of the temple to spread throughout the city with "Holy to the LORD" inscribed on every pot in Jerusalem and even on the bells around the necks of horses (Zech 8–14)![353]

The return from exile that happened in 539 BCE and the renewal efforts described in Haggai and Ezra-Nehemiah seem to be a far cry from the fulfillment of these glorious prophecies. By the time of the New Testament period, even though Israel had returned from exile in Babylon, it could hardly be said that Zion was the center of a world empire, that the temple had been exalted to be a beacon to the nations, or that the Roman soldiers had traded in their spears and swords for ploughshares and pruning hooks after they had visited

---

wrath upon the people, but on a fixed day is re-established by God, described as a rising again from the dead to life. . . . It is particularly interesting to see how this prophet suffers on behalf of the people for their sins, so that he is familiar with the idea of vicarious suffering found in several psalms and prophecies"; Bo Ivar Reicke, "Liturgical Traditions in Mic. 7," *Harvard Theological Review* 60 (1967): 349–67 at 366.

353. This inscription was engraved on a golden emblem, attached to a turban, and worn by only the high priest on his forehead when he was ministering in the tabernacle (Exod 28:36–38; 39:30).

the temple. What did a return from exile mean if one was still a slave to the Romans in one's own land? Where was Zion's king? Where was the glory of Israel? Where was all the divine glory that was promised? Where was the forgiveness of sins and the renewal of nature? Where was David?

Into this melting pot of historical tension, Jesus Christ was born. The Gospels announced his birth as the beginning of the fulfillment of the covenants made to Abraham and Israel (Matt 1-2; Luke 1-2). This birth had taken a long time, and Mother Israel had experienced hundreds of years of gestation before the birth pangs came and the child was born. His birth happened in Bethlehem to indicate that he would be the Davidic ruler, the eschatological shepherd, who would rule in the strength of the Lord unto the ends of the earth (Matt 2:1-18). But if Bethlehem was a sanctuary of world peace it soon became a war zone, as this new king was seen as a rival to others. Another king—specifically one with universal intentions—could not be tolerated by other rulers. But this "one of peace," arrived with his message of peace and called twelve disciples to represent that he was restoring Israel, and all who were weary with sin, who wanted *ḥesed* more than sacrifice, and who would now reorganize their lives under the divine rule.

What about this Son of David with his healing ministry (Matt 4:22-25), with his announcement of divine forgiveness (Mark 2:1-12), with his challenging of the religious authorities (Matt 23), with his call to turn the other cheek to the aggressor and to walk the extra mile carrying the equipment of the Roman soldier (Matt 5:39-42)? What about his call for his disciples to be a city set on a hill, showing everyone their heavenly Father through their good deeds so that they might glorify their Father who is in heaven (Matt 5:14-16)? Could this one from Bethlehem be on the move to conquer the kingdom of Nimrod, the kingdom founded at Babel? In his interaction with people he was constantly showing the importance of doing justice and loving *ḥesed* rather than sacrifice. Twelve times the Gospels use the term σπλαγχνίζομαι "to well up with compassion" (Matt 9:36; 14:14; 15:32; 18:27; 20:34; Mark 1:41; 6:34; 8:2; 9:22; Luke 7:13; 10:33; 15:20). In each case but one the subject of the verb is Jesus or God, and in the other case it is the Good Samaritan, who practices justice—rights a wrong—because he has a Jesus heart—a *ḥesed* heart, a heart that is moved with compassion (Luke 15:20). The religious leaders and their institutional structures were more interested in tithing the smallest herbs than prioritizing justice, mercy, and faith (Matt 23:23). During the last week of his life on earth, Jesus entered Jerusalem on a donkey to announce peace to the nations and to show the utter impotence of the chariot and warhorse. His only act of violence was to cast out the buyers and sellers from his Father's house, who had turned it into a "shopping mall" (using a term from *The Message* in Matt 21:12-13), after which he became the target himself of horrendous violence. One of the accusations against him was that if the temple would be destroyed he would rebuild it in three days (John 2:19; cf. Matt 26:61; 27:40).

As the Messiah, Jesus took up his throne on the cross as he was exalted for all to see, suffering violence for human sin. In true repentance for others, he interceded, asking God not to condemn them for they did not know what they were doing. But he became the one who took the curse in the place of a sinful people so that by his death he might truly produce forgiveness and be the agent of justice and *hesed* so that, as Paul said, God might be just and the justifier of him who believes in Jesus (Rom 3:26). As a result death could not hold him: he was resurrected three days later and spoke a message to his disciples to announce repentance and forgiveness to the nations in the power of the Holy Spirit (Luke 24:44–49).

Interpretation—Micah's Word Now. The new temple of Jesus's literal body leaves earth and ascends on high where the shepherd of Bethlehem reigns, and his new body on earth begins to fill the earth and be a healing stream to the nations. As people stream to the temple, which now is not confined to one location, they find a deep quenching of their spiritual thirst and reconciliation with God and neighbor. "They will come trembling out of their dens and turn with fear to the LORD"—a conversion that leads to another: the conversion of their swords into ploughshares and their spears into pruning hooks. The new symbols of this empire are a Roman cross, a towel and basin, and a meal of fellowship and forgiveness. The "one of peace" has come and is making all things new: he has built a new empire of reconciliation between races, genders, ages, and social classes.

As the message plays out, the new Israel constituted now of Jew and Gentile, made into a holy temple in the Lord, can shout out to its enemy, who has said "Where is your God?": "He is found on the cross, and his tomb is now empty. He is now with us to the end of the age."[354]

God is at work today just as much as he was in Micah's time and in the early church. He calls his people to be the city set on a hill, and even though the nations and peoples worship their own idols, his people are called to worship him alone and so be that beacon to the nations so that they would see his people's good works and say, "Let us go up to Jerusalem to hear the word of the LORD, for he will teach us his ways and we will walk in his paths" (Mic 4:2). His ways form a new society based on his forgiveness and love, which leads to repentance. Canadian novelist Rudy Wiebe captures brilliantly what this society of peace—this city set on a hill—looks like, whose king is the one of peace:

354. Wolff, *Micah*, 233.

Jesus says in his society that you show wisdom by trusting people; you handle leadership by serving; you handle offenders by forgiving; you handle money by sharing; you handle enemies by loving; you handle violence by suffering. You have a new attitude: towards everything, towards everybody, towards women, towards nature, towards the state, towards all and to every single thing. And in a Jesus Society, you repent, not by feeling bad, but by thinking differently.[355]

This is a forgiven society in which everybody is in desperate need and every repentant sinner is forgiven. Because of divine forgiveness, there is the genuine possibility of a new beginning, since forgiveness liberates from a paralyzed past and introduces a new future with possibility and hope. But it is also a repentant society that is forging a new way in the world. It has seen a vision of God, and this vision has made a world of difference. It contemplates the vision and with the ancient prophet exclaims in wonder: "Who is a God like you?" And as it turns back to his world, it transforms that worshipful stance into a daily service of pursuing a life of justice, inspired by a love of *ḥesed*, and it finds that the God of the exalted and lofty vision is walking alongside along the dusty roads of this world to help the needy. This is the gospel according to Micah from the town of Moresheth-gath, in the southwestern hill country of Judah, who lived and prophesied 2,700 years ago, and whose word still speaks today to all who will listen.[356] The wonder only increases: "Who is a God like you?" O come let us adore Him![357]

---

355. Rudy Wiebe, *The Blue Mountain of China* (Grand Rapids: Eerdmans, 1970), 216.

356. "In Micah's famous saying [6:8], with these concluding verses of his book forming its magnificent corollary, the gospel according to Micah is recorded in such plain language that no one could possibly misunderstand it"; Thomas F. Torrance, "The Prophet Micah and His Famous Saying," *Evangelical Quarterly* 24 (1952): 206–14 at 214.

357. Dale Ralph Davis, *Micah* (Welwyn Garden, UK: EP Books, 2014), 169.

Theological Themes of Micah

Micah's Vision of God

One of the main themes in the book of Micah that arrests the attention of the reader immediately is Micah's vision of God. After all, the prophet's name provides the first hint: Who is like Yahweh? This question is not so much designed to elicit new information and therefore rooted in a type of epistemology, as a gasp of wonder and praise rooted in the practice of doxology. It is a rhetorical question expecting an emphatic negative answer. And the audience is not disappointed as the first oracle in the book presents a stunning picture of Yahweh's transcendence before which all creation dissolves (1:2–7). Yahweh is described in breathtaking omnipotence as he emerges from the throne room of his heavenly temple to touch down on the heights of the world, and the natural world disintegrates in his path as he marches toward Samaria and then to Jerusalem.

Such a vision is found countless times in the Old Testament and is a typical description of a theophany in poetry. The first such example occurs at the exodus, when Yahweh destroys the Egyptian armies at the Red Sea, with the blast of his nostrils. His burning anger consumed them like chaff, and as a result the Israelites ended their song of praise with a similar rhetorical question about Yahweh's identity: "Who is like you, O LORD, among the gods? Who is like you, majestic in holiness, awesome in praises, doing wonders?" (Exod 15:11). When this God appears on Mount Sinai, his descent on the holy mountain causes the earth to shake, lightning to flash, thunder to clap, and smoke to envelop the peak of the mountain. The people at the foot of the mountain are terrified and plead for Moses as a mediator. The question is rhetorical again: "For who is there of all flesh that has ever heard the voice of the living God speak out of fire, as we have, and remained alive?" (Deut 5:26). The next example occurs when the Israelites need Yahweh's help in their attempt to claim the promise of the land. They describe the divine aid as follows: "LORD, when you went out from Seir, / when you marched from the region of Edom, / the earth trembled, / and the heavens poured, / the clouds indeed poured water. / The mountains quaked before the LORD, the One of Sinai, / before the LORD, the God of Israel" (Judg 5:4–5). This leads to an Israelite victory over the Canaanite enemies, despite their military superiority.

The language used to describe David's victory over his enemies is similar:

> In my distress I called to the LORD; to my God I cried out for help. From his temple he heard my voice. . . . Then the earth reeled and rocked; the foundations also of the mountains trembled and quaked, because he was angry. . . . The LORD thundered from heaven; the Most High uttered his voice. . . . The channels of the sea were seen and the foundations of the world were laid bare at the rebuke of the LORD at the blast of the breath from his nostrils. (2 Sam 22:7–16)

God emerges from his holy temple, and created reality convulses in terror, making way for the salvation of David.

In the prophets and the psalms there are many of these theophanies. Thus Isaiah describes Yahweh's emerging from his place and going forth to punish sin and the ground of the earth opening up to reveal the innocent blood that has been shed on it (26:21). The consequence of the theophany will be that people "will flee to caves in the rocks / and to holes in the ground / from dread of the LORD / and the splendor of his majesty, / when he rises to shake the earth" (2:19 NIV).

The prophets that follow Micah in the Masoretic order are Nahum and Habakkuk. They respectively begin and end with a similar divine appearance:

> He rebukes the sea and makes it dry,
> and he dries up all the rivers;
> Bashan and Carmel wither,
> and the bloom of Lebanon fades.
> The mountains quake before him,
> and the hills melt;
> the earth heaves before him,
> the world and all who live in it.
> Who can stand before his indignation?
> Who can endure the heat of his anger?
> His wrath is poured out like fire,
> and by him the rocks are broken in pieces. (Nah 1:4–6)

> God came from Teman,
>> the Holy One from Mount Paran.
> His glory covered the heavens . . .
>> rays came forth from his hand,
>> where his power lay hidden. . . .
> He stopped and shook the earth;
>> he looked and made the nations tremble.
> The eternal mountains were shattered . . .
>> the everlasting hills sank low. . . .
>> You split the earth with rivers.
> The mountains saw you, and writhed. (Hab 3:3–10)

This awesome depiction of divine transcendence is found in Micah at the beginning of his collection of oracles. It is a transcendence that is particularly provoked by human evil, which must be judged since God is depicted from the beginning as the divine king who must uphold and maintain his moral order. Throughout the book the assumption is that Israel will be judged because of its sins. Frequently the punishment corresponds to the crime (1:7; 2:1–5; 3:4–6, 12). This judgment is described as a bearing of the anger and wrath of God (5:15; 7:9, 18). To be sure, this is not an arbitrary anger, but it is an anger that is implacably opposed to human evil. This is shown particularly in Yahweh's "war to end all wars" when he destroys all offensive military apparatus and defensive installations, all idolatry and false religion in his reform of Judah and the world, and it is described as a consequence of his wrath and anger (5:10–15).

While such theophanies are not developed as much in the New Testament they provide the background of the day of the Lord, the depiction of God's entrance into the universe to set up his final kingdom. John the Baptist, who was the hinge of the new age, spoke of preparing the way of the Lord, who would appear with eschatological fire signifying impending divine wrath (Luke 3:16–17). Jesus himself spoke of casting eschatological fire upon the earth, and the descriptions of his second coming use language that is redolent of the prophetic theophanies. Jesus will be revealed from heaven with blazing fire to consume his enemies (2 Thess 1:7–9). "The heavens will disappear with a roar; the elements will be destroyed by fire, and the earth and everything done in it will be laid bare" (2 Pet 3:10 NIV). This builds to a climax in the book of Revelation:

> When he opened the sixth seal, I looked, and there came a great earthquake; the sun became black as sackcloth, the full moon became like blood, and the stars of the sky fell to the earth as the fig tree drops its winter fruit when shaken by a gale. The sky vanished like a scroll rolling itself up, and every

mountain and island was removed from its place. Then the kings of the earth and the magnates and the generals and the rich and the powerful, and everyone, slave and free, hid in the caves and among the rocks of the mountains, calling to the mountains and rocks, "Fall on us and hide us from the face of the one seated on the throne and from the wrath of the Lamb; for the great day of their wrath has come, and who is able to stand?" (Rev 6:12–17)

This awesome transcendence in Micah is thus one with the general biblical picture. The divine ruler of the cosmos will judge all evil. Nothing will thwart his judgment; there is no obstacle too formidable to obstruct the divine march to bring the rule of heaven to earth.

Yet, this is certainly not the last word on transcendence, as Micah ends his oracles with the same rhetorical question: Who is like Yahweh? (7:18). But now there is a different depiction of transcendence: forgiveness, pardon, cessation of anger, renewal of mercy, conquest of sin, and eradication of evil. Here are direct allusions to the revelation of God: human dominion over nature, conquest of enemies at the Red Sea, and revelation of the divine name at Sinai. Just as Israel's enemies in the past were conquered at the Red Sea and drowned in its depths, now Israel's own sins will meet the same fate. Second, just as Yahweh revealed himself as the forgiver of all manner of sins at Sinai and as the God of overflowing and abundant *hesed* (Exod 34:6–7), he will do the same for Israel, having compassion on the remnant of his people so that they can experience his love and be agents of reconciliation in the world. Thus the awesome judgment of God that reveals the divine transcendence is overshadowed at the end of the book with the overpowering, transcendent love of God.

This same thread of transcendence in love as overshadowing the revelation of divine transcendence in judgment shapes the biblical narrative from the beginning in the garden. Although the first couple are exiled from Eden, the divine intent is to bring them back and to restore the divine rule in the world. Thus when Abram is called, he is called to be a blessing to the entire earth (Gen 12:1–3). The daunting obstacles of the barren wombs of the patriarchs' wives are removed by the divine transcendence that makes a joke of all attempts to limit or domesticate it in the birth of Laughter—Isaac (Gen 17). The plagues of Egypt that show God's unique power and the exodus demonstrate divine transcendence raising Israel from its Egyptian graveyard (Exod 7–15). At the mountain of God, the decision to save Israel because of Moses's intercession turns out to be due as much to the divine intention because of the divine nature as it was due to the mediation of Moses: God's goodness and mercy overshadow his justice. In the dark days of the judges, God raises up a desolate Hannah who has a child who will bring about the next major epoch in Israel's history—the transition to kingship. But she learns a greater lesson as a result of her own personal reversal from barrenness to birth—that God's transcendence is overwhelmingly used for mercy as he abases the proud and mighty and exalts the humble and weak and brings up the dead from the graveyard (1 Sam 2:1–10)! She discerns that someday this transcendence will bring the rule of heaven to earth. Similarly David, in a dark period in his own life, has to make a decision among alternatives of divine judgment, and he chooses the direct affliction of divine wrath since "I am in deep distress; let us fall into the hand of the LORD, for his mercy is great; but do not let me fall into human hands" (2 Sam 24:14).

In the prophets, the decision to save Nineveh springs from the divine love that desires compassion on a city of 120,000 people who don't know their right hand from their left, and much cattle (Jon 4:11). The problem with Jonah is that he knows this only too well! Hosea describes the battle within the divine mind between justice and mercy and finally indicates that transcendence is defined by mercy:

> How can I give you up, Ephraim?
>> How can I hand you over, O Israel?
> How can I make you like Admah?
>> How can I treat you like Zeboiim?
> My heart recoils within me;
>> my compassion grows warm and tender.
> I will not execute my fierce anger;
>> I will not again destroy Ephraim;
> for I am God and *no mortal,*
>> the Holy One in your midst,
>> and I will not come in wrath. (Hos 11:8–9)

Isaiah defines transcendence in the same way. To a people who are without much hope, the prophet draws a picture of transcendence that inspires hope:

> Seek the LORD while he may be found,
>> call upon him while he is near;
> let the wicked forsake their way,
>> and the unrighteous their thoughts;
> let them return to the LORD, that he may have mercy on them,
>> and to our God, for he will abundantly pardon.
> For my thoughts are not your thoughts,
>> nor are your ways my ways, says the LORD.
> For as the heavens are higher than the earth,

so are my ways higher than your ways
and my thoughts than your thoughts. (Isa 55:6–9)

Similarly Ezekiel's vision of the valley of dry bones shows that God's transcendence is utilized to save, to bring up from the graveyard (Ezek 37).

How are these twin themes of transcendence reconciled? One does not have to wait until the New Testament. The example is found in the description of the suffering servant in Isaiah, who is highly exalted (transcendent) and at the same time stoops to the lowest depths to save many lost sheep, taking their judgment upon himself (Isa 52:13–53:12). This is reflected in the cross and the resurrection in the New Testament, in which the high and exalted One descends to the depths to die for his people, the just for the unjust, and now is exalted to the highest place so that at his name every knee will bow and the heavenly rule will finally come to earth (Phil 2:5–11).[1] Who is like Yahweh? Indeed.

Divine Name and Israelite Credo

The passage that ends the book of Micah in hymnic fashion is based on the Israelite credo found in Exod 34:6–7. This passage in its context is a further explication of the meaning of the divine name, first revealed in Exod 3:14 to Moses at the burning bush. This new revelation at the burning mountain is the most complete definition of Yahweh in the Old Testament. In this passage, after the crisis of the golden calf in which the people of Israel break the covenant and Moses has successfully interceded for them, Moses wishes to see God's face, to know his way, to perceive his glory. God gives Moses a glimpse of the glory by hiding him in a cave so that he might peer out and see the trail of this brilliance and not the full frontal vision, Yahweh's "back" and not his face. To see the front would lead to instant death. Then at the appropriate time Yahweh's glory appears, and it is not so much seen as heard. Yahweh exegetes his own name in a brief soliloquy:

The Lord descended in the cloud and stood with him there, and proclaimed the name, "The Lord." The Lord passed before him, and proclaimed,

"The Lord, the Lord,
a God merciful and gracious,

1. For a sound and perceptive understanding of this particular theme, see Jeremy R. Treat, *The Crucified King: Atonement and Kingdom in Biblical and Systematic Theology* (Grand Rapids: Zondervan, 2014).

slow to anger,
and abounding in steadfast love and faithfulness,
keeping steadfast love for the thousandth generation,
forgiving iniquity and transgression and sin,
yet by no means clearing the guilty,
but visiting the iniquity of the parents
upon the children
and the children's children,
to the third and the fourth generation." (Exod 34:5–7)

Before considering the meaning of this passage, it is important to note how it not only provides the climax for the book of Micah, but also provides the key turning point in the previous book of Jonah and is part of the introduction in the subsequent book of Nahum. The text provides the real reason why Jonah did not want to go to preach to the Ninevites:

But this was very displeasing to Jonah, and he became angry. He prayed to the LORD and said, "O LORD! Is not this what I said while I was still in my own country? That is why I fled to Tarshish at the beginning; for I knew that you are a gracious God and merciful, slow to anger, and abounding in steadfast love, and ready to relent from punishing. (Jon 4:1–2)

Divine compassion forgave the Ninevites because of their repentance. But in the next book of Nahum, which is also aimed at Nineveh a few generations later, the last part of the credo comes into play to an unrepentant city:

A jealous and avenging God is the LORD,
    the LORD is avenging and wrathful;
the LORD takes vengeance on his adversaries
    and rages against his enemies.
The LORD is slow to anger but great in power,
    and the LORD will by no means clear the guilty.
His way is in whirlwind and storm,
    and the clouds are the dust of his feet. (Nah 1:2–3)

This passage also occurs at significant junctures in other prophetic books and in many other biblical books.[2] Various studies on its use show two concerns:

---

2. See, e.g., Nathan C. Lane, *The Compassionate, but Punishing God: A Canonical Analysis of Exodus 34:6–7* (Eugene: Wipf & Stock, 2010); and Raymond Van Leeuwen, "Scribal Wisdom and

the overwhelming mercy and grace of God as well as his justice. Nevertheless it is overwhelmingly weighted toward mercy and grace. The passage can be divided as follows:

the double name	Yahweh, Yahweh
who Yahweh is (ontology)	the compassionate and gracious God, slow to anger, abounding in love and faithfulness
what Yahweh does (praxeology)	maintaining love to thousands and forgiving wickedness, rebellion, and sin; yet he does not leave the guilty unpunished; he punishes the children and their children for the sin of the parents to the third and fourth generation

It is easy to see the significance of pairs in the text. The divine name occurs twice, which is unique in the Old Testament (the closest parallel is Deut 6:4). This double use of the name signals that the text is extremely important and also points out both the compassion and justice of God. There are two pairs of God's attributes and two pairs of God's actions. Throughout this highly poetic text, the second line in the pair further explicates its complementary first line: Yahweh's grace and compassion means forbearance and abundance of covenant love; his maintaining covenant love for thousands of generations means forgiveness of iniquity, rebellion, and sin; and his commitment not to acquit the guilty means that he will punish them down to the third and fourth generation.

Thus the basic divine ontology can be summed up in the first part of the text, and the function of this ontology in the second part. The strategic use of this text in three successive books dealing with the Assyrian crisis shows how crucial this text was for true prophecy. This text clearly shows the importance of repentance and confession in order to experience the mercy of God. This is shown decisively in the Jonah story. The people experience this side of God only when they repent, and at the end of the book it shows that grace and mercy are not forced out of God like water out of a stone or like money from a stingy miser. The water gushes from the sluice gate, which is immediately opened when there is repentance and brokenness. Significantly this mercy is forthcoming in Micah when a confession is given to the people (7:8–20). When the people present such a confession, God will hear and forgive. In contrast,

---

Theodicy in the Book of the Twelve," in *In Search of Wisdom: Essays in Memory of John G. Gammie*, ed. Leo G. Purdue, Bernard B. Scott, and William Johnstone (Louisville: John Knox, 1993), 31–49.

the people of Nineveh in Nahum's time experience God's judgment when they do not repent.

Exodus 34:6-7 demonstrates lucidly the divine nature. God is compassionate and gracious, is ever patient, and is full of loyal love. There is no limit to the expression of that grace, but the sinner's experience of it depends on the willingness to change. At the same time there is a delay even when repentance does not take place, which shows the nature of the divine patience. It must also be remembered that this is the *back* and not the *face* of God!

The divine commitment to justice and righteousness and God's patience in holding back judgment even in the face of overwhelming evil is shown throughout the Scriptures. The flood story presents a world full of violence, but even in the midst of that violence there is a delay in judgment of 120 years, before God as the moral arbiter of the universe washes the evil away in a deluge of cleansing waters (Gen 6:3).[3] At the same time, he saves a man and his family because of his grace, and in the aftermath of the flood, when humanity has not changed, he promises not to disrupt the world order by a flood again despite the presence of the same human evil that caused the flood. After the call of Abram he delays the judgment of the Canaanites for 400 years because their sins are not yet ripe for judgment (15:13-15). This is testimony once again to the divine patience. In the story of Sodom, God is not willing to destroy the cities of the plain if there are ten righteous people in Sodom (18:32). In later times the prophets make it clear that God's patience has borne with Israel for a long period but that there is, alas, even a limit to the divine patience (Amos 1-2).

That God is patient but not infinitely so shows tension within the divine nature. God suffers when he forgives, for someone has to bear the consequences of the sin. What does this say about the entire history of a rebellious people that God has endured? It says something not only about their rebellion but also about the divine forbearance—of suffering love. It also shows that when God judges, it is, as Isaiah says, his strange work (Isa 28:21). Ezekiel presents the same point in a divine rhetorical question, the negative answer of which is obvious: "Do I delight in the death of a sinner?" (Ezek 18:23). In case there is any doubt about the answer to this question, God answers it himself, but before he does, he adds another question: "Why will you die, people of Israel? For I take no pleasure in the death of anyone" (18:31-32).

There is no question that the unrepentant ones suffer as well since God visits on their children the consequences of their sin but limits it to three or four

---

3. Gen 6:3 is difficult but the main alternative to this rendering is to understand the temporal reference as a reduction in human age because of all the violence. But there does not seem to be a drastic reduction in the life spans in the ensuing text (cf. Gen 11:10-32).

generations, which means probably one household family in ancient Israel.[4] In the New Testament Moses finally sees the face of God when he sees Jesus transfigured before him, and he hears the divine word that this is the beloved of the Father, revealing grace and truth to the superlative degree (Matt 17:1–13). Shortly thereafter the tension between the justice and mercy of God is finally resolved in Christ, who becomes the sin-bearer, who experiences the divine judgment for humanity's sins so that forgiveness and love can be extended to the entire human race. God's *ḥesed* now knows no spatial bounds as well as no temporal limits.

This credo thus shows that the fountain of love that springs up from the divine nature cannot be contained to the scope of its initial recipients. Yahweh is the name of the Israelite God but he is also the creator of the heavens and earth, and if the people he has chosen through which he will bless the world experience his forgiveness and grace, then it is clear that this is a foretaste of such blessing spilling over to the rest of creation. This is clearly the message of the book of Jonah, and in Micah this experience will occur when the remnant of his people repent and Zion again becomes exalted to be a blessing to the entire earth. But this period will not last forever, and thus will come the measure of divine justice that even the nations will experience. When they do not listen to the divine appeal, they will eventually experience judgment (Mic 5:15).

The motive to bless the world can be seen in the meaning of the divine name as expounded in the credo. Although the Gospel of John says that the law came by Moses but grace and truth came by Jesus Christ (John 1:17), it is not contradicting the credo in Exodus. In comparison to the face of God revealed in Christ, "the back" has been obscured. A hundred-watt light provides illumination for the darkness, but its light seems insignificant when compared to the shining brilliance of a million-watt bulb. Yahweh is the name that will someday be exalted over the entire earth, and that name will mean that every knee will bow down and praise the person that name designates, because there will finally be a unity to heaven and earth. Jesus Christ, who experienced the drastic descent in the cross and the equally exalted ascent in the resurrection and ascension, now bears that name, but it will be revealed to the entire cosmos only at the end of history (Phil 2:5–11). In him God's ultimate intent for humanity is clearly seen. As Brevard Childs remarks: "To know God's name is to know his purpose for all mankind from the beginning to the end."[5]

4. Families in ancient societies (and in many modern non-Western societies) consisted of three or four generations as opposed to the one- or two-generation families in predominantly modern Western cultures.

5. Brevard S. Childs, *The Book of Exodus: A Critical Theological Commentary* (Philadelphia: Westminster, 1974), 119.

God and the Nations

At the outset of the book of Micah there is a prophetic call for the nations to hear the word of God and to pay attention for the acts that are happening to Israel are supremely relevant to them. Having stressed the authority of the prophetic word in the titulary superscription (1:1), the text addresses a universal audience, the nations, and these become almost a major preoccupation of the central section and last section of the book. In the central section there are no less than seven references to the nations (4:2, 3 [3x], 7, 11; 5:7, 15) and six references to peoples (4:1, 3, 5, 13; 5:7, 8); and in the last section the nations are the principal subject of discourse in two major units (7:11–13, 16–17). It is easy to lose sight of this big picture as one looks at all the various details in the text of Micah.

Perhaps it is best to understand the nations within the grand narrative of Scripture before considering Micah's contribution more closely. The primeval history preceding Israel's national history in Genesis serves to place the calling of Abram against the backdrop of the plunging of the world into curse, death, and alienation. Significantly, the calling of Israel is strategically placed after the great Table of Nations and the Tower of Babel. Israel is thus the divine solution to the human problem: the raison d'être for the election of Abram was to be a conduit of blessing for the nations. As a nation it has been elected to mission and therefore has a universal responsibility.[6] Even with its national covenant at Sinai, it was called out as a holy nation and as a kingdom of priests from among the nations so that it would fulfill its priestly task on behalf of the nations (Exod 19:5–6). The construction of the temple is found approximately at the middle of the Hebrew Bible (1 Kgs 6–8), and it is supremely a place for forgiveness and a locale of shalom, illustrated by the name of the one who built it, Solomon (*šĕlōmô*) (1 Kgs 8). Amos speaks of God's judgment of the nations first before his later judgment of Israel, but that he emphasizes the nations shows their importance in God's plan (Amos 1–2). In fact their crimes against humanity scream to high heaven for judgment. In many of the other prophetic books, unlike Micah, there are many oracles against nations (OAN) (Isa 13–23; Jer 46–51; Ezek 25–32; Zeph 2; Zech 9:1–8), showing that Yahweh is not just a nationalistic deity but the supreme creator and ruler of the universe and ultimately rules the nations. But coincident with this judgment is a focus on salvation. God will have mercy in the latter days on Moab, Ammon, and Elam. There will be a highway

---

6. This is not to suggest that its election could be reduced to mission; election is first of all an election based on love, but this does not eliminate a concern for service. See R. W. L. Moberly, *Old Testament Theology* (Grand Rapids: Baker, 2013), 41–52.

of salvation from Assyria through Israel to Egypt, and the same terminology used of Israel will also be used for these nations:

> On that day there will be a highway from Egypt to Assyria, and the Assyrian will come into Egypt, and the Egyptian into Assyria, and the Egyptians will worship with the Assyrians. On that day Israel will be the third with Egypt and Assyria, a blessing in the midst of the earth, whom the LORD of hosts has blessed, saying, "Blessed be Egypt my people, and Assyria the work of my hands, and Israel my heritage." (Isa 19:23–25)

The Septuagint translators could not accept the radicality of the Hebrew words, which clearly mean that "all three [nations] will be God's chosen people."[7] Their nationalism resulted in a radical revision in which Jewish exiles were the recipients of blessing: "Blessed is my people *in* Egypt and *in* Assyria, Israel my inheritance!"

These two ideas of the nations as the enemies of God and Israel and as worthy of judgment and at the same time as the object of divine love and salvation are sometimes difficult to fathom, not only for later academics studying these themes in the Bible but for Israel itself. The prophetic book of Jonah wrestles with both but not from an academic point of view. There it is seen that as the divine judge, God's holiness cannot tolerate human evil, but the message of judgment sent to Assyria is really because of God's desire to save. The divine nature revealed in the Israelite credo (Exod 34:6–7) to Moses cannot be limited to one nation. When God first revealed the content of his name to Moses, it resulted in Israel being forgiven at Sinai and being spared as a nation from certain divine judgment. But Jonah learns the hard way that the name's saving significance cannot be contained by one nation. Indeed God's plan will finally be fulfilled in a world that is free from idolatry and violence and the nations will dwell in peace. Yahweh will be king in that day over the entire world, and he will be one and his name one (Zech 14:9)!

How do Micah's oracles fit into this schema of world history? The message of Micah opens with a word to the nations in order to force them to see what is happening with God's people so that they can be instructed. The entire world needs to hear that it is ultimately accountable to its creator, who is a witness of its deeds and thoughts. If God will not let his own people off the hook of judgment, the nations can expect the same if they do not pay attention.

But in the book of Micah the so-called schizophrenic or bipolar approach to the nations is extremely prominent. On the one hand, the nations will be attracted to Israel's proclamation of the Torah and will make a pilgrimage to

---

7. Abraham Joshua Heschel, *Insecurity of Freedom* (New York: Macmillan, 1955), 166.

Jerusalem, hear the word of Yahweh, and be literally transformed, turning their weapons into tools for agriculture (4:1–5). On the other hand, they will make a pilgrimage to Zion to destroy it, and there they are destroyed by the Israelites (4:11–13). Are these the result of two radically different approaches to the nations in Israelite thought, a universalistic thrust versus a nationalistic zeal? Or is it possible to integrate both into a coherent whole? For example, they may represent the same theme expressed differently. The basic point is that the nations in their warlike attitudes come to Jerusalem, and their warlike attitudes are totally destroyed. More likely, however, they represent different stages in the divine plan.[8] First, God uses the nations to refine his people and to judge them, but their attempt to destroy the people will meet with final defeat. Then when God reforms his people, this will become the nations' opportunity for salvation. They will see their plight and hear the word of the Lord go out from Zion, and this will result in their pilgrimage to Zion and repentance in which they give up their ways of war. Thus the blessing of Abraham will come upon the nations. These differences, then, between the nations as enemies and the nations as the objects of God's salvation in Mic 4–5 and 7:8–20 are not contradictions but simply reflect differences in the development of the divine plan or the progress of redemption.[9] The kaleidoscope visions of the prophets in which visions of the future are jumbled together contribute to the confusion, but when these visions are untangled and presented in their logical order the confusion disappears.[10] Even within the order of the Twelve, these two perspectives are seen: Jonah witnesses to the repentance and salvation of Nineveh; Nahum to the judgment of Nineveh.

There are similar features in Israel's earlier history. The Israelites fight for their very survival against the nations in the conquest, bringing about God's judgment on the nations, but this is ultimately to save the nations in the end, as the means by which the nations will be saved is preserved. When Israel strays from God's salvific plan, the nations are used by God to judge and purge the

---

8. Burkard M. Zapff argues that Micah systematizes the different view of the nations found in Joel, Jonah, and Nahum as two "diverse temporally differentiated behaviors of the nations and likens it to the view found in Zech 14; "The Perspective of the Nations in the Book of Micah as a 'Systematization' of the Nations' Role in Joel, Jonah, and Nahum: Reflections on a Context-Oriented Exegesis in the Book of the Twelve," in *Society for Biblical Literature Seminar Papers 38* (Missoula: Scholars Press, 1999), 612.

9. John N. Oswalt tackles the same problem for Isaiah and seeks to work out a coherent view in the present text. The only other option as he sees it is "two apparently contradictory pictures. . . . Will the nations come to destroy or will they come to worship?"; "The Nations in Isaiah: Friend or Foe; Servant or Partner," *Bulletin for Biblical Research* 16 (2006): 42.

10. E.g., McKane (*Micah*, 14) likens Mic 4–5 to a "picture show."

people so that eventually God can use Israel to bring about his saving purpose for the world. Thus after the death and resurrection of Christ when the nations seem to be arrayed against the Lord and his Messiah, the early church is born, and it is given a message to the nations. The resurrected Jesus states to his disciples that the divine plan of the Old Testament included the nations, and the opportunity for the salvation of the nations is in the period before his first and second coming: "This is what is written: The Christ will suffer and rise from the dead on the third day, and repentance and forgiveness of sins will be preached in his name to all nations, beginning at Jerusalem" (Luke 24:46–47 NIV). Consequently "now is the day of salvation" describes the period before the final judgment. If the nations do not hear during the divine "now" (Mic 4:1–5), they can expect only the justice of God in the divine "then" (5:15). In summary, the final intent for Yahweh's mission to the nations is not their extermination but their restoration.[11]

Justice

The word "justice" occurs in Micah only five times (3:1, 8, 9; 6:8; 7:9), yet this small number represents one of the highest percentages of the occurrence of the word in a biblical book. According to the standard Hebrew lexica the word has many connotations. The semantic field for justice in ancient Israel was wider than ours because it encompassed as a whole three areas of government that have been separated in modern societies: legislative, judicial, and executive. Consequently the word was used to indicate all three, dealing with law making, the judicial sentencing, and the enforcement of that sentencing. It sometimes indicates the custom of a culture (Judg 18:7; 2 Kgs 17:33); the habit of a person (1 Sam 2:13) or a group (1 Kgs 18:28); a natural law or a quota for a particular product, plan, design, or appearance (Judg 13:12; 2 Kgs 1:7); or a personal right—what is due to one (Isa 49:4; Jer 32:7–8) by being a member of a certain profession. It can also indicate a person's plight or cause (1 Kgs 8:45, 59).

The word is often used with the term "righteousness," and the word pair is a hendiadys for "social justice."[12] In its first occurrence in the Bible it is a way of life that is to characterize Israel. It functions as one of the main reasons why Yahweh chose Abraham:

---

11. John N. Oswalt, "The Nations in Isaiah: Friend or Foe; Servant or Partner," *Bulletin for Biblical Research* 16 (2006): 45.

12. Moshe Weinfeld, *Social Justice in Ancient Israel and in the Ancient Near East* (Jerusalem: Magnes, 1995).

> Abraham shall become a great and mighty nation, and all the nations of the earth shall be blessed in him. . . . For I have chosen him, that he may charge his children and his household after him to keep the way of the LORD by doing righteousness and justice; so that the LORD may bring about for Abraham what he has promised him. (Gen 18:18–19)

The phrase "righteousness and justice" exegetes "the way of Yahweh" (cf. Jer 5:5). In its context this is explicitly a way that is different from "the way of Sodom," where the cries of people rise up to Yahweh, seeking justice and relief from oppression (Gen 18:20–21). The cries from the victims of Sodom are like the blood of innocent Abel, which cries to God from the ground demanding redress (4:10). Thus to practice *mišpāṭ*, justice, is to provide help for people in social distress, who have become the victims of social oppression because of their lack of power. Particularly they are the weak and the vulnerable, the so-called quartet of the marginalized and disadvantaged in society: widow, orphan, refugee, and poor. Within the context of Gen 18, such people are being victimized by the people of Sodom. In the very next chapter, total strangers to the city—people who might be classified as aliens or refugees—are threatened by a mob who want to take them from a house of protection and violate them. This leads to the judgment of Sodom. The "refugees" stand for all the victims of oppression in Sodom, a place whose people abominated justice.[13]

With the growth of Israel as a nation, the legal codes were regarded as a collection of "judgments" that were specific examples of how Israel was to conduct itself as a society. In a manner of speaking this became the embodiment of Yahweh's way. In fact the commitment to the Torah and its judgments is often called "the way of Yahweh." In a number of texts, meditating on the Torah and implementing it is viewed as providing directions for the righteous and came to be known as "the way of the righteous." These judgments, collectively sometimes designated as Torah, constituted the legislative branch of Israel's judicial system. Consequently it was important for judges to deliberate and "do justice" by ensuring that these judgments were applied in society. People would bring their cases to a judge, who would then render a verdict (Judg 4:5; 2 Sam 15:2).

---

13. Another excellent example of the "social justice" significance of this hendiadys is found in Jer 22:3, where justice and righteousness are followed by the following words: "Rescue from the defrauder him who is robbed; do not wrong the stranger, the fatherless, and the widow; commit no lawless act, and do not shed the blood of the innocent in this place" (JPS Tanak). To know the way of Yahweh is essentially to know Yahweh, as is shown in 22:15–16: "Do you think you are more a king because you compete in cedar? Your father ate and drank and dispensed justice and equity—Then all went well with him. He upheld the rights of the poor and needy—Then all was well. Is this not to know me?" declares the LORD" (ESV).

Thus the exhortation is given repeatedly not to pervert justice by showing favoritism (Deut 1:17; Prov 18:5; 24:23) or accepting a bribe. Justice is able to set things straight because it sees things straight. Thus Solomon asks for a discerning heart so that he will be able to discern justice, that is, know the difference between right and wrong, good and evil. Showing favoritism and accepting a bribe blind the eyes of the judge and thus distort the application of justice to a particular social situation, condemning the innocent and exonerating the wicked (Deut 16:18–19; Prov 17:23). This results in the corruption or perversion of justice (Eccl 3:16). This must have been a common practice since it is mentioned many times as the "turning aside" of justice (1 Sam 8:3). Similarly the judgments of a refugee, poor person, orphan, or widow represent their protection under the law, and thus the upholding of their "rights" (Deut 24:17). They were not to be "turned aside" by the courts but must be upheld. In any society it is the most vulnerable who are in need of the most protection under the law, and Israel assured this group of their rights within the law. But practically speaking these rights were the easiest to violate because of the impotence of the vulnerable. There were various verdicts that the courts could pronounce based on the judgments, some of which were sentences of death (Deut 19:6; 21:22; 1 Kgs 20:42; Ezek 16:38; 23:45). The pronunciation of a sentence would mean to speak or decree a judgment (2 Kgs 25:6; Jer 1:16; cf. 1 Kgs 20:40; 2 Chr 19:6).

The executive implementation of justice would ensure that justice would be applied in the society and wrongs righted. Justice would not only be pronounced by the courts but would be carried out within the society. Thus it was the task of the powers within the society, the political authorities, to ensure that the decisions of the judicial branch would be executed. Thus one would "do justice" (Deut 17:8–11). Beginning with the king, this process would filter down through the society. The king was to do justice, to ensure its enforcement. Probably the preeminent example was Solomon, who was called upon to right a wrong at the lowest stratum of society, between two prostitutes, immediately after he became king (1 Kgs 3:16–28). When he determined the injustice, he rectified it and ordered the child to be returned to its rightful mother. But there was a definite sense in which everyone was involved in this process to some degree. The people would come to know what justice was and what was required. And they would seek to apply this in their own spheres of influence, showing compassion and fairness in all that they did. They would thus become advocates of the vulnerable and champions of justice.

The first use of "justice" in Micah excoriates the judicial officials in Israel, who are supposed to know it (3:1). If any group has the expertise in knowing the difference between right and wrong it is this one. They are the ones who are to render the appropriate verdicts and ensure their execution. But in actual fact, they do the opposite, thus ensuring that the rights of the powerless and vulnerable are trampled. They are not just exploited—they are "cannibalized"! Consequently these judicial officials can be described as "abominating justice" (3:9). Clearly justice here has to do with the judicial function of the court system. In contrast, Micah has been given the power, the spirit of Yahweh, justice, and courage to declare to Jacob his sin (3:8). Micah is able to discern the truth about equity and fairness and therefore is able to pronounce the proper verdict—a verdict of truth and justice, whose announcement is empowered by the Spirit of God.

The next example, in 6:8, concerns individuals doing justice, loving mercy, and walking humbly with their God. This unquestionably has to do with the common people living a fair and equitable life, helping the powerless, doing the will of God in their social relationships, ensuring that they are concerned for the disadvantaged and that the wicked be punished and the righteous vindicated. Finally, the last example in Micah indicates clearly the plight and cause of Israel. God will vindicate his people's cause and plight after the judgment (7:9)

By far and above the main meaning of justice in the prophets is the proper administration of justice in the courts and the demonstration of justice in the sphere of influence in each person's life. All of the preexilic prophets have a concern especially for those who usually become the victims of injustice: the socially disadvantaged, the poor. One does not have to read very far in the book of Micah or for that matter in many of the preexilic prophets to realize that there is a deep concern for the socially vulnerable. After the prediction of the destructive theophany that blazes a path of destruction in the northern and southern kingdoms (Mic 1), the reasons for such a terrible swath of judgment are shown clearly (Mic 2). The people have been dispossessed from their homes and estates as a result of covetous land-grabbing by a wealthy elite. These people were probably foreclosing on debts that could not be paid, and as a result the estates would pass into their hands. To do this "legally" the courts would have either had to sanction it or to connive at it as a result of bribery. The text speaks of a lament that the rich will wail when their judgment comes, but this is probably an echo of the poor who were exploited: "We are utterly ruined." Later the prophet speaks of men being stripped of their clothing, women being driven out of their homes, and children being taken away from the blessing of living in their own homes. Micah is irate at injustice.

In the second section of the book the intensity of Micah's rhetoric is ratcheted up as he becomes livid about the court's complicity in depriving the poor of their legal rights. He uses the image of cannibalism to excoriate his audience! Instead of just ripping the people's shirts from their backs, they rip the skin from their bodies! It is clear that bribery has produced further injustice. In the final section of the book, the rich have houses full of violence and have used crooked weights and measures to increase their wealth (6:10–11). Later the land becomes chaos where people seem to hunt each other down, looking to gain some monetary advantage (7:1–6).

Isaiah speaks about justice as being the key ingredient necessary for the flourishing of a covenant society. Using the metaphor of a vineyard to describe Israel, he says that the result was a harvest of bitter grapes: "The vineyard of the LORD Almighty / is the nation of Israel, / and the people of Judah / are the vines he delighted in. / And he looked for *justice*, / but saw bloodshed; / for *righteousness*, / but heard cries of distress" (Isa 5:3–7 NIV). Here the poetic word pair "justice and righteousness" means social justice: righteousness (צְדָקָה/ṣĕdāqâ) is contrasted with cries of distress (צְעָקָה/ṣĕʿāqâ), which come from helpless victims of oppression; justice (מִשְׁפָּט/mišpāṭ) is contrasted with flaying (מִשְׂפָּח/miśpāḥ)! The social nature of the sins is further demonstrated by the list of sins that follows: the greedy acquisition of real estate, the perpetual partying without any care for the law of God, the pursuit of hedonism and alcohol, and the corruption of justice in the courts (Isa 5:8–23). Other prophets present similar themes.

This concern of justice is just as much a key concept in the New Testament as in the Old. It is unfortunate that justice is often pitted against mercy. Interestingly, Jesus unites them, indicating that they belong together. He lambasts the religious leaders of his society for being concerned for the fairly minor points of the law while neglecting justice, mercy, and faith (Matt 23:23). This is probably a direct echo of Mic 6:8, in which the call for Judah was not to be concerned so much with the one-off sacrifices and rituals as to be involved in living a life of doing justice, loving mercy, and walking with God (faith).

One serious problem in the history of Christianity has been the neglect of social justice. In the twentieth century this was particularly heightened by a reaction to certain theological moves that identified the Christian message virtually in an exclusive manner with social justice.[14] The result was that a large segment of the church overreacted by stressing the spiritual nature of salvation and downplaying the social element, thus tearing apart the message of Jesus and the prophets. This has been called the Great Reversal, and it has amply been documented by historians.[15] It is only in the last few decades that Protestant

14. E.g., see Walter Rauschenbusch, *A Theology for the Social Gospel* (New York: Macmillan, 1917).

15. Religious historian Timothy Smith was the first to coin this term as a descriptor for abdication of evangelicals from social engagement in the first part of the twentieth century. See further David Moberg, *The Great Reversal: Reconciling Evangelism and Social Concern* (Eugene: Wipf & Stock, 2007), 28–45.

evangelicals have sought to rectify this serious problem, with a concern for the importance of social justice, but it is still an issue.[16] For Micah it represented a natural outflow of a life of fellowship with God.

Land

Land is a central theme in the book of Micah. God leaves the throne room of the universe and treads on the high places, indicating that he as the divine owner is laying claim to his land. In the first chapter it is clear that God has everything to do with land: Samaria and Jerusalem and many of the towns on the southwestern flank of Judah are to be destroyed. They have not been good stewards of the land given to them by the divine landlord, and they must forfeit those places, and the population is to be driven away from the land to exile.

One of the reasons for poor stewardship of the land is that wealthy Israelites have coveted the lands of their poorer counterparts. As a result land has been expropriated through debt foreclosure. Many owners' indigence would force them to borrow from the wealthy, who would demand payment at an inopportune time. Unable to pay, the poor would have to relinquish their houses and lands. The rich are characterized as merciless, consumed by the objects of their covetous lust: "They covet fields and seize them, and houses, and take them away. They oppress householder and house, people and their inheritance" (2:2). The result is that women are expelled from their estates, and the blessing is taken away from their children forever. Here "blessing" is identified with the children living in the land God has given them in which to grow and flourish.

Sin does not affect just relationships between people; land is defiled, making it unclean. This is why the prophet can say to the greedy land-grabbers of his day: "Get out of here! Immediately! For this is not your resting place, because it is defiled—completely ruined, beyond all remedy" (2:10, my translation). The word "defiled" is normally used in a priestly context to designate ritual uncleanness but here it is clearly used for moral reasons. The violation of Israel's ethical code has polluted the land. Other examples in earlier texts describe the origin of this concept. In Genesis, the blood of a murdered man defiles the land upon which it is shed (4:10–12).[17] In ancient Israel, laws indicated that murder defiled the land:

---

16. See, e.g., Timothy Keller, *Generous Justice: How God's Grace Makes Us Just* (New York: Penguin, 2010). A recent popular book speaks to the problem: Richard Stearns, *The Hole in Our Gospel* (Nashville: Nelson, 2009).

17. Thus Cain cannot farm the land but must be a nomadic wanderer.

You shall not pollute the land in which you live; for blood pollutes the land, and no expiation can be made for the land, for the blood that is shed in it, except by the blood of the one who shed it. You shall not defile the land in which you live, in which I also dwell; for I the LORD dwell among the Israelites. (Num 35:33–34)

When a corpse is discovered—the victim of a murder—and the perpetrator remains anonymous, the elders of the nearest village must perform a peculiar rite (Deut 21:1–9). This was an act of atonement in order to purge the evil from their land. In fact throughout the book of Deuteronomy the formulaic phrase "to purge evil from the land" is one of the motivations for punishing criminals (13:5; 17:7, 12; 19:13, 19; cf. 2 Sam 4:11). This is not just to deter crime: the purity and holiness of the land must be maintained.

Perhaps Westerners can better understand this concept if they compare it to ecological pollution. In the last few decades, it has become clear that huge tracts of land and water have been polluted, showing the drastic consequences for the habitation of life in these areas.[18] Love Canal in upstate New York became notorious as a dumping ground for toxic waste, and the results were horrific; the polluting of the Gulf of Mexico by a damaged oil well in the summer of 2013 caused untold damage to the environment over a period of months. Chernobyl was a nuclear disaster, the consequences of which are still being experienced today. In the biblical view, there is such a thing as moral pollution. The first consequences of it are experienced after the fall when the ground produces thorns and thistles and is resistant to the production of agriculture. Cain's murder of Abel means that the ground that soaked up the blood of Abel is now cursed for Cain, who must give up his occupation as a farmer and become a nomad. The judgment of the flood may be understood as a cleansing of all the innocent blood that was shed because of human violence. Interestingly human beings after the flood must institute a death penalty for murder (Gen 9:5–6). This may be an atonement procedure much as is present in the book of Numbers mentioned above.

The conquest of the Canaanites is viewed from a priestly point of view as one example of this conception. They are "vomited" from the land because of their evil. The moral evil they have practiced, including the shedding of innocent blood, has poisoned the land, and as a result the land expels the poison

---

18. There is a vast amount of literature on this subject. The first "prophetic" voice to be raised against pollution in the West was Rachel Carson, *Silent Spring* (repr. New York: Houghton Mifflin Harcourt, 2002). In a series of articles in the *New Yorker* (1962) she voiced concern about ecological pollution.

(Lev 18:28; 20:22). This understanding lies behind the priestly conception of the universe. When sin occurs whether morally or ritually, it needs to be purged from the community, and it "collects" on the most holy places, the altar, the representation of God, and thus the blood of the sacrificial animal must be poured out at the base of the altar to atone for the sins of the Israelites, that is, to cleanse the sanctuary area.[19] Thus on the Day of Atonement the blood also has to be sprinkled on other objects, particularly the place of atonement, the lid of the ark of the covenant. The transferring of all the sins of the community on the scapegoat that is led out in the wilderness graphically describes what has happened in the atonement rite. The camp has been cleansed.

Micah declares to his audience that the priestly rites are not effective anymore; since the priests themselves have become corrupt and the people are simply using the sacrificial system not as a means to take sin seriously but as a means for license—they always have a scapegoat—the temple itself has become a place of defilement, and no sacrifices can suffice: it is to be destroyed and the people themselves will be "vomited" up from the land as were the Canaanites before them. Although this language is not used, it has a similar meaning. Like the scapegoat, the people of Judah will carry their sins with them out of the land into exile. Other texts complement this picture. The land now is able to receive rest from all the Sabbaths that were not kept (Lev 26:35–43, 44; Jer 29:10; 2 Chr 36:21).

Thus one of the worst punishments of judgment is to be exiled from the land.[20] When God pronounces exile against the people of Judah he describes it in similar terms. They are to mourn for their youth who will be taken away from the blessing of living in the land. Indeed the exile is mentioned at key passages in the book: it is clearly a time of great judgment, and it is viewed on the one hand as a barrier to salvation, and on the other as a precursor to salvation—a means of purification.

Salvation is about coming home. The walls of their exilic prison in Babylon seem formidable, but God will send "a breaker" to breach the walls and lead his people through the rupture as he led them through the Red Sea in the past. God, their king, leads them out of their dungeon back home. Back in the land each can have his portion of land just as it was distributed when they first

---

19. "Insofar as the Tabernacle and later the Temple serve as the holy center of creation, the violation of Yhwh's Torah corrupts all of creation, requiring that the offenders and sanctuary must be purified in order to restore the sacred order of creation as a whole"; Marvin A. Sweeney, *Tanak: A Theological and Critical Introduction to the Jewish Bible* (Minneapolis: Fortress, 2012), 110.

20. The climactic punishment in the curse list in Deut 28 is exile, particularly in Egypt (28:64–68).

entered the land during the conquest of Canaan (Mic 2:5, 12–13). At the same time, this period is viewed as a period of refining judgment, of birth pangs, before future salvation (4:9–10).

When the exiles will finally return, the geography will change. Although Zion will become the highest mountain, the temple, God's presence, will become the focal point of the land, and the city of Jerusalem will become a beacon to the nations—a magnet drawing them from the ends of the earth. How does Zion become such a beacon, a magnet? It comes only after a long time of judgment and exile, which is interpreted as a long period of gestation for Mother Israel. After a long period a ruler is born who will rule the nations with justice. His title, "Ruler" (מוֹשֵׁל/*môšēl*), is an anagram for the result of his rule: "peace" (שָׁלוֹם/*šālôm*)! He will lead the exiles home but he also will reform the nation and destroy every idol (5:10–15). Thus fortified cities and walls will be torn down, as well as instruments of warfare. Peace will become the dominating feature in the land that has come about with trust in Yahweh alone. Zion will be elevated in prominence as the city set on a hill. The resulting peace and harmony will produce fertility, safety, and satiety. The people will be like sheep feeding in the rich pasturelands of Bashan and Gilead, which had been famous places of great fertility in ancient Israel (7:14). Thus the Torah that goes forth from Jerusalem will have authority behind it (חֹק/*ḥōq*; 7:11). It will be a proclamation to the nations of the divine rule in this motley group of rehabilitated exiles and be a universal call to listen and pay homage to the king. Many will be impressed by the difference that Yahweh has made, and when they hear about the proclamation of the Torah, they will be drawn to Zion as iron filings to a magnet, or as the text says, they will "river up" to Zion (4:1). There they will be confronted by the king, and they will change their ways, to walk in Yahweh's way and will take instruments of war and transform them into farming implements in order that they might develop the now fertile earth. Those among the nations that do not respond will experience judgment some day, and meanwhile their own part of the earth will suffer under the weight of their sins (5:15; 7:13).

This view of land in Micah and in the Old Testament can serve as an important corrective on spiritualizations of the promises to the people of God in the Old Testament by Christians. The New Testament is often portrayed as promising life after death in heaven for the believer, and heaven is viewed too often in the popular imagination as a place for disembodied spirits flying around in a vague, ethereal space where choirs and harps abound. But this is a theological distortion of the eschatological hope. The New Testament has a clear concern for the end and an expectation that it will happen within a short time. At the same time there is a great hope in the resurrection from the dead, which implies also the reclamation of the soil of the earth. There does not seem to be a concern for the *land* of Israel as there is in the Old Testament,[21] but there is certainly a concern for the world. Jesus has been granted all authority over the earth (Matt 28:18–20). The disciples of Jesus are to make disciples of all nations. Paul views the promise of a descendant to Abraham and Sarah and the promise of the land of Canaan to them as types of a vast number of believers and the world itself. Thus Abraham by faith was to become "the father of many nations" (Rom 4:18) and "an heir of the world" (4:13). The biblical storyline is concerned for nothing less than the redemption of the earth. It looks forward to heaven coming down to earth and there being a perfect union someday.[22] The result is a new heaven and a new earth!

Temple

Standing at the center of the book of Micah are two visions of the temple: a building at the center of an oppressive world (3:12) and a building in the middle of a shalom society (4:1–4). When people come to the first temple, they are not changed. They come to a place of corruption where the priesthood represents the idol of money and profit rather than Yahweh. And as a result the people who gather to worship leave more ignorant of Yahweh's ways than before, and become more corrupt. When people come to the second temple, they are transformed as they experience truth, healing, and peace (4:1–5). They hear the words of Yahweh and experience conversion and change the society around them. They bring their weapons, and hearing the word of the Lord, they beat them into ploughshares and pruning hooks, productive tools for the flourishing of agriculture. In the first example, the world of idolatry and war has changed the temple, and in the second, the temple has changed the world of idolatry and war.

The first vision is a gross distortion of the purpose and function of a temple while the second is completely accurate. The temple was the holy center of creation, a microcosm of the macrocosm of the world: the place of God's rule. When God created the world it was constructed as a holy place, with lights and food, with his images placed in the inner sanctum, with the responsibility to be his priest-king and queen extending his rule to the entire world (Gen 1–2). This great house of God was his dwelling place, and the first human couple had inti-

21. W. D. Davies, *The Gospel and the Land: Early Christianity and Jewish Territorial Doctrine* (Oakland: University of California Press, 1974).

22. See, e.g., Sandra L. Richter, *The Epic of Eden: A Christian Entry into the Old Testament* (Downers Grove: InterVarsity, 2010), 119–36; and J. Richard Middleton, *A New Heaven and a New Earth: Reclaiming Biblical Eschatology* (Grand Rapids: Baker, 2014).

mate fellowship with God in the inner sanctum, the garden of Eden. Here they lived in a completely transparent relationship with each other and with their creator: the rich garden park of Eden, a holy hill, complete with its fruit trees and tree of life had pure spring waters bubbling up and flowing out to the rest of the world, thereby giving it life. As images of God, the human couple were placed in the inner sanctum of the temple of the universe, with the command to extend that inner sanctum to the rest of the world.[23] But with the fall, humans were banished from the sanctum and giant angelic beings guarded the way to Eden (3:24). Outside Eden, the holy ground of the earth becomes defiled with blood and violence until it has to be cleansed. An ark serves to help continue the created order with Noah and his family and the animals. But in many ways, with the call of Abram, God starts to reclaim his lost dominion and brings the temple back to humanity. When Abram comes into the land of Canaan, he pitches a tent and builds an altar (12:8). This indicates that God is now dwelling with humanity again as the altar and tent foreshadow the altar and tabernacle, which will later play such prominent roles in Israelite society. During Moses's time, God leaves the mountain of God at Sinai and comes down and lives with the Israelites in a tent (Exod 25–40). For the first time in the Bible since Eden, God is now living more permanently with human beings. During the time of Solomon, the tent becomes permanent in a temple, and the temple is named after its builder, Solomon, because it is to be a place of holiness and peace in the world, a place where the word of God might be proclaimed, where forgiveness occurs, and where all the nations might find shalom (1 Kgs 6–8).

The symbolism of the temple indicated the elements of creation: altar = mountain; bronze laver = ocean; pillars = support of the cosmos; decorations of fruit trees on the temple walls = garden of Eden; Menorah or candlestick = tree of life; twelve loaves of bread = people of God; and holy of holies where the ark of the covenant was located = footstool of the invisible divine throne.[24] The high priest who came once a year into this most intimate atmosphere had the holy name of God on his forehead and represented the people with his breastplate of twelve precious gems. Sometimes there is a depiction of the meaning of this glory. Isaiah gets a glimpse of this in his temple vision, when he sees the divine king on his throne towering over everything in the holy of holies with the train of his robe filling the entire temple: the angelic beings thunder

23. For further discussion of these themes, see L. Michael Morales, ed., *Cult and Cosmos: Tilting toward a Temple-Centered Theology* (Leuven: Peeters, 2014); G.K. Beale, *The Temple and the Church's Mission: A Biblical Theology of the Dwelling Place of God* (Downers Grove: IVP Academic, 2004).

24. See, e.g., O. Keel, *The Symbolism of the Biblical World: Ancient Near Eastern Iconography and the Book of Psalms* (Winona Lake: Eisenbrauns, 1997), 113–60.

the words: "Holy, holy, holy, for the entire earth is full of his glory" (Isa 6:1–5). The temple image, with the train of Yahweh filling the entire precincts of this structure, represents the world being filled with the glory of Yahweh. Similar images are found in other passages of Scripture: during the reign of the messianic king, it is stated that not only nature will be transformed, but that no one will hurt and destroy in the Lord's holy mountain and that the world will be filled with the knowledge of the Lord as the water covers the sea (Isa 11:1–9). At the end of Ps 72 the editor of the Psalter appends a doxology for the praise of the God of Israel: "May his glory fill the entire earth." It is no accident that this doxology ends a messianic psalm in which the Davidic king will bring blessing to the entire earth.

With the building of the temple by Solomon, Israel became known as the center of God's plan for the world. God dwelled on his throne in Jerusalem, and it was to be the place of healing and forgiveness (1 Kgs 8). It became a symbol of election and God's promise to bless his people forever. It was the preeminent symbol of God's favor. But as the kingdom became divided and as the people of Judah apostatized, the religious leaders used their offices to exploit for personal aggrandizement. Sin was sanctioned, and the temple as a place of life became a place of death and defilement. More sins resulted in more need to provide salve for guilty consciences through sacrifice, which made more wealth for priests, the custodians of the temple. Thus Micah is the first person in the history of Israel to pronounce judgment on the temple. He basically stated that the sacrificial rituals performed in its locale were all to no avail; God had had enough and was going to destroy his holy place, abandoning it completely. This judgment speech would have been shocking to the people, and in fact history records that a shaken Hezekiah led a national repentance that preserved the nation (Jer 26:19). At the same time the next generations did not learn the lesson, and the people deteriorated to their former state, with the temple being regarded as a sanctuary for criminals (cf. Jer 7 and 26). As a result the judgment fell and the temple was obliterated, with the people being either destroyed or taken off into exile (Jer 52), just as Jeremiah and Ezekiel had predicted (Jer 26; Ezek 24).

With the return of the exiles, their first act is to rebuild the altar; after a considerable delay they finish the temple (Ezra 3; Haggai; Zech 1–8). The prophets Haggai and Zechariah encouraged the builders with promises of great glory to come in the future for this new sanctuary. Micah himself as well as Isaiah had promised a new temple that would be elevated as the highest mountain and be a beacon to the nations and from which the Torah would be promulgated to the nations. Stager states "that on the mountain of Yahweh, Mount Zion, the indissoluble triad of creation, kingship and temple find their most profound literary and visual expression."[25] Zion was a cosmic center where the king would rule, and heaven and earth would be united. In the vision of Micah the nations would come, meet the Lord, the king, be rebuked and instructed by him, and then transform their instruments of war into ones of peace. Thus the temple would live up to the name of its original builder (Solomon) and be a wellspring of Shalom to the wider world. The temple would be like a city set on a hill. In an even bolder move, Ezekiel describes a new temple on a mount, from which a spring of pure water emerges that grows into a mighty river bringing life to everywhere it flows (Ezek 47). A similar motif occurs in Zechariah, where a river of living water arises from an elevated Jerusalem and divides into two branches, with half flowing to the east and half to the west, and the river never dries up—even in the summer (Zech 14).

By the time of the New Testament the temple had been rebuilt, but the promise of worldwide glory had not materialized. The temple had become a place of corruption from which Jesus drove out materialistic, greedy profiteers, whose only interest was to exploit religion for financial gain (Matt 21:1–17). He himself prophesied its destruction as the sign of the end of the age and the coming of a new one.

But in the New Testament there was the dawning consciousness that the temple was only a *type* anticipating its *antitype*, the presence of God. It was the promise of God living with his people, which was there at the original creation in the land of paradise. The supreme fulfillment of that type was the revelation of God in Jesus Christ, God tabernacling among his people, becoming one of them, walking with them, eating with them, conversing with them, teaching them, living with them (John 1:14). Thus he says to a Samaritan woman looking for true life that "the hour is coming when you will worship the Father neither on this mountain nor in Jerusalem . . . when true worshippers will worship in spirit and in truth" (4:21–23). The whole world will become the locus of the presence of God, because Jesus Christ is here and he will give his Spirit free access to anyone who calls on the name of the Lord. In the shadow of the temple from which someday would spring up a river of living water, Jesus says, "Whoever is thirsty let him come to me and drink. Whoever believes in me . . . rivers of water will flow from within them" (7:37b–38 NIV). Jesus is now claiming that he himself—not the temple—is the source of living water and when a person drinks from him, out of that person's body will flow rivers of living water!

This use of the temple as an image for the body of Christ is further emphasized when Jesus remarks in the Gospel of John that if the temple is destroyed, he would raise it up in three days (2:19–22). He spoke, however, of the temple

25. Lawrence Stager, cited in James McKeown, *Genesis* (Grand Rapids: Eerdmans, 2008), 251.

of his body, to the confusion of both his opponents and his own disciples. Thus in the destruction of his body he suffers anew the curses of the covenant for his people, probably in a greater manner than the temple in the time of the Babylonian judgment; his resurrection from the grave represents the beginning of a new world order, the temple elevated to the highest place, a city set on a hill (Mic 4:1–5; Isa 60; Matt 5:13–16)! It is the temple that is lifted on high to become a beacon to the nations. His disciples now constitute his body—living stones that he inhabits through his Spirit, bringing his light and life to the world, a true city set on a hill: a true place of justice. Thus when he returns there will be a world like the first in which there is no literal temple (Rev 21:22). The whole universe will be "one gigantic holy of holies."[26] The signal mark of this place is: "The LORD is there!" (cf. Ezek 48:35).

Messiah

"The term Messiah is used so commonly in the English language that few people ever reflect on its meaning or its origin."[27] Thus begins Fitzmyer's major study of the Messiah. But where does this term originate, and did it always have the idea of a superhuman figure who would right the world's wrongs, as it does in modern parlance? Or was this later connotation a meaning that distorted its original significance? Although the term "Messiah" does not occur in the book of Micah, the concept is important there as the figure of an eschatological shepherd-king emerges from a place in Judah named Bethlehem, who will someday have a worldwide reign (5:2–5; 7:14–15).

The term "Messiah" is an Aramaic loanword that was rendered into Greek (Grecized). This is related to a Hebrew noun derived from the verb, which means to apply a liquid to an object through actions such as rubbing, smearing, or painting. Thus a house could be painted (Jer 22:14), shields could be rubbed with oil before a battle (Isa 21:5; 2 Sam 1:21), or a person could have his or her body massaged with fine oils (Amos 6:6). But most frequently it came to be used to apply to religiously significant objects or persons who were dedicated for sacred purposes. Thus priests were "anointed" with oil when they were appointed to their task, as were the objects in their peculiar environment: for example, altar, tabernacle, temple, and furniture. It also came to be associated with the installation of a king, as God's anointed agent of rule. Thus when the

---

26. Cf. M. Woudstra, "The Tabernacle in Biblical Theological Perspective," in *New Perspectives on the Old Testament*, ed. J. Barton Payne (Waco: Word, 1970), 88–103, esp. 103.

27. Joseph A. Fitzmyer, *The One Who Is to Come* (Grand Rapids: Eerdmans, 2007), 1.

military commander, Jehu, is anointed by Elisha the prophet, it is immediately recognized by his comrades in arms that this is beginning of a coup d'état (2 Kgs 9:12–13).

The noun "Messiah" is a passive participle meaning "anointed one"; the adjective or noun is almost always used of a king or kingly figure who is sometimes called "the anointed of the LORD," although it could be used for the priestly office. Thus David, even though he had already been privately anointed by Samuel and had the opportunity to kill Saul, refused to do so because it would be to attack "the anointed of the LORD" (1 Sam 24:6 [2x]).

The question whether the term functioned in an eschatological sense in the Old Testament is strongly suggested by a consideration of the larger narrative sweep of the biblical story. From the beginning of Genesis there is the expectation of a seed born of a woman, who would reverse the curse (Gen 3:15—the so-called Protoevangelium). This partially explains the genealogical uniqueness of Genesis, which tracks this expectation from its beginning (3:15) through the promise to Abram that through his seed all the nations will receive blessing (12:3) and that kings will emerge from his line (17:6), until its hope in prophecy at the end of the book, where Jacob blesses Judah with the announcement that a king will emerge from his line, to whom the nations will give their obedience (49:8–10).[28] The prophecies of Balaam make the same claim for this king, in virtually identical language (Num 24:9). While it is true that this figure is never named the Messiah up to this point in the biblical story, the concept of a royal ruler who will emerge as a worldwide figure becomes more developed.

The book of Samuel is framed by two poems that can be heard in antiphonal response. Hannah's thanksgiving song for the gift of her kingmaking son, Samuel, is a prediction of the future course of world history. It will not be in the control of "the movers and the shakers," the powerbrokers of politics and economics—the Elis and Goliaths—it will be in the control of the God who exalts the lowly and abases the proud. Thus her final words are "Yahweh will judge to the ends of the earth, and give power to his king, and raise the horn of his anointed" (1 Sam 2:10, my translation). In his final words David resoundingly echoes those of Hannah: "He magnifies the triumphs of his king; he shows unfailing love to his anointed, to David and his descendants forever" (2 Sam 22:51, my translation). While Hannah has an eschatological king in mind, that king has come to expression in David and his seed. This commitment to and singling out of the small shepherd boy, David, from the tribe of Judah, is a core element of the narrative between these two poems, but the fact is that a covenant is made

---

28. T. Desmond Alexander, "Genealogies, Seed, and the Compositional Unity of Genesis," *Tyndale Bulletin* 44 (1993): 255–70.

with David, which promises him an eternal dynasty (2 Sam 7). The promise to David uses language that was used with regard to the Abrahamic covenant, that David and his line would be exalted and provide universal blessing. Despite all the vicissitudes of kingship and the schism between the northern and southern kingdoms, David's line was preserved in the southern kingdom as a hope for this future. The historian called this preservation "a lamp" shining in the darkness (2 Sam 21:17; 1 Kgs 11:36; 15:4; 2 Kgs 8:19). When Judah was destroyed and it no longer had a king, the historian ends the book of Kings with a note that the Davidic king in exile, Jehoiachin, was released and exalted above all the other exiled kings in Babylon (2 Kgs 25:27–30). This suggests that the lamp is still burning, albeit dimly.[29] Consequently Isaiah can regard this as a shoot arising from the stump of Jesse, and the shoot will grow to become a king whose rule will save the wretched of the earth and even transform nature (Isa 11:1–9). Other prophets speak of a new David who will come and save Israel and restore the world (Hos 3:5; Ezek 34:23–24).

The seams of the Psalter also stress the same point. At the beginning, the Davidic king's installation points to his inheritance of the entire earth and his universal rule and the call for rebellious kings to submit and to "kiss the son" (Ps 2:12). This is the only psalm where the words "anointed one [Messiah]," "son," and "king" occur together in the entire Old Testament, and they make the point clearly that the Davidic king is God's son and his representative, who has been set apart (anointed) to rule the world and bring universal peace. Although many scholars assume this language is just hyperbole, characteristic of poetic language in the ancient world, which was used as a type of political spin for ancient Near Eastern kings, it is significant that when the Psalter was finally edited, this psalm was placed at its beginning in a time when no king was reigning in Judah. At other seams in the Psalter, the Davidic king is not only the one who will rule from sea to sea, he will bring justice to the nations, and in him all the promises of universal blessing through Abraham's seed will be fulfilled (72:17).

This probably explains best the idea of a Danielic Son of Man, who both represents the people of God and who triumphs over all evil and saves humanity from the raging beasts of the earth (Dan 7). Indeed Daniel draws from images of humanity reigning over the beasts in Gen 1 as well as the king of Israel and the Son of Man reigning over the ravaging beasts in the Psalms (Ps 8, 80).[30] Daniel

---

29. James R. Critchlow, *Looking Back for Jehoiachin: Yahweh's Cast-Out Signet*, Africanus Monographs (Eugene: Wipf & Stock, 2013).

30. Cf. Andrew Streett, *The Vine and the Son of Man: Eschatological Interpretation of Psalm 80 in Early Judaism* (Minneapolis: Augsburg Fortress, 2014).

is the first to use "Messiah" to describe a coming ruler who will be the fulfillment of the plan of God for history: to bring in everlasting righteousness, which
shows that this term now has explicit eschatological significance (Dan 9:25).
By the time of the New Testament there is the hope in this figure: "A strong
Redeemer, by his power and his spirit, [who] will bring complete redemption,
political and spiritual, to the people Israel, and along with this, earthly bliss and
moral perfection to the entire human race."[31]

Micah and his contemporary, Isaiah, are found midway in this messianic
trajectory. Micah announces a king born from the line of David in Bethlehem
who will someday rule the nations (Mic 5:2–4) after the land has been abandoned for a long period. This period can be compared to the gestation pains
of a mother in labor. But finally the mother will give birth to a child, who will
rule unto the ends of the earth. His exaltation seems to presage or coincide with
the exaltation of the temple at the end of the ages, in the latter days, when the
people will be saved and Jerusalem will be a blessing to the nations. Although
the term "Messiah" is not used by Micah, it is clear that he has a Davidic king
in mind who will be the agent of world peace. In fact a reference to a royal birth
in both Micah and Isaiah has a universal significance, occurring in a period of
crisis. In Isaiah, the Emmanuel accounts seem to climax in the birth of a child,
long after a period of exile, who will shatter the yoke of Assyrian oppression
and bring light to the Assyrian-dominated northern reaches of Israel, Zebulun,
and Naphtali:

> For a child has been born for us,
>   a son given to us;
> authority rests upon his shoulders;
>   and he is named
> Wonderful Counselor, Mighty God,
>   Everlasting Father, Prince of Peace.
> His authority shall grow continually,
>   and there shall be endless peace
> for the throne of David and his kingdom.
>   He will establish and uphold it
> with justice and with righteousness
>   from this time onward and forevermore.
> The zeal of the Lord of hosts will do this. (Isa 9:6–7)

---

31. Joseph Klausner, *The Messianic Idea in Israel from Its Beginning to the Completion of
the Mishnah* (Charleston: Nabu, 2011), 9, cited in Joseph A. Fitzmyer, *The One Who Is to Come*
(Grand Rapids: Eerdmans, 2007), 5.

It is difficult not to see the obvious link between this text and Mic 5:

> But you, O Bethlehem of Ephrathah,
>   who are one of the little clans of Judah,
> from you shall come forth for me
>   one who is to rule in Israel,
> whose origin is from of old,
>   from ancient days.
> Therefore he shall give them up until the time
>   when she who is in labor has brought forth;
> then the rest of his kindred shall return
>   to the people of Israel.
> And he shall stand and feed his flock in the strength of the LORD,
>   in the majesty of the name of the LORD his God.
> And they shall live secure, for now he shall be great
>   to the ends of the earth;
> and he shall be the one of peace.
>   If the Assyrians come into our land
>   and tread upon our soil,
> we will raise against them seven shepherds
>   and eight installed as rulers. (Mic 5:2–5)

Both texts speak of the birth of a ruler, whose domain will eventually reach to the ends of the earth and who will defeat the Assyrian enemy—a powerful symbol of oppression. Along with such texts, others suggest that Micah was not to be read alone, but to be read in relation to Isaiah. One of the main points that emphasizes this bond is the placement of the "elevated temple" oracle in both books. Isaiah 2:1–4 and Mic 4:1–4 are virtually identical and are placed in each book in similar contexts: Zion will be elevated someday after every high and lofty power, every proud pretension, every arrogant ambition, and every idol will be humbled. Yahweh and his king will return to Zion to accomplish this, and the king will be exalted until the ends of the earth. It does not take a great imaginative leap of logic to connect the dots on this trajectory from Genesis to the New Testament. To argue that the Messiah is simply a New Testament distortion of the Old Testament evidence is to read the Old Testament in an atomistic way.

One further important feature of this trajectory is the birth of the Messiah. The Isaianic and Mican texts both stress the birth of the ruler. In Isaiah, there are no labor pains associated with the birth but this is not the case in Micah. This theme resonates with other passages in the Bible, beginning with the promise to the woman that she would give birth to a seed who would deal a fatal blow to the head of the seed of the serpent (Gen 3:15). And in the very next verse, the woman becomes afflicted with the pains of labor, which is associated with the curse (3:16). Whereas before, the woman was told that she was to be fruitful and multiply and have children (1:26–28), now she is told that what will be fruitful and prolific will be her pains in childbirth but that eventually she will have a descendant who will be victorious over the serpent.

The book of Genesis with its repeated reference to "seed" and its numerous genealogies placed at strategic junctures highlights the importance of this descendant who will bless the world.[32] Many of these themes are developed in the rest of the Torah, but most receive their genesis in Genesis. As is often the case, there is fluctuation between the descendants of the patriarch and one of their members, but it is clear that there is the promise of abundant vegetation (Gen 49:11; Mic 4:4), hope for the lame and the limp who have fought with God and won the blessing (Jacob/Israel) (Gen 32:32; Mic 4:6–7), the birth of children after the pain of labor that leads to death near Bethlehem (Migdal Eder) (Gen 35:16–21; Mic 4:8–9), the use of oxen imagery to stress the pulverizing of the enemies of God (Num 23:22; 24:8; Mic 4:13), and the use of the imagery of dew (Gen 27:27–29; Mic 5:7) and a lion (Gen 49:8–10; Mic 5:8) to describe both the positive and negative impact on Israel's friends and foes among the nations. In Micah many of these themes are presented in kaleidoscope fashion. Thus there are the promise of abundant vegetation guaranteed by a royal peace, the promise that the lame and limp like Jacob of old will be regathered and brought home, that Israel's pain will be like Rachel's in labor near Migdal Eder where she gave birth to Benjamin and then died, that Israel will pulverize its enemies who seek to defile it, that Israel will bear a child after a long period of gestation who will be from Bethlehem and rule the nations, and that Israel will also be like dew from heaven among the nations on the one hand and like a lion on the other. Israel's new king will bring about the destruction of the great enemy Assyria, but also the destruction of every false god within Israel, whether representing military offense or defense, sorcery, witchcraft, or idols made by human hands. This same range of images is found in Mic 4–5, where it freely moves back and forth among these patriarchal stories and pronouncements. What they all have in common is the determination to bless Israel and those who bless Israel, and the judgment of those who seek its harm. Throughout Micah are pervasive references to Daughter Zion (1:13; 4:8, 10, 13; 7:8–11) or Daughter of the Troops (5:1), and a woman seized by labor pains in child birth. This traces

---

32. T. Desmond Alexander, "Genealogies, Seed, and the Compositional Unity of Genesis," *Tyndale Bulletin* 44 (1993): 255-70.

its origin to the Protoevangelium and its announcement of blessing and curse and is reshaped at the beginning of the patriarchal narratives, where there is the same narrative-shaping motif:

> I will make of you a great nation, and I will bless you, and make your name great, so that you will be a blessing. I will bless those who bless you, and the one who curses you I will curse; and in you all the families of the earth shall be blessed. (Gen 12:2–3)

That the biblical text can easily move from this text to a king who will crush the serpent's head is suggested in Ps 72, in which Yahweh installs a Davidic king who will bring justice to the nations and reduce his enemies to crawling in the dust, transform nature and be like dew and showers to the fields, and rule from sea to sea, and as a result "all nations will be blessed through him, / and they will call him blessed" (72:17 NIV). A creative imagination is unnecessary to see that a child born in Bethlehem will someday rule the world, bring about an end to war, and usher in a new world in the latter days. The New Testament with one voice announces that such a day has come in Jesus Christ.

That these events do not happen concurrently is due to the unfolding mystery of God's plan. For if they did happen all at once there could be no mission to the nations. The delay between the first and second comings of Christ—the first in suffering the curse of judgment and the second in glory and judgment—allows for the blessing of Abraham to be spread to the nations and to give them hope, so that the entire world can be blessed through Abraham's seed, before God leaves his throne room and steps down to the earth for final judgment (Mic 1:2–4).

Worship

Perhaps more than any other prophet, Micah defines true worship. In a classic definition he contrasts it with false understandings:

> "With what shall I come before the LORD,
>   and bow myself before God on high?
> Shall I come before him with burnt offerings,
>   with calves a year old?
> Will the LORD be pleased with thousands of rams,
>   with ten thousands of rivers of oil?
> Shall I give my firstborn for my transgression,

> the fruit of my body for the sin of my soul?"
> He has told you, O mortal, what is good;
>   and what does the LORD require of you
> but to do justice, and to love kindness,
>   and to walk humbly with your God? (Mic 6:6–8)

Micah contrasts specific acts of cultic service with a life dedicated to God. In his time, the understanding of worship had been bastardized. Worship is one part of a dialogue with God that takes place between two spheres, the cult and the culture. The whole purpose of the cult is to change the culture. Thus there is the dynamic of holiness, in which the Israelites hear in the cult the directive: "'Be holy for I am holy,' says the LORD." They then take that directive outside the cult to the culture, and the holiness of the cult ought to begin to permeate the culture.

If one can think of the cult (the actual place of formal worship in which there is the practice of sacrifice and ritual, the hearing of Torah, and the singing of God's praises) surrounded by a much larger sphere (that of the culture, where there is the area of sacraments and rights, dialogue with neighbor and God outside the formal worship service) the fundamental relationship between them is straightforward. Cult functions as the meeting place between God and worshiper, in which sacrifice is presented for sins, and thanksgiving, where formal praise is offered and the divine word is read and interpreted. Thus worshipers move from the culture to the cult to express remorse and penitence for sin, to give thanks, to hear the divine words of mercy and forgiveness, to receive divine guidance for life, to express praise for God's mighty acts. Thus when they return to the culture, they will seek to live renewed lives of mercy and justice, to follow the precepts of the Torah, and to live a life marked by the qualities of the divine character, which they have praised in their worship service. Thus there is an inextricable relationship between the cult and the culture. Westermann expresses it using slightly different images:

> The relevance of worship in Israel lies in its function as the focal point of the life of the people. What is decisive is not what happens in the isolated service, but rather what happens in worship for the whole people and the whole land. Therefore, the walk from the house to the service, and from the service back to the house, is an important factor of the service itself. What is brought into the service on these walks from the outside life, and also what is taken back into everyday life from the service, are necessarily a part of the act of worship as well. Only in this way can worship be the center of the entire life of the people. Only in this way is criticism of worship

also possible, as in the prophetic criticism of a worship which has become false. The reciprocal event of worship from God to people and from people to God receives meaning solely from the fact *that it becomes the center of events outside the service*.[33]

Thus, as far as Micah was concerned, people were to leave the cult committed to walk with Yahweh, which meant a life committed to *ḥesed* and *mišpāṭ*. They were to walk in "Yahweh's way" in a life that constituted seeking justice and loving *ḥesed*. Humanity becomes like the first human couple before the fall, reflecting the image of God, and once again in charge of creation.

But if this mutual relationship between worship and life is severed, then life starts to unravel and the people of God lose their real identity and purpose. Society breaks down, as the center does not hold. The quartet of the vulnerable (widow, orphan, poor, refugee) who are already on the margins of society are marginalized further, and they begin to be victims of oppression. The concern for the Torah becomes a matter of the letter rather than the spirit. Thus Amos speaks of the entrepreneurs in his day eagerly waiting for the Sabbath to end so that they can return to the business of maximizing profits by cheating their customers (Amos 8:5). They are worshiping Yahweh only in name, but their hearts are worshiping another god. Of course, such ritual performances are repugnant to God, in the same way that an unfaithful spouse would make his or her faithful partner upset with an outlandish anniversary celebration:

> What shall I do with you, O Ephraim?
>   What shall I do with you, O Judah?
> Your love is like a morning cloud,
>   like the dew that goes away early. . . .
> For I desire steadfast love and not sacrifice,
>   the knowledge of God rather than burnt offerings. (Hos 6:4, 6)

> I hate, I despise your festivals,
>   and I take no delight in your solemn assemblies.
> Even though you offer me your burnt offerings and grain offerings,
>   I will not accept them;
> and the offerings of well-being of your fatted animals
>   I will not look upon.

33. Claus Westermann, *Elements of Old Testament Theology*, trans. Douglas W. Stott (Atlanta: John Knox, 1982), 79–80 (emphasis added).

> Take away from me the noise of your songs;
> > I will not listen to the melody of your harps.
> But let justice roll down like waters,
> > and righteousness like an everflowing stream! (Amos 5:21–24; cf. also
> > Isa 1:11–17)

The later prophets (e.g., Zech 7:10; Mal 3:5) are just as concerned for ethics as these eighth-century prophets. This concern does not mean that worship is anticultic or that worship and morality contradict each other. An earlier tradition of scholars used to exaggerate this contrast and pitted the prophets against the priests, but this was more of a reflection of their own times when Protestants saw in the contrast between prophets and priests the difference between their own faith and Catholicism. This is why the prophets were often viewed as the pinnacle of ethical monotheism and the priesthood as part of a cult whose religious muscles had atrophied and who had quenched the spirit of a living faith.[34] But this concern for ethics can be traced back to the beginnings of Israelite history when Samuel informed Saul of the superiority of obedience over sacrifice (1 Sam 15:22); the concern for the heart involved in worship can be traced to the beginning when Abel offered God a better sacrifice than did Cain (Gen 4:3–5).[35] The sacrificial cultus was not wrong: it was defective when unaccompanied by a sincere heart.

Jesus has a similar teaching in the Sermon on the Mount, when he said that reconciliation with one's neighbor needed to take place before worship at the altar (Matt 5:23–24). For Jesus a temple in which sacrifices were being offered insincerely had become an abomination. Thus he used a whip to drive out those who had turned a house of prayer into an emporium (Matt 21:10–13).

In the New Testament church, James describes the essential core of true religion: "If any think they are religious, and do not bridle their tongues but deceive their hearts, their religion is worthless. Religion that is pure and undefiled before God, the Father, is this: to care for orphans and widows in their distress, and to keep oneself unstained by the world" (Jas 1:26–27). Indeed as Paul stressed, the ethical core of the law, as fulfilled in love, is the abiding mark

---

34. Note, e.g., Julius Wellhausen's characteristic description of priestly religion: "The law thrusts itself in everywhere; it commands and blocks up the access to heaven; it regulates and sets limits to the understanding of the divine working on earth. As far as it can, it takes the soul out of religion and spoils morality"; *Prolegomena to the History of Israel* (repr., Atlanta: Duke University Press, 1994), 509. According to Wellhausen, it was this law and cult that later killed the spirit of the prophets with their concern for pure ethical monotheism (55–60).

35. The suggestion that Abel's sacrifice is better than Cain's because of its more generous nature is clearly shown in the reaction of Cain. But the major difference is the attitude.

of the church. Without love, nothing else matters (1 Cor 13). Thus true worship is loving God with all one's heart, soul, and strength. Or seeking justice, loving *ḥesed,* and walking humbly with God.

True and False Prophecy

The fact of prophetic conflict soon emerges in the book of Micah. Micah had a very different view of his prophetic office than others who were engaged in prophesying (Mic 2:6–11; cf. 3:5–12). The latter could not accept Micah's conclusion that God was going to judge Israel. Their message was a positive one of unconditional love, and it was no doubt based on the same texts that Micah used from the Torah. These prophetic foes began with the first principle of election and covenant and concluded that those were the fundamental, indisputable facts. Thus when Micah spoke words of judgment, they responded: "Do not prattle on about these things. . . . You descendants of Jacob, should it be said, 'Does Yahweh ever lose patience? Would he ever judge us?'" (2:6–7, my translation). This text vividly describes Micah in the throes of controversy with these prophets. They focused on the first part of the Israelite credo that stressed God's patience and forgiveness (Exod 34:6–7a) but they omitted the last part, which spoke of God's judgment (34:7b).[36] This was an issue in Israel and Judah to which other preexilic prophetic texts attest.[37] For example, Amos, after stressing Israel's election, prophesied imminent judgment on the nation because of this doctrine (Amos 3:1–2)!

Later, Micah compares these prophets to mercenaries who have sold out their calling for food and money: "As for the prophets who cause my people to wander, they pronounce 'peace' if they have something to eat, but declare war against anyone who won't pay them!" (3:5, my translation). His message stands

36. It is interesting that although the words "love," "patience," and "forgiveness" are all front-loaded, there are an equal amount of words that focus on judgment! Each section matches the divine name, which is invoked twice: fifteen words versus fifteen words (in the Hebrew text).

37. No technical term in Hebrew identifies a false prophet. For the most part the terminology used of the false prophets is also used of the true prophets. The Septuagint uses the term "false prophet" as an interpretation for the Hebrew word for prophet in some contexts where it is clear that a false prophet is speaking (e.g., Jer 26:8, 11, 16 [= 33:8, 11, 16 in Septuagint numbering]). Gerhard von Rad simply concludes that true prophets were prophets of woe and that false prophets were prophets of weal in early Israel. This results in a restrictive reading of the evidence that precludes preexilic prophets from pronouncing salvation that runs counter to what the texts themselves state; "Die falschen Propheten," *Zeitschrift für die alttestamentliche Wissenschaft* 51 (1933): 109–20.

in sharp contrast: "But as for me, I am filled with power, with the spirit of the LORD, and with justice and might, to declare to Jacob his transgression and to Israel his sin" (3:8). The motivation of these prophets is solely material while Micah's is moral and theological. Their message is determined by monetary considerations while his is determined by the Spirit of God. In another text, the prophets are lumped together with the priests and judicial officials: "Its rulers give judgment for a bribe, / its priests teach for a price, / its prophets give oracles for money; / yet they lean upon the LORD and say, / 'Surely the LORD is with us! / No harm shall come upon us'" (3:11).

Micah uses a word meaning divination for the verb translated "give oracles" by the NRSV, which is translated "tell fortunes" by the NIV (יִקְסֹמוּ/ *yiqsōmû*); he is probably avoiding the common word for "prophesying" because these spiritual leaders have become so corrupt. Their final announcement about the impossibility of Judah experiencing judgment originates from a theological distortion. Micah's parody of their message sums up their theological conclusions: Judah and Jerusalem were invulnerable because of the divine presence. They were guaranteed eternal security.

Micah's prophetic conflict was one expression of a perennial problem in Israel's history. Balaam was a hired foreign prophet who was enticed to prophesy against Israel because of wealth (Num 22–24). Micaiah's voice was only one against hundreds of prophets during the time of Ahab, who ate at the king's table (1 Kgs 22). Elisha could not be bought even though his servant could be (2 Kgs 5). During the time of classical prophecy, Jeremiah and Ezekiel sounded this theme at length. They both struggled to contradict the false prophets and described their characteristics almost in summary form (Jer 23:9–40; Ezek 12:23–13:23): (1) they do not speak the truth; (2) they countenance injustice and idolatry; (3) they sometimes prophesy in the name of other gods; (4) they are materialistic; (5) they are sexually immoral; (6) they are addicted to alcohol; (7) they encourage sinners and discourage the righteous; (8) they proclaim false hope with their salvation oracles of peace and prosperity; (9) they have personal inspiration rather than divine inspiration, that is, they were not called by God; (10) they do not demand repentance; and (11) their predictions do not come true. These criteria can be categorized under a few broader themes dealing with the character of the prophet and the message of the prophet, although these categories cannot always be neatly separated. Many of the false prophets probably did not exhibit all of these traits. For example the false prophets in Micah's day could be said to exhibit characteristics 1, 2, 4, 7, 10, 11. It seems that they once had divine inspiration but the delivery of the message was distorted by their venality. Consequently the well of their inspiration was going to dry up. Some scholars argue that other factors such as social location were the major causes of prophetic conflict, but these are largely omitted by the prophetic editors.[38]

Many scholars think that the traits listed above could not infallibly determine the authenticity of a prophet; consequently the judgment of the validity of prophecy was left up to individual decision. Crenshaw reaches this conclusion and claims that this is the reason why prophecy finally failed in Israel and led to a focus on wisdom and apocalyptic. The lack of criteria for determining truth from falsehood in prophecy was its Achilles' Heel.[39] Thus it is claimed that it is better not to use the categories of true and false for prophecy but rather those of conflict and competition.

Crenshaw fails, however, to consider the complexity involved in reaching certain judgments about prophecy. For example, reputation and context would be important factors in making any decision. Consider the example of Micah's predecessor in the northern kingdom, Micaiah ben Imlah. He was well known by King Ahab as someone who did not always prophesy auspicious messages. When on one occasion Micaiah was called to utter an oracle to the king before a major battle with the Arameans, the monarch had already been reassured of victory by four hundred other prophets (1 Kgs 22). Micaiah's message of defeat and death for Ahab was in startling contradiction to his prophetic colleagues, and he blatantly called them liars. But the litmus test of whether his prophecy of judgment and disaster for Ahab and Israel and the false prophets was true was crystal clear. This was not "different strokes for different folks." It was one man's word against four hundred, but the outcome was to be decided in the arena of real life—history! When Ahab told his men to put Micaiah in a jail cell and give him bread and water until the king got home with his army, Micaiah said to the king in a voice that everyone could hear, "If you come home alive, then I am not a prophet!" And then he added so that all might hear: "Remember where you heard it!"[40] That Ahab disguised himself before battle and had the king of Judah wear the royal garb of the northern king shows that he had misgivings about Micaiah's prophecy. Those misgivings were confirmed when a randomly shot arrow found its way to Ahab's heart. History was the anvil on which all prophecy was tested.

One of the reasons why prophetic oracles were collected was to witness

---

38. Burke O. Long, "Social Dimensions of Prophetic Conflict," in *The Place Is Too Small for Us: The Israelite Prophets in Recent Scholarship*, ed. R. P. Gordon, Sources for Biblical and Theological Study 5 (Winona Lake: Eisenbrauns, 1996), 308–31.

39. James L. Crenshaw, *Prophetic Conflict: Its Effect upon Israelite Religion* (Berlin: de Gruyter, 1971). For further insight regarding the distinction between true and false prophets, see R. W. L. Moberly, *Prophecy and Discernment* (Cambridge: Cambridge University Press, 2006).

40. I am embellishing the content of 1 Kgs 22 for the purposes of clarity.

to a later generation of the importance of hearing the word of God. The folly of earlier generations for not hearing the prophetic word was recognized for what it was—sin. When Amos's prophecy begins with the superscription "the words . . . which he saw . . . two years before the earthquake" (Amos 1:1), they are there for a reason—to show that a major prediction that he prophesied actually happened two years after he spoke. Thus his words were authentic, arresting immediate attention for people in spiritual slumber to wake up! Many times it might be difficult to tell the difference between a true prophet and a false one because it was impossible to weigh the hidden motives of the heart, and for a long-range prediction, patience was required to determine truth. Then, again, if people repented, the future could be changed, as was clear from the prophesying of Micah, since his prediction of the destruction of Jerusalem did not happen in his own day. Nonetheless, after the delay of judgment, no one, as far as can be ascertained, considered him to be a false prophet.

An account in Jeremiah's time between two prophets, Jeremiah and Hananiah, shows how difficult it could be to judge the difference between true and false prophecy (Jer 27–28). The historical context for the debate between these two prophets was the recent invasion of Judah by the Babylonian army, which had resulted in the exile of the upper class from Jerusalem as well as of King Jehoiachin and his family. Furniture and valuables from the temple had also been removed. One group of prophets was essentially saying that this judgment was only temporary and that both the people and the temple artifacts would all be returned soon. Jeremiah, however, had a different message. He was told to wear a wooden yoke, which symbolized the importance of continuing to submit to Babylonian rule. Things reached a crisis point when one of the prophets named Hananiah met Jeremiah in the temple and blatantly contradicted his message, predicting that the exiles and temple furniture would be returned within two years. Jeremiah was flabbergasted and left speechless. But he did retort that he hoped Hananiah was right, which shows that prophets of judgment did not necessarily have a jeremiad personality—even if their name was Jeremiah! They also wanted to believe the best. But Jeremiah gathered himself enough to make a statement that shows that he was aware of the test for a true prophet. It is based on Deut 18:15–22, where the difference between a true prophet and a false one is determined on the basis of the accuracy of prediction. Over the years this test had been modified:

> Amen! May the LORD do so; may the LORD fulfill the words that you have prophesied, and bring back to this place from Babylon the vessels of the house of the LORD, and all the exiles. But listen now to this word that I speak in your hearing and in the hearing of all the people. The prophets

who preceded you and me from ancient times prophesied war, famine, and pestilence against many countries and great kingdoms. As for the prophet who prophesies peace, when the word of that prophet comes true, then it will be known that the LORD has truly sent the prophet. (Jer 28:6–9)

The question needs to be asked, Why was the test modified to invalidate only prophecies of salvation rather than judgment? The most likely answer seems to be that the prophet who prophesied judgment had no vested interest in prophesying bad news. Thus it would simply be expected that he or she would speak the truth, because theirs was a message presumably that no one would volunteer to announce. That a predicted judgment would not come true might have been due to the repentance of the people and therefore would not have counted against the prophet. In fact this seems to be the case in Jer 18, where repentance and not the prophecy itself is the key to determining the future. Thus a repentant people abandoning their sin could avert divine judgment. On the other hand, a prophet could easily "profit" from a message of good news, and as a result this probably became the default way in which the test was utilized.

Nonetheless, in the context of Jeremiah, Hananiah was unfazed and removed Jeremiah's wooden yoke and smashed it to demonstrate the irrevocability of Hananiah's prophecy. Jeremiah left the temple but returned later with a prophecy essentially denouncing Hananiah as a false prophet and saying that he would be dead within the year. Hananiah had prophesied that the exiles and temple materials would be returned within two years. He was dead within a few months. This would have been an extraordinary case of divine judgment as he was judged before his prophecy ever had a chance of being fulfilled!

In the normal circumstances of life many complexities would enter into the various contexts when prophets would pronounce their messages; there was probably not one foolproof determinant to help an audience ascertain the truth or falsity of a prophecy. In the end it would require wisdom, experience, and an instinct for the truth on the part of the hearers. When true prophets spoke their message they had to do it out of necessity, and when the word of God was uttered on human lips, it was self-authenticating. If human truth has its own moral compelling power,[41] then surely this must also be the case with divine truth. That additional criteria are given to authenticate a prophecy was part of the human condition after the fall. The combination of supernatural, theological, and moral signs as well as the historical context could be used by hearers to help determine the truthfulness of the message. Surely Jesus made

---

41. Hannah Arendt, *Eichmann in Jerusalem: A Report on the Banality of Evil* (New York: Penguin, 2006), 170–75.

a point about the self-authentication of truth when as the ultimate prophet he discoursed with Pilate on the question of truth: "For this purpose I was born and this is why I came into the world, that I might bear witness to the truth, and everyone who is on the side of truth hears my voice." When Pilate responded with his prescient postmodern question, "What is truth?" Jesus knew that any more talk about truth would be wasted (John 18:38).

Remnant

The remnant theme is an important one not only in the book of Micah but in the rest of the Bible.[42] It is found in all three major sections of the book of Micah (2:12; 4:7; 5:7–8; 7:18). The word "remnant" is a noun form from a verb that has the basic idea of "to remain." Thus a remnant is something that remains or is left. It can describe the residue of wood or land (Isa 44:17; Jer 47:5), but it often designates a group of survivors from a catastrophe (Amos 5:15; Jer 8:3; 44:28; Ezek 5:10; 9:8). Clearly in Micah it refers to the latter, a group that has survived judgment. Theoretically, it can have a positive or negative significance. For the latter, the judgment is so radical and thoroughgoing that there are only a few survivors. Thus Amos speaks of the few pieces of evidence remaining after judgment as evidence for the destruction (Amos 3:12). Ezekiel sometimes speaks of survivors from judgment but it is only to accentuate the judgment (Ezek 5). The four successive survivors who announce to Job the waves of calamitous destruction on his estate and family serve to enhance the comprehensive scope of his loss: "I alone am left" (Job 1:13–19). But for the most part, however, there is a positive significance for the remnant idea: "Unless the LORD Almighty / had left us some survivors, / we would have become like Sodom, / we would have been like Gomorrah" (Isa 1:9). Thus Isaiah describes the survivors of the Assyrian military campaign of 701 BCE.

At the beginning of the biblical storyline, Noah, his family, and the animals—a minuscule group from the great mass—survive the flood to build a new future for the world (Gen 6–9). Joseph was sent ahead of his brothers to Egypt to preserve a remnant on the earth (45:7). Theologically the concept is thus profound, and it becomes an essential idea of the covenant. Since the covenant

---

42. Some key studies on the concept are W. Müller, *Die Vorstellung vom Rest im Alten Testament* (Neukirchen-Vluyn: Neukirchener Verlag, 1973); and Gerhard F. Hasel, *The Remnant: The History and Theology of the Remnant Idea from Genesis to Isaiah* (Berrien Springs: Andrews University Press, 1972). Müller's study was a ThD dissertation at the University of Leipzig in 1939. Unfortunately Müller himself did not survive the war. There has also been an important monograph on the remnant in Micah: Cuffey, *Literary Coherence of the Book of Micah*.

is based on God's commitment and human obligation as well as on the curses for disobedience and the blessings for obedience, a remnant is indispensable for the maintenance of the covenant. Thus God says that he can destroy all the people and start again with Moses when Israel sinned during the golden calf episode (Exod 32). But Moses will have none of it. He intercedes for his people and they are saved, though judged. In Israel's later checkered history, a remnant somehow survives and guarantees a future. Sometimes this is even a remnant of one, as it was when Joash was saved from the assassination of the entire royal line during Athaliah's coup (2 Kgs 11:1–3). Sometimes it is seven thousand, as it was during Elijah's time when, even though he was convinced that he was a remnant of one, there actually were many others (1 Kgs 19:18)!

The idea of a remnant is developed as a positive concept in most of the prophets, but against the backdrop of the negative. Thus Hattori remarks: "To be sure, it is manifest that it is impossible to comprehend properly the idea of remnant without a proper understanding of God's judgment. . . . In biblical and extra-biblical literature, everywhere and without exception, the remnant is defined by judgment, either a judgment already accomplished or a judgment to come."[43]

Isaiah names one of his sons to illustrate the coming judgment: Maher-shalal-hash-baz—"Speedy is the Spoil, Hasty is the Booty" (Isa 8:1, 3). But he named another son Shear-jashub to signify the aftermath of that judgment: "A remnant shall return" (7:3). Return after what? Return after the certainty of judgment and exile. There develops a core doctrine in the prophets that God's people will be judged and purified, and a remnant will be refined through that purging, able to be used by God to bring about healing to the nations (4:2–5). Thus the remnant attests to the judging, but finally, restoring work of God.

In Micah, the concept of the remnant is developed and expanded over the three sections of the book.[44] At first, it is just an assumption. There has been a prediction of exile, and suddenly Yahweh appears in the midst of the exile and breaks his people free from their Babylonian prison, leading them on a march back to their homeland (Mic 1:16; 2:12–13). Whereas before, Yahweh had decimated Judah and led the people away as exiles, this is now reversed. In the second section, more detail is provided for the return of the remnant. Yahweh gathers the stragglers and crippled ones, brings them home, and reigns over

---

43. Y. Hattori, "Ezekiel's Idea of the Remnant" (ThD dissertation, Westminster Theological Seminary, 1968), 86–88.

44. For a similar but more nuanced exposition over four sections of Micah, see Kenneth H. Cuffey, "Remnant, Redactor, and Biblical Theologian," in *Reading and Hearing the Book of the Twelve*, ed. James Nogalski and Marvin A. Sweeney (Atlanta: Society of Biblical Literature, 2000), 185–208. Cuffey does not discuss the New Testament appropriation of this concept.

them *in Zion* (4:6–7). The picture of the remnant as a motley group of crippled survivors evokes the memory of the crippled Jacob returning home after his fight with God in which he is broken but blessed (Gen 32). In Micah's second section these survivors are named "the remnant of Jacob" (Mic 5:7–8), which functions both as a blessing to the nations that bless it and a curse to those who curse it in fulfillment of the Abrahamic promise.

In the final section of the book, the prophet identifies with the remaining people left in Judah who pray to God a prayer of confession, hope, and trust, and from this emerges a hymn that states that Yahweh forgives the remnant of his people because he delights in *ḥesed* and he casts their sins into the depths of the sea and tramples them there (7:8–20, esp. 7:18)! The remnant is both continuous and discontinuous with the Jewish nation. It cannot simply be identified with Israel, but is a part of the nation that emerges to be God's instrument in the world. Eschatological passages speak of the remnant surviving and declaring God's glory to the nations and remnants of the nations joining Israel on Mount Zion and experiencing God's salvation (Isa 66:19–20).

This doctrine is at the forefront of Jesus's mind when he gathers around himself twelve disciples representing a nucleus of the twelve tribes of Israel. They are sent out to the lost sheep of the house of Israel (Matt 10:1–15). And after the crucifixion and resurrection they are sent out to declare his glory to the nations.

When Paul reflects on the vast majority of his compatriots having rejected the message about their Messiah, he uses the concept of the remnant to explain it (Rom 9–11). The nation was never continuous with the people of God, as all Israel was not necessarily Israel. Within the nation there remained a remnant according to grace (e.g., during Elijah's time seven thousand did not bow the knee to Baal). Paul proceeds to show that the vast majority of the nation has stumbled, but this has caused an opportunity for Gentiles to believe and to be saved. After the nations are saved, there will be a massive restoration of the Jews, and thus all Israel will be saved (11:25–26). Thus the remnant is absolutely crucial for understanding Paul's theology and Israel's relation to the nations.

But the remnant is helpful pastorally and theologically for situations of dire difficulty when believers have experienced marginalization, isolation, and persecution for their faith. As in nature, so in history, God has not left himself without a witness. Particularly as understood in the book of Micah, it is from the remnant that world salvation will come, for it is the remnant that becomes the city on a hill, over whom Yahweh rules: it is a beacon in a world of darkness. Thus it is not the people of God at their strongest, but as a crippled and lame remnant, that makes, literally, a world of difference.

Micah's Contribution to Biblical Theology

While many of Micah's themes resonate with those of other prophets, Micah has his own distinctive contributions to make. He is the first person in history to pronounce destruction on the sacred temple of Jerusalem and to announce judgment on the Holy City. This may merit him the title of Amos of the southern kingdom, but he would have had to have formidable courage and boldness to announce such unthinkable judgment. In some of his other oracles he is no less radical: he calls judges and court officials cannibals and describes their activity of taking bribes from the rich to "shaft" the poor as that of cannibals greedily eating some of their victims raw and using the leftover bones to make soup; he characterizes false prophets as greedily gobbling down the payments of food from rich benefactors—they are prophets interested only in profits; with pun after ominous pun he pronounces doom on the cities in the southwestern Shephelah, wailing and lamenting in a dirge of the anticipated judgment; in a chain of hammer blows of destructive verbs he shows how Yahweh will someday destroy war itself; in language unique to the Old Testament he describes the complete breakdown of society as people hunt each other down and no one—absolutely no one—can be trusted. These are clear examples of his radicality in announcing judgment. His graphic and macabre descriptions are a type of high-voltage shock treatment, presented to jolt his audiences back into reality. As such they indicate the lengths to which Micah was prepared to go to accomplish his mission.

How do these features make a distinctive contribution to biblical theology? Frequently, in theology in the quest for the universal and the general, the particular details of individual texts are blurred and altered into more general patterns. But these features of Micah's prophesying should not be blurred, for they show the horror of injustice in God's eyes as oppressors can be described as cannibals, certain judgment can be pronounced on the sacred city and temple, false prophecy can be portrayed as a terrible perversion, and an outpouring of divine grief over judgment is depicted as the prophet wails through the countryside of Judah.

Moreover in Micah, there is contained in a nutshell an eschatological vision of the future, which because of its brevity helps provide an outline for larger books like Isaiah, Jeremiah, and Ezekiel, whose length and detail can sometimes obscure the overall framework. This eschatological vision for the future is largely based on the promises in Genesis; the mountain of the house of the Lord's exaltation, which will serve as a blessing to the nations, serves as a sharp contrast to the story of the Tower of Babel and highlights the promise to Abram and the exaltation of his name; the return from Babylon of a chastened and crippled remnant recalls God's fight with Jacob, in which he wins the blessing but not before being maimed; the description of Zion using the female imagery of a daughter in the pains of childbirth and the final birth of a leader who will be exalted to the ends of the earth recalls Gen 3:15; the description of the remnant as both dew and a lion resoundingly echoes the patriarchal promises to Jacob (Gen 27:28) and Judah (49:9). In fact the conquest of all evil and of all the enemies of Judah (Mic 5:8–15) is like an extended meditation on the triumph of the child born from the woman in Gen 3:15.

The sequence suggested in Micah for these events suggests the following tableau in Mic 4–5, for Micah appears to present a "picture show" in a kaleidoscope of images:[1] judgment on present Jerusalem in which Jerusalem is saved from assaulting nations, although its king is humiliated; judgment on Judah in which it is exiled to Babylon; a chastened remnant as a blessing and a bane among the nations; this remnant returning, with a Davidic leader reforming Judah, exalting Zion and the kingdom to universal prominence, and issuing a call to the nations to cease their warring ways; those that hear making a pilgrimage to Jerusalem, meeting Yahweh and being transformed, then transforming their weapons of war into instruments of peace. Those who do not hear will be judged. This understanding makes logical sense of the variety of images in Mic 4–5 and throughout the rest of the book.[2]

This sheds light on the New Testament message that describes the exaltation of Zion in the message of Jesus Christ, who was born of a Jewish peasant woman in Bethlehem and who came to reform Judah and Jerusalem and make them a light to the nations. He gathered around himself a nucleus of twelve disciples representing the twelve tribes of Israel, and he presented the true way

1. McKane, *Micah*, 14.

2. For a similar scenario for Isaiah, see John N. Oswalt, "The Nations in Isaiah: Friend or Foe; Servant or Partner," *Bulletin for Biblical Research* 16 (2006): 41–51.

of Yahweh, the way of *mišpāṭ, ḥesed*, and walking in the ways of Yahweh. By going to the cross, he was able to conquer the darkness and strip all the powers of darkness of their ability to destroy and to oppress, and to forgive all sins. His body as the very temple of God was destroyed for taking upon itself the judgment due for sin. But by being raised he was able to deliver humanity from the curse and forever signal the beginning of the end for death. As a result he was able to create a new temple not out of cut stone but of stones not cut with human hands. Humans who respond in faith are joined to him and become part of the new exalted temple of the living God in which the divine Spirit dwells, and thus their main message is peace and reconciliation instead of war and alienation. The nations are beckoned to come to this new temple, this new city of Zion set on a hill, and meet the resurrected Jesus, hear his message, and change their warring habits. Now is the day of salvation! Those who refuse will either be judged in the present or judged in the future when the resurrected Messiah will finish his mission and rule from sea to sea.

Micah does not mention an interim period in which the nations have the possibility of being saved, but an interim period as the New Testament sees it clearly makes logical sense out of the twin facts of the nations having the possibility of being saved or being judged as depicted in Micah and the rest of the prophets.

Other prophets speak of the change in human nature that results from this new age as God writing on the heart his law (Jer 31:31–34) or being given a new heart (Ezek 36:26), but Micah simply says that those who will meet Yahweh will turn their swords into ploughshares and their spears into pruning hooks (Mic 4:3) or that they will do justice, love *ḥesed*, and walk humbly with their God (6:8).

Micah's Relevance to Present-Day Theological Issues

Doctrine of God

One of the main problems in popular theology is the pernicious revival of the heresy of Marcionism. Such a view pits the Old Testament God of wrath and judgment against the New Testament God of mercy and forgiveness. One professor recently remarked: "I once had a student say to me in class, 'Judaism was a harsh religion that taught people to fear God's judgment, but Jesus came to teach us to love God with all our heart and soul and strength.'"[1] One of the sadder observations about such a statement is that the scholar had to provide a footnote in his book for readers who might not catch the irony in the student's assertion.[2] But the teacher continued by lamenting the result of such teaching producing a "disastrous effect on the theological imagination of many Protestant churches . . . everything in the Gospels that looks too much like the OT is screened out as 'inauthentic' and theologically dangerous—teachings about the election of a particular people, the mandate for holiness and purity, the expectation of God's ultimate judgment of the world."[3]

Popular Christian theology is clearly Marcionite at its core. In Rob Bell's best seller *Love Wins*, there is the spinning of a narrative that clearly avoids judgment and justice.[4] Bell is concerned that the extreme right of the church has coopted the biblical narrative and has read a fundamentally different story so much so that in truth "the plot has been lost and it's time to reclaim it. . . .

1. Richard B. Hays, *Reading Backwards: Figural Christology and the Fourfold Gospel Witness* (Waco: Baylor University Press, 2014), 5.

2. Ibid., 113n10.

3. Ibid., 5.

4. Rob Bell, *Love Wins: A Book about Heaven, Hell, and the Fate of Every Person Who Ever Lived* (New York: HarperOne, 2011).

Love compels us to question some of the dominant stories that are being taught as the Jesus story."[5] What he has in mind as the aberrant story is a narrative that has been dominant in the history of the church that states that while a select few Christians will spend eternity in heaven, "the rest of humanity will spend forever in a torment and punishment in hell with no chance for anything better."[6] Such a narrative is "misguided and toxic and ultimately subverts the contagious spread of Jesus's message of love, peace, forgiveness and joy that our world desperately needs to hear. And so this book."[7]

To be sure many of the anecdotes that Bell relates in his book reflect encounters with misguided "believers": a woman who was taught the Lord's Prayer by a father who raped her; Christians who spew hatred at homosexuals. While many will debate whether Bell has found the correct solution in his book, it is clear that he has seriously underread the Old Testament. A close reading of the book of Micah makes clear that love wins but not at the expense of justice and judgment. God's transcendence is marked by both justice and love, and the call that God places on the life of humanity stresses the doing of justice, the love of *ḥesed*, and an intimate daily walk with him. In Micah both justice and love, both wrath and grace, are powerfully present. To eliminate one at the expense of the other is somehow to miss something essential to an understanding of God's character.

Bell's book is one of a spate of current books and literature that seeks to attack the Old Testament view of God as one of inferior status and shows that Jesus brought a new understanding of God, a nonjudgmental God, a God who is not "into judgment but only into unconditional love and complete acceptance," a God who might be termed "a best buddy." Thus, theories of the atonement that focus on the appeasement of divine wrath cannot be tolerated since this would be the equivalent of cosmic child abuse.[8] In the words of others, in the cross God was committing suicide, apologizing for his sins against humanity in his judgments in the Old Testament. Thus in the Christ event God is asking for human forgiveness.[9] Many passages in the Old Testament that do not suit contemporary tastes are thus part of not only the sacred word but the broken word.[10] Another scholar can urge the church away from the "monster God of

5. Ibid., viii.
6. Ibid.
7. Ibid.
8. Steve Chalke and Alan Mann, *The Lost Message of Jesus* (Grand Rapids: Zondervan, 2004), 174.
9. Jack Miles, *Christ: A Crisis in the Life of God* (New York: Vintage, 2002).
10. Kenton L. Sparks, *Sacred Word, Broken Word: Biblical Authority and the Dark Side of Scripture* (Grand Rapids: Eerdmans, 2012).

retribution to the Christlike God of the Gospels."[11] The impact upon areas of Christian living are devastating. Otto writes about the impact of Marcionism on the contemporary Western church:

> God is viewed by many as accepting all people and as tolerating all evil. He is, therefore, not feared, but instead is invoked through the name of Christ by a host of political operatives in the service of other deities, resulting in the leading astray of many. The gospel is viewed apart from law, grace apart from sin, faith apart from repentance, and Christ apart from his bodily nature. He who came to save and transform the entire person and the whole of culture for his glory is reduced to a subjective idea of acceptance. Finally, Scripture is viewed as bearing witness to God by the Marcionite method of abandoning the Old Testament and all portions of the New Testament that do not agree with a God of complete acceptance.[12]

All of which reminds one of the Jew who quipped, "It was we Jews who produced the Old Testament, and it was you Christians who gave us hell!" Thus pitting the Old Testament against the New is not even accurate. There are many examples of love and mercy in the Old Testament, and many examples of God's wrath in the New. And it is clear that Micah himself will not have anything to do with such a fundamental separation of key concepts in the Bible. It was not as if Micah was unaware of such an interest in separation, for that was one of the main battles that he had to fight. He cites the words of the false prophets in his time in utter condemnation as a satirical example of famous last words: "Is not the LORD among us? / No disaster will come upon us" (Mic 3:11 NIV). Is this not a similar statement to what is being proclaimed today by many: "Don't worry. Be happy. God loves us unconditionally. God's judgment will never happen to us." But Micah knows that one of the key functions of a true prophet is to declare the transgression of Jacob and to call back God's people to their fundamental identity of people who are to do justice, love ḥesed, and walk humbly with their God (3:8; 6:8). Micah's words to these prophets of prosperity are that they are merchants of death, causing people to wander away from the words of the true and the living God (3:5).

In fact this tension between God's judgment and mercy is something that runs not only through the book of Micah but through the Old Testa-

---

11. Brad Jerzak, "Psalm 7—The God of Everyday Wrath," *Clarion Journal* (April 2015), available online at clarion-journal.com/clarion_journal_of_spirit/.

12. Randall E. Otto, "A Problem with Marcion: A Second-Century Heresy Continues to Infect the Church," *Theology Matters* 4 (1998): 7.

ment and finally reaches into the New Testament and is resolved in climactic form on the cross: "The themes of God's wrath, forbearance and love barrel through Scripture and climax in the cross."[13] The God who casts our sins into the depths descends to the depths to conquer and subdue them (Mic 7:19; Phil 2:5–11).

Modern Ministry and the Role of a Spiritual Leader

If there is one sad fact in the modern church wherever it is found, it is the pervasive presence of false teachers and false prophets. Recently a minister of a prominent church in the United States was receiving negative publicity for seeking to raise $64,000,000 to buy a private jet that was to be used for furthering his ministry, so he decided to forgo the publicity campaign. Later, he defended himself by saying that God expects people to dream big: "Let me tell you something about believing God—I can dream as long as I want to. I can believe God as long as I want to. If I want to believe God for a $65 million plane, you cannot stop me. You cannot stop me from dreaming."[14] This is no doubt true but the question is whether these dreams are biblical or not. One is reminded of Biff Loman at the graveside of his father lamenting that his father had pursued all the wrong dreams, "all, all wrong."[15] His dreams were the stuff of the American dream, from rags to riches, becoming rich and "set for life." They led to his suicide.

There are many examples of spiritual leaders having huge incomes, multiple luxury homes worth millions of dollars, and the very best of automobiles and luxurious conveniences. Megachurches have become huge businesses and virtually corporations in themselves. The scandals associated with these ministries are legion. Whether it is sexual infidelity on the part of the leaders, or their sexual exploitation of minors, or financial exploitation and/or spiritual and toxic abuse of their parishioners, the results are nothing short of outrageous. The message of such spiritual leaders is usually "Christianity Lite," or a variation on a theme of self-help or motivation or entertainment. It helps if the minister has a good physical presence, is laid back and relaxed, is in short "cool." It is

13. D. A. Carson, *Scandalous: The Cross and Resurrection of Jesus* (Wheaton: Crossway, 2010), 71.

14. Sarah Adams, "Televangelist Creflo Dollar Speaks Out on $65 Million Plane Fundraiser: 'You Cannot Stop Me from Dreaming,'" (April 22, 2015), available online at christiantimes.com/article/televangelist.creflo.dollar.speaks.out.on.65.million.plane.fundraiser.you.cannot.stop.me.from.dreaming/52261.htm.

15. Arthur Miller, *Death of a Salesman* (New York: Viking, 1949), 138.

difficult to make generalizations, but criticism of such ministries often results in defensive posturing or overt counterattacks.

"The more things change the more they stay the same." In Micah's time it was not that much different, but he speaks passionately about three important traits that spiritual leaders should possess. The first is truthfulness. They need to speak the truth about sin and God's judgment. There is no mistaking Micah's prophetic calling, which was to announce to Jacob its sin and to Israel its transgression. This virtual definition of his prophetic task occurs in the context of false prophets who are saying the opposite and who are being paid to announce what their audience desires (Mic 3:8; cf. 3:5–7). The true spiritual leader must listen for the voice of God primarily and not the voice of people. It thus behooves the spiritual leader today to keep an ear close to the Scriptures, the canon of the church, to listen carefully for how God would address a contemporary situation. The leader must so inhabit the Scriptures that they provide the vision for understanding the world, for in showing love for the word of God there will be a consequent love for the people. The messenger will have something to give them to keep them from wandering into lostness. Or to change the metaphor, as seventeenth-century Huguenot minister Jean Daillé once remarked: "Ministers are not cooks, but physicians and therefore should not study to delight the palate, but to recover the patient."[16] This means often telling patients not what they want to hear but what they need to hear.

Second is theological balance. Spiritual leaders need to have a wholistic understanding of the Scriptures. The problem of the false prophets and priests and the people in Micah's time was that they emphasized only one part of the biblical revelation. They were very much interested in election and blessing and the Zion tradition (the inviolability of Zion as the place of God's presence). But they were not enthusiastic about the responsibilities of election, blessings, and the Sinai tradition. Micah made it clear that there were two sides to the covenant formulary: "I will be your God" was to be balanced by the consequence "you will be my people." But the false prophets emphasized only one side of the equation. Heresy is usually not an outright rejection of the truth but its distortion through overemphasizing certain aspects and underemphasizing others. It is clear that Micah was in a theological debate with spiritual leaders during his time. They totally disagreed with his message of judgment and told him and his colleagues to cease and desist. In their objection, they said, "Does Yahweh ever lose patience? Would he ever judge us?" (2:6–7, my translation). Their rhetorical questions expected negative answers. They should have had a more comprehensive understanding of the Torah that showed a complete picture of

---

16. Cited in M. Brown, *It's Time to Rock the Boat* (Shippensburg: Destiny Image, 1993), 41.

Yahweh's character: that although he was merciful and gracious and slow to anger and full of *hesed*, he also did not acquit the guilty but punished them down to their third and fourth generation. Micah responds to his interlocutors with a rhetorical question of his own but in contrast, his expects a positive answer and not a negative one: "Do not my words do well to those who walk uprightly?" With these words the false prophets are instantly exposed, particularly with the salvo of accusations that follow the question, proving that sin has gone unchecked within the nation.

The third trait is the exclusive worship of God. Spiritual leaders need to have God as their treasure and not the treasury. Micah shows that covetousness of wealth is the main problem with the spiritual and civil leaders in the nation: the prophets' message was inspired by prosperity; they would prophesy salvation if they were paid, and judgment if they were not; they prophesied only for money. It was the same for civil leaders and for priests. Bribes blinded the eyes of court officials, and priests taught Torah only when they were paid. According to Micah the answer to this was to be filled with the Holy Spirit. This would not only give the courage to tell the truth and describe the situation as it was, but it would provide the God-consciousness so necessary to say "no" to monetary enticements. Amos, like Micah, had that same divine awareness when he responded to the censors of his era: "The lion has roared; / who will not fear? / The LORD God has spoken; / who can but prophesy?" (Amos 3:8). At an earlier period, Elisha refused the treasures of Syria for healing a leprous military commander. He did not need them because he had something far more important—God. That his servant went after the treasures and became afflicted with the leprosy of the Syrian soldier reveals something about the contaminating power of wealth (2 Kgs 5). Wealth not only detracts from spiritual power—it is somehow connected to death, because it leads away from dependence on God, the true source of life. Perhaps this is the reason why wealth is almost deadly. Presciently the sage in Proverbs prays for two requests:

> Two things I ask of you;
>   do not deny them to me before I die:
> Remove far from me falsehood and lying;
>   give me neither poverty nor riches;
>   feed me with the food that I need,
> or I shall be full, and deny you,
>   and say, "Who is the LORD?"
> or I shall be poor, and steal,
>   and profane the name of my God. (Prov 30:7-9)

The danger of poverty is that it might lead to theft and thus a violation of the covenant, but the danger of wealth is that it might lead to autonomy, where there is no need to depend on God. This was Israel's experience in the land when they became prosperous. Thus it became particularly important for prophets and spiritual leaders who depended on Yahweh in a special way to direct the people to stay spiritually dependent. Perhaps this is the reason the true prophets shied away from wealth.[17] The problem can be seen in the early days of Israel's history as a foreign prophet outside of Israel was motivated by wealth and would sell his blessings and curses to the highest bidder (Num 22–24). From early times the stories about Eli's corrupt sons and their monetary and sexual exploitation of the Israelites show the problem in all of its insidious power (1 Sam 1–4). That God was determined to destroy them shows how seriously the betrayal of a spiritual trust was taken.

In New Testament times Jesus predicted that false prophets would arise in the ranks of his disciples like ravenous wolves in sheep's clothing. Perhaps one of the clearest examples of how wealth and spiritual power are incompatible is when the apostles condemned Simon for attempting to purchase the power of the Holy Spirit with money (Acts 8:9–25). In the early church one of the first signs that someone was a false prophet was the request of money for a spiritual service (*Didache* 11). Perhaps the most poignant example of the relationship between the lack of spiritual power and the concern for money comes from the medieval church. When Thomas Aquinas was invited to an audience with Pope Innocent II, the pontiff said to Thomas: "Remember the story when Peter said to the lame man who was begging, 'Silver and gold have I none, but such as I have I give unto you. In the name of Jesus of Nazareth, Rise up and walk!' Well, Thomas, Look around at all the wealth we have now. We don't have to say that first part any more." Thomas curtly responded. "True, Holy Father, but neither we can we say, 'Rise up and walk!'"[18]

There is a lesson here for all spiritual leaders in every age. To serve money is to serve another god, Mammon, and there will never be enough money to satisfy this god's cravings. Spiritual leaders must first incarnate the truth of godliness resulting in material contentment. Perhaps part of the answer is for such leaders to realize to whom their primary loyalty is due. Who is their first love? After answering that question they must constantly remember their answer.

---

17. See the insightful remarks of Samuel A. Meier, *Themes and Transformations in Old Testament Prophecy* (Downers Grove: InterVarsity, 2009), 180–210.

18. F. F. Bruce, *The Book of Acts* (Grand Rapids: Eerdmans, 1988), 77–78.

Cheap Grace

Micah had to fight against a theology of cheap grace. Such a theology was at home with social exploitation of the poor, with injustice in the courts and in the markets, and with purchasing spiritual favors. It could easily be accompanied by ostentatious displays of religious fervor, including expensive sacrifices. Cheap grace guaranteed spiritual favor or "eternal security" without any accompanying change in the life of the recipient. Micah attacked this view with all the passion he could muster. For him there could not be spiritual guarantees for a life not committed to justice, *ḥesed*, and walking in the Torah. Or, if there were spiritual guarantees, they were destruction and exile. Forgiveness was for the penitent or the faithful remnant that survived the judgment.

Such a lesson needs to be heard today. Over a century ago William Booth, the founder of the Salvation Army, feared for the church in the future. He remarked: "The chief danger that confronts the coming century will be religion without the Holy Ghost, Christianity without Christ, forgiveness without repentance, salvation without regeneration, politics without God, heaven without hell."[19] That day has certainly arrived. In the West there is a proliferation of an antinomian, hypergrace movement that specializes in separating the above pairs. It has all stemmed from spiritual leadership that failed to emphasize personal holiness and life transformation. A quipster summed up the present generation in the West as being "a generation that is trying to eat and drink its way to prosperity, war its way to peace, spend its way to wealth, and enjoy its way to heaven."

Bonhoeffer made similar statements in Germany before World War II when he was addressing a church of compromise and laxity:

> Christ has given his church power to forgive and to retain sins on earth with divine authority (Matt. 16:19; 18:18; John 20:23). Eternal salvation and eternal damnation are decided by its word. Anyone who turns from his sinful way and repents at the word of proclamation receives forgiveness. Anyone who perseveres in his sin receives judgment. The church cannot loose the penitent from sin without arresting and binding the impenitent in sin. The key to loose has no serious eternal significance if the key to bind has not the same significance.[20]

---

19. Ray Johnston, *Jesus Called: He Wants His Church Back. What Christians and the American Church Are Missing* (Colorado Springs: W. Publishing Group, 2016), 81.

20. Cited in Eric Metaxas, *Bonhoeffer: Pastor, Martyr, Prophet, Spy* (Nashville: Nelson, 2011), 292.

For Bonhoeffer one of the real problems in the church of Germany was the phenomenon of cheap grace, which means simply experiencing the grace of God without a concomitant change in behavior or lifestyle. Orthodoxy was a matter of simple intellectual assent to a number of doctrinal propositions without orthopraxy. This was different from costly grace, grace that saved one from sin and divine judgment but also saved one to a life of holiness and love:

> Cheap grace means the justification of sin without the justification of the sinner. Grace alone does everything, they say, and so everything can remain as it was before. "All for sin could not atone." The world goes on in the same old way and we are still sinners. . . . Well, then let the Christian live like the rest of the world.[21]

Reflecting on the relevance of Bonhoeffer for modern Christianity, Timothy Keller writes:

> It is impossible to understand Bonhoeffer's *Nachfolge* without becoming acquainted with the shocking capitulation of the German church to Hitler in the 1930s. How could the "church of Luther," that great teacher of the gospel, have ever come to such a place? The answer is that the true gospel, summed up by Bonhoeffer as costly grace, had been lost. On the one hand, the church had been marked by formalism. That meant going to church and hearing that God just loves and forgives everyone, so it doesn't really matter much how you live. . . . By the time of Hitler's ascension much of the German church understood grace only as an abstract acceptance—"God forgives; that's his job." . . . This lapse couldn't happen to us, today, surely, could it? Certainly it could. We still have a lot of legalism and moralism in our churches. In reaction to that, many Christians want to talk only about God's love and acceptance. They don't like talking about Jesus' death on the cross to satisfy divine wrath and justice. Some even call it "divine child abuse." Yet, if they are not careful, they run the risk of falling into the belief in "cheap grace"—a non-costly love from a non-holy God who just loves and accepts us as we are. That will never change anyone's life.[22]

Micah's message simply adds to the message of the prophets in general. The message of grace is inextricably connected with a message of responsibility.

---

21. Dietrich Bonhoeffer, *The Cost of Discipleship* (New York: Touchstone, 1995), 43–44.

22. Tim Keller, "Foreword," in Eric Metaxas, *Bonhoeffer: Pastor, Martyr, Prophet, Spy* (Nashville: Nelson, 2011), xv.

After all, Abraham was chosen to walk in the way of Yahweh, which is further defined as justice and righteousness (Gen 18:19). Israel's election was to holiness and love. When the inextricable bonds are severed, God must judge his own people because they have distorted his fundamental message. As Isaiah says, the divine intention was to make a vineyard that produced grapes for the world to taste the wine of the kingdom. But tragically the wine had become almost toxic (5:1–7)! Consequently the vineyard had to be destroyed and a new one planted.

The New Testament is in harmony with this prophetic view, and the good news in Jesus Christ cannot be separated from the demand to repent and walk in newness of life. In fact when Jesus came announcing the kingdom, his message could be expressed in a single sentence: "Repent, for the kingdom is at hand" (Matt 4:17). His Sermon on the Mount belies anyone who would call Jesus Lord without obeying him (7:21–23). There is no free grace without lordship, as if there could ever be![23] Paul's theology condemns those who would separate the grace and love of God from the importance of a life path of holiness: "Shall we continue in sin in order that grace may abound? By no means!" (Rom 6:1–2a).

> Do you not know that wrongdoers will not inherit the kingdom of God? Do not be deceived! Fornicators, idolaters, adulterers, male prostitutes, sodomites, thieves, the greedy, drunkards, revilers, robbers—none of these will inherit the kingdom of God. And this is what some of you used to be. But you were washed, you were sanctified, you were justified in the name of the Lord Jesus Christ and in the Spirit of our God. (1 Cor 6:9–11)

It is surely a lamentable fact in Western churches that writers speak of "barcode" Christianity, in which people are identified as a Christian only by a correct doctrinal formula and nothing else.[24] Or people can honestly ask whether God's forgiveness will extend to a contemplated act of adultery.[25] Pastors, priests, and spiritual leaders need to have the courage of Micah to call a spade a spade and to challenge their flocks to remember the costly grace that necessitated the Son of God to die a gruesome death for human sin and to urge them to think long and hard about the last stanza of Isaac Watts's hymn "When I Survey the Wondrous Cross":

23. Cf. Zane Hodges, *Absolutely Free: A Biblical Reply to Lordship Salvation*, 2nd ed. (Grand Rapids: Zondervan, 1989).

24. Dallas Willard, *Renovation of the Heart: Putting on the Character of Christ* (Colorado Springs: NavPress, 2002).

25. Philip Yancey, *Finding God in Unexpected Places* (Colorado Springs: WaterBrook, 2008), 225–29.

Were the whole realm of nature mine,
that were a present far too small.
Love so amazing so divine,
demands my soul, my life, my all.

Justice

During the first three quarters of the twentieth century, the evangelical church heard little about the importance of social justice. As a Reformed Protestant, Nicholas Wolterstorff relates (via a personal communication) how a concern for justice became important for him. On a trip to South Africa in 1976 he was in a meeting with Afrikaner and black Christians; as an outsider he was able to see the blind spots of the Afrikaners clearly. They could not understand the plight of their African brothers and sisters since the latter were the recipients of so much charity. But the fact remained that, despite the charity, the same structures of injustice remained in place. Experiencing charity in the form of monetary gifts could not compensate for the fundamental injustice of the apartheid structure in society. In this case "charity" was not love but served to perpetuate injustice. What was needed was love seeking justice, a love that would seek to create a more just society where the rights of all human beings would be respected.

In 1987 a group of concerned Christians in Moncton, New Brunswick, Canada, met and decided to help women who were contemplating abortion because of adverse social circumstances. The group wished to provide a service for these women in order to help them nurture their children in the womb and outside the womb once they were born. They would also seek to provide support for the mothers, whether social, spiritual, or financial. It was their attempt to deal in a positive way with the injustice of abortion. Nearly thirty years later the Pregnancy Resource Centre is not only helping women and their children in trying circumstances but is also involved in education, counseling, and medical services. It is a shining example of justice in action: Christians addressing major social problems with positive solutions.

In 2014 a group of Indian Christians working in a large city decided to add an important dimension to their Christian faith as they worked with the Dalits, sharing with them the gospel of Christ and showing them their precious value in the eyes of God. A five-hundred-year-old custom of a particular caste among a tribal group, the Banchada people, was the practice of prostituting the eldest daughter of a family in order to provide income. This speaks volumes about the horrendous poverty that drives parents to such desperate straits with their children, repeatedly violating and humiliating their daughters and destroying their dignity. But the Christians started to make a difference by making a

251

plan with an organization named Food for the Hungry, to provide housing for the girls and education and training in various skills. In addition, Bible study groups were arranged to help the youth gain a concept of human dignity that is defined by being made in the image of God. This is justice in action. Not only is a difference being made in the souls of people and the concern for their eternal salvation, but a difference is being made in their society, so that the kingdom of God becomes a reality here and now.[26]

In Cameroon, West Africa, an organization called CABTAL (Cameroonian Association for Bible Translation and Literacy) is involved in translating the Bible into the indigenous languages of the country. The workers are bringing the gospel and the word of life into the mother tongues of many peoples so that they can understand the word in their own heart language. In the process they are involved in education and literacy training. When I was at a workshop in a small village, Wum, in northwestern Cameroon in 2013, the question was posed to a group of villagers, "What does literacy mean to you?" Without hesitation one young woman responded, "Enlightenment!" CABTAL has found that when literacy is taught a new world is opened up to people. They are no longer deceived when they go to a pharmacy to purchase medicine. They cannot be duped by charlatans who try to get them to agree to contracts they cannot read. They become more aware of their rights and privileges within society. They can participate more responsibly in the political process since they are able to evaluate better the programs of different political parties as well as to vote with integrity. Literate people are also more likely to see the value of education not only for themselves but for their children. Not only do the people learn the word of life in the Scriptures; they learn about hygiene, sexually transmitted diseases, stories from their own culture, laws of their land, traffic signs, pride that comes from seeing their own language take its place alongside other written languages, and as a result the preservation of their own culture. CABTAL's programs bring about a more just society.

All of these examples could be multiplied many times over but they are reminders of what the contemporary church is called to do. Micah's call for justice was to stand with those whose rights were being infringed, the helpless, the disadvantaged. The gospel is a call to stand alongside the poor and the oppressed, the voiceless and the marginalized, "the quartet of the vulnerable." The question each individual group of believers has to ask is this: Who are these people in our midst? Are we there for them? Are we there for the single mothers, the unborn, the homeless, the aged, the prisoner, the refugee, the foreigner, the stranger, the poor? Jesus reminds his disciples of the importance of

---

26. I cannot name the organization, but I know its leaders and have visited the area.

a concern for the body as well as the soul, the concern for fundamental justice: "I was hungry and you gave me food, I was thirsty and you gave me something to drink, I was a stranger and you welcomed me, I was naked and you gave me clothing, I was sick and you took care of me, I was in prison and you visited me" (Matt 25:35–36).

Idolatry, Covetousness, and Injustice

That the prophets are concerned with idolatry and injustice can be observed from even a superficial reading of their speeches. In some prophets like Hosea, the emphasis is idolatry; in another like Amos the stress is injustice.[27] Nonetheless, both conceptions are important in all the prophets, and a canonical reading ensures this: "When one reads the Twelve Prophets canonically, the question is not whether God cares about idolatry or injustice; rather both are an affront to the holy one of Israel."[28] Although these two concepts often appear together, not many biblical scholars explore the underlying conceptual relationship. One exception is Oswalt:

> What they [the prophets] are saying is that social injustice is ultimately the refusal to entrust oneself to a fair and loving God. Whenever persons begin to believe that the cosmic order is basically uninterested in human welfare and that those who succeed are those who know best how to capture the cosmic forces for their own purposes (the underlying attitudes of idolatry), the relatively more helpless and vulnerable begin to be crushed. The more helpless the individual, the more devastating the crushing.[29]

Oswalt's insightful analysis shows the underlying conceptual link between these two behaviors, which seem very different on the surface. But the prophet Micah adds a third element to the mix: covetousness. When Micah first begins to castigate people for their sins, he speaks of idolatry (1:7), covetousness (2:2), and injustice (2:2). His grouping of these terms together can help show the interrelationships between these behaviors and their polar opposites: true worship, justice, and satisfaction. These are all achieved in the latter days when the nations go up to worship Yahweh (4:1–2) and beat their swords into plough-

---

27. E.g., see the classic distinction between the two prophets in Heschel, *Prophets*, 74–75.

28. Bo H. Lim and Daniel Castelo, *Hosea*, Two Horizons Old Testament Commentary (Grand Rapids: Eerdmans, 2015), 152.

29. John N. Oswalt, *The Book of Isaiah, Chapters 1–39* (Grand Rapids: Eerdmans, 1986), 106.

shares (4:3) and are finally satisfied (4:4). It is when all idols are destroyed that this can be achieved (5:10–15).

But how is one to explain this interrelationship? Clues to this linkage can be shown in the Ten Words given to Israel at Mount Sinai (Exod 20:1–17; Deut 5:6–21). The first three commands stress the transcendence of God. Thus no other god can displace Yahweh; Yahweh's transcendence is not to be compromised by the making of an idol, or the use of his name for ulterior motives. An idol is some object that initially stands for God and therefore compromises divine transcendence, but eventually can be viewed as a stand-in and therefore a replacement for God. As Reno remarks, it is "the *sine qua non* of covenant faithlessness in the Old Testament . . . a final, spiritualized strategy of life based on the . . . spiritualized hope that something other than God has deathless power."[30]

The final commandment is a command against coveting, which is a comprehensive list: "You shall not covet your neighbor's house. You shall not covet your neighbor's wife, or his male or female servant, his ox or donkey, or anything that belongs to your neighbor." Here two issues come to the fore, one the inner thought life of the person. Yahweh, the unseen one, wants allegiance in the person's heart. The point is there will be a consequence if that allegiance is not given here—the coveting of seven different objects: house, wife, male servant, female servant, ox, donkey, or anything else. The number seven emphasizes completeness and suggests a virtual limitless list of desired objects. But the crucial point is that all these objects do not belong to the subject of the coveting, and thus coveting is a form of private injustice, which if acted upon produces social injustice.

There is an inextricable relationship between these different elements. To worship Yahweh as the supreme God is to worship someone whose throne is founded on justice. In him all reality is perfectly integrated and proportioned, for after all he is the creator. His passion is justice. If some thing or person or force is elevated to the position of Yahweh and Yahweh is dethroned, this can lead only to injustice. When Baal was enthroned during the time of Elijah and Micaiah, the poor lost their rights as the poor and, for example, Naboth had his family inheritance seized from him, the result of covetous thoughts that led to murder and theft. Indeed the backstory of Ahab and Jezebel and Naboth is assumed in Micah (2:2). Baal requires no such restriction on King Ahab's and Queen Jezebel's appetites and their coveting. They are royalty, and consequently there are no human limits on their power. How dare someone restrict their desires! Injustice is the consequence.

An essential problem is that when Yahweh is dethroned and replaced by

---

30. R. R. Reno, *Genesis* (Grand Rapids: Brazos, 2010), 90.

an idol, a spiritual insufficiency is expressed in seeking more and more for the self. This is expressed in limitless coveting, which when acted out leads to the proliferation of injustice. This is exactly the picture in Mic 2–3. The rich never have enough and think up and dream of ways they can get more and more because they cannot be satisfied with what they have, since they have abandoned Yahweh. Thus they covet lands and seize them, estates and rob them. And this is also the hidden motive behind the other examples of injustice in the book. The judges in the courts, the priests at the temple, and the prophets wherever they are found can all be purchased with money in the form of bribes. Money has become the idolatrous force that drives their lives and they must covet it, and this covetousness leads to cannibalism in the courts, connivance among the prophets, and corruption of the priesthood. The result is appalling injustice.[31]

Two laws that seem so different are juxtaposed in the Deuteronomic legislation that deals with justice: "Follow justice and justice alone, so that you may live and possess the land the LORD your God is giving you. Do not set up any wooden Asherah pole beside the altar you build to the LORD your God, and do not erect a sacred stone, for these the LORD your God hates" (Deut 16:20–22 NIV). Many commentators see two disparate laws placed beside each other with no real inner connection. But as one rabbi clarifies, other similar texts are found together:

> The truth is that almost every time the Bible forbids idolatry, it is within the context of the immoral behavior which characterized it: Do not bow down to their gods, do not worship them and do not act according to their practices . . . (Exodus 23:24); Guard yourself lest you seek out their gods . . . they burn their sons and daughters in fire to their gods (Deut. 12:30–31); You shall destroy the Hittites . . . in order that they not teach you to act according to all their abominations (Deut. 20:17, 18).[32]

The command not to covet functions as a convenient list of possible idols and is a type of spiritual thermometer. When coveting is happening Yahweh has been displaced from his supreme position. Yahweh and his provision should be sufficient for human desire—if he is not, there is a problem internally, and thus there will be an external problem in the society as coveting leads to injustice.

In the parable of the rich fool, Jesus aims to show a young man who wants

---

31. For a similar analysis cast in systematic theological terms, see Langdon Gilkey, *Maker of Heaven and Earth: The Christian Doctrine of Creation in the Light of Modern Knowledge* (Washington: University Press of America, 1959), 233.

32. Shlomo Riskin, "Parshat Shoftim: To Know God. Pursue Justice," *Jerusalem Post* (September 2, 2011).

his brother to divide the inheritance with him that it is a matter of covetousness and therefore idolatry. He tells the young man, almost rudely, to beware of covetousness, and he supplies the reason in an insightful proverb, which sketches the basics of a theological anthropology (Luke 12:15): a person's life "does not consist in the abundance of things possessed" (King James Version) or "life is not defined by what you have, even when you have a lot" (*The Message*). Coveting cannot fulfill the human person, because his being is defined differently. What can fulfill one's purpose is being "rich toward God," which means, among other things, giving away possessions rather than hoarding them and being concerned for the needs of others (12:21). That is why a little later in the narrative of Luke, treasure in heaven (being rich toward God) comes as a result of selling possessions and giving money to the poor (12:33). But the reason this can be done is that God has become the center of the believer's life: the kingdom of God has supreme place in his or her life and is therefore the ultimate treasure (12:31–34).

Jesus makes a similar point in a parallel saying in Matthew and Luke, when he concludes that it is impossible to serve two masters and therefore impossible to serve God and Mammon (Matt 6:24; Luke 16:13). Here "Mammon" is an Aramaic word that means wealth or riches, but it seems to be personified into a god associated with these. This suggests how coveting money is already a form of idolatry since the money has taken on the power of a god, demanding service and homage. It is as if "wealth is an evil and superhuman power that stands in opposition to God, 'possessing them' and distracting them from devotion to God."[33] In other words, Mammon is clearly seen as an idol: "Where God does not rule, there rules idols, the most powerful of which is Mammon."[34]

Paul connects the theological dots in two parallel sayings in different letters and points out that covetousness is essentially idolatry, meaning that it functions like a god:

> Put to death, therefore, whatever in you is earthly: fornication, impurity, passion, evil desire, and greed (which is idolatry). On account of these the wrath of God is coming on those who are disobedient. (Col 3:5–6)
>
> Be sure of this, that no fornicator or impure person, or one who is greedy (that is, an idolater), has any inheritance in the kingdom of Christ and of God. (Eph 5:5)

---

33. Brian S. Rosner, *Greed as Idolatry: The Origin and Meaning of a Pauline Metaphor* (Grand Rapids: Eerdmans, 2007), 19.

34. Ibid., 20, citing Leonhard Ragaz, *Die Gleichnisse Jesu: Seine soziale Botschaft* (Mohn: Gütersloher, 1990), 42.

In these passages the word "greed" translates the Greek word for covetousness. It is clear from these brief catalogs of sins that covetousness is uniquely linked to idolatry. This is probably because covetousness has an all-consuming nature and thus necessarily must displace God. While this is definitely in the context of sexual lust in the above texts from the Pauline corpus of letters, it also indicates a lust for wealth as well, and these two idols are pervasive in much of modern life. While Paul does not develop the injustice that results from the lust for sex and material things, one does not have to be a prophet to see the link in Western culture where bodies are objectified and commodified, even those of young children. Human trafficking in the sex trade is a worldwide blight, not to mention the destruction of countless marriages and families because of sexual infidelity. The proliferation of sexually transmitted diseases is a sad fact of modern life, never mind the worldwide crisis of AIDS, some of which is linked with sexual promiscuity. Similarly the supreme value of wealth and prosperity makes governments mainly concerned with the economy and employment. Nevertheless, this top priority also engenders political corruption, social stratification, emphasis on economic concerns rather than on ethical and environmental ones. People themselves become viewed as commodities, medicine and social services are delivered only to the ones who can pay. Certain categories of people are treated as nonpersons because they have no economic power, whether it is the unborn, the homeless, the poor, or the aged. In many countries "palms have to be greased" to get any kind of legal action. The wealthy can emigrate if they wish, but not so the poor. Contemporary literature speaks of "the zero people"[35] and "disposable humans."[36]

In a recent speech in Mexico Pope Francis addressed the link between a number of these issues in a speech to government officials at the Presidential Palace without using theological language:

> Experience teaches us that each time we seek the path of privileges or benefits for a few to the detriment of the good of all, sooner or later the life of society becomes a fertile soil for corruption, drug trade, exclusion of different cultures, violence and also human trafficking, kidnapping and death, bringing suffering and slowing down development.[37]

The proliferation of sweat shops, child labor, and human trafficking in the rest of the world as well as Mexico owe their existence to those who seek "the

---

35. Jeff Lane Hensley, ed., *The Zero People: Essays on Life* (Ann Arbor: Servant, 1983).

36. Kevin Bales, *Disposable People: New Slavery in the Global Economy* (Berkeley: University of California Press, 1999).

37. http://www.cbc.ca/news/world/pope-francis-mexico-1.3447218 (Feb 13, 2016).

path of privileges for a few": the idolization of money. Luxury items such as diamonds and jewelry have become polluted by the blood of scores of victims. In terms of the general picture 1% of the people in the world have 48% of the world's wealth, leaving 52% to the rest of the population, while the top 20% account for 94.5% of the world's wealth.[38] Oxfam's report on this incredible injustice is tellingly titled: "Wealth: Having It All and Wanting More."[39] But more importantly, in nations that desire to protect what they have and to seek more, there is the creation of a mass weapons industry, whose production and consumption require enormous expenditures: in the ten years from 2001 from 2011 the average yearly expenditure on arms was 1.6 trillion dollars! Over this period there has been an escalation from 1.18 trillion to 2.09 trillion dollars.[40] This may seem like mere numbers but if one thinks of the other possibilities for which such expenditures could be used it staggers the imagination. In terms of defense spending the United States spends as much as the next nine countries combined![41] Humanitarian organizations estimate that it would cost only 30 billion dollars to eliminate world hunger and 170 billion dollars to eliminate worldwide extreme poverty over the course of twenty years.[42]

The central symbol in the book of Micah and in the book of the Twelve is the temple (Mic 4:1–5). Its exaltation to the supreme place in the world means that Yahweh is exalted and his name has become universal. This means that when the nations come to Jerusalem they are acknowledging that Yahweh is supreme; when they hear his Torah, they are not only corrected and satisfied; they are changed. Their "bloated appetites" for more and their aggression for war to satisfy and defend those appetites are gone. They now have a love for *ḥesed*, and they take that new *ḥesed* heart and fashion instruments of peace from their weapons of conquest. They begin to practice justice in the world—walking in Yahweh's ways—after which each person can sit under their own fig tree in a plot of land, complete with its own vineyard. There are no more "bloated appetites" because Yahweh's leadership supplies what has been lacking—satisfaction,

---

38. Deborah Hardoon, "Wealth: Having It All and Wanting More," *Oxfam Briefing* (Oxford: Oxfam, January 2015). Thus, e.g., eighty billionaires have the same amount of money as nearly 3.6 billion people! Wealth is defined in terms of economic assets such as properties, money, land, investments, securities, etc.

39. Ibid.

40. "World Military Expenditures and Arms Transfers," Bureau of Arms Control: Verification and Appliance Reports (Washington DC: US Department of State, 2014).

41. Thomas C. Frohlich and Alexander Kent, "10 Countries Spending the Most on Military: Analysis and Commentary for US Global Investors," *24/7 Wall Street* (July 10, 2014).

42. Jeffrey Sachs, *The End of Poverty: Economic Possibilities for Our Time* (New York: Penguin, 2006).

and there is a new motive to love *ḥesed* and to practice justice. Thus they learn war no more. West Point, Royal Military College, Sandhurst, and the various military colleges spread throughout the world will become obsolete because people will no longer covet; they will worship Yahweh, and he has given them a *ḥesed* heart. A world of idolatry, and hence covetousness and injustice, will become a world of true worship, *ḥesed*, and justice. Idolatry will finally give way to doxology (6:8)![43]

Peace

At the very heart of the book of Micah is the vision of a restored and elevated temple, with Yahweh speaking words of life to a needy world. His speech addresses the nations and offers them peace to walk in his ways. Later this walking in the ways of Yahweh is defined more fully as doing justice and loving *ḥesed*. It results in repentance and forgiveness, as shown by the people from the nations leaving the temple unharmed but not unchanged. They have been transformed from a hostile military orientation to a peaceful one. Their bloated appetites for more and more are now satisfied with the Messiah's provision as everyone is living under their own fig tree, not desiring any more material goods. Shortly after this vision of an exalted temple is that of an exalted messianic leader, who comes from a place of fruitfulness (Ephrathah) and food (Bethlehem), whose reign provides security, and who becomes literally "our peace." Clearly his rule is a rule of peace. He declares war on war and makes Jerusalem a place of true worship and shalom. That the blight of war can be ended by the beginning of a messianic reign shows that there is no end to the peace that can result from the Prince of Peace's reign in human hearts. The New Testament envisions this happening in the breakdown of racial, social, and gender barriers in the new temple created by Jesus Christ. For example Paul writes in Ephesians about the new relationship Gentiles have in the body of Christ (note the fourfold use of "peace").

> But now in Christ Jesus you who once were far off have been brought near by the blood of Christ. For he is our *peace*; in his flesh he has made both groups into one and has broken down the dividing wall, that is, the hostility between us. He has abolished the law with its commandments and ordinances, that he might create in himself one new humanity in place of

---

43. Cf. some of the insightful thoughts of Walter Brueggemann, *Israel's Praise: Doxology against Idolatry and Ideology* (Philadelphia: Augsburg Fortress, 1988).

the two, thus making *peace*, and might reconcile both groups to God in one body through the cross, thus putting to death that hostility through it. So he came and proclaimed *peace* to you who were far off and *peace* to those who were near. (Eph 2:13–17, emphasis added)

Christ ended alienation between God and humanity and between the members of humanity. This peace is a sign of the new age, the messianic reign, and too often Christians embrace war and militarism when the people of God should be a people who are satisfied with what they have and become instruments of peace in a world of war. Just the same, there are powerful contemporary signs of Christians making a peaceful difference in the world.

As mentioned in the commentary on 4:1–5, an Anglican bishop in Mozambique decided to do something about the proliferation of arms in his country toward the end of a civil war that had decimated the nation. He went to every province and asked people what they thought might jeopardize peace in the future. One person responded: "Guns, we have so many guns in our hands. Both sides have been very generous in dishing out guns just like that, so when peace comes are those guns going to be just left alone?" The bishop was not prepared for this question but after much prayer and reflection he received his theological answer from the books of Micah and Isaiah. The following day he announced that disarmament from a biblical perspective would begin, and he issued a request that guns would be returned to collection centers throughout the land. The guns would then be made unusable and exchanged for instruments for production. Since this program started over one million guns and other weapons have been collected and transformed. The program was called "Turning Swords into Ploughshares." To inspire the future generation, children were encouraged to bring their toy guns to church, where they were smashed, and they were given in exchange toys that did not inspire violence.

A particularly powerful illustration of the same principle emerges from World War II (mentioned in the commentary on 4:1–5). An American army chaplain made a set of communion cups from machine gun bullets by extracting the lead and the gun powder and turning the resulting cases into receptacles for wine, representing the blood of Christ. When he shared communion with a Japanese minister after the war, the lesson was not lost. Bullets that were intended to harm and kill became instruments of life and peace and reconciliation. Whereas the machine gun bullet was once intended to produce blood and death, it had been transformed to contain a drink of everlasting life.

But what about the workaday world for many people that is far removed from the literal battlefields of life, where there are no tanks and bombs and bullets? In Micah, the marketplace and the courts, the city and the temple were places of "battlefield" where people were being cheated, robbed, framed, and hurt in innumerable ways. Judah had become a place where each person was out for his or her own advantage, where there were adversaries even in one's own home, where people were waiting to ambush some unsuspecting traveler (7:1–6). The entire social fabric had been shorn. Micah's advice in such a situation was to hope in Yahweh, to go to the temple and hear the word of Yahweh, to experience transformation, and to live this transformation by laying down one's arms—to meet hatred with love, injury with forgiveness, cursing with blessing—in short to walk in the ways of Yahweh. Why? Because this is the wave of the future.

Similarly for the church. Paul gives similar counsel to Christians at Rome. In light of the coming day of Christ, they are told to remember that the final day has already dawned (Rom 13:11–14). The time for a life of licentiousness and lust is over; the dog-eat-dog world is so passé; the life of alienation, aimlessness and war is finished—it belongs to the past darkness. The wave of the future is to gather together to hear the word of the resurrected Lord, to "put on the Lord Jesus Christ," to embody his values and become agents of forgiveness, reconciliation, peace, and hope.

There are so many lost opportunities, and history could be so different if these qualities had been practiced. One thinks of the amazing possibilities when one considers what might have happened after World War I when Germany lay broken, depleted, impoverished, virtually dead from starvation. England itself was not in much better shape. Since 1914 the United Kingdom had lost 908,371 lives, with 2,090,212 wounded and another 191,652 missing in action. It seemed that this was the classic example of a pyrrhic victory.[44] And yet the "victors" had a chance to show mercy to the vanquished enemy. Winston Churchill proposed to the British parliament that a dozen ships stocked with provisions be sent immediately to Hamburg but his proposal was coolly rejected. Meanwhile

> a twice-decorated German non-commissioned despatch runner, temporarily blinded during a heavy gas attack, sat in a Pomeranian hospital and learnt of Germany's plight from a sobbing pastor. Six years later the soldier set down his reaction: 'I knew that all was lost. Only fools, liars and criminals could hope for mercy from the enemy. In these nights hatred grew in me, hatred for those responsible for this deed . . . I resolved to go into politics.' The soldier's name was Adolf Hitler.[45]

44. Richard Holloway, *On Forgiveness* (Edinburgh: Canongate, 2002), 91.
45. Ibid,, 91–92.

Meanwhile, the church, with its proclamation of forgiveness and peace, is a city set on a hill, called to illuminate the world, called to change history until history ends. The world can be different—it will be different—as the reconstituted community of the Crucified and Resurrected One accompanies its proclamations with deeds that glorify its Father in Heaven. In Micah and in Christ, the church has heard the music of the future. It is called to dance to its tune in the present.[46] "Even though all the peoples each walk in the name of its god, we will walk in the name of Yahweh our God forever and ever!" (Mic 4:5).

46. This is a slight rewording of a quotation by Croatian theologian Peter Kuzmic: "Hope is the ability to hear the music of the future. Faith is the courage to dance to its tune today."

Bibliography

Frequently cited works are listed here and are cited in the commentary by author's last name and short title. Other works are fully documented in the footnotes.

Alfaro, Juan I. *Justice and Loyalty: A Commentary on the Book of Micah*. International Theological Commentary 11. Grand Rapids: Eerdmans, 1989.

Andersen, Francis I., and David N. Freedman. *Micah*. Anchor Yale Bible 24E. New Haven: Yale University Press, 2007.

Ben Zvi, Ehud. *Micah*. Forms of the Old Testament Literature 21B. Grand Rapids: Eerdmans, 2000.

Calvin, John. *Commentaries on the Twelve Minor Prophets*. Reprinted Charleston: BiblioLife, 2010.

Cuffey, Kenneth H. *The Literary Coherence of the Book of Micah: Remnant, Restoration, and Promise*. London: Bloomsbury T&T Clark, 2014.

Hagstrom, David Gerald. *The Coherence of the Book of Micah: A Literary Analysis*. Society of Biblical Literature Dissertation Series 89. Atlanta: Scholars Press, 1988.

Heschel, Abraham Joshua. *The Prophets*. Reprinted Peabody: Hendrickson, 2007.

Hillers, Delbert R. *Micah: A Commentary on the Book of the Prophet Micah*. Hermeneia. Philadelphia: Fortress, 1984.

Jacobs, Mignon R. *Conceptual Coherence of the Book of Micah*. Journal for the Study of the Old Testament Supplement 322. Sheffield: Sheffield Academic Press, 2001.

Keil, C. F. *Minor Prophets*. Translated by James Martin. Commentary on the Old Testament 10. Reprinted Grand Rapids: Eerdmans, 2010.

Mays, James Luther. *Micah: A Commentary*. Philadelphia: Westminster, 1976.

McComiskey, T. E. *Micah*. Expositor's Bible Commentary 7. Edited by Frank Gaebelein. Grand Rapids: Zondervan, 1985.

McKane, William. *Micah: Introduction and Commentary*. Edinburgh: Bloomsbury T&T Clark, 2000.

Renaud, B. *La Formation du Livre de Michée: Tradition et Actualisation*. Paris: Gabalda, 1977.

Rudolph, Wilhelm. *Micha, Habakuk, Zephanja*. Kommentar zum Alten Testament. Gütersloh: Gütersloher, 1975.

Shaw, Charles S. *The Speeches of Micah: A Rhetorical-Historical Analysis*. Sheffield, En-

gland: JSOT Press, 1993. Available online at public.eblib.com/EBLPublic/PublicView
.do?ptiID=436901.

Smith, Gary V. *Hosea, Amos, Micah*. NIV Application Commentary. Grand Rapids: Zondervan, 2001.

Smith, J. M. P. *A Critical and Exegetical Commentary on the Books of Micah, Zephaniah, and
Nahum*. International Critical Commentary. Edinburgh: T&T Clark, 1911.

Smith, Louise Pettibone. "The Book of Micah." *Interpretation* 6 (1952): 210–27.

Sweeney, Marvin A. *The Twelve Prophets*. Collegeville: Liturgical Press, 2000.

Waltke, Bruce K. *A Commentary on Micah*. Grand Rapids: Eerdmans, 2007.

———. "Micah." Vol. 2/pp. 591–764 in *The Minor Prophets: An Exegetical and Expository
Commentary*. Edited by T. E. McComiskey. Grand Rapids: Baker, 1993.

Wolff, Hans Walter. *Micah: A Commentary*. Translated by Gary Stansell. Continental Commentary. Minneapolis: Augsburg Fortress, 1990.

———. *Micah the Prophet*. Translated by Ralph Gehrke. Philadelphia: Augsburg Fortress,
1981.

Index of Modern Authors

House, P., 51n150
Huffmon, H. B., 94n105, 157n267
Hume, D., 79
Hutton, R. R., 158n270, 158n272
Hyatt, J. P., 161n279
Hyman, R. T., 165n286

Innes, D. K., 74n49

Jacobs, M. R., 22n69, 22nn71–72, 24n79,
    27n86, 36n120, 48n141, 105n134, 123n183,
    189n350, 263
Jenkins, A. K., 13n43
Jenkins, P., 173n314
Jeppesen, K., 27n86, 35n116, 49, 142n238
Jeremias, J., 70n39
Jerome, Saint, 5n15, 59n10
Jerzak, B., 243n11
Joel, Billy, 98
Johnson, D., 112n145
Johnston, R., 248n19
Johnstone, W., 21n65, 201n2
Jones, B., 54n157

Kaiser, W., 71n42
Kaltner, J., 94n105
Kapelrud, A., 29, 136n218
Keel, O., 217n24
Keil, C. F., 24n81, 69n34, 70n38, 71n43,
    73n47, 87n82, 136n218, 168n297,
    185nn339–40, 263
Keller, T., 212n16, 249
Kent, A., 258n41
King, Martin Luther, Jr., 150
King, P., 119n168
Klausner, J., 223n31
Klein, G., 102n128, 125n185
Klein, N., 97n117
Kimchi, D., 88n85
King, P. J., 5n15
Kugel, J., 40n126
Kuzmic, P., 262

Laetsch, T., 92n101, 106n136, 139n229
Lane, N. C., 200n2
Lang, A., 12n40, 53n156
Lawson, J. N., 114n150

Leithart, P., 69n35, 168n296
LeMonchek, L., 117n162
Leuchter, M., 113n147
Levenson, J. D., 159n273
Levin, Y., 59n10, 60n13
Lewis, C. S., 78
Lichtheim, M., 101n126
Lim, B., 253n28
Limburg, J., 99, 120, 157n267
Long, B. O., 232n38
Luther, M., 47, 147

Maclean, J. B., 98n122
Maclellan, J., 3n9
Maltby, L., 131
Mann, A., 242
Marrs, R., 129n203, 136n218, 142n243
Mays, J. L., 1n5, 3n8, 7n2, 12n41, 22n71,
    23n74, 29n101, 47n138, 58n5, 67n28,
    74n53, 95n110, 104n133, 112n144,
    126n189, 127, 130n204, 137n224, 140n236,
    142n240, 159, 165, 170n306, 76n323, 63
McCarter, P. K., Jr., 5n16
McComiskey, T., 22n73, 24n80, 69n38,
    75n56, 144n250, 175n317, 263
McKane, W., 28–29, 67n26, 74n50,
    86n79, 88n85, 89n91, 126n192, 176n324,
    189n347, 206n10, 239n1, 263
McKenzie, J. L., 68n32
McKeown, J., 219n25
McNeil, J. T., 172n313
Meier, S. A., 47n137
Mendenhall, G., 142n239, 179n330
Metaxas, E., 120n176, 248n20, 249n22
Middleton, J. R., 216n22
Miles, J., 242n9
Miller, A., 244n15
Miller, D. E., 22n72
Miranda, J. P., 78n62
Moberg, D., 211n15
Moberly, R. W. L., 121, 204n6, 232n39
Morales, M., 217n23
Muilenberg, J., 140n233, 147n257, 157n267
Müller, W., 235n42

Na'aman, N., 59n11, 74n54, 175n319
Nasuti, H. P., 94n105

Torrance, T. F., 193n356
Treat, J. R., 199n1
Turner, M., 36n121
Tutu, D., 150

Vadas, M., 118n164
Van Leeuwen, R., 21n65, 200n2
VanVonderen, J., 112n145
Volf, M., 31–32, 33n114
Von Rad, G. 47n135, 137n223

Waldow, H. E. von, 80n64
Waltke, B. K., 9n30, 17n57, 18n58, 22n73,
    24, 25n82, 73n44, 81n67, 86n77, 88n87,
    91n95, 120n174, 125n186, 264
Watson, W. G. E., 40n126
Watts, I., 250
Watts, J. D. W., 52n153
Weinfeld, M., 161n277, 207n12
Weiser, A., 28n96
Weissenberg, H. von, 53n156
Wellhausen, J., 27n87, 28, 229n34
Wessels, W. J., 65n25
Westermann, C., 227, 228n33
Wheaton, B., 120n172
Whitfield, G., 79
Wiebe, R., 192, 193n355
Wiesel, E., 68n33
Wifall, W. R., 147n255
Wiklander, B., 48
Wildberger, H., 127n196

Willard, D., 121n179, 250n24
Willis, J. T., 17n56, 23n76, 24n79, 69n38,
    128n201, 162n280, 170n308
Wiman, C., 97n119
Wöhrle, J., 56n158
Wolfe, P., 125n185
Wolfe, R.-E., 29n99
Wolff, H. W., 5, 7, 8n22, 13n45, 22n71,
    30nn103–5, 58n6, 71n43, 73n46, 74n54,
    85n73, 91n100, 93, 94n102, 95n107,
    95n109, 96n114, 99n124, 110nn139–40,
    113n148, 115nn151–53, 116nn154–56,
    117n158, 119n72, 125n188, 126n193,
    142nn241–42, 145n251, 150n263, 152n265,
    58n271, 167n292, 169n298, 170n309, 179,
    180n334, 186n342, 188n346, 189n349,
    192n233, 264
Wolterstorff, N., 3n6, 78n62, 91n97
Wood, J. R., 22n72, 26, 67n26
Woude, A. S. van der, 8n24, 28n96,
    104n132, 110n141, 127, 128n199
Woudstra, M., 220n26
Wright, C. J. H., 4n10
Wright, G. E., 157n267
Wurm, Bishop T., 121

Yancey, P., 250n25
Yoder, J. H., 131n208

Zapff, B. M., 56n158, 206n8
Zimmerli, W., 17n55, 106

Index of Subjects

Aaron, 8, 157

Abraham, 29, 95, 149, 160–63, 177, 187, 191, 206–8, 216, 222, 226, 237, 250

Absalom, 72, 111

absence of God, 35–36, 108–10, 184

Achzib, 42, 59n10, 66

Adullam, 59n10, 66, 73–76

Ahab, 63, 69, 86, 93, 114n150, 130, 168, 170, 177, 231–32, 254

Ahaz, 9, 11–12, 60, 73n48

"alas, woe!" (*hôy*), 83, 85

alcohol, 85, 93, 98, 170, 175, 250, 260

anacrusis, 83, 110

Armstrong, Lance, 172

Asherah, 77, 141, 142n238, 255

Ashkelon, 159

assembly of the Lord, 42, 84, 87, 94

Assyria, 2, 8, 9n28, 10–15, 19–21, 31n111, 35, 38, 41–42, 52, 54–55, 60, 61, 70, 71n43, 73, 74n54, 77, 87n81, 89, 104, 105, 111, 114, 116, 134–37, 140–45, 169, 176, 177n327, 183–88, 201, 205, 223–25, 235

Athaliah, 147, 236

Atrahasis Epic, 12n40

Auschwitz, 68n33

authorship, 16, 26–33, 136n218

Azekah, 14

Baalam, 8, 29, 95, 150, 157–58, 163, 221, 231

Baal-perazim, 102

Babel, 122, 130, 136n218, 137n222, 140, 144, 191, 204, 239

Babylon, 14, 21, 31, 34, 52, 73, 103–7, 122, 125, 133–36, 140, 148, 150, 183, 190, 214, 220, 222, 233, 236, 239

Balak, 8, 157–58

Baruch, 16n50

Bashan, 185, 195, 215

Ben Sira, 53, 70n41

Benjamin, 86, 135, 225

Bethlehem, 8, 26–27, 73, 123–24, 132, 134–35, 137–38, 143–44, 148–52, 185, 189, 191–92, 220–26, 239, 259

Beth-leaphrah, 42, 66–67

Beth-ezel, 66

Boaz, 164n285

"Breaker," 33, 99–107, 214

cannibalism, 12n40, 33, 45, 103, 108, 111, 115, 117, 210, 238, 255

canon, 15, 18–19, 21n66, 37–39; 48–52, 57, 126n190, 127n194, 139n230, 143n245, 200n2, 245, 253; canonical placement of Micah, 20–21; canonical orders of the Twelve (Minor Prophets), 51–56

Carthage, 159

cheap grace, 2, 96, 114, 121, 166, 248–51

Chronicler, 6, 11n35, 12

clothing, 90–92, 96, 118, 160, 210, 253

cohesion: alliteration, 83–84, 174; assonance, 41, 83–84, 124, 156; coherence,

270

Index of Scripture and Ancient Sources

283